WITNESSING
HISTORY

WITNESSING HISTORY

One Chinese Woman's Fight for Freedom

真善忍

JENNIFER ZENG

Translated by Sue Wiles

First published in Australia by Allen & Unwin Pty, Ltd in 2005 under the title
Witnessing History: One Woman's Fight for Freedom and Falun Gong

Copyright © Jennifer Zeng 2005

First published in the United States of America in 2006

Soho Press, Inc.
853 Broadway
New York, NY 10003

10 9 8 7 6 5 4 3 2 1

I dedicate this book to all those
who are stepping towards a brighter future.

Contents

真善忍

Preface

真善忍

THROUGHOUT MY SCHOOL YEARS, I disliked writing compositions and when I enrolled in science at the university I was delighted that I would never have to write another. Not in my wildest dreams did I imagine the day would come when I would consider writing a book.

However, our lives often take unexpected turns, and twelve years after graduating from the university I was sentenced to twelve months' re-education through forced labour for simply writing a letter to my parents-in-law explaining why I practise Falun Gong. The letter was sent by email and I was subsequently charged with 'using the Internet to voice grievances on behalf of Falun Gong'. Initially I was sent to the Beijing 'Re-education Through Forced Labour Despatch Division', where conditions were unimaginably dreadful. Within the confines of the labour camp, I sometimes spoke jokingly of writing a book to expose the horrors of the place. Halfway through my sentence, I started to take the idea more seriously. By then I had witnessed and experienced far more brutality and darkness than I ever thought existed and certainly more than I could bear. I was determined to expose these evils and wrote this book in my heart from then on.

I thought carefully about starting with an account of my first arrest, but realised that this wouldn't work because my story is about practising Falun Gong. Had I not embarked upon this journey, given the Chinese Central Government's suppression of Falun Gong, it would have been almost impossible for me to disregard my personal safety and risk arrest, beatings and death—for defending what I believe to be true. As this is the story of what happened to me as a Chinese practitioner in China, I have used my Chinese name (Zheng Zeng) throughout, although I now use my English name in my new, English-speaking country.

I was among the first group of people in Beijing to be sentenced en masse to re-education through forced labour for practising Falun Gong. Within a few months, the number of inmates at the Beijing Xin'an Female Labour Camp had swelled from around 200 to about 1,000. I witnessed the vast changes in the camp as a result of the large influx of Falun Gong practitioners. I also witnessed the ever-widening and deepening impact that Falun Gong was having on Chinese society and the whole world.

There is an old Chinese saying, 'Still water runs deep'. Although we can hardly see or feel the rapid current underneath the 'still' surface, what is occurring below can be truly terrifying. This is what is happening to the countless innocent Chinese Falun Gong practitioners locked behind the oppressive walls of the hundreds of forced-labor camps throughout China; the world is still largely unaware of the vastness of the current. With the world now at such a critical moment, I feel that documenting my experiences through writing this book has become my responsibility to history.

I also wanted to work unflaggingly with the untold thousands of decent people who long to bring this brutal suppression of Falun Gong to an early end and so save more lives. I feel that writing this book was a mission set for me by present reality.

After I was released from the labour camp in April 2001, to avoid further harassment from the police I left my home and went to my hometown in Sichuan province, thousands of kilometers to the south-west. That was when I found out that my younger sister had been forced to leave her home several months earlier because of her involvement with Falun Gong. Her daughter was almost eighteen months old and just starting to talk. When my mother and I went to see her, she ignored her well-known grandmother and ran unsteadily to my arms, calling 'Mummy, Mummy' instead of 'Auntie'. Her expression was one of joy and her voice so innocent. I embraced this little child tightly, not knowing whether to answer her or not. Words fail to express how I felt at that moment.

My brother-in-law stood motionless, his head bent, and didn't make a sound while I held my sister's daughter in my arms. I realised his heart must be bleeding within him at hearing her repeatedly crying out 'Mummy'. As I looked at the broken family in front of me, my heart bled too.

I also visited relatives implicated to varying degrees because of my sister and me. For generations, these good and decent people had never had any dealing with the police and now the police came to their homes constantly to search for my sister as an 'escaped criminal'. They now pass their days in a perpetual state of anxiety over the police and worry themselves sick over her.

And then there are our friends . . . I have discovered through world human rights organisations that more than 1,000 Falun Gong practitioners have been persecuted to death, and tens of thousands have been incarcerated in forced-labour camps and prisons. It is impossible to calculate how many others have been sentenced, detained or forcibly enrolled in government-run 'brainwashing classes'; how many have effectively been deprived of their freedom through being under constant surveillance by local police; how many have become destitute and homeless; how many have been dismissed from their jobs for no apparent reason, finding themselves with no means of earning a living. The true number of innocent people affected by this oppression must be in the tens of millions.

So my book is dedicated to them too. I appeal to all kind-hearted people around the world to take note of what is happening to the Falun Gong practitioners in mainland China. Extend your helping hands to these millions of innocent beings, save them and, at the same time, save yourselves. For this, I am prepared to sacrifice my life.

At this point, tears cover my face and I am unable to continue. I can but turn to an ancient Chinese saying, 'Kowtowing with a bleeding heart'. I want to kowtow with a bleeding heart to those who are willing to read my book. With all my strength and my entire being I offer this book. I offer my heart, and the essential principles of the universe that I validated through my life.

I do not know when this human calamity that is the Chinese Communist Party's persecution of Falun Gong will cease, so most of the names in this book have been changed to protect the identities of innocent people. All the events, however, are absolutely true.

Zheng (Jennifer) Zeng
China, May 24, 2001
Revised in Australia in September, 2004

Part I

A NEW EXISTENCE

真善忍

I **WAS BORN IN A** small town in Sichuan province in 1966, the year the Great Cultural Revolution began. My father had graduated from the University of Politics and Law and had been assigned to a teaching post in a metropolitan polytechnic in Mianyang City, Sichuan province. However, during the Cultural Revolution he was accused of being a 'reactionary capitalist-roader lackey' and was sent off to a remote township of 30,000 people called Han Wang in Mianzhu County, where I spent my childhood.

In the early 1980s, the public security departments, procuratorial organs and people's courts that had been dismantled during the Cultural Revolution were resurrected, and my father was recalled and given work in the new metropolitan judicial bureau of Mianyang City, where he had worked before. There was no position available for my mother, however, so she had to remain in Han Wang with my youngest sister. It would be more than three years before our family was reunited. I returned to Mianyang City with my father and my middle sister, and enrolled in senior middle school.

I was a quiet and conscientious student—my only act of rebellion was to refuse to obey the restrictions the school system tried to place on our reading. I would beg or borrow books from anyone, devour them instantly and begin the search again.

I graduated in 1984 at the age of 18, and sat the entrance examination for Beijing University. I was accepted into the Geology Department and in my third year was recruited as a member of the Chinese Communist Party, the first person and one of only two persons in my class to join. After graduating in 1988 with excellent results, I was taken straight on as a graduate student without having to sit any examinations.

My husband and I met on the university's Martial Arts Team. We took an immediate fancy to each other and quickly fell in love. We were married in 1988, while I was still a graduate student, and in 1991 I was assigned to the State Council's Development Research Centre. We were very happy, the envy of all our friends. Until 1992.

When I gave birth to our daughter, Shitan, in 1992, a botched medical procedure caused me to have two massive hemorrhages. I almost died, but the blood transfusions that saved my life left me with hepatitis C and, for the next few years, my life became an endless series of treatments and hospitalisation. I was given every medication imaginable, and underwent expensive Interferon treatment. In a desperate effort to improve my health I practised qigong breathing exercises, but nothing worked. In 1995, an abdominal ultrasound showed early indications of cirrhosis of the liver. Four years after giving birth I still could not go to work and was so weak a breeze would almost blow me over. I had constant vertigo and dizziness and had held my beautiful daughter only a handful of times. As I was so weak, I couldn't carry her, feed her, nurse her—in fact, we had decided it was better that her grandparents bring her up. I was only 30 years old; I had a wonderful husband and a precious daughter, but I felt so wretched that life hardly seemed worth living.

I had become a virtual prisoner in our apartment. The vertigo and dizziness that I was experiencing became almost unbearable if I went outside. Movement of any sort made me nauseous, whether it was busy traffic or the branches of the trees shaking in the wind. I had to force myself to go out, to overcome the panic attacks that swept over me.

After four years of misery I finally decided that I was not going to be enslaved by my illness forever—I'd rather 'overdraw' my life and die earlier. Consequently, I went back to work at the beginning of 1997, taking many precautions for my health. I didn't go back to the Development Research Centre, however. While I was sick, China's Stock Exchange had opened, and my husband's company was one of the first two flotations on the market in Bejing. Employees had been given share certificates, but many had refused them, or discarded what they thought were worthless pieces of paper. It surprised many that this 'paper' could really be exchanged for money.

My husband was so busy that he didn't have time to go to the stock market to sell his shares. He suggested I go instead. In fact, selling the shares was far less important to me than finding a way to kill time. Shitan was with her grandparents, and I was bored to death with nothing to do and nobody to talk to during those long, long days. My husband often came home very late at night. After talking to all sorts of people for a whole day, he was too exhausted to talk to me while I had spent the whole day calculating what I was going to say to him when he came home. So my going to the stock market appealed to him. He didn't mind whether I earned or lost money— at least I, too, would have something to do in the day time. And I didn't have to go if I felt unwell or tired.

I entered the market when it was almost at its lowest point. Most of the time I ended up playing billiards, offered to the investors by brokers, instead of trading. However, by observing the ups and downs of the market for a few years, learning from the experiences of others, doing some 'experimental' trades and reading a lot of relevant material, I began to feel that I had obtained quite a lot of knowledge in the area. It was then that I came across an advertisement for a position in an investment consultant company. I already knew that I didn't want to go back to the Centre—it was a government-run organization, and everyone there was very keen to be seen to be on the promotion ladder. After what I had been through, this didn't seem as important any more.

After an interview, I was offered the job, and I took the plunge back into full-time employment. I diligently took my medicine every day and also kept up a form of qigong. Although it did not help much, at least I could tell myself that I was trying my hardest. I thought I was taking every precaution to ensure that my health did not take a further setback, until I started practising Falun Gong (a form of qigong), which brought a new beginning to every aspect of my life.

1

THE MISTS OF BELIEF

I WAS ONE OF THOSE docile grade A students who were criticized so roundly during the Cultural Revolution. From primary school through senior middle school, I was always first in my class, head of my grade, and at the top in every test. I remember myself as exceptionally obedient, sensible and disciplined. However, at that time in China, there were two very famous revolutionary slogans: 'The more knowledge you have, the more anti-revolutionary you are' and 'To rebel against the authorities is encouraged'! So grade A students were regarded as out of date and no good.

In the small factory in Han Wang where my father worked our family was classed as intellectuals. This placed us ninth on the list of class enemies, and we weren't really able to identify with what were called the 'laboring people'. To forestall any quarrels, my mother discouraged my playing with the other children, so I spent most of my time after school reading anything I could get my hands on. I went to endless trouble to read: I would read by flashlight under my quilt, on summer nights tucked up safely under my mosquito net, and would even feign illness to get out of gym class so that I could sit in the classroom reading. I would use a length of bamboo to jiggle books off the top shelf where my father had put them out of reach of childish hands. I would read during class through the cracks in my desk and use my lunch money to borrow books. Reading was my greatest pleasure, but there were so few books to read.

Yet despite all my reading I developed little worldliness, and had no greater plan in my head than studying hard to become a scientist.

Beijing University, one of the most famous institutions of higher learning in the country, opened my eyes to the whole world around me. The greatest thing for me about 'Beida', as Beijing University is affectionately known, was the opportunity it afforded its students for independent thought and the chance to be ahead of the times. I began to awaken in that environment and, like so many others who had attended Beida before me, I began to ponder many things, especially my place in the world.

From the beginning of time, philosophers have contemplated questions such as 'Who am I?', 'Where did I come from?' or 'Where am I going?' I took to the magnificent collection of texts in Beijing University Library like a fish to water, and I dipped into every book of philosophy I could find—Rousseau, Schopenhauer, Nietzsche, Kant, Hegel, Sartre, Freud, Socrates, Aristotle, the cynics . . . these giants of philosophy were leading me into uncharted waters: my understanding was growing but, as time went on, I felt as confused as ever. I still had no satisfactory answers to life's fundamental questions. Our graduating class wrote a few parting words to each other in a book and my own comments sum up how I felt then: 'Growing older day by day, and day by day realising how little I know; I don't understand why we are here.'

CHINA'S *QIGONG* CRAZE

Ever since I was little I had wanted to be an outstanding scientist, just like Marie Curie. After studying science at the university, however, I began to think that science had not really achieved any substantial leaps forward since Einstein, and that much of our recent progress has been in technology rather than science. I was convinced that any qualitative scientific leaps in the new century would have to be in the life sciences because, while we 'can ascend to the highest heavens and embrace the moon, plumb the depths of the five oceans and catch the soft-shelled turtle', we know too little about ourselves. I believed, and still believe, that this is the direction in which we can achieve the greatest development precisely because we still understand so little.

It so happened that at that time in China, there was a surge of interest in extraordinary human abilities—what Westerners would probably call the 'paranormal'—and qigong (the practice of mind and body improvement through exercise and meditation). Two professors in the Biology Department at Beida had begun researching such things in 1979, when the first case of 'recognising written characters by ear' occurred in China.

This phenomenon involves a character being written on a piece of paper, without the test subject seeing the character. The piece of paper is then rolled up into a little ball and placed in the subject's ear. The subject is then asked to 'read' the paper, without moving it or touching it in any way. The case in 1979 involved a young boy, so the Beida professors decided to focus on primary school children, as being old enough to concentrate, but not old enough that their minds were starting to close. Rather than putting the pieces of paper in the children's ears, they asked them to hold the ball of paper between their two palms and concentrate on visualising the characters on the paper. Exhaustive research showed that over 60 per cent of the children were able to concentrate enough to 'read' the word with their hands.

They pursued their rigorous scientific research for over ten years, accumulating a great deal of first-hand data and scouring a great many ancient books. Then they offered 'The study of the paranormal and qigong' as an elective subject open to all students; I took it while I was a graduate student. The meticulous scholarship of these two professors impressed me greatly, and to this day I can still see them shaking with anger as they stand at the lectern, denouncing the degenerate frauds who were discrediting the good name of qigong. Along with the other students taking this elective, I was part of a number of well-designed experiments that indicated the existence of the paranormal; these experiments also showed that such powers could be induced in subjects in a particular age group – confirming their research at the primary school. They also carried out many other experiments on mental telepathy, telekinesis, remote vision and hypnotism.

Their many experiments may have proved the existence of the paranormal but they did not make any significant theoretical breakthroughs and in their classes they relied mainly on records of the paranormal contained in a few ancient books. I recall them telling us quite frankly that they were unable to come up with a theory that could explain paranormal capabilities so they had concentrated on the preliminary stage of collecting a body of authentic first-hand material for later researchers to work with. Their enthusiasm, and commitment, inspired a spirit of scientific endeavour in their student. I studied several styles of qigong, writing up my qigong practice diary every day to provide authentic first-hand data.

These experiences showed me how marvellous we humans are and confirmed my belief that the next major scientific breakthrough would be in the life sciences. I also realised that current scientific theory is seriously lacking in really penetrating, satisfactory explanations.

This was all about science *per se*, but at some stage I began to have thoughts of a different kind about science. I began to think about the social function of science. I thought that science should be done not for the sake of science alone but for the sake of humankind, in the pursuit of the greater happiness of humankind. It is true that people have always enjoyed the material comforts and convenience of technological advances, which today are happening ever more rapidly. But do these advances ever bring true happiness? Over a thousand years ago the poet Tao Yuanming wrote: 'Gathering chrysanthemums by the east hedge, my lazy eyes meet South Mountain.' But what do we sing of today? There was a time when almost everyone was echoing the famous rock and roll star Cui Jian's song: 'It's not that I don't understand, it's just that the world is changing too rapidly'. Our pop songs are all 'I'm so lonely', 'I'm so sad', 'I'm so heartbroken'. We no longer possess the leisure, comfort, tranquillity, harmony and grace revealed in the literature, music and art of the ancients. People today are anxious and uneasy, worried about the world and what lies ahead. Family relationships are fraught as never before and the pace of society places enormous pressure on everybody. Traditional social ethics and moral values are being seriously challenged, making it difficult to establish a new equilibrium because of the new problems that are constantly emerging. I remember those popular T-shirts with 'So tired' printed on them or 'I'm edgy. Don't mess with me.' Such pithy comments really summed up what people were feeling.

Have scientific developments really given humankind a corresponding degree of happiness? Indeed, could any scientific or technological advance bring with it true happiness? Happiness ought to be deeply felt, not just a matter of material possessions or technologies. If science has not made people happier, what do we want with science? By this point I had become deeply sceptical about science and its benefits.

———

The first Buddhist text I came across was a handwritten copy in regular script of the *Diamond Sutra*; I used it when I was practising calligraphy. As I copied this sacred scripture over and over, the words 'All beings are led by me to the final Nirvana for the extinction of reincarnation' drifted through my consciousness like wisps of mist but I could never quite grasp the substance behind the mist.

I also roamed the world of Daoism, poring over texts like the *Daodejing* (also known as the *Tao Te Ching*). The perfection of the unique Oriental wisdom and art of Laozi and Zhuangzi took my breath away. As a graduate student I developed an interest in the *Yijing* (generally known in the West as the *I Ching*). I bought heaps of reference books and had begun to delve into them seriously, an obsession that lasted until I had my baby.

Three times during my pregnancy I consulted the *Yijing*, wanting to know how the birth would go, and each time the hexagrams indicated great peril. I didn't take much notice though, let alone consider how I might avoid this peril, because at that stage I was really only dabbling. I was still unsure whether I believed that everything can be foretold and whether a person's fate is decided at birth. These were big issues that brought into question my whole worldview, and for the moment I was unable to take a stand.

Things did indeed go wrong during Shitan's birth and I very nearly died. I was overwhelmed by fear of the gods of fate then, and willing to acknowledge allegiance to them: I had no choice but to believe that destiny had a hand in everything. The next question, of course, was: If there really is a certain inevitability about our destiny, are we able to change it at all?

While thus afflicted I met the Chair of the Taiwan Daoist Association, who advised me to study *Qi Men Dun Jia*[1], one of the three

---

1 *Qi* usually means 'mysterious' or 'strange', but could mean 'valuable' or 'holy' here. *Men* means 'a gate', and *dun* means 'hidden' or 'escaped' (to make hidden), and *jia* is the first one of ten stems, which is considered as the most sacred in this method.

most amazing divination learnings in ancient China. It is believed that by mastering *Qi Men Dun Jia* you can not only foretell both good luck and bad luck in aspects of time and space (direction), but can also manage to change them—and that this is the only way to change one's fate. I bought a lot of books and off I went, but became dispirited very quickly and abandoned the whole thing. My years of delving into the tortuous arts of prophecy based on the interaction of yin and yang suddenly wearied me with their over-elaborate jargon and their tedious and complicated calculations.

Quite early on in my philosophical journey, I had begun to think in the following way: the universe moves in a regular fashion, everything from a galaxy to a microscopic particle following its own orbit; we can even write the molecular formula for mud. So, why is it that human beings are so chaotic? I believed that the cosmos remained stable and in harmony because everything in it followed certain common laws. In other words, the universe must contain an ultimate truth. And this truth must be simple yet profound.

It took Buddha Shakyamuni (Siddhartha Gautama) six years before he suddenly perceived that deliberately seeking hardship and punishing oneself was not the path to enlightenment; then he renounced it. I, too, came to the realisation that it was futile to seek the truth of the universe through studying the yin–yang arts of prophecy. It was not the way, so I renounced it.

My search for the truth of the universe and my musings about life came to a standstill. Preoccupied with trying to get through each pain-filled day, I gave these seemingly irrelevant questions no further thought. Over all, however, my worldview gradually became more and more Buddhist. I had a vague feeling that this was where the truth of the cosmos lay but I was still unable to find out what was behind those mists.

2

ZHUAN FALUN[2] REVEALS
NATURE'S MYSTERIES

I SHALL NEVER FORGET JULY 2, 1997. Hong Kong had been handed back to China the day before which had been declared a national holiday. When I returned to work, a colleague said as she placed a set of books in a broken package on my desk, 'Here you are. *Zhuan Falun!*' The package was from my younger sister back home in Sichuan. I had rung her a few days earlier when she told me she had started practising Falun Gong. The name sounded vaguely familiar; I may have seen books in the bookstalls or people may even have recommended it to me, but it hadn't really registered. So when my sister said she would send me some Falun Gong books I didn't say no. I had once been very keen on *qigong* and was actually still practising one form for the sake of my health.

I opened the package and found four books: *Zhuan Falun*; *Zhuan Falun: Volume II*; *Essentials for Further Advancement*; and *Explaining the Content of Falun Dafa*[3]. My sister suggested I start with *Zhuan Falun*; I took her advice.

I was one of those people described in *Zhuan Falun* who had learnt many forms of *qigong*, who had a stack of certificates to prove it, and who felt they knew all there was to know about it. I thought

---

2 *Turning the Law Wheel,* the main book of Falun Gong teachings.
3 'Great Law', 'Great Way'; principles. *Falun Dafa* means 'great way of the law wheel'.

I'd have a look at the book anyway. I started reading the first few pages: the author, Li Hongzhi, began to describe the origins of human life and I was immediately captivated.

Over the next two weeks I read all four books through twice, muttering to myself all the while, 'Good heavens! So that's it!'

It's no exaggeration to say that these four books shook me more than all the other books I had ever read put together. I felt like a blind person suddenly given the gift of sight, as if a paper window had been pierced and the endless panorama of nature's mysteries revealed to me. I thought my head would burst. I had the solution to all those questions I had agonised over for so many years, and all those things I had never understood were suddenly clear to me.

Zhuan Falun explained very clearly, for example, the paranormal and *qigong* mechanisms that had perplexed my two professors at Beida and that I had felt were so inexplicable—the third eye, remote vision, telekinesis, mental telepathy and the healing power of *qigong*. It also clarified the relationship between matter and consciousness, an issue that philosophers and scientists had long wrestled with. Another thing I had never been able to work out was how Shakyamuni attained supreme understanding after sitting beneath the bodhi tree for 49 days: if I sat for 49 days, could I attain supreme understanding, too? Just what was supreme understanding? Was it something that only Shakyamuni had, or was it something that we ordinary mortals could attain if we used certain methods? What did Daoists mean when they spoke of how 'the conscious soul dies, the true soul is born'? Have we had previous incarnations and is there an afterlife? Can we vanquish sickness, senility, ignorance and death? Is there a universal ultimate truth? What is the ultimate truth? And so on and so on. I had found the solution to all these questions.

I also discovered that I was gazing upon the whole of humanity and human history with new eyes, as if from a great height—the history of human civilisation, of religion, of social systems. Take religion, for instance. Like so many people who had grown up under Marxist dialectical materialism, I believed that gods were artificial constructs, that people who knew little about science had imagined these idols into existence for the purpose of providing spiritual sustenance. Religion to us was simply an intensification of this sort of group consciousness that then became 'a tool in the hands of the ruling class to hoodwink and anaesthetise the masses'. But now I understood: 'In fact, a religion has two aims: one is to really make those who are good rise by cultivating the proper way of living; the other is to maintain the morality of human society on a high level. These are the two things a religion has to do.' (*Zhuan Falun: Volume II*). So that's what a true religion is, I thought to myself!

Another thing. Whenever I had tried to find a way to transform my life through the yin–yang prophetic arts, the complexity of it all had completely baffled me. But everything was now so simple and so clear: do good more, do evil less; accumulate merit more, create karma less. And that was it.

My greatest discovery, however, was to understand, finally, the significance and the meaning of life. Li Hongzhi says in *Zhuan Falun*: 'We see that in this universe a human life isn't created in ordinary human society; the creation of one's life takes place in the space of the universe'. So our true purpose as human beings is not simply to be human but, in the midst of perplexity, to practise and return to our original, true selves and our original source. And that's what *Zhuan Falun* is all about: the hows and whys of practice.

Within a few short days the whole world had changed for me. I had been transformed from an atheist into a believer. Not only did I believe that Buddhist, Daoist and spiritual higher beings existed, I also recognised that for an even happier and eternal existence, each one of us need only want to practise to be able to reach the realm in which those beings exist. This process may be difficult, it may be easy, but it is simply a matter of continually shedding ideas and practices that are not good enough, raising ethical standards and continually assimilating Truthfulness, Compassion and Forbearance (*zhen, shan, ren*). It says in *Zhuan Falun*: 'One should return to one's original, true self; this is the real purpose of being human'. Finally, I had discovered the reason for my existence! That which I had been seeking for so many years was all here! How could I not believe?

I remember the day I finished reading the four books for the first time. I sat staring at the stock market quotations scurrying across my computer screen. A sense of crisis surged within me. Instinctively I felt that, even though I now knew of 'heavenly' things, I had spent too long in this earthly quagmire and unless I read the books again immediately I might be dragged back into that quagmire. I didn't have a moment to waste. Straight away I read *Zhuan Falun* again from cover to cover. Only when I had read through all four books for the second time was I at peace; the sense of crisis had passed. I knew I had become a completely new person. I said to myself, calmly and clearly: I know what I am here for. I came here to practise, and I firmly believe that there is no power on earth that can drag me away from it.

I PRACTISE TRUTHFULNESS, COMPASSION AND FORBEARANCE AND SHED ATTACHMENTS

As soon as I had finished the books for the second time I phoned my sister to ask where I could find people in Beijing to teach me the exercises of Falun Gong. I already knew from the books that there were five exercises to do. She told me I should be able to find volunteers teaching them at practice sites in any of the large parks.

I went to the nearby Temple of Heaven Park and quickly came across a practice site. The lessons were free, of course, and the five movements that made up the set were not all that difficult. Exercises 1, 3 and 4 could be completed in ten minutes; Exercise 2—the Falun Standing Stance—took as long as you could hold the pose. The other tranquil exercise was sitting in meditation and it was up to you how long you did this. There were no specific requirements as to place or time, so you could practise whenever and wherever you liked; you didn't even have to go to a practice site. How much time you spent on your practice was up to you: if you had the time you did more and if you were pressed for time you did less.

It took me about a week to learn all the movements, but for me they were only a small part of practising Falun Gong. Li Hongzhi says in *Zhuan Falun*, 'If you only practise the exercises without improving *xinxing*,[4] and without the powerful energy that strengthens everything, it cannot be called cultivation practice . . .'. In other words, the ideological content is more important. My outlook on the world and on life had been thoroughly transformed. I now had completely new goals in life and new ways of looking at the world, and because I demanded different things of myself I was a very different person.

This sounds abstruse, but when put into practice, it was really concrete. For example, not long after taking up Falun Gong I was help-

---

4 Mind or nature; moral character.

ing my husband prepare noodles for dinner and I spilled some as I scooped them out of the water.

'God, you're clumsy!' my husband snorted. He immediately glanced at me anxiously, certain he'd put his foot in it again.

As I mentioned before, since giving birth I had had a host of health problems. Illness had not just ruined my health; it had ruined my career and left its mark on my life and on my moods. After I came out of the hospital, my husband and I had paid a visit to my workplace to put in a claim for my medical expenses. I learned from a colleague that all of the graduate students who had been assigned to the unit at the same time as I had been promoted to bureau cadre or acting mayor, had gone overseas, had been assigned an apartment or had been given a professional post. My illness had put my career on hold, however, and there was nothing for me but a monthly pittance for basic living expenses.

I didn't say a word on the way home in the car. Sensing my mood, my husband tried to comfort me, pointing to the beautiful flowers alongside the road in an effort to raise my spirits a little. I turned to the window but tears streamed down my face. I thought of how women were always likened to flowers—but what flower would I be? I hadn't had the chance to burst into bloom before I withered and fell. All through my life, when had I ever lagged behind others in anything? And now, to see the grudging expression on people's faces when I put in a claim for some medical expenses—I had become a burden to everyone and everyone loathed me! It wasn't that we needed the money—we were fortunate that my husband had a good enough job to support us all—but that earning an income was a sign of my independence, of what I had achieved with my life, and now it had been taken away from me.

One day my husband and I were chatting and I said I had not been into the office to collect my pay for several months.

'Well, you can't have anything to eat then,' he said.

I knew very well he was only joking but I burst into tears all the same. He had hit a nerve, divided as I was between self-pity and competitiveness, and what I was really crying about was the hopelessness I felt about my future.

I consulted medical books and read magazines, looking everywhere for a cure. But instead of 'becoming a self-taught specialist', my study made me feel I had received a death sentence, with a reprieve of maybe eight or ten years. According to the literature, because the hepatitis C virus had not yet been isolated and extracted from human blood, no antiviral medicines had been developed for it. And hepatitis C could lead to cirrhosis of the liver or liver cancer much sooner than other forms of hepatitis.

I cried for days until, with some difficulty, my husband finally coaxed me out of my depression. He gradually became very, very careful lest a word out of place upset me. I was touchy so he always had to be extremely careful. Hence the anxious look when he'd blurted out, 'God, you're clumsy!'

Admittedly, my first impulse was to throw down the bowl and storm out. But then it occurred to me that I was practising Falun Gong now and since practitioners are supposed to abide by Truthfulness, Compassion and Forbearance, I shouldn't lose my temper. Not only that, I must get along well with people no matter what; I must be broad-minded and tolerant. Besides, I knew he had not said it maliciously.

With a bit of an effort, I gave him a smile.

'Who made you pick a clumsy wife?' I said. Then I quietly cleaned up the noodles while he stood there looking as though he had just seen the sun rise in the west.

Li Hongzhi says in *Zhuan Falun* that 'cultivation depends on one's own effort while the transformation of *gong* is done by the master'. After I started practising, I found myself able to easily do things that had once been impossible for me. For example, surely I could have been a little nicer to my husband before. Yet whenever I started to get angry with him I would lose my temper and then, because I couldn't control myself I would hate myself for losing my temper, and on and on the vicious cycle would go.

I CAST OFF MY OLD SELF

Not long after I began practising Falun Gong, the company I worked for applied for accreditation as one of the first Chinese investment consultancies qualified to carry out securities work. One of the requirements for accreditation was that the company have five individuals qualified in such work. It was a very great honour for the company and for those five individuals who would be part of 'China's first group'. Management notified me to prepare to be listed among the five.

I got my material ready for the application as requested and several days later heard a colleague say that the five individuals had been chosen and everything had been finalised. I was not one of the five. But the worst thing was that no one had breathed a word to me about why I had not been chosen.

If this had happened before, I would have surely lost the balance within my heart even if I refrained from approaching management to ask why I hadn't been selected. This time, however, I immediately recalled that *Zhuan Falun* states, 'If something is yours, you will not lose it. If something is not yours, you will not have it even if you fight for it'. What practitioners seek is to improve their moral character and cast aside harmful attachments, not this world's fame and gain. I felt much calmer then and went on with my work conscientiously, not giving the matter another thought.

My husband quickly realised that I had changed. They say it's easier to change the course of rivers and move mountains than to change a person's nature, yet my temperament and my mental state had really been transformed. My mood swings were gone, I had stopped being pessimistic and, more importantly, I was actually optimistic and magnanimous, qualities that were new to me. I no longer had any 'petty bourgeois worries' and I was even able to help him when he was worried, something I had never done before.

My husband was soon telling people that the world might be full of books but few were actually capable of changing people.

'*Zhuan Falun* has changed my wife,' he would say. 'It's terrific, even if she's the only one it's changed, that's terrific!'

A little later he confessed to a group of friends that his wife was well on her way to becoming a saint.

My practice also had a dramatic effect on my health. A little over a month after I started practising Falun Gong, everyone at work had to undergo their annual physical examination. My blood tests came back completely normal, indicating that the hepatitis I had lived with for over four years had vanished without trace. You would think this would have made me wild with joy, but I didn't get excited because I had somehow expected such a result. I knew that the first thing that happened when you started practising Falun Gong was a drastic improvement in your health. So, given the transformation I had experienced in my mind and heart, it was not surprising that I would experience a similar change in my physical health.

I took my daughter to the hospital for an injection one day when she was running a temperature. Suddenly, seeing all those emaciated patients in dreadful pain—a pain that no longer had anything whatsoever to do with me—I understood the meaning of gratitude. Once a regular visitor, I knew that I had said goodbye to hospitals forever. The days when I hovered between life and death had become as remote as if they had taken place in a previous existence and I felt, with great clarity, that I now belonged to a different existence.

This, then, was the reality of cultivation. It appears not quite possible. Nevertheless, I felt happier and more peaceful than I had ever felt and I understood what Buddhists mean by 'utter fearlessness' and 'great ease'. Utter fearlessness is the courage and rationality that comes with wisdom once one understands the ultimate truth. Great ease is the ease and wonder that comes with casting aside improper pursuits, attachment and selfish preoccupation with gain and loss.

Slowly, I became part of a new group of friends. We called ourselves fellow practitioners. There must have been about 60 or 70 people practising at the Temple of Heaven Park exercise site I went to. Every morning as soon as the gates opened we would go to our spot with hardly a word, turn on the cassette player and begin. If you had time you would do all five of the movements, if not, you would do as much as you had time for; it was up to each individual.

I hadn't been practising there long when I was approached by one of the volunteer assistants. The assistant asked if I'd like to join a group to study the *Fa* (the law and principles in the Buddha School). At these *Fa*-study groups, people who lived near one another met once a week in somebody's home to read Falun Gong books and discuss their experience of practice.

I managed to attend only one *Fa*-study group meeting, mainly because evenings were the only time I had to help Shitan with her homework, but I made every effort to practise the exercises in the park. I didn't really have time to chat but I saw the other practitioners who believed in Truthfulness, Compassion and Forbearance as belonging to the same family, people who were striving to be unselfish, and therefore had little need for talk. Here there was no need for the anxiety and guardedness of everyday life. Everybody was concerned with cultivating their character and ridding themselves of attachments, improving their moral standards and eliminating from their thoughts all that was not good. What we shared was how each of us had gone about improving and the insights we had had into our practice. In a world where people's relationships had become extraordinarily strained, this place was truly a paradise.

The only thing I took part in besides morning exercises was weekend activities to introduce Falun Gong to the public. Although there is no requirement within Falun Gong to convert others, after they had experienced its benefits most practitioners were very eager to introduce this practice to their family and friends. We would go to new places where there were no practice sites in order to let others know about Falun Gong. We went to many different places to practise, sometimes an hour or two's ride away in the suburbs, sometimes quite close to home. Rain, hail or shine, if we said we'd go, we'd go.

One weekend we went to a shopping centre in Fangzhuang, not far from Temple of Heaven Park. The assistant said that only those from the several practice sites in the park had been notified of our visit but several thousand people turned up, filling the soccer field outside the shopping centre. There must have been a lot of local practitioners who did not go to the practice sites in the park but somehow heard about the activity. It really was a splendid sight, several thousand people in orderly rows practising as one, and all around the field banners were fluttering in the breeze—'Falun Dafa', 'Truthfulness, Compassion, Forbearance', 'Free Falun Dafa instruction'. Onlookers crowded around, with many people making enquiries and coming to learn.

By the summer of 1998 I was only able to go to Temple of Heaven Park to practise on weekends because of my work as a consultant which took me out to different locations. So during the week I would bundle up my meditation cushion, cassette player and the loose clothing I wore while doing my practice, and get up before six each morning to catch the first bus to where I would be working that day. I would find a secluded spot, do my practice and then have something to eat at a nearby foodstall before starting work.

However, I quickly discovered that wherever I went there was a practice site close by, sometimes several. Some sites held several sessions and I was able to choose a time that suited me. At various times I practised at all four of the large temple parks in Beijing:

the Temple of Heaven south of the Forbidden City, the Altar of the Earth to the north, the Altar of the Sun to the east, and the Altar of the Moon to the west. Eventually, as I rode the early-morning buses through the quiet streets, I realised that groups of people were practising Falun Gong wherever they could—in parks at intersections, in plazas outside large markets, in town squares and even in open areas on the pavement—sometimes different sites were only 100 metres apart. When I went home to Sichuan at Spring Festival in 1999 I found it was much the same there.

The soft music, the leisurely movements, the brightly coloured banners, the peaceful expressions on the faces of practitioners even when it was windy or raining: this was a beautiful early morning spectacle. Falun Gong practitioners, with their Falun Gong insignia, were like a garden of exotic flowers blossoming all over the land of China.

Part II

THE CRACKDOWN

1

THE FIRES OF ENVY

IN THE MEANTIME, MANY THINGS had quietly been happening of which I was completely unaware. I did not know, for instance, that *Zhuan Falun* had been one of the ten bestsellers of 1996. Nor did I know that in the same year China News Press had put out a memorandum 'for Chinese eyes only' banning the publication and distribution of *Zhuan Falun*. This restricted memorandum was apparently not circulated, however, and the ban was not implemented. As far as I was concerned there had never been a shortage of Falun Gong books in the city, probably because they were so popular and pirate book dealers would never pass up such an opportunity. The owners of the little bookstalls on the streets were very familiar with how many Falun Gong books had come out. Whenever a new one was published they would rush to stock up. I frequented a small bookstall near Yongdingmen and all I had to say was 'I need a set of Falun Gong books' and the owner would put aside a full set for me. I often bought extra copies in case any of my friends wanted to have a read. Most people would stand at bookstalls for hours browsing without buying anything, but people who came for Falun Gong books would take them sight unseen, so the bookstall owners were more than willing to handle these books.

There is a saying that 'a storm hits the tallest tree first'. When the *qigong* craze hit mainland China in the early 1980s, *qigong* styles of every description sprang up like bamboo shoots after spring rain; at one stage there must have been several thousand. By the 1990s, however, most of them had disappeared and a great many *qigong* teachers were finding it difficult to attract students. When Falun Gong emerged in 1992 as a form of *qigong* it was in much the same situation, except that it made quite a splash at the 1992 and the 1993 Oriental Health Expos. Only a couple of hundred people attended the first Falun Gong study class and by the end of 1994, when the founder of Falun Gong, Li Hongzhi, conducted his last class in Guangzhou, between 30,000 and 40,000 people had attended the 54 classes he personally conducted in China. Then, after only a few short years, it was estimated that the number of Falun Gong practitioners increased to 70 million and then to over 100 million. This happened without any media coverage or advertising across the country, simply by word of mouth. People who had been introduced to Falun Gong and had experienced its health benefits warmly recommended it to their family and friends, to their work colleagues and to their neighbours.

You must remember that China is a one-party autocracy in which every aspect of society is tightly controlled by the Communist Party. How, then, could such a large group of people escape the attention of those in power? The people in power—who were not democratically elected—feared nothing but destabilising of the system. What were this many people up to, they wondered, practising one style of *qigong*?

Also, those who had studied Falun Gong spoke with unconcealed respect and tremendous gratitude about the teacher, Master Li Hongzhi, and about all they had gained from their practice. Later on, when the authorities suppressed Falun Gong, everyone said that Falun Gong was 'competing with the Party' for the people. Was this oppression sparked by jealousy? It seems hard to believe, but it is probably true.

Many foreigners who had grown up in Western democracies found the crackdown against Falun Gong inconceivable. 'Why do they want to suppress Falun Gong?' they wondered. But China had already been through the anti-rightist campaigns, the Great Leap Forward and the Cultural Revolution. It hadn't taken the people of China long to realise these things were absurd, yet they happened. Is it that this land, this country, this system is a breeding ground for such absurdities?

In some respects it was inevitable that the dictatorship would fear Falun Gong, which burst forth as a completely new and independent ideology in a land that has never had genuine freedom of thought. Falun Gong has never had any political motivations; it is all about individual faith and self-cultivation, and yet China's fearful dictatorship created for itself a fictitious enemy that could only be defeated by struggle. From its very inception, the Communist Party has believed implicitly in force. Communism is responsible for the three largest killing sprees of the last century, outstripping the Nazis, genocide and war. More than 84.5 million people were either butchered or died an unnatural death in communist countries, twice as many as died in both world wars. And more people died unnatural deaths in China than in any other communist nation. A conservative estimate of those deaths is 20 million, and international societies and Chinese experts suggest that the true total may be closer to 80 million. One could say that the 80-year-long history of the Chinese Communist Party has been written in blood. Didn't Mao Zedong say long ago that power comes from the barrel of a gun and that there is nothing more enjoyable than battling heaven and earth—and men?

On the surface there was much greater economic freedom in China after the reform and opening up of the 1980s but in reality the despotic nature of the system had not changed in the slightest. In some respects it was even more stringent once Jiang Zemin assumed the posts of General Secretary of the Central Committee of the Chinese Communist Party and President, and Chairman of the Military Commission of the Central Committee. No one person had ever occupied these three posts simultaneously, taking Party, political and military power to himself, and thus being able to utilise the resources of the entire country at will, for whatever he wished. At the height of the student democratic movement in 1989, one million people took to the streets in Beijing on one day. But who was going to dare say 'No' once the tanks entered the city and the machine-guns opened fire? And all the Great Powers resumed normal relations with China not long after, didn't they?

Ever since the publication of an article attacking Falun Gong in the official *Guangming Daily* in 1996, a hidden current against Falun Gong began to surge underneath the 'still' surface. In 1997, the Ministry of Public Security started a secret nationwide investigation, during which public security personnel penetrated Falun Gong by masquerading as students and practising alongside Falun Gong practitioners to find out just what they were up to. The information they gathered from all over the country was the same, however: Falun Gong practitioners simply dedicate themselves to the practice and like to share Falun Gong with others. When something happens they say 'do not hit back when attacked, or talk back when insulted', 'look inwards', 'cultivate your character', 'cherish virtue'; they avoid committing 'misdeeds' or causing 'problems'.

On top of that, one after another, the officers of the Public Security Ministry became interested in the practice. The following incident, which took place at an experience-sharing meeting, was typical. A former drug addict whose whole body was a testament to his habit spoke of how he had given up drugs and turned over a new leaf after practising Falun Gong. He said that when he went around to repay his debts to people he had deceived and stolen from, they thought at first he was up to his old tricks. As soon as this ex-drug addict had finished speaking at the meeting, a member of the audience leapt onto the podium, brandishing a tape recorder.

'Do you know who I am?' he said excitedly. 'I am from the Ministry of Public Security, assigned to spy on you. I had no idea this was what Falun Gong was about. In all my years bringing in drug addicts I have never seen anyone kick the habit. Falun Gong is miraculous! I won't be part of this rotten business any longer; I want to learn Falun Gong, too.'

In front of everyone, he pulled the tape out of the machine and tore it to pieces.

There were many incidents like this, which apparently frightened some people. There is a line in a poem that goes something like 'Nobility is the motto of the noble-minded;/the base use sordidness as a pass'. Base souls cannot comprehend noble hearts and noble actions, nor can they believe that people can live magnanimous lives. When the Ministry of Public Security issued a notice in 1998 that Falun Gong was being investigated, groups of practitioners all over the country were disrupted and dispersed, homes were searched without proper authority and private property was confiscated. This was just an indication of the crackdown to come.

At that time, however, I was concerned only with my own practice, and filled with ceaseless admiration for the personal realisations it was affording me. I was not paying much attention to the world around me and knew nothing of what lay beneath the surface of things. This went on until the Beijing TV station incident of 1998.

One Saturday in the summer of 1998 I went to the park to practise and heard that earlier that week Beijing TV had broadcast a misleading report slandering Falun Gong. Some practitioners had decided to go to the TV station the next day to request that the facts about Falun Gong be presented. I decided I would go, too, and made appropriate arrangements.

When I got home, however, I grew uneasy. I remembered that June Fourth—the day of the Tian'anmen massacre in 1989—was approaching and this was a politically sensitive time. Our teacher, Li Hongzhi, had stressed repeatedly that practitioners were not to take part in politics, and when questioned about why he no longer made personal appearances, he had said that he wanted to avoid large gatherings of people in case it caused 'misunderstandings'. The more I thought about it the more I felt I shouldn't go. In the end, I didn't.

Quite a few local practitioners did go, though, along with some people who had come in from Hebei province—several hundred people altogether. Management of the TV station met with them and listened as they talked about their own practice. Management realised that these people had no evil intentions and wanted only to present the facts about Falun Gong and have errors in the TV program corrected. They all agreed this was important because such misleading reports harmed the reputation of the TV station almost as much as they damaged Falun Gong. The station later corrected its mistake by broadcasting a positive report about Falun Gong. The reporter who had put the slanderous report together was sacked. So the matter was put to rest.

After that I felt that everything was pretty much the same as before and went on with my practice, until April 25, 1999.

THE PEACEFUL APPEAL OF APRIL 25

A fellow practitioner phoned me on April 24, 1999—a Saturday—to ask if I had heard about Tianjin. Apparently a fellow of the Chinese Academy of Sciences named He Zuoxiu had written an article attacking Falun Gong. Its title was 'Why young people shouldn't practise *qigong*'. In the article, he cited some already discredited cases, claiming that practising Falun Gong caused mental disorders. He had received nine reports of people jumping from buildings, eight of whom had died, the other person sustaining serious injuries. He implied that Falun Gong would destroy China just as the Boxers had in 1900, poisoning our youth far more seriously than any 'killing with theory'. The impression the article gave was that practising Falun Gong was very dangerous and could lead to people having mental disorders and even leaping to their death from buildings.

The first Chinese report on exceptional human abilities (the paranormal) had been published in 1979 and had sparked off a lively debate in academic circles on whether such things, if indeed they existed, should be the subject of serious research. Qian Xuesen, the famous scientist who had been in charge of building and launching China's first artificial satellite, was the leading figure in favour of paranormal research. Yu Guangyuan, a deputy director of the Chinese Academy of Social Sciences, headed up those holding the opposite view.

Debates such as this are a perfectly normal and useful step in the scientific process. However, because Marxism–Leninism labels the paranormal and *qigong* as 'feudal and idealistic superstition' this academic debate quickly became a political issue and as both viewpoints were supported by senior members of the Central Committee and the Academy, Hu Yaobang, General Secretary of the Chinese Communist Party Central Committee, felt compelled to comment. So in June 1982—ten years before the appearance of Falun Gong—the Propaganda Department of the Central Committee proclaimed its 'three-nots policy' with regard to *qigong* and the paranormal: that the media should not be for it, should not be against it and should not debate it.

Therefore, when He Zuoxiu published his article in the Tianjin Teachers' College journal *Teenager Expo*, Falun Gong practitioners in Tianjin felt that he had slandered Falun Gong's good name. They also believed he had violated the three-nots policy and that this should be rectified. They made their way to Tianjin Teachers' College and other government bodies to make their views known and request these be publicised along with a factual account of the matter.

However, they were confronted there by riot police, who beat them, injuring some and arresting 45. When the rest of the students demanded the release of their fellow practitioners, the Tianjin municipal administration told them that the Ministry of Public Security was now involved and they would have to take the matter up with the Central Committee in Beijing.

The friend who telephoned me was going to the State Council Petition Offices the following day, with another practitioner, to make an appeal. The function of the Petition Offices, incidentally, was 'to hear the views, suggestions and requests of the masses, to accept supervision by the masses and to serve the people'. My friend asked if I wanted to go and I told him I would let him know after I had read He Zuoxiu's article.

I was shocked by the article and couldn't believe it had been written by an academic, a member of the Chinese Academy of Sciences. In it he said that science was still unable to explain just why *qigong* caused mental disorders but that there was no question that it did. Such statements were not only scientifically wrong; their logic was flawed.

If everybody who practised *qigong* developed a mental disorder then, in terms of logic, practising *qigong* was a sufficient precondition for developing a mental disorder. If it was necessary for all those who developed a mental disorder to have first practised *qigong*, then practising *qigong* was a necessary condition for developing a mental disorder. But what were the facts? Most people who practised *qigong* exhibited no signs of any mental disorder, and very few patients in psychiatric hospitals had practised *qigong*. Therefore, practising *qigong* was neither a sufficient nor a necessary precondition for developing a mental disorder, much less a full and necessary precondition. In this sense, there was absolutely no causal relationship between practising *qigong* and developing a mental disorder. What more could be said?

I came to an immediate decision: I would go to the Petition Offices the following day.

A MIRACLE

Just after six on the morning of the twenty-fifth, my two fellow practitioners and I cycled to the State Council Petition Offices on Fuyou Street outside Zhongnanhai, the residential compound for the nation's leaders. The police on duty said the office didn't open until eight and told us to wait. We moved back into one of the small lanes so as not to disrupt traffic and sat down quietly to wait. Gradually the lanes filled with people.

I had a suspicion that practitioners from other places would turn up but I had no idea so many would come. Everybody spoke quietly and looked very solemn. As I sat on the steps outside somebody's house watching people file into the lane, tears came to my eyes. For some reason, I was deeply moved, and very proud.

I found out later that some people had left notes in case something happened to them. Given the brutality of the Chinese Government, and with the gunshots of the Tian'anmen massacre of ten years before still ringing in our ears, who knew what might come of a group petition of this size? Alongside me that day was a woman in her forties. She seemed very gentle and quiet and said with a smile that if the police threatened to shoot anyone, she would still find the courage to stand up in the name of Falun Gong.

What happened that day made a great many people aware of Falun Gong and many of them later took up the practice. On the first anniversary of April 25, the immunologist Professor Feng Lili from Baylor College of Medicine in the United States published the article 'Truth! Eternal April 25' in which she wrote:

> I read in a local newspaper about Falun Gong people going to Zhongnanhai on 25 April to make an appeal. Knowing how stern the government is, I trembled when I saw their serene composure and gentle expressions. What kind of people were these who would risk their lives to make an appeal? What kind of people would so innocently petition a government as notoriously brutal as this? It was inconceivable that an idea could enable these very ordinary Chinese people to be so courageous. I looked into my heart and knew I couldn't have done it. The harsh realities of human relationships and the toil of living had dulled my righteous ardour; but who does not feel this?
>
> As soon as I found out that these people lived by 'Truthfulness, Compassion and Forbearance' I resolved without the slightest hesitation to practise Falun Dafa. A teaching that in seven short years could transform Chinese people into something so unusual is simply extraordinary. I used to be an atheist but I am even more convinced that human nature and the nature of a nation cannot be changed. This must be a miracle created by the gods!

ZHUAN FALUN GOES INTO ZHONGNANHAI

About eight o'clock we moved out of the lane onto Fuyou Street. The police told us to wait on the western side of the road, opposite Zhongnanhai, until someone came out to speak to us. There was quite a crowd by now and we moved back into a cul-de-sac off the pavement so we wouldn't obstruct traffic. There was not much room but everybody stayed back. Someone suggested we sit down to wait but another said that it might look as if we were meditating as a protest and it would be better to stand. However, quite a few of the elderly among us were beginning to tire and before long we had formed into two or three standing rows with the elderly sitting down behind us. Everybody was very quiet and orderly, despite the crush.

I was standing almost directly opposite the western entrance to Zhongnanhai and could not tell how many of us there were by looking down along the lines. I heard later that the crowd stretched along Fuyou Street, along Chang'an Street from Xidan to Tian'anmen, and filled the street to the north of Zhongnanhai. Official reports later said that over 10,000 people had 'besieged' Zhongnanhai.

About nine o'clock I heard someone say, 'Look! Zhu Rongji!' And there, across the road, I saw Premier Zhu Rongji coming out of the main gate escorted by five or six rather tense-looking men, clearly bodyguards. His appearance caused a bit of a commotion and part of the crowd surged forward, immediately retreating when somebody called out 'Don't move!'. This all happened very quickly and Zhu Rongji had just walked to the middle of the street.

A few seconds later the crowd began to applaud him for coming out in person to meet us. The whole atmosphere was extremely friendly. He approached the crowd and said a few words to the students standing opposite the main gate, then after a few minutes he and several Falun Gong practitioners, one of whom was carrying a copy of *Zhuan Falun*, went back through the main gate.

I was elated by this.

'Well,' a fellow practitioner beside me commented, '*Zhuan Falun* has gone into Zhongnanhai. Isn't that great!'

The first group soon came out and then a second group of practitioners went into Zhongnanhai; a third group went in but I didn't see them come out again. Tired but very determined, we waited calmly to hear what was happening.

There were some police cars and police officers around throughout the morning, but buses and pedestrians went about their business. Some people just hurried by but others stopped to ask what we were doing. As the afternoon wore on, the police presence increased and the officers were constantly on their walkie-talkies to each other. The atmosphere grew a little tense as pedestrian and bus traffic ceased and we guessed that the police had sealed the street at both ends. I was amused to see the police rushing up and down in a lather while we stood quite still and calm.

At about three o'clock the police passed a circular among the crowd. It had a red seal on it and apparently emanated from the Beijing Bureau of Public Security. The gist of it was that we should not heed rumours, we should leave quickly, we should maintain public order, and so on. However, there was not a word about the arrest and beating of the Tianjin Falun Gong practitioners.

We read the notice but not a single person left. No further notices were issued, and a number of police were stationed across the road to watch us.

We stood or sat quietly, chatting among ourselves or reading. From time to time somebody would emerge from the crowd with a plastic bag and collect empty mineral water bottles and disposable food containers, picking up the rubbish and cigarette butts discarded by passers-by and the police.

It was exhausting standing there all day but the time passed quickly and almost before I knew it, it was beginning to get dark. When it was quite dark and the streets were quiet we decided we could finally sit down and rest.

Around nine o'clock a youngster brought word from our representatives in the Petition Offices that we should return to our homes and asked practitioners who lived in Beijing to help find accommodation for those who had travelled from elsewhere.

But how could we just turn around and go home after waiting all day, with nothing to show for it? Someone in the crowd challenged the youngster, asking him if he was a Falun Gong practitioner, but a pregnant woman to my left spoke up for him.

'Yes, he is a practitioner. I know him,' she said.

In the absence of anything concrete, my intuition told me we should go home.

'We mustn't suspect each other. I believe him; let's go home,' I said and immediately left with my two companions.

Some others came with us and I heard later that within twenty minutes everybody else had slipped away in an orderly fashion.

After we left there was not a scrap of paper on the ground, as Falun Gong teaches us to be good people in all circumstances, and always to consider others first. We could not leave any litter behind for others to clean. This may seem a trifle, hardly worth mentioning, until you realise that it is not common in the nature of the Chinese people en masse to be so civilised. When the suppression of Falun Gong got under way, Chinese Central TV (CCTV) broadcast an informal discussion between two people on the topic of Falun Gong. Referring to April 25, one of them remarked on how highly disciplined the petitioners were since a gathering of that size had been so orderly. That Falun Gong could carry off this unprecedented feat seemed simply to confirm to him that it was a major conspiracy.

Rumour has it that policy makers were even more determined to suppress Falun Gong when they noticed how exceptionally well Falun Gong practitioners had behaved. They believed the group was a formidable political adversary whose members had undergone rigorous training.

A statement by a spokesperson for the Petition Offices of the Central Committee and the State Council later appeared in newspapers. It said that 'the government has never forbidden the practice of *qigong* exercises for health' and that the people had the freedom to practise any kind of *qigong*. It was a matter for each individual, the statement went, and the government didn't take a stand either way. Then it reiterated that people should not listen to rumours, that they should maintain stability and unity, etc.

That appeared to be the end of it, since the Tianjin practitioners were also released on April 25. Foreign media spoke in glowing terms of how April 25 had seen the beginnings of 'the Chinese Government's enlightened acceptance of a proposal from the people' and 'an improvement in the quality of the Chinese masses'.

MISLEADING THE PUBLIC

In China, however, serious undercurrents were becoming evident. The authorities adopted a policy of being strict underneath while apparently easing up on the surface. Within China they blocked all foreign reports and commentaries on the affair, keeping the people completely in the dark, and then they called urgent meetings to formulate countermeasures against what they saw as a formidable foe. On the evening of April 25, President Jiang Zemin had written to the Standing Committee of the Politburo and to other leaders, saying, 'It will be absolutely absurd if the Communist Party cannot vanquish Falun Gong.' It was reported that this letter was passed on internally from the highest level of the Chinese Communist government to the bottom units as an official document. Public security bureaus stood in readiness and rumours were flying that Falun Gong was on the move again.

Soon afterwards, all military units received secret 'three nots, one strictly forbidden' orders. These stipulated that military personnel must not believe in Falun Gong, must not practise Falun Gong, must not take part in Falun Gong activities, and were strictly forbidden to set up Falun Gong practice sites in military camps or industries and business enterprises.

From then on, Falun Gong practitioners throughout the country were harassed to varying degrees in their practice. Assistants were watched and followed; their phones were also tapped. It turned out that the person who had set this whole bizarre episode in motion—He Zuoxiu—was not simply an academic. He was also the brother-in-law of Luo Gan, head of the Central Committee's Commission of Politics and Law. Luo Gan later masterminded the setting up of the notorious 610 Office, specifically to suppress Falun Gong.

On May 4, 1999, Taiwan's *Central Daily* quoted a reliable source as saying that Luo Gan was seeking political advantage in his 'meticulous distortion' of Falun Gong and that the April 25 incident was a case of 'Luo Gan's bragging calling down disaster upon the Central Committee'.

One day in early May I was dumbfounded when a work colleague suddenly said to me, 'Now, are you Falun Gong people really going to go to the Fragrant Hills on your teacher's birthday to commit suicide?'

Where had this rumour come from? For a moment I didn't know what to say. For one thing, I had no idea when Li Hongzhi's birthday was. For another, while Falun Gong might hold that 'the great *Dao* is formless' and it might not have an external form or regulations and commandments, there were still explicit rules against killing living things and against suicide. Once I had begun practising Falun Gong, I did all I could not to kill even a mosquito, so why would I suddenly decide to be part of a mass suicide? My life was fine; why should I want to commit suicide? It was cultists who killed themselves! What was he thinking?

It was not the right place to say all of this so I just shrugged and said no. But my colleague's question had been prompted by a terrifying conspiracy. I didn't find out until much later that the notion of the 'birthday suicides' had been concocted and deliberately spread about by the Public Security Bureaus in the hope of providing a justifiable reason for the suppression of Falun Gong.

Rumour has it that the only people who went to the Fragrant Hills that day were the police. But while there were no suicides, of course, the rumour did have a deep impact: it left a negative impression about Falun Gong in people's minds without their realising it.

2

MASS ARRESTS

O N JULY 20, 1999, WHILE people still slept, a plot that had been brewing for a long time finally became a dreadful reality.

Just after four o'clock in the morning I was startled from sleep by the shrill ring of the phone by my bed. It was the fellow practitioner with whom I had gone to Zhongnanhai. Something big has happened, he told me, and he was going to the Petition Offices in Fuyou Street again; would I go, too?

Clearly it had to be something important for him to ring at this hour, but it was a Tuesday and I had to go to work. I hesitated for a few seconds then decided that since it was so early I could go to the Petition Offices to see what was happening and still get to work by nine o'clock.

My husband was awake by then so I asked him if he would come with me. We had a car and my husband usually dropped me off at work and picked me up on the way home; if he was away on a business trip, I would drive myself. His parents lived with us, so we didn't have to worry about finding someone to look after Shitan. They would just think that we had gone to work early.

He had strongly opposed my going to Zhongnanhai on April 25. The shock and grief of the Tian'anmen massacre in 1989 had left many Chinese people feeling very dispirited. Recovery was slow, with some people moving from numbness, to acceptance, to tacit approval of those in power. Others gradually became 'realistic' and were happy to make a little profit or even just live out their lives, so that they considered everything else a bonus. Yet others didn't care whom they had to swindle to make a buck. There may not have been signs in teahouses saying 'Don't discuss state affairs', but that is how many people operated. My husband understood politics and he was worried about the consequences of my going to Zhongnanhai. We had been divided over this topic for three days after I got back on April 25, but in the end we agreed to disagree and dropped the subject.

But, for some reason, this time my husband replied straightaway. 'I'm coming too,' he said, partly, I suspect, because he was genuinely concerned about the Falun Gong situation and partly because he wanted to be there to prevent me from getting into trouble.

We were in Fuyou Street a little after six so we waited in a small lane, as I had the previous time. A few others were there whom I recognised as Falun Gong practitioners but nobody could say with any certainty what was going on. All they knew was that the government had moved simultaneously in eighteen provincial capitals, arresting Falun Gong assistants and searching their homes, and it looked like there was a complete crackdown ahead.

I was astonished by this news but at the same time it made me glad I had come. I thought that if lots of people turned up that day it would lend more weight to our cause and would give the government pause, so that it might not act rashly.

The others disappeared after a while. I assumed they had gone to find out more information. My husband and I strolled up and down the lane, intending to go out onto the street when the Petition Offices opened, just as I had before.

Pretty soon, we noticed a minibus parking in the lane; in it were several police officers who looked like they'd slept in the van. A senior officer, an older man, approached us.

'Are you Dafa disciples?' he asked.

Before I had a chance to speak, my husband answered with a flat 'Yes'.

The word was hardly out of his mouth before a young officer jumped out of the minibus.

'I'll take them,' he said.

Then he told us to get into the vehicle. I asked him where he was taking us and he said we would know when we got there. He also told us they had indeed spent the night holed up in the van in order to 'perform a mission' in the morning. I thought he was probably going to see us on our way from Fuyou Street.

As the minibus sped up Fuyou Street I saw police cars and officers lined up on both sides of the street in a ferocious display of force. A few minutes later we drew up alongside a large bus. Our driver hopped out and told us to get out. A male and a female police officer immediately came forward.

'Open the parcel,' one of them said.

Numbly, I undid the parcel I was holding. Without a word, the female officer grabbed it and tipped everything out. She fished out my copies of *Zhuan Falun* and *Falun Buddha Law: Lectures at the Swiss Conference* and handed them to the male officer, then ordered us to get on the bus. I had brought these books with me so that I would have something to read if we had a long time to wait for the Petition Office to open.

Everything was happening so quickly I was dumbstruck, and we climbed onto the bus as we were told. There were many people in the bus already. Some sat quietly, others seemed a little anxious; nobody said much and nobody knew what they were going to do with us. My brain seemed to have shut down entirely.

As people walked along the street they were detained if they admitted to being Falun Gong practitioners, and pretty soon the bus was full. I saw the assistant from my practice site grabbed as soon as she walked by but she wasn't hustled onto our bus. I don't know how many buses were parked in Fuyou Street.

As soon as our bus was full it took off, travelling west along Chang'an Street. The police officers said not a word and we detainees remained silent. About seven o'clock the bus stopped outside Shijingshan Stadium in the west of Beijing behind several other similar vehicles, all full of detainees, and some police buses. Police on point duty were busily directing buses in and out of the area.

Our police escort hopped off the bus and after conferring with some other officers told us to get out and form a line in front of the gates to the stadium. Police and some other people in civilian clothes—they didn't look like police, more like people who had been brought in from somewhere to help—sat at tables that had been set up outside the stadium. Police were stationed a couple of metres apart keeping watch as, one by one, we wrote down our names, where we worked and our home addresses.

Then some other officers escorted us into the stadium. It was vast; the stands must have seated over 10,000 people.

When we walked in, the stands were almost half full—about three or four thousand people were there already. They were reciting poems from Li Hongzhi's anthology, *Hongyin*, and in among all those voices you could hear the piping voices of two precious children, echoing across the stadium:

The heart harbours Zhen-Shan-Ren,[5]
Cultivating oneself while benefiting others.
With Dafa always at heart,
One would certainly surpass others in a future year.[6]

Tears welled up and poured down my cheeks. It was exceptionally muggy and with all the windows closed the stadium was completely airless. I made my way to a seat right up at the top, unable to stop crying.

'Don't get upset, don't get upset,' my husband kept saying, thinking I was upset at so many people being detained.

I didn't know how to respond. I didn't even know why I was crying. Perhaps it was because on some deep level I had a premonition about exactly what these Falun Gong practitioners were destined to go through, and about the marvellous courage and magnificent deeds they would be capable of.

People kept coming into the stadium. The police guarding the exits were dripping with sweat. We later found out that the same thing was happening at stadiums all over Beijing. The assistant from our practice site was being held with over 10,000 other practitioners at Fengtai Stadium. The police had pulled her right arm out of its socket and she spent the entire day in the stadium with a dislocated shoulder, at times nearly passing out with the pain. To hold people in stadiums was indeed an emergency measure of some genius, one that possessed Chinese characteristics.

5 *Zhen*—'truth', 'truthfulness', 'honesty'; *Shan*—'compassion', 'benevolence', 'kindness'; *Ren*—'forbearance', 'tolerance', 'endurance'.
6 *Hongyin*—'harmonious and bright', Li Hongzhi, February 1994.

Eventually I stopped crying and calmed down; I began to wonder if my unit had started work yet. Fortunately, my husband had a mobile phone, so I rang my office and explained that I was being held in the stadium and wouldn't be able to get to work. A few others used his phone to ring work and ask for time off or to contact people at home to tell them what was happening, while some tried to contact practitioners to find out or pass on information. The few police there were fully occupied guarding the exits and couldn't do anything about our using the phone. After a few of these calls my husband turned his phone off to conserve the battery, just in case we needed it should things turn bad—who knew how this situation would turn out?

Slowly, everybody began to lose the sense of calm we had experienced on April 25. Surely we wouldn't be kept here? Just what were they going to do with us? What was happening outside? How many people were being detained? What was the situation in other cities? At one point, a young girl suggested we all stand up and call on the police to tell us on what grounds we were being detained. A lot of people stood up but the police immediately changed their tone.

'Sit down!' they called out sternly. 'Somebody could get trampled to death!'

They were right. With several thousand of us and only a few of them, they had good reason to be anxious about a riot breaking out and people being hurt.

'Maintain your *xinxing*! Maintain your *xinxing*!' a group of practitioners called out in unison. This familiar phrase was much more effective than the police order and everyone immediately sat down. The police heaved a collective sigh of relief and leant against the railings, mopping their brows.

I had been sweating since I walked into the stadium and my clothes were sticking to my skin. It was so humid I felt I was breathing underwater, and everybody else was gasping for breath, but we all exercised admirable restraint. Someone turned on a portable cassette player and the gentle, solemn, somewhat sorrowful strains of the Falun Gong music *Salvation*[7] and *Benefit Humankind*[8] echoed through the stadium, filling us with the beauty and majesty of

---

7 *Pudu*, in Chinese.
8 *Jishi*, in Chinese.

Buddha's paradise. We sang along quietly with the melody and felt uplifted, blending with another world beyond human experience.

Someone started reciting a verse from a poem in *Hongyin*:

> In the vastness of the cosmos,
> A wheel of golden light.
> The enlightened one descends to the world,
> Towards whom both heaven and earth face.
> The universe is bright and clear,
> Assimilating to the light of the *Fa*,
> Fly and ascend upon Consummation,
> Together returning to the heavenly paradise.[9]

The stadium rumbled as several thousand voices joined in and the guards gazed up at us in amazement, shaken without understanding why.

———

At about five o'clock, the corridors echoed to the thud of massed footsteps and several dozen police jogged into the stadium and up the aisles in single file. As one, they halted, turned and stood ramrod straight, like a group of well-trained, cold-blooded killers. An aura of foreboding suddenly filled the stadium.

A moment later, a man who had the air of a cadre came in with a loudspeaker, through which he told us that the local governments of each district had sent vehicles to collect us. If we went straight back on the bus to our own district the government would treat us properly. We were not to take to the streets again—if we did we would have to accept the consequences.

He turned and left and the police began clearing the stands. Someone said we couldn't just go. How could we just leave after being held all day for no apparent reason and having our books taken from us? At least we should make them return our books. People linked arms and refused to leave.

The police had little to say. Four to one they descended on those who refused to leave, picked them up bodily and dropped them at the bottom of the stands. One white-haired elderly woman landed

---

9 Hongyin, *Assimilation and Consummation*.

face down; blood was streaming from her nose when she stood up. Some people called out, 'You mustn't beat people!', but most of us remained silent.

My husband and I were among the last to be dealt with because we were right at the top of the stadium. By that time the police were exhausted, their clothes drenched with sweat. I had linked arms with the person beside me, intending not to leave, but when I saw the state the police were in I could not find it in my heart to make it more difficult for them. So I walked down, my husband following me.

A thunderstorm had been brewing all day and now, finally, it began to rain. It was chaos outside the stadium, with police, local government employees and detainees all splashing around in the rain. My husband and I battled our way through the crowd and eventually found the coach for Chongwen District. When the coach was full it took us back to our district government offices. It was quite dark by then and after we got off the bus we turned to leave, thinking that was it.

'Don't move,' a voice suddenly rang out. 'A vehicle is coming for you.'

Each of us was asked in turn which police substation we were under, and this information was noted down. In a little while a minibus screeched to a halt, and a police officer leapt out, announced which substation he was going to, and told all the people who lived there to get in the van. My husband and I got in our van with five or six others. When we reached our police substation, one by one we had our details recorded: name, address, phone number, when we had started practising Falun Gong, and who had introduced us to it. I couldn't see any harm in telling them this—our practice was all above board, wasn't it, so what was there to fear? So I answered all their questions fully.

After taking our details, they put my husband and me in a room together with several police officers.

'You are so difficult,' one of them said. 'You'll behave yourselves when the Central Committee documents are made public in a couple of days, eh? So many people went to Zhongnanhai on April 25, but it was an illegal gathering. Do you understand? Well, just you wait and see.'

'Excuse me,' my husband said. 'Is it against the law for a citizen to appeal to the Petition Offices?'

'For one person, no, it's not breaking the law.'

'If it's not breaking the law for one person to do it, then on what grounds is it breaking the law for 10,000 people to do it?'

The police officer didn't reply.

'Good for you!' I said to myself. My husband might have been against us going to Zhongnanhai, but here he was standing up to the police. And he was right. If a thing is wrong it's wrong, whether one person does it or 10,000 people do it. And if a thing is right it's right, whether one person does it or 10,000 people do it. Why hadn't I thought of that?

After everybody's details had been taken, we were finally released. It was only when we were outside in the cool night breeze that we realised we hadn't eaten or drunk anything all day. All of a sudden we were hungry, thirsty and tired.

We didn't dare go home and cook because we didn't want to have to explain to my husband's parents why we hadn't yet eaten. So we grabbed a quick bowl of noodles and went home, trying to look as if nothing had happened.

JUNE FOURTH, TIAN'ANMEN REVISITED

On the morning of the following day—July 21—I went to practise as usual at Altar of the Moon Park near my new work premises. I had just found this practice site and I resumed my daily practice there on weekdays while going to Temple of Heaven Park on weekends. As I hadn't been going to Altar of the Moon Park for very long, I hardly knew anyone there. I found that there were fewer people than normal that day and I overheard some of them quietly discussing going to the Petition Offices again. I really wanted to go with them but on second thought realised I had to go to work. Beijing's large stadiums were crowded again that day, much the same as the previous day.

On the morning of July 22, a Thursday, as we were halfway through our practice, two of the park's administrators appeared and told us to take down the Falun Dafa banner we hung up every day. When we asked why, they said curtly they didn't know, that it was an order from above. After a moment's hesitation our assistant did as she was told and so, for the first time ever, we silently completed our practice without a banner.

That afternoon I had to go to an investment office some distance from work. When I drove off in my office car, just after three o'clock, I reached over to turn on the tape player to listen to one of our teacher's lectures, as I often did while driving. I accidentally hit the wrong button and on came the radio instead.

Good grief! What on earth was this? The station I usually listened to played music but this time I heard a harsh male voice loudly reading out a draft criticism. From his manner and tone I thought for a moment I was going mad: surely the Great Proletarian Cultural Revolution hadn't started again? I felt as if I had gone back ten years to when I was still a graduate student at Beida. On the morning of June 4, 1989, I had gone to the student broadcasting station at Sanjiaodi in Beida as soon as I got up to find out what was happening with the democracy movement. I had heard that the previous afternoon there had been a clash between police and demonstrators in the vicinity of Xidan, not far from Tian'anmen, and things were quite chaotic. Just as I got to Sanjiaodi a male voice, choked with emotion, came over the radio. 'At the hospital . . . I saw . . . a hundred . . . more . . . corpses.' The man was sobbing and couldn't go on. 'Corpses?' I thought numbly. 'What does he mean by corpses? This word is familiar; why can't I think what it means?' It was ages before I really understood, simply because I couldn't have imagined the government would really give the order to fire.

Now I felt exactly the same. Dumbstruck, I heard that harsh male voice read out the editorial 'Li Hongzhi: the man and his deeds' from the *People's Daily*, then the Ministry of Public Security's six prohibitions, then the Ministry of Civil Affairs' outlawing of the Falun Dafa Research Association. Each groundless allegation was more bizarre than the one before, each false charge more venomous than its predecessor, each prohibition more fierce than the last. This affected me as the word 'corpses' had and I found myself unable to think. The only words in the editorial that were not fabricated were 'Li Hongzhi' and 'Falun Gong'. The rest of this editorial, the printed version of which was over 10,000 characters long, consisted of completely unfounded rumours: 1,400 persons had died because of Falun Gong; such and such a person cut open his belly and killed himself because Falun Gong had made him insane; such and such a person hanged himself from a tree; such and such a person drowned herself in a well; Falun Gong is extremely dangerous to society; Falun Gong is anti-human, anti-society, anti-science;

Li Hongzhi cheats all his students and has made huge sums of money by doing so; Li Hongzhi frightens people into believing Falun Gong by telling them that the earth will explode.

How long had it taken them to concoct so many contemptible lies? Drowning in this tsunami of allegations, it was impossible to know where to start to refute them.

I was stuck in traffic on the way back to work and the radio just kept repeating this drivel, but when I changed the station I found the same message was being broadcast.

My husband picked me up after work.

'Have you heard?' I asked as I got into the car.

'A bit.'

I switched on the radio but as soon as he heard the first sentence—'. . . talks about the earth exploding . . .'—he reached out and clicked it off.

'What?' he said impatiently. 'He actually says the earth is *not* going to explode!' He grasped the wheel and gazed straight ahead.

Neither of us spoke for several minutes. Suddenly, through gritted teeth, he said bitterly, 'Jiang Zemin has gone mad.'

RELATIVES ON THE OFFENSIVE

When we got home I found my mother-in-law and my six-year-old daughter, neither of whom usually watched TV at that hour, glued to the screen, the expression on their faces reflecting the enormity of what was happening. My husband and I had agreed in the car that we would not rush to prepare dinner; that way we could eat a little later and not turn on the TV until after the news. We didn't want his parents to see it and be frightened to death.

The instant my daughter saw me come in she rushed up and asked: 'Mama, are you still practising Falun Gong?'

Trying hard to look normal, I smiled at her.

'Yes,' I said. 'Mama will keep on practising no matter what they say.'

This seemed to satisfy her and she ran off quite happily.

The evening meal was eaten in silence; nobody knew what to say. I went to bed early, as I intended to go to the park the following morning to practise as usual. I was just about to get into bed when my mother-in-law came into my room.

'Zheng Zeng,' she said tearfully, 'please don't practise Falun Gong any more.'

My parents-in-law had come to live with us when they had retired eight years before. My husband was their only son and they were of the generation that felt they could never live with a married daughter, only with a son, so that's how it had been with us. There is a saying in China: 'To have your parents in your home is to have a treasure'. Retired couples have traditionally cared for the children of their working sons and daughters; I was unwell from the time I gave birth and was very fortunate to have them care for our daughter when I was really not up to it.

It's difficult to avoid disagreements, though, when you have three generations under one roof, two with their own attitudes and habits and ideas about raising children. The atmosphere in our home was often not the best, especially when I was unwell. I would sometimes drive my mother-in-law to tears and she would do the same to me; it was very common in China for a woman to be on bad terms with her daughter-in-law. These days, fewer and fewer elderly people want to live with their offspring, and young people, too, think the same.

After I started practising Falun Gong, my health improved and I became more cheerful so the endless trifles I had haggled over no longer worried me. Seeing this change, my mother-in-law encouraged me to practise; she even made me a pair of warm cotton leggings so I wouldn't freeze when I meditated outdoors in the winter. Relations at home grew increasingly genial and we all came to a deeper understanding of each other. So as soon as my mother-in-law saw the expression on my face she knew I was not about to obey the government's ban.

I had recovered from my initial surprise by then and understood very well how difficult it was going to be to go on practising, but I said nothing as my mother-in-law carried on about how, if the government wanted to do something, it would do it; how we little people couldn't go against the government; how opposing the government could only damage our family; and so on. There wasn't anything I could say to her. The only thought in my mind was that I must not give in. By that time I had been practising for exactly two years and I knew, based upon both my miraculous recovery from my illness and my own reasoning, that what I had embraced was truly a magnificent path. History taught that almost every traditional belief had experienced some kind of tribulations before it was fully accepted. Christians were persecuted for more than 300 years. It is not easy to be a practitioner. How you react in the face of tribulation and trials is a testament to true belief. On the first day I practised Falun Gong I had told myself that nothing in the world would drag me away from it. Though I did not know of the challenges yet to come, and so soon, I was sure my faith wouldn't be shaken.

When my mother-in-law realised she could not change my mind she burst into tears.

'Mother goes down on her knees to you!' She wept and actually made to kneel down.

My husband quickly ushered her out the door. I was still speechless. Attempting to make light of the situation, he said, 'When the police do that it's called intimidation, but when our relatives do it it's called love. She's no different from the police in this sense, but you can't get angry with her.'

The next morning my husband persuaded me not to go out. I practised silently in our cramped bedroom, all the while conscious, even without seeing her, of my mother-in-law outside the room, her eyes fixed on our firmly closed door. Not for a second would she have relaxed her 'revolutionary vigilance'. My heart wasn't in it and I did not do the meditation that morning. By the time I came out, my father-in-law had already prepared breakfast. My mother-in-law watched us eat and said nothing, but her reproachful gaze never left us.

I was not a willing participant in this, however, and as we drove past the practice site I asked my husband to stop the car; it was still early and I wanted to see if anyone was there. We walked into the park and could see from a distance that not a soul was at the practice site. My heart was unspeakably empty as I stood there. Then I turned and walked away.

THE LOCAL POLICE KEEP A CLOSE WATCH

On the morning of the second day after the prohibition—July 24—I again shut myself in our room to practise my exercises. That day was Beijing's hottest on record: 42.5°C★. The temperature had climbed

---

★ 108° Fahrenheit

10°C in two days. That morning, the air was so thick and hot it was difficult to breathe.

It was a Saturday and should have been our day off but my husband had arranged to meet someone about a work matter. It was so hot that we had decided that Shitan and I would go with him and cool off in the air-conditioned market near his meeting and, when he was finished, we would all go swimming. There was nothing else you could do on a day like that.

We had just finished breakfast and were on our way out when somebody knocked heavily on the door. My mother-in-law opened the door to a burly policeman. He stepped inside, blocking the doorway.

'You two,' he said, pointing to my husband and me. 'Come with me.'

My mother-in-law was stunned but quickly pulled herself together. She realised that she knew this man, Local Police Officer Wu. In mainland China everybody has an ID card. In addition, the registered residents of every city are assigned to the jurisdiction of a specific police station according to where they live. These police stations then divide the area under their jurisdiction into a certain number of localities administered by local police. Local police normally patrol the beat, which is how my mother-in-law knew this officer. Those of us who went off to work every day never had anything to do with them, however, and I had never laid eyes on Officer Wu.

'Young Wu,' my mother-in-law said with an obsequious smile, 'fancy you coming out on such a hot day! Where are you taking them?'

'Where? To the police station! All Falun Gong practitioners have to go.'

This knocked the wind out of her. It was just what she'd feared. Her daughter-in-law had not reported to anybody that she was practising Falun Gong, so how did the local police know? Surely they hadn't been watching? She thought the game was up, that nothing could be concealed. She wasn't to know that our details had been recorded at least three times on July 20 and that we'd long ago been blacklisted.

'I'm sorry,' my husband said, 'I have some business to attend to today. I have already made arrangements for a meeting and I have to go now. How about we talk about whatever this is when I come back?'

'What! What did you say?'

Officer Wu obviously hadn't anticipated a refusal. He drew a breath and was about to seize my husband by the collar.

I stepped between Officer Wu and my husband.

'I don't have anything on today,' I said. 'How about I go with you now? Would that do?'

Officer Wu took off his cap and wiped the sweat from his brow, eyeing my mother-in-law and my daughter. He hesitated a few seconds, as if to ensure he had a hostage.

'OK,' he said to my husband. 'I'll let you go about your business; then you come to the police station tonight. I'm on duty all day.'

I asked him to wait while I changed, because my clothes were wet through from doing my exercises in the heat.

'I'll wait for you at the station,' he said to me. 'You come along when you've changed.' Without waiting for a reply he turned to go, with an I-know-you-wouldn't-dare-not-come look on his face.

I splashed some water on my face, slipped into some fresh clothes and started out the door. My mother-in-law was right behind me.

'Be nice at the police station,' she pleaded. 'Whatever you do, don't be difficult!'

Outside it was like an oven. By the time I got to the police station Officer Wu had prepared the documents for the record of my questioning. My mother had worked in the courts so I had seen these sorts of papers when I had helped her sort out her legal documents. It had never occurred to me that one day I'd be questioned and a record made.

It began as usual with 'What's your full name?', but this time there were more detailed questions about the practice site.

Are you the assistant?

Who is the assistant?

Who is your normal contact?

Whose place do you usually go to?

Were you involved on April 25, on July 20? And so on.

When he had finished this line of questioning he frowned.

'Do you know that Li Hongzhi changed his date of birth?' he asked accusingly.

The *People's Daily* editorial had devoted a great deal of space to what was in fact a very ordinary matter of correcting a wrongly recorded date of birth. Blowing it out of all proportion, the paper had said that by changing his birthday Li Hongzhi was claiming to be the reincarnation of Shakyamuni so that believers would follow him blindly.

I felt a great weight pressing down on me. In a single night, heaven and earth had changed places and this formless thing, weightier than the earth itself, was consuming the very air, leaving me gasping for breath in the insufferable heat. Wu, with his colossal misconceptions and hostility born of listening to and believing those rumours, was part of that thing.

I decided that no matter what I would speak frankly and strive to dispel his misconceptions and his hostility.

'I will be honest with you,' I said slowly. 'I really have no idea when my teacher's birthday is. I practise Falun Gong because I feel it is good and because what he says makes sense. We do not worship him. I have read all of our teacher's books and listened to all of his taped lectures. Never on any occasion has he implied or indicated that he is the reincarnation of Shakyamuni.'

Apparently this was not what Officer Wu had expected. He said nothing for several seconds then continued in accordance with the procedure laid down.

'Do you know that 1,400 practitioners have died from practising Falun Gong!' he yelled. There was such hatred in his voice I almost felt responsible for all 1,400 deaths.

I didn't let his hatred rattle me and took my time to reply.

'I have never seen any such thing, nor have I heard of any such thing,' I said. 'As they say, good news never goes beyond the gate but bad news spreads far and wide. If people could die from practising Falun Gong, we practitioners would be the first to know and we would be the first to stop doing it. All I can say is that I have derived great benefit from practising Falun Gong and so have those I have practised with. My father also practised Falun Gong. He had high blood pressure, pharyngitis and tracheitis for over twenty years and now he's better. He's given up smoking, which he'd been trying to do for years, and even the presbyopia he suffered from for over ten years has got better. He's nearly 70 and he can read better now without glasses than he could before with his prescription glasses.'

I spoke very slowly and he took down everything I said, word for word, with machine-like accuracy. Looking at his notes I felt the weight over my head lighten somewhat.

'Do you have any Falun Gong flags, banners or posters at home?' he asked.

'No, only the assistants have those.' As soon as the words were out of my mouth I realised what I had done. I was telling him clearly that I was not an assistant and I was betraying the assistants.

Sure enough, he spotted my slip.

'Which assistant has them? What is her name? Where does she live?'

I couldn't satisfy him on this, telling him again that I really did not know the assistants' names, nor where they lived.

Eventually realising that I did indeed not know, he changed his tone, becoming almost confidential.

'Do you have Falun Gong books at home?'

'Yes.'

'Which ones?'

'*Zhuan Falun; Zhuan Falun: Volume II; Essentials for Further Advancement . . .*'

I was about to reel off all the books I had when it suddenly occurred to me: No! Why is he asking this? Could they be going to search my home? I quickly stopped myself.

'My copy of *Zhuan Falun* was confiscated on July 20,' I said.

'Uh-huh. Confiscated. Do you have any Falun Gong tapes?'

'Yes.' The first thing you learn when you take up Falun Gong is that under no circumstances must you tell lies, so I had to say yes.

When he had written down all the questions and my answers he got me to sign the record. This seemed to bring everything to a close and he told me I could go. He followed me to the front entrance and suddenly stopped, speaking to me in his confidential tone again. He told me to write a guarantee that I would no longer practise Falun Gong when I got home and to get my husband to bring it when he came to the station that night. I was to get my husband to write one, too. My husband was to bring along my *Zhuan Falun: Volume II* and the tapes as well. If we handed them over ourselves, Officer Wu wouldn't come and search to see if we'd held anything back.

'You've got a youngster and old folks at home and we're as good as fellow townspeople—Is it worth it?' he said.

I murmured noncommittally; he took this as agreement and let me go.

By the time I got home my brain was in a whirl. Two days before, when my mother-in-law asked me to give up my practice I was determined to keep on with it. But I never imagined I would be tested again so soon. Should I hand over the books? Should I write the guarantee? If I handed over the books and wrote the guarantee could I still be said to be a practitioner of Falun Gong? But what would happen if I didn't hand over the books and I didn't write the guarantee? A house search? Imprisonment?

I got out the reprint of the Ministry of Public Security's six prohibitions that had been published in the newspaper and studied them carefully:

1. It is prohibited for anybody to hang or post banners, pictures, symbols and other tokens in any place or any occasion to promote Falun Dafa (Falun Gong).
2. It is prohibited for anybody to distribute books/magazines, video/audio materials and any other means of promoting Falun Gong, in any place or occasion.
3. It is prohibited for anybody to gather crowds to do 'group practice', 'Fa promotion' and other similar Falun Gong activities, in any place or on any occasion.
4. It is prohibited for anybody to hold 'conferences', 'parades' and 'demonstrations' that support or promote Falun Gong by means of 'meditation' or 'making an appeal'.
5. It is prohibited to fabricate or distort facts, spread rumours deliberately or instigate and interfere with the social order with other means.
6. It is prohibited for anybody to organise, assemble or lead events that are against government policies.

Nowhere did I find anything about individuals not being allowed to practise alone in their own homes. I remembered the look on Officer Wu's face as he told me to write the guarantee and hand over the book. I had the distinct impression that if I just went through the motions and did as he asked his superiors would be satisfied. He wouldn't pursue the matter and would not fuss about whether I continued to practise at home. Besides, my words had already made him believe that Falun Gong was beneficial to one's health.

I decided to accept his hints and wrote a three-line guarantee that I would comply with the Ministry of Public Security's directive, observe discipline and obey the law, all without mentioning Falun Gong. Then I dug out a copy of *Zhuan Falun: Volume II* and an old tape I had used when I was learning English many years before. I copied the music we listened to when practising onto the tape and packed it all up for my husband to take to the police station.

When he came home, my husband read my guarantee and wrote a similar one. That night he took both guarantees, the book and the tape to the police station and before long he was back. I asked him what he and Officer Wu had talked about but he didn't want to tell me in detail.

So that was where my husband and I stood: guarantees written, book handed over, practice tape handed over. Officer Wu was able to report to his superiors that 'these two people under my jurisdiction are now behaving themselves and will not cause any further bother'.

At that time, those who had formulated the crackdown policy, police officers like Officer Wu, and the public, probably all believed that the Party's show of strength and propaganda offensive had been successful. All the key members had been arrested and locked up, all the outlets for Falun Gong books had either handed over their stocks or hidden them and you couldn't buy a book anywhere. Just as the saying goes, 'The tree fell and the monkeys are nowhere to be seen'; it was now expected that Falun Gong would surely disappear from mainland China without a trace—within a mere three months.

SECRETLY PRACTISING AT MY HOME 'JAIL'

While we were detained in Shijingshan Stadium on July 20, I had told the fellow practitioner next to me how sorry I was I had brought along my copy of *Falun Buddha Law: Lectures at the Swiss Conference*. I had just purchased it and now it had been confiscated. He said he had some extra copies and could let me have one, so we arranged to meet the following Sunday—July 25—at the entrance to Temple of Heaven Park.

We didn't know then that two days later everything would have changed. As soon as the ban was promulgated my house became a prison, policed by my mother-in-law. As a 'volunteer' she didn't cost the state a cent but she was much more conscientious than any police officer drawing a salary. How would I be able to keep my Sunday morning appointment? To make matters worse, I hadn't asked this fellow practitioner's name or gotten his phone number so I had no way of letting him know I couldn't come.

All Saturday night I racked my brains trying to think how I could get out the next day but to no avail. My only hope was that, since I had not gone out to practise for two days, my mother-in-law might be a little less vigilant.

A little after five on Sunday morning I crept out of bed, opened the door a crack and peeked outside: so far so good. All was quiet and it looked as though she wasn't up yet. I made my way stealthily to the bathroom then dressed in my room, picked up my bicycle key and got ready to slip outside. I opened the door again, very quietly, and got the shock of my life. My mother-in-law was lying right across the doorway, her eyes fixed on the ceiling, an I-dare-to-die-for-my-country look on her face.

'Zheng Zeng!' she shouted as soon as she heard the door open. 'You'll go out this door over my dead body!'

As I stepped back in surprise she rolled over and sat up then began wailing, yelling abuse about Falun Gong that she had heard on TV and declaring she couldn't go on living; she was going to cut her own throat, hang herself. Never in my entire life had I seen such a performance. I stood there, dumbstruck.

The ruckus woke my daughter, who sat up in bed wide-eyed with amazement.

When she had howled herself hoarse, my mother-in-law tried to get me to admit that what they said on TV was true, that Li Hongzhi was a political careerist, a big cheat, and so on.

I have always been timid by nature and never very good at quarrels. Even before I opened my mouth I would tremble like a leaf. And that's how I was now. Listening to her regurgitating rumours from the TV, I felt a tightness in my chest and it seemed to take forever before I managed to speak.

'In all my life I have never learned to tell lies,' I said.

My daughter finally burst into tears.

'Are you going to get breakfast ready? I'm hungry,' she wept.

She was six years old and had never seen anyone in her family quarrelling. She knew that what Grandma cared most about was whether she was hungry and that the most important activity in the family was preparing meals. She might have been young, but she was astute enough to figure out that saying this should focus Grandma's attention on food instead of on quarrelling with me.

But her question, not even finished, only brought on a further round of wailing.

'Ai-ya-ya!' my mother-in-law cried, slapping her thighs. 'I'm finished! Let the whole family starve to death! There'll be nothing to worry about when we're all dead!'

My husband was up by then and he pulled me back into the room, sat me down and went out, closing the door behind him. I heard him say something to his mother in a low voice.

'Don't try to fool me,' she shouted. 'Fetching a book! It's reading so many books that's poisoned her mind! Oh, with these sorts of ideas in her head she says she's not going there to practise but when she gets to the park and sees others doing it, you don't think she's not going to fold her legs and sit there with them, do you? With things so tense, now the whole family will be carted away! You might think you don't need a wife but my granddaughter still needs a mother!'

'I think you're going to have to leave it for today,' my husband said when he came back.

From then on I practised every day shut up in our small room, not even daring to play the music. The most memorable thing about that summer was the heat, and with the door of our 10-metre-square bedroom closed it was like being in a steam basket. Sometimes, sweating through the pain of sitting in the meditation pose, I felt I was exercising in a sauna.

My mother-in-law watched me intently and continually. She was not sure whether I was still practising but didn't ask me straight out. She believed that I wouldn't admit it so she had no option but to keep listening at our door in a trial of strength, her nerves stretched to their limit. One morning she couldn't stand the suspense any longer. She grabbed the spare key to our room from the kitchen, shoved it into the lock and charged in. There was a tremendous bang as the door slammed against the wall behind it. My husband woke with a start.

'What's going on?' he said, annoyed, still half asleep.

Unfortunately for my mother-in-law I had finished my practice not two minutes before and was just getting dressed. All that fuss and nothing to show for it, besides which she knew it was really inappropriate for her to have charged into our room like that. Ashamed, she rushed into the living room and sat crying on the sofa. That morning she wouldn't even eat breakfast.

'THE MOUNTAINS SHAKE, THE SEAS CHURN, AND THE FEROCIOUS WAVES BILLOW'

Another memorable thing about that summer was the smear campaign conducted against Li Hongzhi and Falun Gong. CCTV's half-hour news program was extended to an hour and then to an hour and a half, and whichever channel you switched to, an attack on Falun Gong was being aired.

The most relaxing and enjoyable part of the day used to be when the whole family gathered in front of the TV after dinner. If there was something good on we'd watch it but if there wasn't we'd spend time playing with Shitan or chatting about our day. Now, however, this was the most painful part of the day for me. Quite apart from the venom of the programs themselves, what upset me even more was to look on helplessly as my parents-in-law absorbed every rumour they heard, learning to hate 'the behind-the-scenes manipulator who was using Falun Gong practitioners to set the Party and the people off against each other'. My heart ached, yet I did not dare explain anything or clarify anything for them; their nerves were already frayed and I didn't want to risk another run-in.

Once, my mother-in-law was watching a slanderous program on how much money the Falun Gong 'organisation' had made.

'And how much have you spent learning Falun Gong?' she asked me casually, in a slightly mocking tone.

I tried to explain that learning Falun Gong hadn't cost me a cent but my mother-in-law had thought this through.

'Don't tell me all those books you bought didn't cost anything!' she responded.

She was right. I had spent quite a bit of money on Falun Gong books to give to people. But what she didn't know was that Falun Gong books weren't exempt from the flourishing trade in pirated editions. All the books I had bought were pirated editions and no matter how many copies of pirated editions were sold the author didn't get a cent.

Another thing she didn't know was that, while other authors went to court over copyright infringement, Li Hongzhi handled this problem differently. On the many occasions on which he was asked whether we could buy pirated editions, he had said that so long as the text had not been tampered with it was not an issue. Later on, overseas Falun Gong practitioners put all the Falun Gong publications up on their websites so that anybody could download the books, teaching videos, music, tapes of lectures, CDs, etc., completely free of charge. If he'd wanted to make money from Falun Gong, surely this was not the way to do it!

Yet when I explained all this to my husband's parents they didn't believe me.

'Not make money? Really!' they said disdainfully. 'You won't believe the Party, but you'll believe a charlatan, eh?'

This hurt so much I was speechless and retreated into my room to shed silent tears. This seemed to ease the pain a little but I couldn't let myself cry for long. If my daughter noticed I wasn't there she would come looking for me. And if my husband's parents knew that I had got this upset about Falun Gong they wouldn't be able to sleep at night.

That summer I told myself over and over again: I am a Falun Gong practitioner; even if they collapse, I can't.

3

FROM SMALL 'SELF' TO
GREAT WAY

THIS IS ESSENTIALLY HOW IT was the entire summer, right up until autumn: enduring in silence the stress and pain of practising in secret. I had lost almost all contact with other Falun Gong practitioners and only spoke on the phone with two or three of them from time to time.

Just before I finished work on October 25, 1999, six months after the April 25 incident, a fellow practitioner called An Xiulan phoned and asked me to come around to her place. I stopped by after work and found ten or so people there already. I knew only a couple of them, from the practice site. They were chatting when I arrived and of course the main topic was what to do about the crackdown.

I sat and proceeded to tell a story my husband had told me about an old peasant. This old peasant had a shabby old violin that had been in the family for many years. One day a man who collected violins discovered that it was actually a priceless antique; he offered the old peasant a large amount for it and arranged to come and get it a few days later. The old peasant was very happy with this arrangement but the more he thought about it the guiltier he felt at profiting at the collector's expense. Eventually he decided to buy some paint and give the whole violin a thorough coat of paint.

'Now I feel content that I'm not conning this man who is buying it,' he said to himself.

The collector came with the money a few days later and almost cried when he saw the freshly painted violin. The old peasant couldn't understand why he no longer wanted it, after he'd gone to all the trouble of buying paint and making it look so beautiful.

My husband's point in telling me this story was that the best thing we could do in the face of the government's crackdown was to do nothing. I agreed entirely with his idea that we should avoid doing as the old peasant had and worsening the situation.

As I finished telling this story a young woman in her early twenties, wearing a red sweater smiled. She was from Chongqing in Sichuan and she said I reminded her very much of herself just a month ago. She told us how her ideas had changed and that she had come to Beijing to lodge an appeal on behalf of Falun Gong. Then others in the room started to say how they felt. There was even a former policeman from Changchun who had come to Beijing with his wife and child to lodge an appeal.

As I sat there, I was not so much listening to their words as trying to follow their train of thought. All I could remember later was that all of them had stories to tell of what had happened to them or to other practitioners since the crackdown began.

But suddenly a tremor ran through my whole body, as if my brain had exploded, and I knew at once where the difference between us lay. Until then I had had a fairly good sense of self. My faith in Falun Gong had never wavered, I had not bowed to outside pressure; despite the difficult situation I had never let a day go by without practising. But all of this was nothing more than just 'me', while they had long ago done away with 'me'. They had dissolved into the Dafa, the Great Law in which they had faith. This was the major difference between us.

Once I saw this I realised that the guarantee I had written was wrong. Did a government have the right to say black was white and to do exactly as it pleased simply because it had the power to do so? It was fortunate for the nation and for the people that Falun Gong was spreading, because those who practised it benefited from it; some even gained a second life. If we did not speak up during this vicious attack on Falun Gong, we would be undeserving of the good it had done us. The Ministry of Public Security's circular on the six prohibitions violated the constitutional rights of Chinese citizens to freedom of belief, association, speech, assembly, procession and demonstration. What was especially absurd was not being allowed to make an appeal and being forbidden to hang Falun pictures anywhere. This was completely unconstitutional. How could I guarantee to comply with something that was unconstitutional? Here I was, practising this, practising that, and I hadn't even understood this principle.

It all came down to selfishness. When a catastrophe hits, people instinctively look after themselves and theirs. As our teacher said, 'In fact, your previous nature was founded on selfishness.' Our teacher has also demanded this of us:

> From now on, whatever you do, you should consider others first, so as to attain the righteous Enlightenment of selflessness and altruism. So from now on, whatever you do or whatever you say, you must consider others—or even future generations—along with Dafa's eternal stability.

I believed I had been steadfast but had I done this? Wasn't China's biggest problem the serious decline in moral standards throughout society? If we didn't speak out against these slanderous attacks on Truthfulness, Compassion and Forbearance, what kind of society could we expect to have? Didn't practitioners talk of compassion, of saving all sentient beings? But where was our compassion, much less our saving all sentient beings, if each one of us remained silent in the face of such a catastrophe?

As I came to this realisation I was suddenly more at ease than I had ever been in my life. In an instant, the pressure I had felt since the crackdown had lifted. Suddenly everything was different and I no longer felt as if I was suffocating. With vivid clarity, my whole being felt, 'With heavens clear and celestial bodies transparent, the cosmos is rectified; the mega-havoc is over, and the universe is illuminated'.[10] So beautiful, so pure, so fresh. My body seemed to have taken on what our teacher describes as an intangible life, expanding and diffusing into infinity and becoming one with the boundless universe.

'This must be what is meant by transcending the self,' I thought. Once you can genuinely lay aside self-interest you feel at ease. After selflessness comes fearlessness. And then I understood what I had to do: I had to stand up for truth and principle.

---

10 from Li Hongzhi, *After Havoc.*

It was very late by the time we had finished talking and the buses had stopped running so I gave a lift to three people who lived a long way away. That was how I found out there were so many Falun Gong practitioners now living on the outskirts of Beijing and that since the ban dozens more arrived in the city every day, all intent on making an appeal. But the State Council's Petition Offices had simply removed the name plaque from the door and stationed police officers from all over the country to wait there. As they arrived to make their appeal, these newcomers were quietly taken into custody and escorted back to their home districts. So strict was the news blackout that even a Beijinger like me had heard nothing of this.

The morning after I had been to An Xiulan's, I managed to sneak out of the apartment while my mother-in-law was still asleep and I went to the park. Shutting my eyes gently, I began to do the Falun Gong exercises on the pavement at the entrance to the park, with people coming and going around me. Although I had decided that I must stand up for the truth, I really had no idea how I should go about defending it. So I chose to go and practise at the entrance to the park—this was a first step and at least it would show I was not afraid of the prohibition and not prepared to compromise with those in power.

I would like to say that I was not afraid, but my legs were shaking uncontrollably and I kept picturing myself being arrested and taken away. What amazed me, however, was how quickly I settled down. After about ten minutes into the second exercise, I was completely calm and finished the four exercises in as calm a state of mind as I had been before the crackdown. I even stopped picturing myself being arrested. From that moment on, no matter where I was or how momentous the occasion, I don't remember ever being frightened to the point that my legs were shaking.

After my practice I went to Beijing No. 2 Infectious Diseases Hospital, where I had been when I had hepatitis and where my voluminous medical records were kept. At An Xiulan's the night before I had heard that more than three months after several members of the former Falun Dafa Research Association had been imprisoned, their families had finally been told they could have lawyers and that there might be a trial. Their lawyers were looking for evidence that practising Falun Gong was indeed beneficial to one's health so I volunteered to go to the hospital for a blood test and provide the lawyers with medical proof that I had fully recovered from hepatitis after practising Falun Gong.

I was a bit early and the nurse who had just come on duty hadn't had time to set up the equipment so I waited in the corridor. Glancing at the *Beijing Morning Post* the person next to me was reading, I saw on the front page a story about Jiang Zemin being interviewed in France by a journalist for *Le Figaro*. The story was reported under the headline 'The "Falun Gong" is an evil cult'.

The night before I had vaguely heard someone say that there would probably be an escalation of the crackdown on Falun Gong and that they intended to label us an evil cult. My fellow practitioners had vowed that the instant they heard the news they would go to Tian'anmen to present a petition. Who would have thought that hearsay would become a reality so horribly soon? I borrowed the newspaper from my neighbour and tears streamed down my face as I read through the article. My heart was aching so much that I didn't register everything in it. I gave back the newspaper but my tears kept falling. Patients and staff gave me sympathetic glances as they passed, thinking I must have been told I had a terminal illness. I had no physical symptoms, but my pain was unspeakable.

That night Officer Wu knocked on our door again. I knew that his visit must have something to do with the escalating push against Falun Gong.

As soon as she saw who it was, my mother-in-law bundled my daughter into the other room and made herself scarce.

'Are you still practising Falun Gong?' Officer Wu asked in his admonishing-a-criminal voice, frowning fiercely.

I wasn't intimidated by him though, and felt no animosity towards him. At that moment I felt like a naughty child sharing a tremendous secret with another.

'I'm doing it on the sly at home,' I said with a smile.

He clearly hadn't expected this.

'Have you seen the TV?' he asked, his brow still fiercely furrowed.

'No.' My husband had just returned from a business trip and we'd only been back a few minutes when Officer Wu came in.

It goes without saying that the broadcast would have been about the evil cult issue. Since I said I hadn't seen it, he couldn't do as he had planned and browbeat me with what the program had said. He seemed to lose heart a little and was unable to muster his former ferociousness. After beating around the bush for a bit he said there were two things he had come to say. One was that since members of my family in Sichuan were also practitioners it was possible that fellow practitioners from Sichuan would come to Beijing and contact me. I was not, however, to have anything to do with them. The other thing was that in the last few days a great many people from outside Beijing had been going to Tian'anmen and we were not to get together with them to 'make trouble'.

After Officer Wu had gone I kept remembering what he had said: 'In the last few days a great many people from outside Beijing have been going to Tian'anmen'. Here were people travelling long distances to get to Beijing and I was only five bus stops from Tian'anmen. Why hadn't I gone? Should I go the next day? I asked myself a thousand times but I couldn't make up my mind. I was starting to feel suffocated again, as if my chest was stuffed with rotten cotton.

That night Beijing was hit by a Force 6 or 7 gale that wailed like a banshee. I tossed and turned in bed, my mind in turmoil, and finally fell into an uneasy sleep just before daybreak. I dreamed I was in a burning house desperately squirting a fire extinguisher.

When I woke up I gritted my teeth and made my decision: I would go to Tian'anmen, and I would go that very day!

I climbed out of bed and got dressed, putting on more clothes than usual, and pulled out a white T-shirt to wear on top. Then I put a pen in my bag. I was going to go to work first and make arrangements for 'things after I leave', then I would write 'Truthfulness, Compassion, Forbearance' across the front of my T-shirt and 'Falun Gong is not an evil cult' on the back. I would put on the T-shirt and walk to Tian'anmen. My thoughts were in a whirl: Right, today's the day! Let's do it!

My husband saw the look on my face and didn't say a word. We didn't speak in the car but just as we got to work he said, 'It would be better if you didn't go today.'

'Why?'

'No, not why. Your going like this is flirting with death.'

'Well, you tell me. What am I supposed to do?' I said, and burst into tears. I knew that if I were arrested in my present state I would either fight with the police or just start snivelling. So should I still go? But how could I *not* go when they were branding us an evil cult? I wanted to hold him close and have him give me a strategy that would not fail.

'Crying won't do you any good,' he said. 'Remember what Lu Zhaopeng said to Bai Ling in *The White Deer Plain*? "When you have learnt how to swallow a knife, then you'll be up to it."'

Being likened to the girl communist revolutionary Bai Ling immediately brought me to my senses and made me realise where I was going wrong. Right then I was aggrieved and resentful at our being labelled an evil cult and was feeling extremely emotional. I wasn't going to Tian'anmen for rational reasons, to uphold truth and justice; I was going on an impulse. And practitioners were not supposed to act impulsively.

So I gave up the idea. Several days later, when I had calmed down, I decided that I would put my views forward in a letter, where I could pursue my train of thought at leisure and without interruption. So I wrote letters to each of the Central Committee, the State Council, the Standing Committee of the National People's Congress, the Supreme People's Court, the Supreme People's Procuratorate and the State Council's Bureau of Religious Affairs, calling on them to handle the Falun Gong issue peacefully. My husband suggested I not put my name to the letter but I paid him no heed. I felt it was not right to write to the government and not give my correct name and address, besides which they might not think I was writing in good faith. The TV programs attacking Falun Gong were always saying things like 'they write a great many anonymous letters', and I didn't want this to be said of me.

After writing the letters I remembered my parents-in-law's about-face in their attitude towards me practising Falun Gong. Even though they had seen with their own eyes how much good Falun Gong had done me, the violence of the smear campaign had been able to make them discount their own experience. The power of these rumours was terrifying. And the role played by the news outlets in concocting these false reports was shameful. I wrote this open letter, reproduced in full at the end of this book, to the nation's journalists from my heart.

I faxed and mailed dozens of copies of my letter to all the larger provincial newspapers and TV stations. For the next few days every time there was a knock at the door I jumped, thinking, 'They've come to get me.' But when nothing happened it slowly faded from my mind.

A month or so later, Officer Wu phoned and ordered me to pay a visit to the local police station. When I got there he pulled out a Record of Questioning form.

'You wrote to Premier Zhu Rongji?' he said.

'Yes, how do you know?'

'How do I know!' He seemed half-angry, half-amused. 'You thought your letter would actually get to Zhu Rongji, did you? It got as far as a Grade 18 secretary. Do you know where your letter is now?'

I shook my head and he waved a sheaf of papers at me.

'Here it is! This time, as luck would have it, you didn't go to Tian'anmen. But you've made just as big a mess of things; the whole police station knows about it. The head of the police station and the head of this substation will be here shortly.'

Then he told me that my writing that letter was considered just as serious as going to Tian'anmen, so he had to record it. He was still doing that when his superiors arrived. I was still full of the feelings that had inspired me to write the letter, so I told them the whole story, from beginning to end. Every word I said was true and I spoke honestly, from my heart. They were stunned. They listened without saying a word, but half-way through they poured me a glass of water. When I had finished they still said nothing, just indicated that I could go.

WITHIN A HAIR'S BREADTH OF GOING TO PRISON

An Xiulan rang me on the morning of December 3, 1999. She said that the trial of former Falun Dafa Research Association members Li Chang, Yao Jie, Wang Zhiwen and Ji Liewu might be starting that day in Beijing No. 1 Intermediate People's Court and did I want to go? I knew of these people only because their names had been all over the propaganda material since the crackdown—I had never heard of them before that. By this time they had been in detention for several months. Ordinarily, the maximum period people can be held in custody is one month, but because there were no legal precedents about how to deal with Falun Gong and no relevant laws to go by, the courts had no idea how to deal with them. They had just been locked up, awaiting the Party's 'policy'.

I decided to ask for time off to attend the trial. It was to start at nine o'clock so I got there twenty minutes early and wandered around the court environs while I waited. A few minutes later I bumped into An Xiulan, who had just arrived, and we walked together to the court entrance.

We saw some people walking away from the court towards us. We knew instinctively they were Falun Gong practitioners even though they were complete strangers. These fellow practitioners told us court staff had told them that there would be no trial that day. We stood at the side of the road debating the source and authenticity of this information. A woman in her sixties said the person who had told her this was directly involved and could not have been mistaken. We eventually decided that putting the word around that the trial was to start had been a ruse on the part of the authorities designed to gauge the reaction of Falun Gong practitioners, to see how many people would turn up.

Once it became obvious that there was not to be any trial, many people left. An Xiulan suggested we find a more convenient place to gather and share views and since I had already arranged to take the day off, I went with her.

That was the day I met Xiao Ya and You Min.

Xiao Ya was from Shenyang. She was in her twenties and sang in a Beijing singing hall. She seemed very sincere and honest, not at all how I imagined a singing-hall girl would be.

You Min was the last to arrive at our meeting place and said that people were being arrested when she left the court entrance. She had seen two plainclothes officers putting an old woman in a police car. She herself had quickly jumped in a taxi and slipped away. You Min was also in her twenties and, like me, was from Sichuan. She had been teaching in a school in Beijing until the crackdown, when she lost her job. That day, she had a Falun badge pinned to her chest and a backpack full of Falun Gong books. She had been prepared to read them out in court to make the judges realise that Zhuan Falun taught people to be good. It was a pity she had not had the opportunity to carry out her plan.

We heard later that over 1,000 people had been arrested that day so we counted ourselves lucky to have left early.

Part III

THREE STRETCHES IN THE DETENTION CENTRE

1

THE NIGHTMARE BEGINS

OFFICER **W**U CALLED ON US for a third time on the night of December 25, 1999.

He sat himself down and started to chat. He told us how he had written out an application to join the Party nine years before but had not handed it in; instead he had carried it around in his pocket all that time. Why? Because he realised that he was better than many Party members, he said, and that Party members did many bad things. Not long ago, however, he had finally handed his application in. He didn't see what else he could do, he explained, because you couldn't expect to stand out from the crowd in his line of work if you weren't a Party member. He was well into his thirties and he didn't want to remain a junior policeman all his life. It wasn't being a junior policeman that was the problem. These days, everything was connected with money and you earned much less when you weren't promoted regularly. His son was growing up, and household expenses were rising; how could you get by without money?

He said that society these days had gone to the dogs and started talking about the son of the chief of the police station. This boy took up drugs when he was in his teens and before long his habit had plunged the family into debt. No matter how much power the chief had in the station, he could do nothing to control his own son.

Eventually he and his wife made the very painful decision to send their son to a detox centre.

When the son was told of their decision he was beside himself. He rushed into the kitchen, grabbed a knife and *choong!* chopped off his left thumb. The chief was a public security man, however, and he didn't panic. He called a car and took his son, and his thumb, to Beijing's best surgical hospital where they were able to sew the thumb back on.

Their son's hand was on the mend when the chief and his wife sent him, as planned, to the detox centre. Naturally enough, the young man's mother was worried about him and they paid him a visit after a few days. As soon as he saw his parents, he shouted, 'Give me 500 *yuan*! Come on. Give it to me. I want 500 *yuan*, are you going to give it to me or not?'

The implication was that, if he had the money, he could get his hands on drugs even at the detox centre. When his parents didn't respond straight away he pulled his thumb off again.

Hearing this story, I felt as though a part of my own heart had been pulled out: as a parent, it was an extremely difficult situation to bear.

Officer Wu stopped. He pulled a cigarette out of his pocket and lit it.

'How old is your son?' I asked.

'Three. He's just started kindergarten. I often wonder what I would do if my own son turns bad when he grows up. It's a dreadful thought.'

His concern was infectious. My daughter's school was only five minutes' walk from home, but in those five minutes she walked past two brothels, one purporting to be a hair salon and one a massage parlour. How could I not worry, when her innocent eyes gazed curiously at the heavily made-up 'girls' in their gaudy attire standing outside?

Having had his little chat, Officer Wu finally came to the point. For the next day or two things would be a little chaotic outside, he said, so it would be best if we didn't go out. I asked him what would be chaotic.

'It's Christmas Day today,' he said evasively. 'It's chaotic outside.'

'What is chaotic about Christmas Day?' I asked, quite puzzled.

He couldn't give any reason but continued to insist that we were not to go out for a couple of days.

'Don't worry,' I said. 'We're not going to do anything foolish.'

After he left, my husband and I talked about how it would be a miracle if the government didn't bring itself down, the way it was carrying on; why on earth were they getting so anxious about Christmas?

———

An Xiulan rang me very early the next morning—December 26, 1999—to tell me that the trial of the members of the former Falun Dafa Research Association would probably start that day. I was about to ask her how reliable her information was when I suddenly remembered Officer Wu's warning not to venture out for a couple of days. I realised that Officer Wu hadn't turned up by chance: his visit undoubtedly meant that the trial would start that day.

They had arrested over 1,000 people on the previous false start-date of the trial. It was quite obvious what would happen this time, when the trial actually did start. Yet, once I had resolved to go and speak up for the Falun Gong practitioners, I felt completely calm. In *Journey to the West*[11], when Monkey King (Sun Wukong), disguised as Tangseng (the Tang monk), cuts open his chest, a pile of hearts roll out: a miserly heart, a greedy heart, a jealous heart, an argumentative heart, a heart that seeks to outdo others, an ambitious heart, a disrespectful heart, a murderous heart, a venomous heart, a terrified heart, an over-cautious heart, a rash heart, an indescribably deceitful heart—all kinds of bad hearts. All these states of mind are attachments that practitioners must rid themselves of in the course of their cultivation. Once I realised I had to stand up for the truth, one after another my fearful heart, my over-zealous heart, my prideful heart—my competitive heart and my impulsiveness were laid bare. Only then did I finally feel that they were gone, that all that was left in my chest was an equable heart. Everything became very simple and very easy.

'I FOUND UNIVERSAL TRUTHS'

I had never been in prison and didn't know what I ought to take should it come down to that, so I just threw two packets of sanitary pads into my bag.

---

11 *Journey to the West* is a classic of Chinese literature.

Again, I asked my husband if he was coming. I had already decided that if he wasn't I would take the underground railway to the court but, almost immediately, he said he was coming. It was a Sunday, and we had planned to go and buy some paints and other materials for the new house we had just bought. Instead, we got in the car and drove to Beijing No. 1 Intermediate People's Court in Shijingshan District. From quite a distance we could see that there was tight security in the area, with sentries every three or four paces. Cars were not allowed in so we drove around for a while and finally parked in a nearby residential area and walked to the court.

Pedestrians were not being allowed on the same side of the street as the courthouse, but the police blocking off the end of the street let us walk along the other side, saying the court was cordoned off. We walked along the footpath until we were opposite the court. Outside the entrance was a large bus and I remember wondering why a bus would be parked there.

A policeman was standing in the middle of the road.

'Go and ask him if the trial is on today and if we can go in,' my husband said to me. 'I'll ring Officer Wu and see if he knows anything.'

So I went up to the policeman.

'Could you tell me if the trial is on today, please?'

'Why?'

'I'd like to go in.'

'Are you a Falun Gong practitioner?'

'Yes.'

'Any more Falun Gong practitioners?' he said to some passers-by, raising his voice.

'We are,' a young couple responded as they stepped forward, holding hands.

My husband appeared out of nowhere to stand alongside us.

'So it's just you four?' the policeman said loudly, eyeing the pedestrians across the road.

Nobody answered.

'You four come with me,' he said.

'Can we go in?' I asked as I followed him. 'Can we go in?'

The policeman ignored me until we were beside the bus I had noticed before.

'Get in, please,' he said to us.

Only then did we realise we were being arrested.

'If you won't let us go in, OK,' someone protested, 'but why are you arresting us?'

'Get in,' the policeman repeated, blocking our exit.

As soon as I got on the bus I saw that An Xiulan had been arrested, too, but I didn't recognise any of the others. As on July 20, the bus was soon full and in no time we were lined up outside Shijingshan Stadium again, having our details taken down.

When my turn came, the policeman seemed surprised that I had done postgraduate studies and had a master's degree.

'Have you read their books?' he asked, laying down his pen.

'Yes.'

'What did you learn from them?'

'I found universal truths,' I said slowly and clearly, looking him straight in the eye.

<hr />

This time we weren't taken into the stadium. Strips of paper had been stuck to the stadium wall at intervals of 20 or 30 metres with the names of the districts written on them. We were told to find the name of our district and wait there.

The police and other personnel were running around in circles.

'How come we've got Tongzhou?' I heard one of them say.

'Where is Jiamusi?' another complained. The city of Jiamusi was a long way from Beijing, almost on the Russian border, and they hadn't prepared a strip for it, not expecting anyone from so far afield. Now they had to go to the bother of writing one out, cursing under their breath.

About half an hour later a police car skidded to a halt outside the stadium and out jumped Officer Wu. He looked dreadful.

'You really did the dirty on me this time!' he said when he saw us. 'We had such a good chat last night I swore to the local chief that you two wouldn't cause any more trouble. It was just sheer laziness that I didn't go and check on you this morning, and here you are making me come all this way to get you! What am I going to say to the chief now? You've got me into real trouble.'

The only other person from our locality arrested that day was a middle-aged woman named Yu Jie, who worked in an almost defunct honeycomb-briquette factory. Her husband was also a Falun

Gong practitioner and had been fired from his job and expelled from the Party for having made a call to the premier's hotline during the People's Congress to say Falun Gong should not be suppressed. They had a teenage son and things were difficult for them.

We sped off in the police car, back to our local police station.

This time, however, we were made to sign a statement when we went in. The expression on Officer Wu's face was growing uglier by the minute.

Our statements were taken down and we were put in a room with four women who were also Falun Gong practitioners. They had been there all night, having been brought in the night before. The oldest, Wang Jin, was a plump woman in her fifties with the rosy cheeks of a young girl. As soon as we came in she offered us some fried griddlecakes that her son had just brought her.

'You probably haven't had much breakfast,' she said. 'Here, have some fried cakes.'

Her warm greeting almost made me feel I hadn't been arrested but was a guest in her home. I suddenly realised how hungry I was so, without standing on ceremony, I took one.

The police officer on guard left the room after a bit, apparently having other things to do. His place was taken by someone wearing a red armband who looked like a Neighbourhood Committee public security person.

We were kept in this room all day. As we talked, it became clear that these four women had been guests of the lockup before, which was why the local police had taken them in to prevent their 'making another mistake'.

This was the longest I had been able to talk with other practitioners since the crackdown and, in fact, since I took up Falun Gong. The weirdest thing was that if the seven of us had come together outside to talk about Falun Gong we would immediately have been considered an 'illegal assembly' and been arrested. Yet here we were, arrested and thrown together, an assembly. What we were not sure of was whether this assembly was legal, or still illegal?

Some time after eight o'clock that evening, Officer Wu took my husband and me into another room. He looked at us and sighed.

'Give your mother a ring,' he said to my husband.

'How long do you reckon it'll be?' my husband asked.

'Don't know. Depends on the higher-ups.'

My husband pulled out his phone and tapped in the number.

'Mum, Zheng Zeng and I might have to go away for a little while,' he said guardedly to his mother. 'You take care, and don't wait up for us.'

He rang off straight away, without giving her time to ask questions.

———

We were put into a paddy wagon along with Yu Jie. Apparently our 'misdemeanour' was of a serious nature because we had been arrested at the court. Wang Jin and the other women were later released because their stay in the police station had prevented them from 'making a mistake'.

Only then, as the paddy wagon sped along the dark streets, did I feel I was losing my freedom. It was like a dream, blurry pedestrians moving along indistinct streets in another world outside the wagon.

My husband, however, still seemed to be living in reality. He pulled out his mobile phone and rang his work colleagues and my workmates to ask them to apply for leave on our behalf. He even had the presence of mind to ring the person in charge of decorating our house, telling him that we hadn't gotten the materials yet and not to do anything further for the time being.

'That's the way. Make your calls now,' an old policeman sitting alongside him murmured. 'They won't let you ring anyone once you're in the lockup.'

I had thought the detention centre would be quite a way from the city proper but we were there in no time. It was too dark to see where we were but I had the impression we'd stopped in a large courtyard. Armed police were on sentry duty in front of a big iron gate, which was closed and cordoned off with a yellow line on the ground and a warning sign that entry without permission was forbidden.

The police accompanying us jumped from the wagon and told us to wait at the cordon. Carrying what appeared to be dossier files, one of them entered the building. I supposed he was handing over our 'data' and a few minutes later we were waved in.

In the dim light we passed through the gate into Chongwen District lockup, which was surrounded by a high wire fence. We were led in single file to the detention area and through a large door into a custody room, where registration formalities were completed. Once we had been officially handed over our local police had fulfilled their responsibilities and we were off their hands.

The upper half of one of the walls in the custody room was glass, and through it you could see the control room, with its bank of closed circuit television monitors and a wall full of small wooden tags on which were written the names of all the detainees and the cells they were in.

The officers in the custody room flipped through our dossiers while we waited, as instructed. Suddenly an officer in the control room spoke.

'Bloody shameless!' he yelped. 'Sleeping with her bum hanging out in the middle of winter!'

I looked up at the officer. His eyes were fixed on a television monitor on which could be seen a group of sleeping women. One of the women, wearing only a bra and panties, lay fully exposed to the gaze of the male officers in the control room; her quilt must have slipped off when she turned over. The officer who had damned her as shameless could hardly take his lascivious eyes from the screen. Apparently there was a camera in every cell and the police could monitor the occupants' every move.

When the officers in the custody room had finished going through the dossiers they got us to fill out yet more forms. Someone grabbed them to have a look.

'Hah!' he snorted in surprise. 'We've got a couple here, both postgraduates.'

I gathered this conveyed a range of conflicting ideas. 'So postgraduates also practise Falun Gong? Could this Falun Gong have some real substance?' 'A couple coming in together—what about their families?' 'So even postgraduates can come here as prisoners!' 'What's the point of opposing the government?' 'That's really stupid, all those years of study wasted.' 'They've fried their brains with all that study!'

After completing the forms, they went through the things we had brought with us. All we could bring in was toilet paper and sanitary pads. Hairpins, metal buttons and clothing labels were all confiscated, apparently to prevent us harming ourselves by swallowing them. We also had to take our shoes off in case we used them as weapons.

So these things were taken away and there we stood, the three of us, with not a thing to our names. My long hair fell loose down my back. A policewoman brought in a sleepy woman aged about 30, dressed in fairly lightweight pink pajama trousers, and placed her alongside us. She really stood out in that mass of green-uniformed police. I had no idea why she was there, this strange person in her underwear and with dishevelled hair.

Then I suddenly remembered some printouts An Xiulan had shown me from the Clearwisdom (Minghui) website, which overseas Falun Gong practitioners had established a month or so before the crackdown. Telling of their experiences in detention centres, many of them mentioned 'jail leaders', sometimes calling them 'cell leaders'. Perhaps this lightly dressed stranger was the cell leader.

I was not wrong. She was indeed a golden girl here. All the lock-ups, labour camps and jails in China are run on a system whereby prisoners were placed in charge of other prisoners. Every cell in a lockup had its own head, generally called the 'head student', the idea being that this person learned the social etiquette of the prison and imposed it on the others. They went by various names: their fellow prisoners called them 'cell leader' or 'jail leader' or 'head honcho'. The police relied on them to manage the prisoners, so they had considerable power.

There were also 'labour leaders', sometimes known as 'section bosses', whose status was even higher. They did work outside the cells—sweeping the washhouse, washing officers' clothes, issuing food and water—and thus had direct contact with the police, who would get them to do things that were not 'convenient' for the police to do themselves. Their sentences were often reduced because of their great 'contribution'. A great many of them were given protected status either because they had connections or pull or because they bribed the police, and ordinary prisoners did not dare upset them.

Lockup society was as complex as human society anywhere. Some people were protected and lived quite comfortable lives. Others rode roughshod over everyone else, demanding a cut of their money or other perks. If you had no power, no money, or were not aggressive enough, you got bullied. Before Falun Gong practitioners started to be detained, those who had committed financial crimes had the highest social standing in this prison society. Next came brawlers, murderers, robbers and peddlers of pornographic CDs, followed by drug addicts and petty thieves. Call girls and prostitutes were at the bottom of the pile. In the Beijing lockup, prisoners from out of town were also targets for the bullies. All in all, the more serious the crime, the more prestige a prisoner had, because the serious offenders received longer sentences and therefore had seniority. 'Long years of suffering turn a daughter-in-law into a mother-in-law.' If you don't bully a newcomer, who *do* you bully?

I was still pondering whether or not this woman was a cell leader when the policewoman ordered me to go with her. I realised then that I was going to be separated from my husband and from Yu Jie. I glanced at my husband, who quickly pulled a small handkerchief from his pocket and pressed it into my hand. In his eyes I saw a look I cannot describe.

I clutched that small handkerchief, my only possession, as I followed the policewoman and the cell leader into the corridor outside the control room and into the bowels of the jail.

Almost immediately we came to a large iron grille. The policewoman pressed a buzzer and the officer on the other side opened it to let us through. Once inside, I saw several passageways stretching out ahead of me. The cells lining one side of each passageway made up what I later heard was called a section.

I was led to the duty room of East Section 1 on the extreme right where, without blinking an eye, the cell leader suddenly thrust her hand under my clothes and felt around with deft but exaggerated movements, as if she feared the duty officer would think she wasn't doing her job properly. This, then, was my first experience of a body search. After that I was led to a cell, which had a solid door with a grille behind it. The first rule I learned in the detention centre was never to touch a door; to do so was deemed to be trying to escape.

The officer opened the grille door and I went straight into the cell. It was about ten square metres in size, with a passageway less than a metre wide. The rest of the room was taken up by a large wooden plank. Sleeping, 'sitting the plank', eating and resting were all conducted on this plank. At the end of the passageway was a washbasin and, opposite that, a lavatory pit. From the plank you could see everything that went on in the lavatory pit through a clear glass panel, the intention being to prevent suicides. It was then that I realised I had lost more than my freedom; I had lost every last shred of privacy.

'Sitting the plank' is a common physical punishment in the lockup. The prisoners must sit in a line along the edge of the plank with their backs straight and legs together and their hands on their knees. No one is allowed to move, to speak, to go to the toilet. For most of the day we had to 'sit the plank'.

We had two meals a day. We were allowed three *mantou* (steamed wheat rolls) each a day and could top this off with *wotou*, (a type of stale corn bread) that was as dry and unpalatable as sand. Our vegetable was always cabbage soup, which was actually just a few tired old cabbage leaves floating in a broth. Prisoners called it 'swimming cabbage'.

The *mantou* were given out once a day and were cold by the time we got them. We would eat one and had to keep the other two for later in a plastic bag; in winter they went dry and hard and in summer they went sour. The labour leader brought our meals to the grille door, the cell leader brought them into the cell, and then the second honcho dished them out. The second honcho also wielded the soup ladle, which gave her considerable authority.

The hierarchy in the cells was harsher than anything that operated in the real world. The head honcho slept closest to the door, with the second honcho next to her, the third honcho next, the fourth honcho next, and so on, in strict order. The order in which we sat on the plank, the order in which the bedding, the washing utensils and the food basins were laid out, the order in which we received food, did our ablutions and went to the toilet—everything had its own strict sequence. If anyone got it wrong or newcomers didn't adapt quickly enough they were in for it, usually getting a beating and a tongue-lashing.

Sleeping arrangements were generally that the first four honchos took up half the plank and the rest of us, no matter how many there were, all squeezed into the other half. If you couldn't fit, you slept on the floor.

There were two sets of jobs in the cells: cleaning and doing the night shift. Cleaning consisted of cleaning the bench, mopping the floor, cleaning the washbasin and the lavatory pit, and emptying the rubbish. The night shift, which was designed to prevent suicide attempts in the middle of the night, consisted of two people, each doing two shifts. The head honcho decided who did what and for how long.

This was how it was in the Beijing lockup. Detention centres in other places had set jobs as well. My younger sister said that where she was they were forced to sort through dwarf lilyturf tubers (*Ophiopogon japonicus*, used in traditional Chinese medicine) and were set daily quotas.

The police responsible for managing detainees were called corrective officers. They did the day shift and looked after routine affairs. The police on night shift were called squad leaders and they patrolled at twenty-minute intervals to ensure there were no suicides, escapes, fights, and so on. The police responsible for hearing cases were attached to a different department. They were called interrogation officers and were concerned solely with judicial cases, not the prison lives of individuals.

I MASTER 'SLEEPING AT ATTENTION'

When I first entered the cell I thought it was just full of old quilts. On further inspection I saw that under the worn quilts the plank was full of women, some of them asleep. Quite a few curious heads were raised when I went in.

'What's she in for?' came a chorus of voices.

'Falun Gong.'

'That explains why she doesn't look anxious. She's prepared herself.'

'You Falun Gongers are good people,' the cell leader said to me in all seriousness. 'You are very compassionate. Don't give us any trouble and don't practise Falun Gong here and I won't make things difficult for you.'

'What's your name, please?' I asked.

'My surname is Yang. If anything goes wrong, see me about it.'

Having satisfied their curiosity, heads were laid back down and people went back to sleep. The cell leader instructed me not to go to sleep yet.

'They will interrogate you shortly,' she said.

It was so crowded there was no room on the plank and someone was already sleeping in the passageway. I sat alongside her and waited. There was a very strange and awful smell in the cell.

About midnight a corrective officer came to take me to the interrogation building across from the cell area.

The interrogation was conducted by a very young policewoman

who looked as though she was new; perhaps just because of that, she behaved according to the rules. Before questioning me she showed me a sheet setting out the rights of detainees. There were seven or eight items but I remember only two: 'You have the right to remain silent' and 'You have the right to call a lawyer'.

The questions she asked were along the lines of, 'Why did you go to the law court?', 'Who told you to go?', 'Do you know the government has outlawed Falun Gong?' She recorded my answers in a businesslike manner without any comment and then told me I could go.

By the time I got back to the cell nearly everybody was asleep. In the back row, behind the four honchos, women were lying close up alongside each other with no gaps in between.

'Excuse me,' I said, turning to the cell leader, 'where do I sleep?' 'Sleep there, under her quilt,' she replied, pointing behind her.

With some difficulty I squeezed in between two of the women, discovering I had to lie on my side with my legs out straight and my body quite straight. Later, I found out that the special term for this posture was 'sleeping at attention' but I had to learn this most economical style of sleeping all by myself.

That night I slept very deeply, and had no dreams.

I quickly discovered that there were two more Falun Gong practitioners among the fourteen or fifteen women in the cell. Li Xinming was 52; she and her son had been arrested when they went to the Petition Office to appeal and had been in detention for about three weeks. Her son was in the men's cells, where he had been dubbed Little Falun because of his height—he was in his twenties, but just over 1.4 metres tall. Before practising Falun Gong he had found life very difficult because of this physical defect, but Falun Gong had transformed him into a happy, self-confident person. Artistically gifted, he had been accepted into the Central Academy of Fine Arts as a special student. Now that he was incarcerated, however, he didn't know if he would be able to retain his student status. The detention of a mother and son together had been big news in the detention centre for a time, as was the arrival of my husband and me as a couple.

The other Falun Gong practitioner was also in her fifties and had arrived only a few hours before me. She had come from Shandong province to make an appeal but as soon as she stepped from the train a police officer had approached her and asked if she practised Falun Gong.

'Yes,' she replied, and was taken straight to the detention centre.

Several others who had travelled with her were also arrested. There was another group behind them who saw all this taking place but she didn't know what had happened to them.

'Good grief!' one of the prisoners exclaimed when she heard this. 'How stupid can you be? Couldn't you just have said you didn't practise Falun Gong?'

The woman smiled ingenuously, not knowing what to say, so I answered for her.

'What she practises is Truthfulness, Compassion and Forbearance,' I said. 'She could not lie, even if a knife were held at her throat. And anyway, the reason she came to Beijing was to make an appeal, and anyone who makes an appeal is arrested so she would have been arrested sooner or later anyway.'

Several of the prisoners sighed, unable to comprehend how the older woman could have been so 'stupid'.

THE SECRET OF HOW NEWS IS MADE IN CHINA

Most of the other women in the cell were young: one was in for some financial crime, one for drug dealing, one was an addict and the cell leader was in for theft, but the rest were in for prostitution.

At eight o'clock, right on the dot, we began the day's 'sitting the plank'. After about an hour, corrective officers suddenly came to announce that the closed circuit TV in all cells would be coming on and we must watch an important program. We were all in the dark as we gazed up at the screen mounted over the grille door.

Snow, static, then the program started. Lo and behold, it was a special report on the trial of the members of the former Falun Dafa Research Association. So it *was* on the day before! We had watched the news avidly the night before at the local police station, but there had not been a single word about the trial, and we had come to the conclusion that this had been another feint to draw us out.

The report said that at nine o'clock the previous morning such-and-such a case had begun at Beijing No. 1 Intermediate People's Court, in accordance with the law, and that a large crowd had flocked to hear the proceedings. Then they announced that Li Chang had been sentenced to eighteen years' imprisonment, Wang Zhiwen to sixteen years, Ji Liewu to twelve years, and Yao Jie to seven years.

Such heavy sentences! A ripple of surprise ran through the cell. I couldn't help thinking about how there had been nothing on the seven o'clock news the night of the trial. Surely CCTV wasn't that inefficient? I was sure that this report we were hearing in the detention centre had been doctored in some way. They had arrested everyone who went there to attend the trial and apparently had netted over 1,000 people, so where did their 'crowd' come from? And where did their crowd get the visitors' permits necessary to attend the hearing?

One of my relatives had graduated from Sichuan University's Department of Journalism and gone to work at a TV station. He hit the nail on the head once, when he said to me that China has no news. All of the media are propaganda tools, mouthpieces for the Party; even entertainment programs must be politically 'correct'. Journalists who do not understand this, he said, would be better off not working in the journalism profession at all.

Given this, it is no wonder that the June Fourth Movement, which centred on freedom of the press, was suppressed in such a bloody fashion—because once the media's hands are untied it is impossible to preserve that kind of political power.

After this special report had been repeated seven or eight times, the prisoners grew impatient and began to whisper among themselves. Then the grille door clanged open: Corrective Officer Zhang wanted to talk to me.

Officer Zhang took me into her office and pulled out some notepaper. Instead of starting off asking me my full name, she launched into a diatribe.

'Don't think you're the most persistent we've had. I've had lots who were more persistent than you. There was a mother and daughter from rural Shandong who rode an old bicycle hundreds of *li* to Beijing with just four *yuan* fifty in their pocket. They took turns and when they were tired they slept on piles of straw by the roadside. When they were hungry they nibbled on the dry *mantou* they had brought with them. And when they reached Beijing they still had the whole four *yuan* fifty they had set out with. They were illiterate, and when we questioned them all they said was Falun Gong is good. How's that?'

By then I was in tears.

'What are you doing?' Officer Zhang said nervously as I reached into my pocket for my little handkerchief.

When I was washing my face that morning I had realised I didn't have any toiletries, so as a facecloth I had to use my husband's handkerchief. But the head honcho wouldn't let me hang it up to dry, saying that a handkerchief was not 'regulation', so I had to put the damp handkerchief back in my pocket.

'I'm not doing anything,' I said as I fished it out and started wiping my tears away. 'I'm just deeply touched.'

She relaxed when she saw it was just a handkerchief. She went on to ask me what I thought when I found out that our 'leader' Li Chang had been sentenced to eighteen years. I told her that Li Chang was not our leader, that we didn't have a leader, and that I had no opinion about the sentence. I told her I believed Li Chang would not serve the full eighteen years but would be let out early. I saw that she didn't believe what I was saying. For my part, it was just too difficult to explain it to her, but she was no longer interested anyway and hurriedly filled in the rest of the form before sending me back to the cell.

The day passed quickly. I was very calm and untroubled, the people and things around me as unreal as in a dream, as if it all had nothing to do with me. When it came my turn to do the night shift, I finally managed to carve out a little space for myself among the women, pillows and quilts on the edge of the plank. Crossing my legs, I closed my eyes and began to meditate.

A few minutes later the head honcho called out sternly, 'Zheng Zeng! What are you doing?'

Everybody woke up.

'If you practise Falun Gong,' she continued, 'the corrective officers will think I'm not doing my job properly. I don't want to get you into trouble, so how about you go back to sleep and I'll do the night shift for you?'

I did not want to affect the others or have her do my shift, so I decided to give up. At the end of my shift I wriggled back into my sleeping slot but I couldn't get to sleep. The head honcho was only following the orders, I thought. I would have to say openly to the police that I wanted to practise Falun Gong and if they refused I would go on a hunger strike. I had to persevere! But I wondered if I could do it; I found myself hoping I could, telling myself I could.

So moved was I by my own determination that tears began to ooze from under my tightly closed eyelids. The other young woman on night shift must have thought I was having a nightmare.

'She's in here for merely practising Falun Gong,' I heard her murmur sympathetically. 'That's not fair.'

I said nothing, silently resolving to fight for the right to practise Falun Gong.

———

We were sitting on the plank in the afternoon of my second day when the grille door clanged open.

'Zheng Zeng!' an extremely impatient voice called from the corridor. 'Here!'

I followed the voice and was confronted by a plump policewoman who proceeded to turn out my pockets.

'Why have you still got these?' she shouted at me.

'These' were the tokens that were used in the lockup in place of cash. Ready cash was not allowed—it was kept in the custody room—so if you needed money the labour leader issued you with tokens with which you could buy things; she kept records of these loans. That morning I had changed 300 *yuan*. I had handed over 150 *yuan* for bedding and 30 *yuan* for 'communal expenses', so I had just over 100 *yuan* left. The 'communal expenses' was a sort of kitty for daily necessities. The head honcho handled it, buying general items from it or dipping into it to help penniless women or women who had no one outside to send them money.

I didn't understand what was so wrong about me having tokens.

'Don't you know you're being released?' she shouted in my face at the top of her voice. 'How am I going to find somebody now to change these things for money?'

Released! The thought had never occurred to me. Li Xinming had been there for three weeks with no sign of being released.

Seeing how impatient the officer was, I pointed to Li Xinming.

'Can I give them to her?' I asked.

Lockup rules said that no money of any kind could change hands between detainees, but the reality was quite different.

'It's up to you,' she said irritably.

I stepped back into the cell and handed the tokens to Li Xinming. Her husband had died a long time ago and, with her son also in detention, she didn't have a penny to her name. If she had been released she probably wouldn't even have had her bus fare. I had tried to give her some tokens when I first changed my money but she had refused to take them. Now I was counting on the presence of the policewoman, that she wouldn't be able to not take them. I turned away quickly lest she try to give them back and in that instant I saw the looks on the faces of the other women in the cell. They envied me being released and they envied Li Xinming her windfall; some clearly were annoyed that I hadn't given them the tokens.

My head was awhirl as I followed the plump policewoman out of the cellblock. We went back to the custody room the way I had come in earlier. And there was my husband. I had never seen him so unkempt and my heart went out to him. He told me later that he hadn't shaved for two days; he hadn't even washed his face or cleaned his teeth, because he didn't have a facecloth or toiletries. He had shared a moth-eaten old quilt with a drug addict, sleeping on the stone-cold floor. He had been frozen all night and nauseated by the drug addict, who was having withdrawal symptoms and kept dribbling all over the floor in his sleep. He had been let out just once in those two days for exercise, but at the end of December the temperature in Beijing is below zero, and he had been barefoot and frozen stiff.

Finally our belongings were returned to us and we were escorted through the main gate of the detention centre. My husband let out a huge sigh. He told me that when they had taken him to the custody room he had seen a detention note with my name on it on the table, saying I was to be detained for seven days. His heart had sunk when he thought he was to be released without me. I had seen no paperwork and nobody had said a word to me about anything.

Later, when I was taken to the detention centre for the second time, I was told that because I had spent less than 48 hours in detention the first time, my file had been changed to 'held for examination'. In other words, this first time was not counted as 'detention'. This technique of arresting people, locking them up and then filling in the legal documents after the event on the basis of how long they had been held certainly opened my eyes.

Deputy Chief Niu Jun, who had been made responsible for Falun Gong matters in our local police district, was waiting for us at the gate. He was about 30, a clean-cut young man with ambition written all over his face.

In the police car Niu Jun adopted the friendly approach, cloaking his threats as advice.

'Political struggle is about methods, you know,' he said. 'It's not about who's right and who's wrong. Do you know how the Nationalist Generalissimo Chiang Kai-shek punished the Communist Party in the old days? His theory was that it's better to wrongly arrest 3,000 than to let that one Communist you want slip through your fingers. You know that, don't you? Or were all your years of learning history completely wasted?'

I was about to argue back but for some reason I didn't want to talk to him. Also, I really didn't think it proper for him to compare us with the Communist Party, so I kept my mouth shut.

In an apparent show of concern, just before we got to the police station he suggested we have a good long shower when we got home and go to work the following day. But it seemed to me what he was really saying was: Did you two 'honourable citizens' learn your lesson this time? Did you enjoy your stay in the detention centre? You'd die of the filth there; I suspect you won't dare go there again!

Niu Jun gave us another talking to at the police station before ushering us out the door. Finally, we were free. Our car was parked at the court, 20 kilometres away, and my husband said I should go home and he would catch a taxi and go and fetch the car.

Just three days before I had been quite fearless when confronted by the police but now, suddenly, I was afraid.

'No,' I said, clutching my husband's arm. 'I'm going with you and when we get home you're going in first.'

I might not be afraid of the police but I didn't dare face my parents-in-law by myself.

2

'LET LIFE DISPLAY ITS SPLENDOUR IN *FA*-RECTIFICATION'

THE STORM OF BLAME I had expected didn't eventuate when we got home. My husband went in first, but his parents acted as if nothing had happened and made no enquiries. In fact, they had had their suspicions right from the start. The Chinese people have been through so much that nothing can surprise them now. His parents had done their utmost to stop us and keep us out of danger, but when the worst did come to pass and we emerged from the detention centre such sorry figures, it cut them to the quick. How could they bear to make more trouble for us? A day or so later, my father-in-law had a quiet word with me. When we were out all day the day we were arrested, he told me, they had taken it as a bad sign. And after my husband's phone call my mother-in-law nearly passed out. She took to her bed, repeating over and over again, 'I can't collapse, I can't collapse. There's the child, there's the child . . .' He said that if it hadn't been for Shitan, whom she loved more than her own life, she probably would have 'handed in her ration book' and died.

'Oh, you must listen to him who is in power,' he went on, as if he were talking to himself. 'Even if he is just a whelp you have to listen to him as he is still in power.'

This really surprised me. My father-in-law had been a chairman of the peasant association before liberation in 1949. He had served in the Korean forces resisting US aggression, joined the Party, rendered meritorious service, heeded the Party line and waged revolution. He had been faithful and true to the Party. He had come under attack during the Cultural Revolution and had been more or less dropped when he retired. He couldn't quite work out whether what the Party was doing now was socialism—that thing to which his entire generation had devoted a lifetime of struggle. But, despite that, he had never contemplated saying no to the Party's directives. To hear him suddenly refer to the highest authority of the Party as a 'whelp' really staggered me.

After I was released from the detention centre I kept in touch with Wang Jin and the others I had met during our 'legal illegal assembly' in my local police station. One afternoon in mid-January, about three weeks after I was released, Wang Jin took me to see her daughter Zhang Xiaomei, who shared a two-room flat with several fellow practitioners.

There was no furniture in the apartment apart from a few mattresses on the floor and, when we arrived, people were sitting on these mattresses eating a very simple meal of *mantou* with salted vegetables. I knew immediately that these people had come to Beijing to make an appeal.

Among the practitioners I met that day who made a deep impression on me was Sister Ping, a woman in her forties from Wuhan.[12] On October 28, 1999, just as the crackdown was escalating and Falun Gong had gone overnight from an 'illegal organisation' to an 'evil cult', she and several others had somehow managed to set up a secret press conference in Beijing with foreign journalists. Running an enormous risk, they had exposed the cruelty of the suppression. The press conference was extremely effective in letting in a little light at a time when public opinion throughout the mainland was being totally manipulated. It was also the first direct exposure the foreign media had to the plight of Falun Gong practitioners in China. The journalists were enormously impressed with these practitioners, saying how extraordinary they were to put their lives at risk in that way. 'If we

12 In China, the term 'sister' is a title of respect for someone who is of similar age. Similarly, 'auntie' and 'uncle' are used as respectful titles for someone who is older.

are found out the worst that can happen is that we will be deported; you could be killed,' they said.

Sister Ping was one of the organisers of the 1999 Guangzhou Falun Dafa Experience-sharing Conference, which was attended by over 100 people. At that time, under the sort of pressure where 'dark clouds press down on the battlements and the city is about to be destroyed', many practitioners were quite at a loss as to what to do. They received much-needed encouragement when the experiences of fifteen practitioners were posted on the Clearwisdom website. Due to the Internet blockade in China, public access to many websites is restricted. However, some practitioners who have the skill have been able to side-step the blockade and print out these very precious experiences. They then distribute them among fellow practitioners.

I so wish I were capable of describing the magnificence of this conference. I remember being in tears by the time I finished reading the experiences, and wiping the tears from my face. These practitioners' tales of risking their lives to defend their beliefs shook me to the core. The article 'Let life display its splendour in *Fa*-Rectification' by the 32-year-old practitioner from Shijiazhuang, Ding Yan (her real name), inspired countless others around the world.

Before the conference, Ding Yan had once been arrested in Tian'anmen while presenting a petition for Falun Gong. The police handcuffed her in exceptionally heavy brass cuffs, with her hands behind her back. They trod on her back, then lifted both her arms, in the cuffs, like a handle and carried her back and forth, back and forth, torturing her for a full three hours, trying to get her name out of her. Many, many times she thought she could bear the agony no longer but she gritted her teeth and said not a word throughout the entire nightmare. The police then softened, handcuffing her in a slightly more humane fashion.

'You'd better talk,' they told her. 'These brass handcuffs will eventually cripple you.'

By this time she had lost all feeling in both hands, yet she held her tongue except to tell them, with the force of justice behind her words, that she could not cooperate with wickedness. Apparently the police were finally moved to tears, took off the handcuffs and rubbed her ice-cold hands to get her circulation moving again.

Ding Yan was arrested again, when she took part in the Guang-zhou experience-sharing conference, and sentenced to four years' imprisonment. She was transferred between Shijiazhuang and Baoding prisons and died as a result of torture in the water dungeon of Chengde Prison, in September 2001.

Run? Or stay?

On the ninth day of the Guangzhou conference the police burst into the practitioners' room in a hotel where Sister Ping and several other practitioners were staying. The others had all gone out, so while the police moved about ransacking cases and cupboards she quickly tore to shreds all incriminating documents—those containing addresses or phone numbers—and swallowed them with considerable effort with the help of a bottle of mineral water. She was discovered by the police just as she forced down the last mouthful and roughly handcuffed. The police waited for her fellow practitioners to return, leaving Sister Ping, handcuffed, in a police car. She kept her cool and somehow managed to slip the handcuffs off, then made off under the nose of the officer assigned to watch her.

She made her way back to Beijing, where she renewed her extensive contacts with other Falun Gong practitioners and convened three quite large experience-sharing gatherings in a two-room flat, events which attracted participants from all over the country. Tapes of these talks were put up on the Clearwisdom website and had a significant impact.

Inspired by these gatherings, over 1,000 Falun Gong practitioners from China and elsewhere gathered in Tian'anmen on Chinese New Year's Eve—February 4, 2000—to display banners and practise Falun Gong, infuriating those in authority.

Sister Ping and several other Falun Gong students were hiding out in the residential area of a Ministry of Space Research Institute. The Ministry of Public Security was monitoring this area as well as all office blocks and public phones. Sister Ping and Xiaomei were among several Falun Gong practitioners arrested on the sixth day of the first lunar month in 2000—February 10—given away by their use of public phones. During my second stay in the detention centre, I saw on TV that Sister Ping had been sentenced to eight years' imprisonment; she is still in prison somewhere. Zhang Xiaomei was sentenced to five years and is now in Beijing Women's Prison; her boyfriend apparently received a three-year sentence.

I went to that flat several times and met many fellow practitioners from all over the country. I also participated in two experience-sharing gatherings. Many of these people were preparing to deliver their petition in Tian'anmen on Chinese New Year's Eve but I had already arranged to take my daughter home to Sichuan to visit relatives and celebrate the Spring Festival.

The morning after we arrived in Sichuan, I had just woken up and hadn't even had time to greet my parents when the phone rang. It was the Deputy Chief of our local police station, Niu Jun, ringing from Beijing.

'Do you know You Min?'

'Yes,' I said, wondering how he knew her.

'And Xiao Ya?'

'Yes.'

'Where did you take them on January 19?'

'I'm sorry, I can't tell you that,' I replied, remembering that I had taken them to an experience-sharing gathering in Zhang Xiaomei's flat.

'You must tell me!'

'I'm sorry, I must not tell you.' Although Falun Gong practitioners will not tell a lie, this does not mean that they will endanger other innocent practitioners by telling everything they know to the police.

'If you don't, I'll get your local police there to escort you back to Beijing!' he declared and hung up.

My parents were in shock, my mother incredibly distressed. I was stunned, and on top of everything else, I hadn't been able to see my sister to give her the written experiences from the Guangzhou conference I had brought for her.

Mother got out three sweaters, two pairs of woollen long johns and a cotton-padded overcoat.

'Put them all on,' she instructed me. 'The detention centre is very cold and we can't be certain the police won't beat you.'

Thus garbed I sank down on the sofa to wait. Everything felt cold and miserable, under overcast skies, with heavy sleet falling outside.

Shitan had been overexcited on the train trip and hadn't slept well, so she wasn't awake yet. As I gazed down at her precious little face I wanted to tell my mother to send her back to Beijing, to make sure she did her homework, but I knew my mother would move mountains for the sake of her granddaughter, so I said nothing.

By noon the police hadn't come so I decided not to wait any longer. I lay down for a nap after lunch but my mind was too busy and I couldn't get to sleep. Was I being stupid, just waiting for them to come and get me? Should I run away, to avoid being arrested again? How could they find me? But if I ran away I'd have to go into exile and then I wouldn't be able to return home and I wouldn't be able to work. Where would I run to? Was I really going to roam the world? I wasn't ready for this, nor was I able to make a decision.

I spent that night struggling with the dilemma of whether or not to run away.

Niu Jun rang again early the next morning to ask when I was returning to Beijing. In ten days, I told him. Then he spoke to my father, telling him that since I had made the long trip home he wouldn't have me arrested but would let me enjoy my family over the Spring Festival. Then he told my father to 'straighten me out', saying the other things could wait until I got back to Beijing.

Not arrest me? Did the sun rise in the west? My mother said she knew what this was all about. It was like the law courts, she said. When we have to apprehend a criminal outside our own area, we need the cooperation of the local courts and if we don't get it there's nothing we can do about it. It's the same with the Ministry of Public Security: they are so busy with their own cases at the end of the year that even many homicides are not dealt with. What you did in Beijing isn't an issue to them. The Ministry of Public Security here would be more concerned about who would be liable for the travelling expenses.

Whether or not she was right I couldn't say, but I breathed a sigh of relief that they weren't coming to get me. At least now I didn't have to decide whether to run away or not.

For Shitan's sake, we went through the motions for the Spring Festival but our hearts weren't in it, knowing I was to be arrested when I went back.

THE POWER OF COMPASSION

I got back to Beijing very late on February 10, 2000, as arranged. My husband told me that the police had come looking for me the day after I left and had taken him to the police station in my stead. They said they had discovered my connection with You Min and

Xiao Ya after they and Xiao Ya's boyfriend were arrested for displaying a 'Falun Dafa is good' banner in Tian'anmen. The Ministry of Public Security apparently had a deadline for closing the matter and believed I could help them locate the premises at which several large Falun Gong experience-sharing gatherings had been held.

They told my husband that I was to go to the police station immediately upon my return and, if I behaved and gave them the address, they wouldn't be too hard on me. If I didn't, well, there could be no guarantees.

It was from this point on that my husband and I differed violently as what I should do. He insisted that I should tell the police the address. Zhang Xiaomei and the other Falun Gong practitioners who lived there would have moved out immediately after the others were arrested. What could the police do to an empty flat? I said the owner of the flat could be fined heavily.

'Well,' he replied, 'we could compensate the owner and thus he or she wouldn't lose a penny. And you'll be *jailed* if you don't tell them.'

But I just could not see things his way. This crackdown on Falun Gong was totally immoral. Why should I cooperate with something this *wrong*? Besides, if the owner of the flat were also a Falun Gong practitioner, he or she would be arrested too.

My husband and I debated for a long time. The following morning I finally came to a decision that was somewhere between running away and not running away. As luck would have it, the refurbishment of our new house had just been completed and I had been transferred to a new department at work. I quickly packed a few changes of clothes and set off before they started work at the police station, leaving the whole family at home. As soon as I had settled in at our as yet unfurnished home I rang my old workplace, asking them not to tell the police where I was if they rang.

A week later my old workplace called to tell me that a 'Wang Bin' had left his number, asking me to call him back at my convenience. I didn't know any Wang Bin but thought perhaps he was a fellow practitioner I had met in one of the gatherings, so I returned his call.

Wang Bin was a policeman, however, and trapped me into revealing my location. Half an hour later, I was on my way back to the detention centre.

We were almost there when Wang Bin suddenly spoke.

'Do you know why the government is so afraid of you?' he asked.
'No. Why?'

'Because your Falun Gong is too genuine; you are too cohesive a force.'

'Really? Have you read *Zhuan Falun*?'

'Yes.'

'What did you think of it?'

'If I had read it earlier,' he said with a note of regret in his voice, 'I may well have gotten right into it. But now I'm looking at it through different coloured spectacles, seeking from the book ways of dealing with you, so I'm not into it.'

We had reached the detention centre by then so I left it at that. As Wang Bin got out of the vehicle he told me that because so many Falun Gong practitioners were being arrested a special group had been set up to examine their cases. Somewhat apologetically he said he would have to hand me over to someone else because he did not belong to the special Falun Gong investigation task force.

'It doesn't matter,' I said. 'If you could, though, would you ring my husband and ask him to send me a few things I'll need?'

Every day for the next three days he turned up while I was being interrogated, strolling about looking for something to do.

'Did your husband send you those things?' he asked me the first day.

At the time, the interrogators were trying to force me to divulge the location of the experience-sharing gathering. I wanted to taunt Wang Bin, 'Do you think that you've done a great job by arresting me?' But I restrained myself as I realised that to do so wasn't expressing the compassionate nature of a Falun Gong practitioner. So I simply nodded. 'Yes, thank you.' He was there again the second day and asked the same question: 'Did your husband send you those things?' I now realised he felt bad about bringing me in and wanted to apologise but didn't know how, so he just kept repeating the same question. Again I nodded. 'Yes, thanks.' On the third day he arrived with a police dog. He played with the dog for a while before he finally asked me again. 'Did your husband send you those things?' But this time he sounded close to tears.

I didn't look up to answer him. I was beginning to feel uncomfortable on his account. How many other people were there who still had a conscience, but were forced to take part in the persecution?

I also remembered that Li Hongzhi once said that compassion is a most powerful force. Because I hadn't responded to Wang Bin with harsh words, something in his conscience had been awakened.

———

From the moment I was taken into the detention centre three members of the special Falun Gong task force took turns interrogating me: Zhang Qiang, Ma Ying and their section head Wan Jie. On day one, they tried to persuade me. On day two, they threatened me with the safety of my fellow practitioners, turning on my pager and placing it on the table. If I talked, they said, everything would be all right; if I didn't they would arrest each person who called me and say that I had 'fingered' them. In other words, they would say I had turned police informer.

On day three, they wouldn't let me go to the toilet. In the end, when my bladder was about to burst, I gritted my teeth and decided to resolve the matter on the spot.

On day four, Zhang Qiang looked at me as if he had found a priceless treasure, his eyes gloating and triumphant.

'If you won't talk, fine,' he said. 'Someone else will. Your husband went to that meeting, too!' How had he found out? That was the day I had taken a taxi with Xiao Ya and You Min to the gathering and had rung my husband to ask him to pick me up afterwards.

'If you won't talk I'll bring him in. Then we'll see who's the stronger of you two. Uh-huh. And your daughter's going back to school tomorrow. Let's see how that affects you!'

He dangled my husband's phone number in front of me.

'Hello,' he said into the mouthpiece, all sweet geniality. 'Is that X————? This is Zhang Qiang. You know your wife is here, don't you? Could you come over? We'd like to discuss a few things with you.'

My husband agreed readily, unaware of Zhang Qiang's true intentions. I looked at the high wire fence outside and felt tears welling up but fought them down, not wanting Zhang Qiang to see them.

Zhang Qiang reached for a newspaper and appeared quite cool. 'Your husband will be here in half an hour. You've still got time to tell us.' Then he buried his head in the newspaper as if he'd already forgotten I existed.

The interrogation room hadn't been this quiet for four days. I could almost hear Zhang Qiang's fast-beating heart.

He couldn't keep it up, though, and ten minutes later he looked up. 'You ready now?' he said. 'You've still got twenty minutes.'

I gave a thin smile and said nothing.

He buried his head in the newspaper again, pretending to read for another ten minutes. Then he asked me again; still I said nothing.

Ten minutes later my husband rang from outside the detention centre.

'Go back to your cell and wait,' Zhang Qiang told me. 'If he doesn't cooperate I'll detain him, too.'

A bit over an hour later Zhang Qiang came to get me. Not knowing what had happened with my husband, I knew that if I asked he would taunt me so I kept my mouth shut. Without a word, Zhang Qiang led me to the interrogation room. My husband was still there!

'Your husband is more sensible than you,' Zhang Qiang said. 'He's taken us to the site and we know which building it is. Now we just need you to tell us the floor and the apartment and we'll let you go. Otherwise, we'll search the building room by room. Do you think we won't find it? Your husband agreed that he might be able to persuade you. Family members are not normally allowed in but we're making an exception for you.'

He turned to my husband.

'We haven't got much time,' he said. 'Let's get on with it.'

'Could we have some time alone?' my husband asked.

'No.'

I could see that my husband wanted to tell me something but now he was going to have to do it indirectly. It was dark when we went to the meeting, he began, and you probably can't remember which floor the apartment was on, can you? So how about we take them down there and have a look around? I remember we had other things to do when it finished, didn't we? So-and-so had come to Beijing and we had arranged to go and see him, hadn't we?

'So-and-so' was a deputy to the National People's Congress. We had arranged to see him when he came to Beijing for the National People's Congress meeting with the idea of asking him to raise the issue of treating Falun Gong peacefully. Feeling sure this would work, my husband had given Zhang Qiang a guarantee that he could talk me round.

I said nothing to all this.

'And doesn't our teacher say that Dafa is perfectly harmonising?' my husband finally blurted out in desperation.

'Dafa is also serious!' I replied sternly.

Zhang Qiang had had his head down pretending to read the newspaper while my husband was talking, but he looked up at me in astonishment when I said this, obviously forgetting what part he was supposed to be playing.

After half an hour Zhang Qiang saw that my husband wouldn't be able to persuade me and he ordered him to go. There was such despair and grief in my husband's eyes as he left. Caught between harsh reality and his own powerlessness, he felt as if he had been torn apart and the pieces scattered to the four winds. 'Five Horses Splitting the Body' was a famous method—one of the cruellest—used to execute people in ancient China. The victim's head and four limbs were tied to five horses. The executioners would then drive the five horses in five different directions to split the person, alive, into pieces.

My husband told me that he once discussed Falun Gong and my arrest with a friend of his. The friend was not supportive at all, feeling it had nothing to do with him. He felt that he was a very good and honourable person and that his own life was going very well, thank you very much.

'Do you think it is honourable to live in a country where Red Guards can rough up even the Chairman whenever they like?' my husband nearly shouted at him. 'Will you stand by and applaud as they storm your home, as they rape your mother, your sister, your wife? How honourable are you, really?'

This was exactly how my poor husband felt about my being arrested while he could do nothing to rescue me. Although he chose to cooperate with the police, he himself was honourable enough not to blame me for not making the same choice. Falun Gong had restored my health and renewed my joy for life. On top of that, he respected his wife's own free choice.

'THE EARTH WILL EXPLODE' SAVES ME

Furious at my husband's lack of success, Zhang Qiang took me to the interrogation room again the next morning. That afternoon, after hours of going around the same well-trodden track, a police officer brought in a great stack of books that had been confiscated from the home of another Falun Gong practitioner. Apparently determined to provoke me, Zhang Qiang asked me if I wanted to have a look at my teacher's books. Then he said, casually, as if the thought had just occurred to him, 'Oh, will you have a look and see if they're complete?'

By some good fortune, when I went over to his desk I found in the pile two copies of *Falun Buddha Law: Lecture at the First Conference in North America*. I opened both copies at page 42—page 16 in the English-language version—and handed Zhang Qiang and his section chief Wan Jie a copy each.

'Please read this section,' I said.

'What's this about?' Zhang Qiang asked in bewilderment.

'I'll tell you when you've read it,' I said and went back to my place to watch them.

Misgiving written all over their faces, they took the books and began to read. This book had been compiled from tapes of Li Hongzhi's lecture in New York in March 1998 and page 42 contained a mention of previous talk of the world coming to a catastrophic end in 1999, something that simply was *not* going to happen. After the crackdown, CCTV repeatedly broadcast a documentary about Falun Gong, which included some of the lectures, but they had deleted the 'not' in 'not going to happen' when Li Hongzhi talked about the discussion about the catastrophic end of the earth. They also edited the lectures in such a way that everyone who watched the documentary would hear Li Hongzhi saying 'the earth will explode'. At the end, the narrator claimed that many people had been terrified into practising Falun Gong by 'talk of the earth exploding'. Thus, Falun Gong practitioners were presented to viewers as ridiculous 'insane devotees'. I had written to the Bureau of Religious Affairs who played the program, and had looked up the page where it said that the explosion of the earth was not going to happen. And that was how I was able to turn straight to page 42.

Sure enough, I watched the expression on Zhang Qiang's face change as he read. When he finished and looked up at me his face was blank.

'Well?' I asked. 'Did our teacher predict the earth would explode? Why did the government say he did?'

For the first time in five days, he struggled for an answer.

'When did the government say that?' he said. 'How come I didn't know?'

'You really didn't know?' I said. 'And you're in the special Falun Gong task force! It looks like you need to do a bit more study.' I realised it must be hard enough to work for an apparatus that told lies, so I didn't want to kick Zhang Qiang—too hard—when he was down.

'You should read the *People's Daily* editorial of July 22, 1999,' I went on. 'It's called "Li Hongzhi—the man and his deeds" and there's a subheading in it that states "Preaching that the world will explode".'

Zhang Qiang opened his mouth to say something but Wan Jie, who had carried on reading after the bit about the world exploding, suddenly looked up.

'OK,' he said in a tone that allowed no argument. 'Let's wind this up. She's not going to talk. Write "Wouldn't talk" on the record. Get her to sign it and that'll do it.'

Zhang Qiang gave him a surprised look but was quick to do as he was told. He scribbled a series of questions on my file, writing "Wouldn't talk" alongside them, and got me to sign it.

'OK, Miss Postgraduate,' Zhang Qiang said, not really happy with this outcome. 'So you've put all your learning to use for Falun Gong. You know everything your teacher said and which page it's on!'

My case was closed. They put me back in my cell and, finally, left me alone.

<hr />

A couple of weeks later, Zhang Qiang summoned me to the interrogation room, where two police officers were waiting.

'Ah, so we've found you!' the younger one stated as I entered. He went on to explain that they were from Shenyang (a city nearly 700 kilometres north of Beijing) and had been looking for me for over a week before they found out I was in the detention centre.

At the mention of Shenyang I wondered if this could have something to do with Zhao Zhijian. I had met Zhao Zhijian at an experience-sharing gathering a couple of months before. A 28-year-old university lecturer, he had been the first Falun Gong practitioner from Shenyang to come to Beijing to make an appeal. Just four days after the ban was announced he courageously made the trip south, alone.

He was immediately detained and escorted back home. There, the governor of the province and the secretary of the Municipal Party committee both took a personal interest in his case. When the police told members of his family they were going to execute him as an active 'counter-revolutionary', his mother fainted on the spot and it took eighteen Quick-Acting Heart Pills to stabilise her. Day after day, his father abused the young man's despairing wife. He blamed her for not stopping her husband from going to Beijing and demanded she compensate him for losing his son. Zhao Zhijian's wife lost over ten kilos in weight in a fortnight.

Zhao Zhijian was the first Falun Gong practitioner to be placed in a detention centre and suffered greatly from being isolated from other practitioners. However, he soon earned the respect of other prisoners in his cell, who began to refer to him as 'Teacher Zhao'.

'You are the only one amongst us here detained for being a good person, Teacher Zhao,' they said. 'If you want to practise Falun Gong, do it; we'll cover for you.'

The police interrogated him over and over, but couldn't get anything out of him. They couldn't discover any manipulator 'behind the scenes', a charge the government had continued to use when defaming Falun Gong. They even brought in a police officer with a university diploma, to try to talk him round. However, after a day of this, instead of getting anything out of him, the police officer ended by asking, 'Well, do you think I have the sort of inner quality required to be a practitioner?' Zhao Zhijian was released two weeks later and I met him when he came to Beijing again after Falun Gong was labelled an 'evil cult'.

This all flashed through my mind before the other police officer said, 'Do you know Wang Yan, from Shenyang?'

I was about to say no, when I remembered that Wang Yan was Xiao Ya's sister-in-law and also a Falun Gong practitioner. She had gotten hold of two copies of written material that had been spirited out of a psychiatric hospital in Shenyang. They had passed through many hands before finally reaching her. Written by Falun Gong practitioners detained there, they described in detail the horrors they were suffering. Xiao Ya had given my address to Wang Yan, who sent me both copies in the hope that this information could be made public.

The material must have had many adventures on its long journey because by the time it had reached me it was crumpled almost into illegibility. One was written by a woman in her sixties who had been detained in the psychiatric hospital with her daughter and who had been subjected to innumerable bouts of electric shock treatment. The other was by a woman in her forties, who had been arrested when she came to Beijing to appeal. Before she was committed to the psychiatric hospital she had been shunted around to no less than eight different lockups in Beijing and Shenyang. According to her notes, there were rat droppings, cockroach legs and the heads of flies in the food in one of these lockups.

I had transcribed these two pieces onto my computer and saved them to a disk, which I gave to a fellow practitioner who knew how to access the Clearwisdom website and submit the information. I asked him to submit it. This had all happened over two months ago and I hadn't seen him since, so I didn't know if he had managed to send the material.

This was why these policemen had travelled all the way to Beijing from Shenyang. They told me that the two diaries had been published on the Internet, and this had infuriated certain people. The Secretary of Shenyang Party Committee and the Mayor of Shenyang, both of whom were in Beijing for the National People's Congress meeting at that time, had been made personally responsible for discovering how this information had made it out of the hospital. Although busy with their conference, they still found the time to summon the two policemen and instruct them on the line of action they were to pursue.

I wondered if they were going to attempt to extort another confession from me. Sure enough, they asked me if I had received the material Wang Yan had sent me. I replied that I had. They asked me what had happened to it. I replied that after I typed it up on the computer I had given it to another practitioner.

'You gave it to which practitioner?'

'No comment, I'm sorry.'

I steeled myself to maintain my silence, no matter how much they pressured me. However, to my surprise, they didn't seem angered by my response. The younger one was actually smiling as he wrote his notes.

'You Falun Gong practitioners are all the same,' he said. 'You'll talk about yourselves, no problem, but when it comes to other people you clam right up, don't you?'

His tone conveyed both sincerity and a genuine admiration. Suddenly I was deeply moved, thinking of Zhao Zhijian. There must be many Falun Gong practitioners like him in Shenyang, I thought, for these policemen to be so well disposed towards us.

The younger policeman passed his notes across to me to obtain my signature. This, his record of interview, consisted only of my name, where I lived, and the short dialogue that had just taken place between us. Could that be it, then, I wondered, when they had come all this way and gone to all that trouble to find me?

Apparently it was. As soon as I had signed the document and put my fingerprint on it, the other policeman stood up looking even more anxious than I was to get this over and done with, so he could report that their task had been accomplished. Clearly, both of them were just going through the motions.

I looked around for a piece of paper or something to wipe the ink off my index finger.

'Use the washbasin,' the older policeman said quickly. 'There's some soap there you can wash it off with.'

This was unheard of. The washbasin in the interrogation room was only for police officers; people being questioned were never permitted to use it. After I had washed my hands, the younger policeman pointed to a clean towel draped over a line.

'Dry them with that,' he said.

'Hmm, so concerned, eh?' the other man said when I hesitated. 'Don't worry; it's state property. You can use it.'

They waited while I dried my hands then gathered their papers and escorted me back to my cell. As we parted, they even invited me to visit Shenyang when I could, as if I were an old and respected friend, instead of someone—a suspect—they had met only half an hour ago.

3

真善忍

ALL LIVING BEINGS HAVE BUDDHA-NATURE

THIS TIME I WAS PUT in Cell 3 in East Section 1 at the detention centre. As the cell door closed behind me I caught sight of Wang Jin, her plump face aglow and wreathed in smiles, just like Maitreya. It turned out she had been arrested before the Spring Festival while she was doing her exercises in a park. The whole time the police had been interrogating her about me she had been trying to get word to me to be careful.

There were eight Falun Gong practitioners in the cell, including me. Most of the other ten or so occupants were in for prostitution. Four of the Falun Gong practitioners had been arrested in Tian'anmen, where they had gone on New Year's Eve to practise. Another had been arrested for putting up a banner in Tian'anmen and one had been passing a practice site one morning on her way to buy vegetables when she was swept up in a police raid. The other was an elderly woman from Sichuan Province who never made it to Tian'anmen; she had been arrested as she left the railway station.

They were eating when I arrived and Wang Jin beckoned to me to join her little group, just as she had in the local police station the first time we met. I picked up a bowl and was immediately accepted as part of the group.

As far as food and drink went, all Falun Gong practitioners in a cell shared and shared alike. They paid no attention to prison rules prohibiting us from eating and drinking together that had been designed to reduce the likelihood of scuffles and even fist fights breaking out over food. I was taken away for questioning so often during the first few days I was there that I kept missing meal times, but the other students always saved food for me. I didn't even realise at the time that each person was rationed to three *mantou* a day.

Falun Gong practitioners saw this as quite normal but it was very strange for the others in the cell, who were apt to squabble or make a fuss over the slightest thing. Many of the girls brought in for prostitution had been scantily dressed when they were arrested, so of course they had no cash. It was extremely difficult to get by in the detention centres without money; you couldn't even get cotton for when you got your periods. The head honcho was in charge of 'the kitty' and the 'communal articles' but she would only let you use these when she was in a good mood.

Some of the girls had no relatives in Beijing, some had relatives but they couldn't be bothered getting in touch with them, and others were too ashamed to tell their family they were in prison so they simply had to grit their teeth and suffer in silence.

But Falun Gong practitioners were family to each other and the other prisoners envied this closeness. It was this that created such a favourable impression on many prisoners whose admiration for Falun Gong eventually led to their taking it up.

A BROKEN PERSON FAR, FAR FROM HOME

That was what happened with Duan Lili, the head honcho of East Cell 3. She was of the minority Hui nationality, many of whom are Muslims. She was in her thirties and had been jailed on suspicion of drug dealing. By the time I arrived she had been in prison for several months, during which time she had come in contact with a good many Falun Gong practitioners.

It was a rule in the detention centre that Falun Gong practitioners were not to sit together, sleep alongside one another, or even talk to each other. Duan Lili would not let us sit on the plank together during the day, but only because that was when the police had their eye on us. The rest of the time she would let us chat away among ourselves and even arranged for all of the Falun Gong practitioners to sleep alongside one another. 'It doesn't hurt anyone if they talk to each other,' she said once. 'What's the point of separating them? They could be twenty metres apart and they'd still want to talk to each other. There are fewer fights with them here, anyhow!' Things would not have turned out as they have if the people in power had been even half as sensible as she was.

Still, even though she didn't interfere with us, neither did she have much to say to us at first. She seemed intent on playing her role as head honcho. She had little time for the other prisoners, either, and kept very much to herself, seeming to be heavy of heart. One day, about two or three weeks after I arrived, quite out of the blue she told us something she had not told anyone else.

As the eldest child in her family, she had always felt a keen sense of responsibility and, out of a desire to satisfy her parents' wishes, she had married a man of the Hui nationality, even though she didn't love him. She bore him a son but at some point her husband had started taking drugs. Because she loved her son so much and didn't want to lose him, she never considered divorcing her husband. Then, seeing how much pain his habit was causing him, she felt sorry for her husband and started helping him procure drugs on a regular basis.

The restaurant she ran was doing quite well so her husband's sister attempted to blackmail her. When Duan Lili refused to comply, the sister-in-law reported her to the police for buying drugs and bribed the police not to be lenient with her in the hope that this would bring Duan Lili down completely and deliver her property into the sister-in-law's hands.

Now, several months later, her case was still in limbo. Drug trafficking draws a very heavy sentence, so she was naturally worried about her eleven-year-old son, who was still with his drug-addicted father.

By the time she had told us all this, the tears were streaming down Duan Lili's face. Wiping them away, she turned to Wu Ping, the teacher. 'You are a good person, Miss Wu,' she said. 'When you get out, could I tell my son to go to you? Could he study with you and practise Falun Gong with you?'

The youngest person in our cell was just sixteen years old. Her nickname was Little Fatty and she sat next to me on the plank during the day.

Little Fatty was from Jiangxi Province, in central China. She had been fourteen when her mother died and in no time at all her father had taken up with another woman. This woman and her daughter had taken over the room that Little Fatty's mother had given her and Little Fatty couldn't stand them. They quarrelled all the time and Little Fatty and her father turned on each other as well. As soon as she could, she went to live with her boyfriend, planning to get married so that she could leave home altogether. Her father disapproved of the marriage, however. In a fit of anger she had an abortion: she had been over seven months pregnant with twins. So she came to Beijing with somebody and set up as a prostitute in a 'beauty salon'. She was a very rebellious girl, and stubborn: she would die before she would yield. If someone bumped into her there'd be an argument, and she wore a perpetual frown.

'Why is it,' she asked me one day, 'that I don't get annoyed when you Falun Gongers bump into me? How come I don't want to quarrel with you but when other people get in my way I want to hit them?'

Her question threw me at first but after giving it some thought I replied that it was 'because you feel we're good people'.

Carefully, I told her about the need to be well intentioned, for only by being such a person could you gain the respect and affection of others. I told her some other things about the principles behind being human and she took in a lot of it. Eventually, she asked me to teach her the *Hongyin* poems. I began at the beginning, teaching her the first poem, 'Tempering One's Mind and Heart', and explaining as we went along what the poems meant. The third poem, 'Enlightened Being', goes like this:

Everyday people don't know me,
I sit in mysterious pass
Amidst greed and desires, no me
After a hundred years, only me.

I did my best to explain this most profound poem to her in words she would understand, but of course I had no idea just how much of it she really understood. She had had very little education and had not even completed primary school.

One day she was having a bit of a grumble. 'We eat Cabbage Swim every day in this damned place. When I get out I'm never ever going to eat cabbage again! The first thing I'm going to do when I get out is have a decent-sized meal!' She paused, then went on despondently: 'Looks like I'm still no good. I'm still thinking about eating. "There I am . . . amidst greed and desire." My cultivation is still not up to scratch.'

We Falun Gong practitioners were astonished and gazed at each other in wonder, for it was indeed just as Shakyamuni had said: all living creatures have Buddha-nature. We must never underestimate anybody.

By the time she had memorised the fifth *Hongyin* poem, I noticed that her perpetual frown had gone, her temper had improved and she was actually beautiful. Every time I saw her mumbling to herself, striving to learn these poems by heart, I thought of the old Pure Land cultivation practice. Death held no fear for people who had devoted their lives to that practice. As they approached the end of their lives they would go on chanting the name of Buddha with great joy, for wasn't Buddha coming to welcome them? I, too, was full of joy as I watched her earnestly memorising *Hongyin*.

GASPING WITH ADMIRATION AND DELIGHT

Tang Yao, a girl from Sichuan Province, was also in for prostitution. A poor girl from the countryside, she had thought she could earn good money selling her body and that this would enable her to bring her parents to Beijing for a treat. Get rich quick was the order of the day and, as always, people thought it OK to 'ridicule the poor but not the whore', so a great many young girls who came to the cities for work didn't see anything wrong with prostituting themselves. Tang Yao was one of those girls.

One day she came back from her sentence review all flushed and excited, saying that they had promised to release her if she paid a 2,500-*yuan* fine. It so happened that she had a little over 2,000 *yuan* so she wrote asking a friend to fetch it for her. People in detention were not allowed to communicate with the outside world by mail before their sentence was handed down so the police posted the letter for her. Her friend sent her the money straight away and after she handed it over to the review people she waited, on tenterhooks, hoping every day she would go home that day. A few people observed all this with a sneer.

The fifteen-day administrative detention period passed with no sign whatsoever of Tang Yao being released. One day, two days, three days . . . little by little her hope evaporated . . . until finally she could bear it no longer and there, sitting on the plank, she covered her face with her hands and wept hopelessly. Only then did those who had sneered tell her that the review people had deceived many prisoners in this manner and that she had been an idiot to actually believe them.

A few days after this she was taken away to the review again and when she came back she sat on the plank and bawled. She had indeed been duped. Those 2,000 *yuan* had been all she had in the world: now she was penniless, and on top of it she had been sentenced to two years in a women's re-education-through-labour camp. The review officer had made fun of her: 'How much do you charge for a trick, hmm? I might look you up when you get out and maybe you'll give me a little discount . . .'

Tang Yao couldn't seem to stop crying and I really felt for her. An experience like that would surely leave her feeling hostile and that left little hope that she might be transformed into a good person.

One morning as we were getting up she told me she'd had a dream. 'I was shitting in my pants,' she said, 'it was revolting. What do you think that means?'

I was honest with her and told her that her dream revealed how filthy her life had been up until then and that she could not go on like that. Then I talked to her about how harmful her lifestyle was.

She was the most put-upon person in our cell; her family never sent her any money and everyone looked down on her. Falun Gong practitioners were the only people who showed her any kindness so we became as precious to her as an oasis in a desert. I realised that my words had lodged deep in her heart because she really believed every word I said: according to her simple logic, someone who would rather go to prison than tell a lie was incapable of deception.

She told me later that there were Falun Gong practitioners in her village and that she intended to study with them when she went home after her release.

And thus it was that almost everybody in the cell came to admire Falun Gong. Wu Ping even said she would adopt Chen Yuan, who was in for robbery and was a very intimidating person, in the hope she would commit no more robberies. 'Miss Wu,' Chen Yuan said to her, 'I have lived on the wrong side of the law since I was a child. No one's ever got to me and I've never said thank you to anybody, but I know who's good and who's bad. And to you I say—thank you.'

I don't know when it started, but at some point I noticed a change in the behaviour of the other prisoners. Like us, they were now unwilling to let everyone else do all the work and when there was a problem they would 'look inward', learning to forgive others. Just before they left they would wash their prison clothes so they would be clean for the next person. If someone didn't have something, they would give them theirs, of their own volition. When we practised Falun Gong exercises on night shift, they would stand guard and cover for us . . . We all became very close, like one big family.

One Sunday afternoon when we didn't have to sit on the plank, we were chatting together in twos and threes and I had a sudden thought. 'How about I do some of the hand signs (*shouyin*) for you!' Assuming the lotus pose, I did the fifth exercise, 'Strengthening Divine Powers'. As soon as I finished someone said: 'Do it again!' So I closed my eyes and did it again but this time I heard Tang Yao say, 'It's beautiful! I don't know if it's you that's gorgeous or the movements, but it's just beautiful!'

I opened my eyes and saw all the girls watching me intently. Their faces shone with a pure and holy glow and I saw in them what they themselves were quite unaware of—the profound joy of their uplifted souls. It was as if they were no longer despised prostitutes in an earthly jail but pure beings in the Buddha world gasping with admiration and delight at hearing the wonderful Buddha law . . .

———

No Falun Gong detainees were released while I was in the detention centre, for the sole reason that the National People's Congress was being held during that time. After it was over we were released in dribs and drabs. I was the second to last of the nine practitioners in my cell to be released on bail, with my husband acting as my guarantor. On my release, interrogator Ma Ying told me that I was on probation for a year. If I caused any further trouble within that time, my guarantor would be taken into custody along with me.

Niu Jun came to fetch me again, but after giving me a talking-to at the police station he realised that 28 days in the detention centre had had little effect, for I still showed no sign of repentance.

'I'm telling you,' he growled, a malicious grin on his face. 'If you keep giving me trouble like this then I'm going to keep giving *you* trouble! I'm going to make life *impossible* for your husband, *impossible* for your daughter, *impossible* for your parents and *impossible* for your parents-in-law!' I felt a knife go through my heart with each *impossible*, not because I was frightened, but because of the pain of seeing another human being actually be this vicious. 'I'm going to smash your family to smithereens!'

This wasn't an idle threat; he meant it. My 28 days' experience in the detention centre was fresh in my mind, but the most vicious criminal in the detention centre was in a minor league compared to this policeman.

I returned to work the following day. The deputy manager was delighted to see me back and set aside some time for us to have a good talk. In this respect I was much better treated than many other Falun Gong practitioners who were either expelled from the Party or dismissed from their jobs.

The company I worked for was not a state enterprise so it didn't have a Party branch. The few Party members in the company had to be registered under the Party branch of a shareholding unit. Once a year we would grudgingly send someone there to pay our Party membership dues but we secretly regretted ever having joined this senseless Party. It had been such a long time since any of us had gone to a branch meeting that we had stopped getting notifications, so the Party didn't actually know I was practising Falun Gong.

A similar paralysis apparently afflicted grass-roots Party organisation across the country. After the global collapse of other communist regimes, it would be fair to say that none of the tens of millions of Chinese Party members really believed in communism. In the 1980s I had joined the Party in the genuine belief that by doing so I could inject new blood into an organisation that was becoming stale, and help the people. By the 1990s, joining the Party was simply a prerequisite for promotion.

So, because our company wasn't state owned and had no Party branch, the Party was pretty well irrelevant to its day-to-day affairs. The shareholders ran the company and they turned a deaf ear to the Party's strictures on Falun Gong practitioners.

I worked as an investment consultant dealing with the finance sector. The greatest risk in this profession was the moral hazards to which we were exposed. The securities and capital markets are completely new to China and the regulatory system has little relevance to what is happening on the ground. Policy is formulated and laws amended as problems arise. Those who have made money consider themselves lucky and those who haven't redouble their efforts to find new opportunities.

The emerging financial markets staggered many mature investors, who saw the share price of junk stocks, worth a few *yuan*, soar to over 100 *yuan* after being labelled 'composite' or 'high tech'. Organisations and financiers made their fortunes by rigging share prices and small and medium-sized retail investors showed their mettle by resolving to dance with wolves; some were rewarded with a small windfall, others were completely devoured, but nobody imagined that the fairytale of becoming rich overnight would not become a reality. The extreme turbulence of the marketplace could be attributed to speculation of an inflationary nature and a greedy, get-rich-quick mentality that made it difficult to guard against risk.

If I held a managerial position, for example, I could use insider information to my own advantage. I could conduct useless transactions on the company's accounts and get a commission from the traders while the company did not make a cent. I could even broker to my account shares that the company had gotten at a low price or broker worthless shares to the company at a high price, and so on. This was all completely legal and the company wouldn't even be aware of it.

So, an individual's moral character became extremely important in a profession full of temptations and legal loopholes. As a Falun Gong practitioner, I always put the interests of the company first, no matter how wildly share prices fluctuated and no matter how many opportunities I had to make a killing. Unfortunately, many of my colleagues did their work in a perfunctory manner, spending most of their time tracking share quotations, so management considered staff members like me, who were not concerned with personal gain, to be as precious as rubies. They assigned to me the tasks they were uneasy about giving to others, some of them involving hundreds of millions of *yuan*. At a time when a regulatory system had not yet been put in place, they had no option but to trust my integrity.

Because of this, and because we were on good terms, the fact that I had spent a month in jail did not alarm either of my managers. On the contrary, as soon as they had satisfied themselves that I was okay, they talked with me at some length about the plight of Falun Gong practitioners. One believed there was no point in appealing to the Communist Party because it only had another three or four years of life left in it anyway. He said it would be more constructive to concentrate on making our business viable and rescuing our country through its economy.

ABANDONING ATTACHMENTS TO THE SECULAR WORLD

After I returned to work I remained in close contact with the fellow practitioners I had met while in prison. Some of us drafted a letter of appeal to the UN Commission for Human Rights and collected signatures for it. We also discussed asking for an explanation from the detention centre we had been told had tortured Falun Gong practitioners by acupuncture with electric stimulation. The day after we discussed this by phone, the local police station summoned us and questioned us about where we had obtained our information. Our phones were obviously being tapped.

Wang Jin's daughter, Xiaomei, had been held in Beijing Ministry of Public Security's Division Seven—a high-security unit for serious offenders—for two months before she was able to get a message out to her mother asking her to get her a lawyer. Wang Jin eventually managed to find a lawyer willing to take the case and as my parents and my sister all worked in the court system, she asked me to go with her to her appointment.

Our meeting with the lawyer was scheduled for ten o'clock on April 3. I hadn't told my parents-in-law that I was going to see a lawyer with Wang Jin. They had been in a heightened state of vigilance since I returned from my second term in the detention centre: their eyes hardly left me and they seemed able to sense my very intentions. That morning, my mother-in-law barred my way as I was about to leave, her countenance dour, and asked me where I was off to.

I don't recall exactly what I said; probably that I had something to do and I was going out. Nor do I recall at precisely what point she let forth a torrent of abuse. After attacking Falun Gong, she went on to curse my mother and father. Here she was, she screamed at me at the top of her lungs, over 60 years old, and she had had enough. She didn't care about anything; she was going to Sichuan to have it out with my parents. Having always believed it was my parents' fault I had taken up Falun Gong, she was quite prepared to risk death seeking them out as the root cause of all this trouble.

I had never seen my mother-in-law in such a state, not even when she lay in front of my door to stop me going out.

I was so upset I didn't know what to do. I know I was crying as I blindly gathered my things together. I had no idea how to stop her cursing me.

When she realised I really was going out, she saw red.

'If you go out today,' she shouted, blocking the door, 'you will have to divorce my son!'

My heart lurched, but I couldn't help feeling this threat was ridiculous.

'Whether or not we divorce is up to my husband and me,' I said. 'Unless, of course, you're divorcing me?'

'Yes! Yes, I am!' She had completely lost it by now. 'I'll go to court with you today and file for divorce!'

Deep down I knew she was just threatening me. She didn't really want us to divorce; she was just desperate to protect her family. But I had to make it clear that I would not yield to pressure. If I gave in this time, not only would going out become a problem, I would also forfeit my right to practise Falun Gong at home. Besides, Wang Jin was waiting for me. I was running late and I wasn't prepared to go back on my word.

I picked up a pen and began scribbling a 'divorce agreement', not to divorce my husband of course, but to show that I was not to be coerced: 'Of my own free will, I divorce X——.'

'She's not worried about getting divorced,' my father-in-law interjected. 'She's got the money!'

I had always looked after the family's financial documents and affairs because my husband didn't want to do it. Quite some time earlier, however, I had handed everything over to him and tidied up our affairs as I could not guarantee that I would not be detained again. My father-in-law didn't know this. His words cut me to the quick and without a moment's hesitation I added the words 'and I give up all the property of the family in its entirety'. Then I signed the paper and handed it to my mother-in-law with an air of finality.

She hadn't expected this, as I was by nature normally very timid; an angry look used to be enough to upset me for days and any outburst would reduce me to a quivering mess. I used to live in fear of what others thought of me, which left me feeling exhausted. A paragraph from *Zhuan Falun* freed me from this completely, however. It was in the section entitled 'Zhen-Shan-Ren is the Sole Criterion to Discern Good and Bad People' and it said:

> As a human being, you are a good person only if you can follow this universe's characteristic of Zhen-Shan-Ren. A person who deviates from this characteristic is truly a bad person. In the workplace or in society, some people may say that you are bad, yet you may not necessarily be bad. Some people may say that you are good, but you may not really be good. As a practitioner, if you assimilate yourself to this characteristic you are one who has attained the Tao—it's just such a simple principle.[13]

I deeply identified with this, I believed this, and from then on I no longer took other people's opinions of me to heart. Instead, I viewed myself only in terms of whether I had acted with Truthfulness, Compassion and Forbearance. The feeling of lightness I experienced when I was suddenly free of that 30-year-old burden was exquisite.

At the same time that I gained confidence in myself, I found I was becoming much more tolerant about many different things. For example, I used to get very annoyed whenever my father-in-law would put what I considered to be an ugly tablecloth on an elegant piece of furniture. But every time I took it off, he would put it back. His agenda was convenience, mine was appearance, and therein lay the conflict, just one of the speed bumps that make our lives that little bit less smooth.

I became more tolerant through practising Falun Gong and, as time went on, these things loomed less large in my eyes. I renounced my power to make decisions about nearly everything to do with the family, deferring instead to my husband and his parents. I felt it didn't cost me anything and everybody was happy.

So the last thing my mother-in-law expected was for her meek and obedient daughter-in-law to become so resolute and unmanageable. She was completely thrown and didn't even reach out to take the divorce agreement I was holding out to her.

---

13 *Zhuan Falun*, page 16.

We stood there, unmoving, for a couple of minutes and then I put it on the table and asked her to stand aside and let me leave.

Once the spell was broken she panicked and became almost incoherent.

'Call Security! Call Security!' she shouted.

My father-in-law hit upon an even better plan. 'Dial 110! Dial 110!' he yelled, blocking the door with his burly frame.

'You can call Security and you can dial 110,' I said evenly, 'but I'm a free person and no policeman can stop me from going out. You can keep watch on me for a day but you can't keep watch on me for the rest of my life. Please get out of the way. I want to go out.'

Apparently realising that I would not be swayed, my father-in-law was the first to come to his senses. My courage came, I knew, from the conviction that what I was going to do was absolutely correct. He moved aside, leaving only my mother-in-law blocking the door. I slipped past her and she followed me outside still shouting, 'Call Security! Call Security!'

This all happened at our new house, to which the whole family had recently moved. It was in one of Beijing's top residential areas and security officers were on patrol 24 hours a day.

'You'd better not call Security,' I said, turning to my mother-in-law. 'We've just moved in and nobody here knows I practise Falun Gong. They just might find out if you call them.'

At this, she shut up like a clam.

I walked away without a backward glance. For some reason, as I walked along in the spring sunshine, a phrase from the book *A Dream of the Red Chamber* came to my mind: 'leaving only a vast expanse of dazzling white'. A sentence of Li Hongzhi's to which I had never paid much mind also came back to me. Talking about how he had to bring lunch to work as the canteen at his workplace had been shut down, he said, 'I don't like to carry things with me everywhere I go.' I suddenly understood what he meant.

'Ahh,' I thought, 'so this is "abandoning attachments to the secular world".'

HIRING A LAWYER IS A WASTE OF MONEY

I caught a bus to the lawyer's office and arrived on time to find Wang Jin and her husband already there.

This was one of the most expensive law firms in Beijing. They usually only handled financial cases for big companies but had agreed to see what they could do for us because a cousin of Xiaomei's was an old client.

In the autumn of 1999 I had indicated that I intended to attend the trial of the members of the former Falun Dafa Research Association and that I was willing to testify on their behalf. I had intended to say that they had not incited me to be part of the incident on April 25, but that it had been my own decision. However, my father said this was futile, telling me that the judicial office in his city, Mianyang, had brought all the local lawyers together and circulated documents relating to defending Falun Gong practitioners. Three main points had emerged from this exercise:

1. Detained Falun Gong practitioners are different from ordinary criminals. Thus, while lawyers can apply for bail for criminals they cannot do so for Falun Gong practitioners.
2. The general orientation of Falun Gong practitioners is wrong so that, unlike with other cases, 'trivial issues' such as whether the prosecution has ample evidence and whether the facts are irrefutable must not be pursued when defending them in court.
3. Lawyers' complaints must be submitted to relevant leaders for prior examination and the issuing of instructions. When defending cases in court, lawyers can only read out the approved written defence and must not say anything that is not in that complaint.

So why, when I knew so well that hiring a lawyer was a waste of money, did I go with Wang Jin to see one? It was simply in the hope that a trial might bring more people to an understanding of Falun Gong. Besides, I felt no opportunity should be lost to mount a defence of our innocence.

Two lawyers, a man and a woman, had been assigned to our case. I told them a little of what I had heard of Xiaomei while I was in the detention centre. This was that when the police had searched her flat they had found a dozen or so mobile phones and a quantity of ready cash. They were thus preparing a case against her on the grounds that she had swindled people.

'What do they know!' one of the Falun Gong practitioners in my cell had said when she heard this. 'A Falun Gong practitioner from Shenzhen who came to Beijing to make an appeal brought tens of thousands of *yuan* with him. Before going to Tian'anmen he left all his money and his mobile phone with my cousin, because he said he wouldn't be able to use them if he were to go to prison and that other practitioners might need them. How could you call that swindling? It's ridiculous!'

Slowly, I explained to the two lawyers how Falun Gong practitioners view money and property. In these exceptional circumstances, nobody makes a distinction between 'yours' and 'mine'. I heard about a practitioner from Changchun who sold his house and brought the proceeds to Beijing in a leather suitcase, giving a bundle to every hard-up fellow practitioner he came across. It was clear that Falun Gong practitioners must have left the money and mobile phones at Xiaomei's of their own volition; there was absolutely no question that anybody had been swindled.

At this point the female lawyer expressed interest in taking the case. With some embarrassment she told Wang Jin that their fees were very high, ranging from 30,000 to 100,000 *yuan*. She was not sure Wang Jin could afford this much money.

I had only recently received a bonus of 60,000 *yuan*, which should still have been at my disposal despite my having just signed a 'divorce agreement' and given up all my assets, so I said the fee wasn't a problem. If they didn't have enough money I could help them.

'Have you Falun Gong people really reached that level?' the lawyer asked, clearly impressed. 'Perhaps we should make lawyers practise Falun Gong, then they could waive their fees for the poor.'

I then raised the matter of the difficulties inherent in the case, referring them to the restricted documents my father had told me about. The lawyer said they had not received any such documents and that even if Xiaomei had killed someone or purchased explosives and set them off in Tian'anmen, she still had the right to be defended.

On our second visit, however, the male lawyer who had remained silent throughout our initial visit took me aside. He explained that the judicial office in Beijing was much more sophisticated than that in Mianyang. Instead of calling a meeting, it had sent a 'reminder' to all those handling Falun Gong cases. Our lawyers had received this reminder, which consisted of the same three points. Then he just shook his head.

I don't know if these two lawyers ever actually defended Xiaomei, but I do know that it is very difficult to be a lawyer in China. After my mother retired from the courts she handled some cases as a lawyer. Two years later she handed back her accreditation, saying that the system made it just impossible to be a lawyer. As a judge, she would receive informal notes from certain VIPs before she had even looked at the files of a case. As a lawyer, if you didn't bribe the judges you wouldn't win a lawsuit.

A LETTER GETS ME TWELVE MONTHS' LABOUR RE-EDUCATION

After Wang Jin and I had left the lawyer's office, I rang my husband to tell him what had happened with his parents. I suggested it might be better if I stayed somewhere else for a few days until they had cooled down. From this, he gathered that this time it was no small matter and that it would take some time to iron out, so he agreed.

That night I stayed with Yang Runze, a fellow practitioner I had met during my last term in the detention centre. I woke very early the next morning and thought back to the clash with my husband's parents. I realised I hadn't been composed enough and had not explained things to them in a sufficiently calm manner. I imagined they would have been very upset after I left, dreading having to tell their own son about their demand that I divorce him. I thought I should write to them, taking full responsibility for the altercation so as to ease their consciences. I also wanted to let them know that whatever they had done to me I understood them, loved them and didn't bear them any grudge. I wanted to explain why I couldn't renounce my heartfelt beliefs, and why I had to do things that appeared to them stupid and futile.

After making this decision, my heart felt light and my mind clear. Yang Runze was still asleep and I crept out of bed, found a pen and some paper and poured out the letter for which I would be sentenced to twelve months' re-education through forced labour.

Dear Papa and Mama,
After some thought, I have decided not to come home for the time being. I hope you will understand.

1. *I could not change my belief even if my life depended on it. The government has committed a major error in its treatment of Falun Gong and I*

cannot rest until it acknowledges and corrects this. On this point I will not be moved. Given that for the time being you cannot identify with my belief and with what I am doing, my remaining at home and continuing to read Falun Gong books, practise Falun Gong and keep in touch with other practitioners can only cause you pain. For this reason, I am moving out for a while; this will be best for everybody concerned.

2. *I have thought about my responsibility towards the family and am quite willing to accept it. However, what is our real responsibility to the family? I'm sure you remember how, when I first took up the practice, I encouraged you to do the same. You couldn't have known at the time, but when Papa was being treated in Kaifeng for gallstones and he rang telling us how painful the treatment was I was so distressed I went into the next room and burst into tears. Nor could you know how I said, tearfully, to your son in the dead of the night, 'You say you have a strong sense of responsibility to your family, but how strong is it, really?' He just said his mouth pained him so he didn't want to talk and turned over to sleep, while I cried and cried and couldn't get to sleep. Our lives are so short that unless we practise we cannot free ourselves from the pain of life, old age, illness and death. No matter how much responsibility I feel for you, I cannot take your place when you are sick. And when it is time for you to depart this world I cannot make you stay here. It is an unalterable fact that my sense of responsibility cannot save a single soul.*

And Shitan. Both times I was in the detention centre I saw girls of fourteen incarcerated for stealing put in with young women prostitutes of sixteen. They called me Auntie and when they asked me questions I saw in them the same childlike innocence of my own child. They were not bad, by any stretch of the imagination; they had been corrupted by society. They had no one to tell them what was really good and what was really bad, and had unwittingly turned to crime! It is sometimes very difficult for the family to combat society: when two thinly disguised brothels opened virtually at our old front door, I thought 'How can I guarantee my child won't go bad as she grows up, especially since she has to walk past those brothels several times a day?' A society without beliefs is a frightening society and I have many regrets about my child living in such a society. Whether you have seen it or not and whether you believe it or not, those who genuinely practise Falun Dafa make up their minds to live according to Truthfulness, Compassion and Forbearance and to strive continually, wherever they are, to be good people. The more of this kind of person there is in a society, the better that society will become and, as a mother,

I would rest easy if my daughter were living in such a society. From these few years of practice and my observations of society I have become deeply aware that neither the government's efforts to educate nor legal punishments nor imbuing the people with knowledge can transform human hearts. Only genuine belief can do that.

3. *Having practised for this long, I really am setting higher and higher standards for myself. It is not that I don't love my husband, my child and my family; it's just that my love has expanded to include all people. Our teacher often says it is not satisfactory if you do not love your enemy. Regardless of whether I actually achieved this, this is the sort of demand I make of myself. Therefore, my heart of compassion is not limited to just our little family. Isn't there a saying, 'The streams rise when the river is high'? Only when our nation and our society become well, will our small family truly become well.*

4. *I know there are many like you who believe that there has to be a better way to do whatever it is we Falun Gong practitioners are trying to do; that our present method of defending our belief is not having any effect and is not politically apt. I couldn't agree more that it is not politically minded, because we simply don't do politics; we practise Buddha law. Therefore, what we believe in is truth, and truth is indestructible. I believe it won't be long before you see this.*

5. *I completely understand that, as the older generation, you may oppose us or you may support us. But whichever it is, you love us, cherish us and want to protect us. You do not want to make us endure hardship and you want a happier life for us. What I am trying to say is that my three years of practice have shown me that my belief is absolutely genuine. And through my practice I have become happier and more understanding—even when I was in the detention centre. On this score, you need not worry. I am incredibly happy because I understand why we are alive. I am conforming to cosmic laws and that's why I am so happy.*

6. *My purpose in not returning home for a while is so that I will be able to return all the sooner to resume my work and my life with my family as it was before the government banned us. As long as the Dafa I believe in and the teacher I respect are being treated unjustly in this world it is exceedingly difficult for me calmly to carry on with my work and my life as before. It would be the same if you were being treated unjustly: I would not resign myself to that but would speak up for justice. It is not our way to 'be worldly wise and play safe' or to be like the 'wise man' who submits to circumstances. We demand of ourselves that we be selfless, putting*

others first, and when we truly manage to do that we do not lose anything; instead we gain so very, very much. Those who have given something for us, who bear our pain for us, will gain immeasurably. I probably can't make you believe this right now but maybe one day you will understand.

7. *All of this is simply so that while I am not living at home you will not worry about me. 'One does not say thank you for great kindness.' I understand very well everything you have done for this family and do not intend to offer empty thanks. All I wholeheartedly wish for is that you are better able to negotiate this short transition period.*

Zheng Zeng
April 4, 2000

Yang Runze was up by the time I finished the letter. When she read it, she thought it was so wonderful that she wanted to make copies to give to her mother and her brother. Because of the ceaseless propaganda against Falun Gong, many practitioners had this problem of their families not understanding them.

4

真善忍

SHOOT THE ARROW FIRST,
THEN DRAW THE BULL'S-EYE

ON APRIL 12 I RETURNED to our old apartment in Chongwei District. It was almost exactly as we had left it except that no one was living there. We had bought new furniture for our new house, so many things, including some clothes, were still there. After a week of living like a vagabond, spending different nights at different friends' places, I wanted some rest and a change of clothes. I had hardly slept all week, having stayed up late almost every night talking with my fellow practitioners, so I slept very soundly that night. For a fleeting moment in the middle of the night I thought I heard someone trying the door but I just turned over groggily and went back to sleep.

Then my pager went. It was my husband. I heaved myself out of bed and rang him, wondering what could be so urgent that he would page me in the middle of the night. He said Niu Jun was looking for me and wanted me to ring him straight away on his mobile.

Still half-asleep, I tapped in Niu Jun's number. While he kept me on the phone chatting about inconsequential matters, Officer Wu was dispatched to pick me up.

I was still on the phone when Officer Wu arrived at my door. It turned out it had been he who had tried the door earlier; when there was no response, he had gone away thinking no one was there. As I had been moving around all that week, I would never have been found if it hadn't been for my husband. He had become an unwitting accomplice of the police and could not have imagined what would come of my ringing Niu Jun.

Officer Wu drove me to the police station and I was put in a small room, empty except for a small bed on which was a pile of bullet-proof vests. I was so tired that I lay down, pillowed my head on the vests, and went back to sleep.

All the next day Niu Jun, Officer Wu, and another officer I had never seen before took turns questioning me about what I had been doing for the past few days. I didn't answer their questions but asked instead for a sheet of paper. On this I wrote a statement declaring invalid the guarantee I had previously given the police station. Niu Jun groaned with rage.

'You won't talk, eh!' he snarled. 'Don't talk, then, and I'll send you off same as before!'

And that was how I came to be put in Chongwen District lockup for the third time.

This time I hadn't expected to be arrested and I wasn't mentally prepared. When I was in the detention centre last time, I developed the intention of going to Tian'anmen Square to unfurl a Falun Gong banner. I reasoned that if all of us made a stand there would not be enough room in the jails and the ban would therefore be lifted a little sooner. Unfortunately, too few practitioners were making a stand. On the other hand, I could not criticise others for not making a stand if I didn't do it myself.

In the week before I was arrested I had arranged with fellow practitioners to display banners in Tian'anmen on the anniversary of April 25. But what was I to do now, locked up while everyone else went as planned? I decided that I would go on a hunger strike and try to get released before the anniversary.

I didn't get much of a reaction the first two days 'sitting the plank', doing the night shifts and my chores together with the others.

'Are you on a hunger strike?' was all the corrective officer said to me casually as she was doing her rounds.

Only on the third day, when I was showing signs of exhaustion and palpitations, did Officer Zhang finally take me to the clinic. There was only one member of the medical staff on duty and a length of brown rubber tubing lay coiled on the table, alongside a big glass beaker. The beaker was full of some liquid.

Officer Zhang shot a glance at the rubber tubing then jutted her chin at the icy-cold concrete floor.

'You don't really want me to fetch some hefty fellows to hold you down while we pour this into you, do you, Zheng Zeng?' she said. 'It'll save everybody time if you just drink it down.'

I looked at the rubber tubing with some dread, recalling the time a few years before when I had accompanied my husband to hospital for a gastroscopy. It had been quite difficult to get the gastroscope down his throat and into his stomach and they had just succeeded when a patient approached the doctor who was carrying out the procedure. The doctor ushered the patient out into the corridor, where their discussion became heated.

My husband lay on the bed with the tube stuffed in his mouth, alone and apparently forgotten by the doctor. He couldn't swallow and he couldn't throw up but he could hear them quarrelling and couldn't call out. Several times he almost passed out while I sat in the waiting room, completely oblivious to what was going on. When he finally came out he was deathly pale and sweating. It was quite some time before he was up to walking out of there and telling me what had happened.

I hesitated a few seconds. Then, before I had time to imagine how it would feel when the tubing went through my nose—that was the method used to force-feed—I quietly lifted the beaker to my lips and drank. It tasted so dreadful it almost brought tears to my eyes.

I managed to drink half the beaker, I still don't know how. By the time I got back to my cell I was vomiting and had diarrhea, so I got rid of the whole lot.

By the end of the fourth day I was extremely weak; my heart was racing and I was bathed in sweat. Officer Zhang took me off to the clinic again but when I told her there was no point in making me drink because I had vomited everything up and had diarrhea, she said they would put me on a drip. No one in the clinic could find a vein, however, so eventually they fetched a male prisoner to insert the needle. He swaggered in, laughing and joking with the police in a very familiar manner. He was much more skilled than any of the clinic staff and made the job of inserting the needle look easy.

'Go on your hunger strike when you see Jiang Zemin,' he said to me as he inserted the needle. 'Otherwise you'll die in here and no one will ever know. And they'll say that you've committed suicide to escape punishment.'

When the saline solution began to drip from the infusion bottle into my vein everyone moved away, chatting among themselves and paying no attention to me. I leant back against the cupboard feeling a dreadful faintness seeping through me. I hardly had the strength to sit up but didn't want to show any weakness by asking to lie down. Propping myself up with some effort, I tried to focus on the infusion bottle. Officer Zhang started talking about giving electric shock needles to punish a Falun Gong practitioner in the detention centre and I wondered how they could be so cruel. Then I went blank, too weak even to think.

As I grew physically weaker, I became less determined and aware, until my senses began to dim and all I saw was a vast expanse of white before my eyes, like a trick fade-out in a movie.

'You're very tired,' a voice said gently, from far, far away. 'Rest. Rest.'

Seduced by this gentleness, little by little my will slipped away.

'Take the drip out. I'll eat,' I blurted at the last moment, like a drowning person clutching at a straw.

PUNISHED FOR MY THOUGHTS

When I returned from the clinic this time I was given into the charge of Zhang Qiang and Ma Ying again. For the first few days they beat around the bush and wouldn't tell me why I had been arrested.

'Do you know Wu Ping and her husband?' Zhang Qiang kept saying. 'Do you know Li Li? Where did you go on the eleventh and the twelfth?'

I didn't answer and he didn't force me, but I knew where his questions were leading.

Li Li and Wu Ping were fellow practitioners with whom I had shared a cell the last time I was in the detention centre. They had been released about the same time as me and we had arranged to meet and share our experiences at the home of another practitioner on the eleventh. We met at the subway station. Wu Ping's husband had brought another man along, saying he had been studying Falun Gong for a week and wanted to go with us. The man seemed a little tense and I felt something was not quite right, but he was with Wu Ping's husband and Falun Gong had always stressed being open to everybody, so I really couldn't say anything.

The next day—that is, the day before I was arrested—we went to a similar gathering at another fellow practitioner's place and this man came along again. We read aloud from *Essentials for Further Advancement* but when it came to his turn he stumbled over the words and seemed to find them very difficult. I remembered that he was new to Falun Gong, decided that was normal and thought no more about it.

So now, when Zhang Qiang questioned me I knew straight away that this man had not been what he claimed to be. Of all the places I had been, Zhang Qiang knew only of these two, where that man had also been. What mischief had he been up to?

But the word of a spy could not really be used as legal evidence so Zhang Qiang told me that the confessions of Li Li, Wu Ping and her husband could be used as testimony to convict me. But when I challenged him, he was unable to produce these confessions.

A few days later Zhang Qiang excitedly waved some sheets of paper in my face.

'Let's see what you have to say about this, Zheng Zeng!' he crowed. 'Are you going to tell me you didn't write this?'

I saw at a glance it was the letter I had written to my parents-in-law. There was a mess of hieroglyphics along the top of each sheet, indicating that the Ministry of Public Security had downloaded it from some email they had intercepted. And there at the bottom was my name.

I groaned inwardly, wondering who had been responsible for this masterpiece of carelessness. A fellow practitioner must have sent this letter out without thinking that perhaps my name should have been taken off it. Many Falun Gong practitioners had no fear of being detained at that stage, giving little thought to their own safety and protection because they did not fully understand that 'the people's police' did not regard us as 'people'.

There was no point in my denying that I had written this letter.

'"I have nothing to say",' he cried triumphantly. 'This says it all, doesn't it! Only out one month and we've got originals! Your article went up on the web! I *knew* all along you shouldn't have been released!'

And so Zhang Jiang finally had something 'tangible' to justify my arrest.

Two weeks later, I was called to the interrogation building one evening. A section head I had never seen before had summoned me. He said he had no intention of interrogating me but just wanted to have a friendly chat.

He had a Buddha statue on the windowsill in his office and knew a lot about Buddhism. He acknowledged that all the Falun Gong practitioners he had met were very good; he was very impressed with how they managed to abandon everything a practitioner should abandon within such a short period of time. What puzzled him was that Buddhists also preached great compassion and forbearance. 'Why can't you be like Mother Earth,' he said, 'and silently endure sunshine and rain, accept garbage and excrement, and transform it all into nourishment so that all things on earth may thrive?'

'I will share with you my understanding of Forbearance,' I told him. 'There are different levels and realms of Forbearance. When I was a novice practitioner and someone struck me I would feel terribly angry. But then I would remember that I was a practitioner whose teacher said, "As a practitioner one should not fight back when being punched or insulted, but should conduct oneself with a high standard,"[14] so I would forbear and not flare up. However, that anger remained deep within me for a very long time as a question: "Why did you strike me?"

'As I continued my practice I improved and became more tolerant. Now when someone struck me without rhyme or reason I could go cheerfully on my way without any thought of payback.

'Then the time came when someone struck me unjustly and fiercely. I was able to remain cheerful and not get angry, but that person's action would produce bad karma for him and thus harm his life. Out of compassion and a sense of responsibility to him, I had to tell him that it was wrong to strike others and that he must make amends, otherwise he might hit someone else tomorrow. This was Forbearance of another realm.'

14 *Zhuan Falun*, page 150.

The section head thought this over and didn't raise any objections to it, but then he asked, weren't practitioners indifferent to reputation and gain? If so, why did our teacher write to the Central Committee and the State Council after the ban was announced attempting to defend himself? Wasn't that him caring about his reputation?

'I'll tell you a story,' I said to him. 'The famous Song dynasty writer Su Dongpo was very friendly with a monk with whom he used to contend over matters occult. One day Su Dongpo asked the monk, "How do you see me?" The monk replied, "I see you as a statue of the Buddha." Su Dongpo answered this with, "I see you as a pile of stinking dog turds." The monk didn't lose his temper but just smiled, while Su Dongpo went home happy in the knowledge that he had won the day.

'When he got home, however, he had second thoughts. "Damn, that's no good," he thought. "He outwitted me! By telling me he sees me as a statue of the Buddha he's saying that he's got Buddha in his heart, so he sees everybody as Buddha. But as for me, it's because I've got stinking dog turds in my heart that I saw him as stinking dog turds!'

I sat quietly, looking at the section head.

He looked back at me blankly. Then he laughed.

'OK,' he said. 'So when you abuse others you don't use bad language, but you're saying that I'm stinking dog turds?'

I smiled.

'No,' I said. 'I'm not calling you a stinking dog turd, I'm just telling you this reasoning. It's because you're still concerned about your own reputation that you think our teacher wrote that letter to defend himself. But he didn't; he got beyond that long ago.'

The section head asked me lots of questions about Falun Gong and we talked until 2 a.m. Just before he dismissed me, he asked me if I was aware that I now had a reputation.

'Beijing's top leaders all know of you,' he said, 'and they all agree that you are a key member of Falun Gong. They were going to arrest you sooner or later.'

I said I was a very ordinary Falun Gong practitioner; I was not even an assistant, so why did they see me as being key to anything?

'Because of your thoughts,' he said, after a long pause.

'The law can punish people for their thoughts?' I smiled.

He smiled, too, aware that with that one remark he had inadvertently laid bare the 'mystery' of Chinese law.

An ultimatum

It's hard to say how many Falun Gong practitioners passed through the detention centres after the ban. The first time I was taken in the police told me it was over 200 but it was probably double that. The oldest person detained was 83. Most were released after a month, except in special circumstances such as the National People's Congress, when some were held for more than 40 days. At that stage no one in the Chongwen District had been sentenced to re-education through forced labour.

So the day my month was up—May 12—my cellmates began to speculate as to what time I would be released. Some begged me for my extra clothing and other articles of daily use. I passed out what I could then packed my little bag and sat down with them to wait.

We waited and waited, but by nightfall nothing had happened.

The second day passed, the third day, the fourth day . . . endless days with nothing happening. I don't remember exactly when, but it must have been on the seventh or eighth day that a corrective officer finally stopped outside the cell and called out my name.

I was taken to the room in which lawyers conferred with prisoners. Waiting there was the head of the police station I had met when I was taken to the local police station after writing that letter to Premier Zhu Rongji. He told me my husband had come with him and was at the main gate. Unfortunately, he couldn't come in but he had sent his regards. I thanked him and waited to see what was coming.

After beating about the bush for a while, he said he had the authority to release me, on condition I gave him my word I would not go to Tian'anmen. He also said I could practise Falun Gong at home after I got out. In fact, as far as he was concerned I could practise all over the house, so long as I didn't go to Tian'anmen.

I suspected this was a compromise my husband had negotiated on my behalf, at great cost to himself, but I rejected it. I said I couldn't promise anything.

'What if you were sent for re-education through forced labour?' he said, after a moment's silence.

'The birth of any new thing comes at a price. My being sent to re-education through forced labour could be a part of it.'

'But why should it be you?' he blurted out.

'Because I am willing,' I replied softly.

I AM SENT TO PENAL SERVITUDE

Two days later I was called to the lawyers' reception room, where two bureaucrats from the Chongwen District Politics and Law Office presented me with the decision to send me to re-education through forced labour. This is what the decision said:

> In April 2000, Zheng Zeng used the Internet to voice grievances on behalf of the 'Falun Gong' evil cult organization, inciting resistance to the enforcement of the law . . . she has been sentenced to twelve months' re-education through forced labour . . . If she refuses to accept this decision she may, within 60 days of receiving this notification, lodge with the higher authorities an application for administrative review.

Three days later, early on the morning of May 26, before we had even had time to wash our faces, someone called shrilly from the corridor, 'Zheng Zeng! Get your things. You're going!'

People in the cell looked at each other in dismay: they couldn't send me away just three days after I had received my papers! The usual procedure was that no one was sent to the re-education camp or to prison until the process of lodging an appeal and having it heard had been completed. Two of my fellow inmates had been there for nearly a year waiting for their appeals to be processed, and I had made it clear to the police that I intended to seek a review of my sentence.

There were all kinds of people in the detention centre and they all had different ideas. Some played for time, lodging what they knew perfectly well was a hopeless appeal because they didn't want to endure the harshness of a forced-labour camp or prison. Others felt they would rather be exhausted through hard work than be bored stupid sitting the plank day after day. There was always the possibility that their sentence might be reduced if they went to a camp or prison so they lived in hope of being sent away sooner rather than later.

When I got to the custody room I was surprised to see You Min, whom I hadn't seen for ages. She had been in the centre since her arrest at the end of January for putting up Falun Gong banners in Tian'anmen and had been on a hunger strike for eleven days. She was extremely thin, but was also being sent to re-education through forced labour. Wang Jin, too, had been sentenced to forced-labour camp re-education, along with another fellow practitioner called Gu Hua, who had also been a member of our 'legal illegal assembly' at my local police station the first time I met Wang Jin.

As we stood waiting for the others to be processed, a young woman in her twenties called out timidly to You Min. She was in for prostitution and was being sent away with us.

'You Min,' she said, 'did you hear? Number Three has died.'

'Died? When? What happened?'

'She died when they took her to hospital to force-feed her.'

This news reduced You Min to tears. A couple of weeks before, a group of about twenty Falun Gong practitioners had been brought in but none would give their name so they simply became Number One, Number Two, Number Three, and so on. One of the reasons practitioners might refuse to give their name is that once they know your name, the authorities not only have leverage to sentence you, they also can penalise your workplace and threaten your family. They immediately went on a hunger strike in protest at being detained and You Min, who was in the same cell as Number Three, joined in as a show of support. You Min was placed in isolation, away from the others. After twelve or thirteen days, Number Three was carted off to hospital. She never came back. Nobody knew whether she had died on the journey or in hospital. She remained nameless even in death: all that was known about her was that she was 45 and was from Heilongjiang provice in the north.

Then I realised that I had actually met her and spent a few hours with her. She and three others were put in our cell the day they were brought in.

The head honcho of our cell had been sentenced to fourteen years for a serious crime and her only hope of an early release lay in winning over the police, so she spared no effort in carrying out their orders. Clearly, they had instructed her to find out the names of these four women and she began her interrogation at first light.

One of the four was a little older than the others. Another, a woman with short hair who had the air of an intellectual, said she would like to be called Number Three.

'Number Three?' the head honcho spat. 'Number Three pig? Number Three cat? Number Three dog? If you won't talk I'll beat you until you don't have a tooth left in your head! You listen to me. You walked in here upright, but they'll have to carry you out flat!'

Number Three looked at her without saying a word. There was an awkward silence and then a girl from the northeast whom the head honcho habitually bullied courageously offered her *mantou* to the four newcomers.

'Are you hungry?' she asked. 'Would you like something to eat?'

I went and stood beside Number Three.

'I am a Falun Gong practitioner, too,' I told her. 'You are right not to give your names. I'm with you on this.'

Number Three gave me a deep look and nodded.

Half an hour later the cell door suddenly clanged open and all four were whisked away. There had been a noticeable difference in how I was treated during this—my third—term in the detention centre. I was now regarded as a ringleader and all the other Falun Gong practitioners had been moved out of East Section 1 Cell 6, where I was to be kept, before I arrived.

The group that Number Three was part of had arrived in the dead of night and the night-duty police had assigned four of them to my cell, unaware of this policy. As soon as Ma Ying came on duty and realised what had happened she had them transferred out: the policy of segregating me was to continue.

———

Three years later, statistics would show that of the 800-plus deaths of Falun Gong detainees proven to be due to maltreatment, 10 per cent were caused by force-feeding through a tube. The even more disturbing issue here is that in many detention centres and forced-labour camps tube-feeding became another form of torture, its aim being not to keep the sufferer alive but to end his life. It was very common for prisoners without a shred of medical knowledge to insert the thick rubber tube into the nasal cavity. Wang Jin had once been force-fed so brutally that her nasal cavity ruptured and they couldn't stop the bleeding.

———

Once everyone had been processed, those of us going to the labour camp were squeezed into the prison van, each clutching a bedding roll and a bag containing our clothes and personal items. There were five or six other prisoners besides we four Falun Gong practitioners.

The van sped out of the detention centre and away from the city.

Half an hour later we arrived at the high-security Beijing Criminal Despatch Division where prisoners who had been sentenced to jail terms were sorted out from those going to a forced-labour camp, and from whence each individual was sent to his designated location.

Criminal. That one word depressed me infinitely more than any other element of this nightmare time. If there were a hell, for me this would be it. Throughout my life I had trodden the path of a 'three-goods student' (one who excelled academically, adhered to discipline and was of high moral character). I was an outstanding Youth League member, a Party member and had a recommendation as a post-graduate student. The last thing I could have imagined was that I would become a target of the dictatorship of the proletariat.

Our van negotiated several checkpoints before pulling up in front of a large building. One of the officers escorting us went into the building carrying a thick wad of documents and we were told to await further orders.

About ten minutes later the officer emerged from the building and told those of us with criminal sentences to get out of the van. Those of us destined for the forced-labour camp were to stay where we were.

Criminal sentences were handed down for violations of the penal code; these were people who had been through legal procedures and been sentenced to a fixed term of imprisonment and sent for *reform* through forced labour (*Laogai*). *Re-education* through forced labour (*Laojiao*), however, was simply a form of 'administrative punishment' and did not, therefore, have to follow any legal procedures. In theory, decisions about re-education were made by municipal 're-education through forced labour management' committees, but they were handed down at the district level by the district Party Committee's Politics and Law Office. The 610 Office established specifically to deal with Falun Gong was set up on June 10, 1999, on the eve of the crackdown, hence its name. This office was initially under the Commission of Politics and Law of the Communist Party's Central Committee but after the crackdown it was elevated to the level of a ministry, just as the Cultural Revolution Group had been during the Cultural Revolution. Tens of thousands of 610 organisations were set up, from the Central Committee down to the local level, employing millions of full-time and part-time staff. It assumed a unique form in that it straddled administrative, legal and Party organisation functions and it had absolute power over the life and property of Falun Gong practitioners.

China's system of re-education through forced labour was set up in the 1950s, to deal with the remnants of the idle pre-liberation exploiting class. Its purpose was to remould these 'remnants' through forced labour into 'socialist new people'. Gradually the re-education through forced labour system was extended to petty and non-criminal offences like pilfering, brawling, prostitution and drug-taking. With the crackdown it became a major tool for persecuting Falun Gong. In most cases no legal procedures were necessary, making it extremely 'convenient', and all the major provincial cities already had their own labour camps anyway.

AN ACTIVE COUNTER-REVOLUTIONARY

By the end of the 1980s, the Chinese mainland had begun to try to fall in line with international society and the government had rescinded the penal code clause relating to 'counter-revolutionary' crime. The people, however, were still deeply imbued with the class-struggle ideology of the Cultural Revolution.

'If you had carried on like this in the Cultural Revolution,' a police officer in the forced-labour camp once bellowed at me, 'you would have been counter-revolutionaries! You would have got fifteen years, minimum! You get off lightly now that they just sentence you to twelve months' re-education through labour.'

During my previous stay in the detention centre, Zhang Qiang had followed written procedure in his questioning.

'Do you know the state has banned Falun Gong?' he asked. 'Do you know the state has designated Falun Gong an evil cult?'

'No, I don't know,' I had answered.

He'd slammed the desk and jumped up as if I was deliberately trying to anger him.

After he had calmed down a little I told him a couple of things. First, it was the Falun Dafa Research Association that the Ministry of Civil Affairs had banned, not Falun Gong. Falun Gong is simply a style of *qigong*, an ideology; it's not an organisation, so how can it be banned? Second, the Constitution stipulates that citizens have the freedom of association. Yet when the Falun Dafa Research Association withdrew from the Chinese Association for Scientific Research into Qigong, its members applied everywhere to gain registration. They applied to the Ministry of Civil Affairs, the United Front Work Department, the National People's Congress, the Administrative Office of the Bureau of Religious Affairs, the National Physical Culture and Sports Commission, and the State Physical Culture and Sports Commission. No one would accept them. Where, then, does that leave the citizens' freedom of association that is enshrined in the Constitution?

As for the state designating Falun Gong an evil cult, that statement was even flakier. All that had been written about an evil cult was in an editorial in the *People's Daily*: 'The "Falun Gong" is an evil cult'. The *People's Daily* is the same paper that a number of years before carried an editorial called 'Carry the Great Proletarian Cultural Revolution through to the end'. And was the Great Proletarian Cultural Revolution carried through to the end? No, it wasn't. Do the *People's Daily* editorials carry the weight of the law? No, they don't.

Zhang Qiang disagreed so I asked him to show me proof of the legal basis for the evil cult claim. He and Ma Ying practically turned the interrogation room upside down in their frantic search and finally, after about half an hour, they unearthed the judicial interpretation for handling punishment of the evil cult, compiled by the Supreme People's Court and the Supreme People's Procurator. I had long ago pored over this document but Zhang Qiang obviously had not. I asked him if he could see anywhere in it the words 'Falun Gong'. He couldn't. So even if he were to mete out punishment to evil cults, I said, what would that have to do with Falun Gong?

It is really sad that so few Chinese people understand the law and that the authorities have taken advantage of this to perform such a gigantic sleight of hand. It is no wonder that in China, where one party controls everything, the people have never had much use for the law. It is only people who are pedantic in their reading as I am who discover the lie.

In the days when the people were called upon to heed the Party in everything there used to be a slogan: 'We will go in whatever direction the Party points us'. And in the 1950s and 1960s that is indeed what many Party members and ordinary people did. By the 1980s, however, people had lost confidence in the Communist Party and had become more adept at avoiding Party strictures. So at some point this slogan became: 'We will point in whatever direction the Party goes'.

An old story tells of an archer whose arrows always landed in the ten-point ring. When someone asked him the secret of his success he replied, 'I shoot the arrow first, then draw the bull's-eye.'

China today under the Communist Party is just like that. First they decide they are going to suppress Falun Gong; then, one by one, they formulate appropriate 'laws'. So however you look at it, those who have chosen not to understand the law are right. They are sensible, for what is the point of trying to understand this kind of law?

⌒

As soon as the people with criminal sentences had left, the van turned around and headed back the way we had come. Our police escort explained that reforms were being carried out whereby sentenced prisoners were to be kept separate from those being sent for re-education. We had to wait until the new re-education through forced labour despatch division was ready for us.

So we spent another six days back at the detention centre.

I found out later that the despatch division had been unable to cope with the influx of Falun Gong practitioners that the city of Beijing had sentenced to re-education. They had had to set up a new one dedicated to handling Falun Gong, signalling an escalation in the ruthless suppression.

Part IV

RE-EDUCATION THROUGH FORCED LABOUR: TEARS OF BLOOD

1

HELL ON EARTH

Very early in the morning of June 1, 2000, we four Falun Gong practitioners, a drug addict and a prostitute, were taken from the detention centre to Beijing's new Re-education Through Forced Labour Despatch Division, located at Tuanhe in Daxing County.

There wasn't a cloud in the sky that summer morning and the sun beat down on us as we waited outside the tightly secured gate. Our police escort went in through a small door beside the gate with our files, as before, and Wang Jin was just about to say something to me when the gate opened.

'Attention!' a rough male voice called out. 'Pick up your luggage with your right hand and form a line!'

We hurriedly did as we were told and on the command, 'Quick march!', walked in single file into the despatch division.

As soon as we were inside, before we had any time to take stock of our surroundings, a voice from above shouted 'Squat!' This sudden voice, coming out of nowhere before we had time to get our bearings, completely threw me, and involuntarily I squatted down. I could hear the crackle of an electric prod.

'Lower your head!' the voice called sharply. 'Clasp your head! Look at your toes!'

In spite of myself I lowered my head and looked at my toes, but I didn't understand what clasp my head meant.

A pair of feet in black leather shoes materialised beside me and my hands were suddenly pulled up and clasped behind my head.

'Learn this!' a voice ordered. 'This is lowering your head and clasping your head.'

This, together with the variant 'lower your head and clasp your hands', turned out to be an extremely important posture in the despatch division. *Standard conduct for people undergoing re-education through labour*, which we later 'studied', described these variations thus:

> Two-legged squat: both legs bent, feet together, hands clasped behind the head, head lowered.
> Standing position: feet together, hands clasped over the abdomen, right over left, head lowered.

A correctly lowered head enabled you to see your own toes; it also prevented you seeing anything else.

After squatting for five or six minutes I broke out into a sweat. All I could see was my feet and I had no idea what was going on around me. For some reason, the frightening experience of riding my bicycle right into a pond in the rain came back to me. After the initial shock I had felt an indescribable dread that the water was very deep and the bicycle and I would go straight to the bottom. It was almost as if I was hallucinating, that the pond was a big hole right through the earth and the clouds reflected on the surface of the water were actually clouds in the sky at the other end of the hole and that I could just fall right through the hole and come out on the other side of the globe. In a way I knew this was just my mind playing tricks on me, but at the same time I couldn't control my dread, having no idea how deep the pond was.

Lowering your head and clasping it had the same effect. You could hear the crackle of the electric prod but you couldn't tell when it was going to be your turn. And it was even worse when you didn't hear the prod. Then it would come like a bolt from the blue when you least expected it and frighten you half to death.

Whoever dreamed up this position would certainly gain at least a place in any major methods-of-torture competition.

A SECOND FEELS LIKE A YEAR

Eventually the order came to 'Stand up! Pick up your luggage!' We struggled up and were immediately ordered to lower our heads.

Anyone careless enough to lift her head got a poke with the prod or had her head forced down by a police officer. After that our days were spent looking at our toes, our heads lowered. Sighted people abruptly deprived of the power of sight, we did what the blind do: our sense of hearing became sharper so that we could perceive something of what was going on around us.

For now, we trotted blindly along in single file behind a police officer. Able to see little but the feet in front of us, we didn't dare to let those feet out of our sight, no matter what. We crossed what seemed to be two small courtyards and passed through two iron gates, then went down a passageway, passing by two little stools on which people dressed in white were sitting. At the end of the passageway a coarse concrete floor appeared beneath our feet.

The leading feet stopped and those coming up from the rear skidded to a halt.

'Put down your luggage! Lower your heads!'

The first real sign of the dictatorship of the proletariat in the despatch division was the boorish camel-driver tone in which orders were given.

'Attention! Get out all your ready cash, valuables, papers and keys!'

I fished my belongings out, as ordered.

'Zheng Zeng!' a voice shouted. 'Step forward!'

Newly blind, I couldn't work out from sound alone where the voice was coming from so I lifted my head slightly and glanced quickly around. I spotted some table legs two or three metres away that seemed to harbour the source of the voice. Lowering my head, I stepped forward and placed my things on the table.

A pair of hands counted the money, then a form was placed in front of me on which was written the amount of cash I had just handed over and a description of my papers. I was asked to sign the form, and told to return to my place, where I waited with lowered head. One by one the six of us were called to the table; we all signed our forms and then returned to stand alongside our luggage, still with lowered heads.

'Attention!' another voice roared at us. 'Your luggage will now be checked! You are advised to hand over any contraband goods and any Falun Gong texts or accept the consequences!'

A pair of legs in police trousers came over to me and led me to a plastered wall.

'Open your luggage!' the voice belonging to the legs ordered. 'Separate your quilt and your mattress! Take off your clothes!'

A pair of hands in disposable plastic gloves immediately started flicking through my things. The disembodied hands went through everything, tearing open each individually wrapped sanitary pad and strewing them all over the ground, and picking through a packet of tissues one by one before dumping them in a messy heap. Every item of clothing was picked up and shaken out. Once my luggage had been gone through carefully, my bedding was ripped apart and the hands carefully kneaded the cotton wadding. All that remained now was the business of taking off my clothes. Again, I chose to comply and with lowered head I took off everything, including my shoes and socks.

The person who had inspected my luggage hunkered down on the ground and went through my clothes.

Naked, I breathed in and lifted my head, looking up at the little square of sky above me. It was very blue. Out of the corner of my eye I caught the glare of my white skin in the sunlight, stark against the grey buildings. None of the officers busily inspecting luggage noticed my lifted head and I saw people's things strewn all over the ground. But I kept my inspection impersonal, careful not to let my gaze linger on the naked bodies of others.

After about ten minutes of this, a white shirt and a pair of blue shorts were thrown on the ground in front of each of us.

'Put this on!'

'This' was the outfit for people being re-educated through forced labour. We were no longer free to wear our own clothes.

Once dressed, we were lined up facing another plastered wall and ordered to squat, hands clasped on lowered heads. The scorching sun beat down on my back and the sweat began to pour off me, wetting my hair until it stuck to my face. My neck began to ache—I never knew my head was so heavy—and it got harder and harder to keep my hands clasped behind my head. If I pressed down on my head my neck couldn't take it, and if I didn't then my aching arms took all the strain. My legs went numb and started to tremble, I could hardly breathe and I thought I was going to vomit. I had heard people talk of a day feeling like a year but now I knew in the deepest recesses of my being what it was for a minute to feel like a year, for a second to feel like a year. So many times I felt I couldn't take any more. I wanted to collapse on the ground and desperately hoped that I might pass out so that I would be numb to this terrible anguish. But no matter how I longed to pass out, it just wouldn't happen. Instead, I vividly felt every intense second of excruciating pain.

Finally, someone fell to the ground with a thud, only to be goaded with shouts of 'Get up! No pretending!'

It was Wang Jin who had collapsed. Re-education centres weren't used to having older women inmates, so that the one-size-fits-all outfits they provided were made to fit the average young woman. The waistband on the shorts was at least ten centimetres too small for Wang Jin and she had tied a pair of stockings around the waist to pre-serve her modesty. The legs of the shorts were so tight they acted like the Golden Hoop around the Monkey King's head; Wang Jin lost all feeling in her legs and simply keeled over backwards.

I began to stand up and go to help her but several voices berated me. And then I heard the crackle of the prod. I quickly adjusted my centre of gravity and hunkered back down into a squat. Even that small movement was enough to ease the numbness in my legs a lit-tle and allow me to keep going for a while.

Time seemed to have stood still. Very soon I felt I had reached my limit but I gritted my teeth and persevered, quietly hoping that the next person to collapse would be the woman nearest to me, for then I could seize the opportunity to adjust my position and perhaps take advantage of supporting her to stand up for a minute, or even for half a minute.

We squatted in the sun all day. I cannot imagine how I got through those hours, minutes and seconds, nor can I imagine how older women such as Wang Jin endured for as long as we younger women did. All I know is that I do not have the words to describe the taste of going beyond the limits of your endurance, time and time again.

THEY ACT IN COLLUSION

We gathered from the voices that two more groups were arriving, at noon and in the afternoon, from Haidian District and Fengtai Dis-trict. Once they had been frisked and given their uniforms, they were brought in to squat with us. By now there were more than twenty of us in the yard.

After an eternity, the sun finally ceased its persecution and sank below the horizon.

A tall woman and a short woman, both wearing the same clothes as us, swaggered into the yard.

'Get up!' one of them said. 'Now we're going to teach you how to behave.'

I have mentioned previously how in Chinese lockups, re-education camps and prisons it is the prisoners who manage other prisoners. These two women, then, were the squad leaders; if they did a 'good' job for the police, they might get a remission on their sentences. The tall one was in for prostitution and procuring; the short one was a thief.

I found out later that the other women who came in at the same time as us Falun Gong practitioners called these squad leaders 'the black dogs' or 'the Rottweilers'. As far as I was concerned, these two no longer qualified as members of the human race so I didn't waste any energy thinking up names for them. Practising compassion and forbearance does not mean losing your judgement of right and wrong, nor does it imply cowardice or that you will ignore terrible crimes. It doesn't mean you will give free rein to evil beings who no longer have any human nature or righteous thoughts but do evil without limit. In Chinese the phrase 'the wolf and the *bei* do evil together' has come to mean to act in collusion. This is derived from the image of the *bei*, an imaginary creature with short forelegs, riding on the back of the wolf, a creature with short hind legs. Never before had this saying been so perfectly personified for me as in these two women, the taller of whom I called Wolf and the shorter of whom I called Bei.

My brain was so numb from squatting in the sweltering heat all day that when I heard the order to get up I didn't even feel relief. All I could do was place my hands on the ground and very slowly and mechanically stand upright; I couldn't make any other movement for some time.

We were led to a large board.

'Attention!' Wolf shouted at the top of her voice. 'Repeat after me! Points for attention for people entering the re-education through forced-labour camp!'

Numbly we repeated, 'Points for attention for people entering the re-educa . . .'

'Useless!' Wolf bellowed. 'Twenty of you and I can't even hear you! Again!'

All of us together weren't making anywhere near the sound she was producing by herself so we did it again. The points for attention were things like being checked in the head-lowered-head-clasped posture and not smuggling contraband goods in. This had already been well and truly drummed into us but we shouted our way through it a few times.

'Attention!' Wolf yelled. 'From now on, no more talking. You're only allowed to say three words: "Reporting! Present! Yes!" When you come in, it's "Reporting!" When the team leader calls your name, it's "Present!" And when the team leader has finished speaking, it's "Yes!" Now call them back to me and I want them good and loud.'

Like mad things the whole lot of us started shouting over and over.

'Reporting! Present! Yes! Reporting! Present! Yes!'

While we were shouting this we had to do the squat–stand: squat with heads lowered clasping our heads, then stand up with heads lowered clasping our hands, down, up, down, up, over and over again. Over twenty of us going up and down, all out of time, and shouting, with Wolf and Bei yelling, 'Louder! Louder! Come on, let's hear it! Shout it out!'

If I hadn't known better I would have thought I had somehow found my way into an insane asylum.

Many of us developed a tear in our vocal chords from this shouting and after that whenever we spoke or sang at a certain spot in our vocal range we would start coughing uncontrollably.

After a few dozen collective rounds of this Wolf and Bei assessed us individually. If you could shout the words twice through loudly enough you passed; otherwise you had to do it over and over until they gave you the nod.

It had been getting darker while we shouted like mad things and by this time it must have been nine or ten o'clock. It was at least fifteen hours since we'd left the lockup that morning and I was so exhausted that I did as I was told, numbly.

Somehow everybody managed to pass the shouting test but Wolf and Bei weren't finished yet.

'Attention!' they shouted. 'Now you're going to learn the reform songs. The first one is *Shout one-two-one!*'

The first two lines of this song went: 'Shout one-two-one, holding our heads up high / Striving to remould ourselves we start our lives anew'. We sang mechanically, as if we were completely unaware of the absurd incongruity between the words of the song and the reality of our situation. The whole time we were in the despatch division we had to keep our heads lowered, except when we were asleep, so with lowered heads we sang out in a loud voice our resolve to start our lives anew holdings our heads up high.

THE RETURN OF THE EVIL SOCIETY OF OLD

I have no idea what time it was when we finished learning the two reform songs and Wolf and Bei ordered us to lower our heads, face the wall, clasp our heads and squat.

'That's it,' I thought despairingly. 'The evil society of old is back.'

During the Cultural Revolution, it was drummed into us that without Chairman Mao and the Communist Party we would return to 'the vicious society of old' and suffer oppression and exploitation all over again. Thus from a very young age I was taught to dread the evil society of old. When Mao Zedong died, the year I turned ten, I genuinely thought the sky was going to fall and we would go back to the evil society of old with all its suffering and hardship. I cried my eyes out the day of the memorial meeting at school. With time, however, I became more reasonable and recognised the Cultural Revolution and Mao Zedong for what they were, but childish impressions are very deep and these phrases came back to me at certain times.

Having to squat again, now, was much more frightening than the evil society of old and my aching legs started to tremble almost straight away. What frightened me most was that I didn't know how long I would have to squat.

At long last I heard Bei call someone's name and tell her to stand up and go over to her.

Under cover of darkness I quietly turned my head far enough to see the woman sitting on a chair with a piece of plastic draped around her neck and Bei cutting her hair. Inside the camp we no longer had the freedom to dress as we pleased and now we were no longer to have the freedom to do our hair as we wished. Everybody was to have a basin cut, our hair chopped off all round at ear level.

I clenched my teeth waiting to be called and when I finally sank into the chair I remembered a discussion I had once had with some colleagues on just what constituted happiness. One of them had said happiness was an icy-cold beer on a sweltering summer's day. Now I could have told him categorically that happiness is feeling your bottom on a chair after a whole day of squatting with your head lowered, clasped in your hands. Later on, I heard someone say, 'In labour camp this bed is dearer to me than my own mother.' I remember this comment almost reducing me to tears.

But happiness is short lived. My haircut took only a few minutes and I was sent back to my place to squat in the evil society of old.

After everyone's hair had been cut, a police officer called the roll. Three groups, totalling 24 women, had arrived at the despatch division on that, its first day of operation, and twenty of us were Falun Gong practitioners. We were divided up into three squads of eight women each, with the four who were not Falun Gong practitioners sprinkled through the three squads as group leaders responsible for keeping an eye on us. I was put in Squad 4 with six other Falun Gong practitioners and a drug addict.

Utterly exhausted, with lowered head, I lugged my bedding after the police officer to the room marked Squad 4. Our cell was about eight square metres, with four double bunks in it, two each along facing walls with a space of 60 to 70 cm in between and a similar space between the door and the bunks. A single small window was located alongside the door. I was assigned to bunk three, a lower bunk, and I wrestled my bedding onto the bed board, longing for sleep.

'Fold your quilts!' I heard Bei call from the corridor.

This meant folding your quilt into a square with edges and corners even, like a cake of dried beancurd. This was really quite difficult and demanded special skill, particularly since the cheap quilts we had bought at the lockup were filled with wadding of some unknown material that went all lumpy, making it impossible to pummel them into a perfect square. I broke out into a sweat again. Just then the woman in the bunk above leaned down and spoke to me.

'I hope you don't mind my suggesting it but you could use my mattress instead of your quilt. It might be a bit easier to manage. I could use your quilt as my mattress.'

Filled with gratitude, I looked up to see a pretty young face, the living image of sincerity, apparently about middle school age. Her name was Wang Ke and in reality she was a 29-year-old Falun Gong practitioner, a graduate of Nanjing University. She had been working in Beijing for a foreign company and her husband was head of the State Family Planning Commission secretariat, so they were very well placed. Yet here she was, undergoing re-education through forced labour.

Realising this was no time for niceties, I quickly exchanged my recalcitrant quilt for her more amenable mattress.

Finally, after countless tries, all eight of us managed to get our quilts into something resembling a square. Wolf, Bei and a police officer made a tour of inspection and eventually gave us the order to go to bed.

We fell in dejected heaps on our bunks and within seconds were dead to the world around us.

The next day we stood in our cell with lowered heads and clasped hands, without moving, for sixteen hours straight, from 6 a.m. until 10 p.m. Four of us stood in the space between the two rows of bunks and the other four stood between the bunks and the door. Two 'little sentries' placed a small stool at the door and took turns watching us, so that we had not a second to ourselves. (Little sentries were fellow inmates who had been assigned to keep guard over us; there were six little sentries in the despatch division just then, two for each squad.)

We were allowed two minutes total, morning and evening, to wash, rinse our mouths and use the toilet, and we had five minutes for each of our three meals, which we ate squatting on the floor since there was nothing in the cell besides the bunks. The floor was bare earth, but to be fair I don't think the reason it hadn't been concreted was because the government was stingy; it was more likely that there had not been time to get it done. There was a tiled floor in the little sentries' room and I think that was supposed to have been standard throughout the despatch division. But the 'struggle with Falun Gong' was clearly far more pressing than fixing floors.

So, apart from meals and two minutes morning, noon and night for going to the toilet, we spent the rest of the time standing with lowered heads and clasped hands.

But just standing wouldn't do. For the entire sixteen hours we had to recite Order 23. Order 23 covered the re-education through forced-labour camp regulations: *Rules for people being re-educated through forced labour, What people being re-educated through forced labour must conform to* and *Everyday rules for people being re-educated through forced labour*. The first article was that we were to 'support the Communist Party and socialism as a system and not disseminate hostile opinions or incite enmity'. The rest were various prohibitions drawn up for local ruffians, things like we 'must not mix with pimps and bad types, must not bully the weak or use blackmail, must not read or disseminate pornographic publications or spread about licentious ideas, nor in [our] dealings indulge in vulgar or barbarous behaviour'.

The day before, as I squatted half dead in the sun clasping my head, I had thought there could be no greater hardship. Now I understood that hardships of the flesh were not the worst, because at least I still had some freedom of thought and could draw upon my willpower to endure and overcome physical limitations. Here, though, it would be a miracle indeed if I were not driven mad by the humiliation of prohibitions each more vile than the one before, by the constant violation of my thoughts and the havoc this wrought on my willpower, by my dispirited body being mercilessly ripped apart like a defenceless lamb.

Day three was simply a rerun of the day before: we got up at six and stood motionless with lowered heads and clasped hands reciting without a break.

By midday I felt my head was going to burst and my nerves were shot to pieces. If they kept this up I knew I would be utterly 're-educated' in no time. In the detention centre they had stripped us of our right to appeal and now to whom was I going to be able to appeal if the entire 60-day appeal period was spent doing this? I realised I had to get hold of a police officer in order to lodge an appeal.

Once this thought entered my mind I couldn't stand there reciting a moment longer. I didn't give myself time to consider what they might do to me if I were the first to break ranks and request an appeal.

'Would you tell the team leader I wish to make a report, please?' I said to the little sentry before my courage failed me.

I had thought she would refuse, but instead she just looked at me and went off to the duty office, returning two minutes later.

'Off you go,' she said to me. 'Team Leader Liu is waiting for you. Don't forget to keep your head lowered and your hands clasped and to call out "Reporting! Yes!" when you go in and when you come out.'

We had to call out 'Reporting! Yes!' even when we went to the toilet.

'Reporting! Yes!' I barked at the door of the cell then made my way with lowered head and clasped hands to the duty office opposite.

ELECTRIC SHOCKS FALL LIKE RAIN

We never had any idea how big the entire despatch division was. Re-education through forced-labour camps were run along military lines and we were organised into battalions, companies, squads and so on, while the police were called 'team leaders'. We were Company 4 and were housed in two rows of single-storey buildings about ten metres apart, with a small courtyard of about 50 square metres on the eastern side. Our company consisted of eleven squads.

The duty office was in one of the facing buildings and only one officer was on the noon shift. I went in and, with lowered head, explained what I had come for. One, I wanted to appeal and, two, I had not committed any crime and did not accept re-education through forced labour. Therefore, I said, from that moment on I simply would not comply with such requirements as lowering my head and clasping my hands and calling out 'Reporting! Yes!' on entering a room. At this point, I lifted my head and looked directly at the officer.

It was customary in the despatch division that whenever you spoke to a police officer you kept your head down and looked at your toes. You never looked directly at an officer. Officers would let you stand with lowered head and clasped hands when they were in a good mood, otherwise you had to squat with lowered head clasping your head while you talked to them.

This was the first time I'd had a good look at any of the police officers in the division. Team Leader Liu appeared to be in her forties; she had dark skin and a squint. She said my request was something she could not decide. It would have to be referred up. I asked her for some paper and a pen and set down my two points in report form. She promised to send it on then told me to return to my room.

I walked out with my shoulders back, without calling out 'Reporting!', and I swung my arms as I walked towards Squad 4. It felt so good not to have to keep my head down. Team Leader Liu caught up with me just as I got to the door of my cell.

'Come back,' she said in a low voice.

I looked at her without moving.

'Come back,' she repeated.

She seemed to bear me no malice, there was even a touch of pleading in her tone, and I felt I could not refuse, so I went back to the duty room with her.

She led me to the back of the room and asked me if I would give her a little time. Until her superiors responded, she said, I still had to obey the regulations or I would be making things difficult for her. How was she supposed to control the others if I carried on like this? Couldn't I spare her feelings a little, seeing as she just happened to be on duty when I decided to take this action?

I saw her point and agreed to abide by the rules until the following day, by which time she would have passed on my complaint. I was just about to call out 'Reporting!' and leave when I almost collided with a very tall young police officer who was entering. Team Leader Liu hastily told me this was our company team leader; her name was Wang.

'What's up?' Team Leader Wang said sternly.

I said I was reporting something to the leadership of the despatch division.

'I am the leadership,' she replied. 'If you've got something to say, say it to me.'

So I started to make my two points, but she cut me off and reprimanded me in a loud voice, saying that I ought to know my place and that I had to do exactly as I was told.

Shoulders back, I walked out in the middle of her tirade without calling out 'Reporting!' and headed back to Squad 4.

She overtook me, blocking the doorway to my cell.

'Call out "Reporting!"' she ordered.

'No,' I said quietly.

She started yelling right into my face. The women in my cell stopped reciting to watch us.

'Team Leader Wang,' I said, looking her in the eye, 'saying something loudly doesn't make it right. Will you stop yelling at me, please.'

Shamed into anger, she became flustered.

'Go over there and squat!' she said.

'No,' I replied, shaking my head.

Another officer came from nowhere and she and Team Leader Wang dragged me toward a corner of the building. They frog-marched me several metres then dropped me on the ground.

'Squat!' they shouted.

I sat facing the wall with my arms wrapped around my knees without saying a word, tears rolling down my face. How could they be so vicious! How could they treat me like this!

I didn't know what the police officers were doing; all I could hear was Wolf taunting me.

'Hah!' she snarled. 'So you can still cry? Aren't you supposed to embody Truthfulness, Compassion and Forbearance? And you can't bear such a small thing as this?'

I was so choked up I couldn't say anything and just sat there crying.

'Squat for me!' Wolf said, giving me a kick.

I managed to stop crying and, looking up at her, I said, 'I want to make a report to the despatch division leadership. You have no business speaking to me.'

Wolf frowned and gave me another kick.

'The team leader told me to deal with you,' she said. 'That's the business I have with you!'

Ignoring her, I turned away and saw Team Leader Wang and the other officer emerging from the duty office with thunder on their faces and electric prods in their hands.

I was dragged into the middle of the courtyard and electric shocks rained down on my body, each jolt making me tremble uncontrollably as it pierced me with a violent burning sensation. I sat on the ground clenching my teeth to stop crying out, my head spinning.

I don't know how long this lasted. Then I saw Wang Ke being dragged out into the courtyard. In her white shirt and blue shorts and with her short hair she looked like one of those pure young students you see in films of the 1919 May Fourth period. When they used the prods on her, she instinctively ran around the courtyard trying to evade the shocks. At one point my mind seemed to go blank and I just felt enormous sympathy for her. After a bit she wasn't there any more and the two officers came after me again.

Both of them were prodding me but I wouldn't let go of my knees. The crackle grew louder and I could feel the current rippling through my body. As it grew in intensity I squeezed my eyes shut, mustering all my will against the black despair sweeping over me and against this monstrous evil threatening to engulf me.

Suddenly something snapped in my brain and I felt the whole world collapse into darkness with a great roar. 'Hundreds of hardships befall one at once, to see how one lives!' I cried out deep within my soul. Then I collapsed, unconscious, on the ground.

I don't know how long I was unconscious, but as I slowly came round I was amazed to find myself actually squatting on the ground with Wolf trying to put my hands behind my head in the correct 'head lowered, head clasped' posture. They must have lifted me up as I started to come to. My hands were so weak that every time Wolf put them up behind my neck they slid off, but eventually she managed to get them to stay put.

I no longer had the capacity to resist as I squatted under the blazing sun, with Wolf standing behind me ready with a kick every time I moved a muscle.

I watched each drop of sweat as it splashed down onto the burning concrete, a tiny stain that shrank to nothing and evaporated without a trace. I watched the drops of sweat until they stopped, not because the sun was less fierce and the temperature had dropped below 38°C but because my body had no more sweat to give.

And as the sun moved across the sky and the shadow of the building fell onto me, a voice behind me would call out, 'Move forward!'

All afternoon I did this, inching forward, head down, clasping my head, until my whole body was exposed again to the full blast of the sun.

I remembered a scene in some film or other where an unkempt prisoner was tied to a post under the scorching sun awaiting execution. A large crowd was taunting him but a beautiful maiden took pity on him and lifted a bowl of cool water to his parched lips. I ran my tongue over my lips, knowing that no one was going to offer me any water. Knowing also that as soon as I moved I would be kicked, I slowly got the knack of enduring without moving my feet. First I would put my weight on my left foot and then, when I really couldn't take any more, I would move it onto my right foot. Then I would spread it evenly over both feet. I would do the same with my hands, letting them rest on the back of my head for a while then, with my hands still interlocked, bringing my elbows in to rest on my knees so that my legs took the weight for a while. Then I would go through the whole process again.

I discovered some ants having a scuffle on the ground and concentrated on them as if my life depended on it, anything to divert my attention from my aching legs.

The next day the back of my neck was covered in blisters. My whole body was black and blue with the marks of the prods and my buttocks were grazed and torn, the wounds exposed through the gaping holes in my shorts and underpants.

And yet, as I squatted in the sun, covered in bruises and with my clothing ripped, I felt luckier than the others inside reciting 'must not mix with pimps and bad types, must not in our dealings indulge in vulgar or barbarous behaviour, must not use vulgar language or obscenities'.

I squatted for eight or nine hours straight that day. Just before bedtime they let me stand up and go back to the cell.

There is no sun and no moon in a cave, and in the despatch division there were no TV, no newspapers, no calendars, no watches. Our days, indeed our entire lives, were filled with reciting Order 23. After three days of squatting and standing, everybody's feet, hands and bodies swelled up from the immobility. Our feet were like big steamed buns and we couldn't get our shoes on, so we would stealthily kick them off and then have to somehow jam them back on when we used the toilet.

After we had stood for eight whole days we were given small folding campstools to sit on. But our right to sit could be taken away at any time for any reason; the decision was at the discretion of the officers or of Wolf and Bei. And the reciting of Order 23 was never to be remitted.

We gradually lost all sense of time, merely longing for nightfall every day from the moment we got up. After I don't know how many days had passed a new element was introduced to our career in recitation: formation drills.

Everybody, young or old, had to undergo the formation drills, and do them to military standard: mark time, stand to attention, stand at ease, quick march, at the double, parade step. We had to do it again if we didn't do it properly the first time and were just as likely to receive a kick as a reprimand.

This particular day we had been training for a long time when Team Leader Liu told us to sit on the ground to sing the reform songs. She told You Min, who was in Squad 2, to start us off.

You Min stood up and began to recite 'Lunyu'[15], the preface to *Zhuan Falun*:

'Lunyu: The Buddha *Fa*[16] is most profound . . .'

---

15 Statement or comment.
16 The universal principles and law; the way of the universe.

'Stop! Stop!' Team Leader Liu shouted wildly.

The air suddenly became tense. You Min was taken off to the office and an officer named Jiang also rushed over.

A torrent of abuse poured out of the office while tears dripped from my lowered eyes onto the ground. I was filled with remorse that I had not stood up and started reciting with You Min, that all twenty of us had not stood up and started reciting. I deeply resented that every day we would recite that disgraceful Order 23 but did not dare recite 'Lunyu'.

I was still crying when they sent You Min to squat facing the wall. As soon as she squatted down a violent wind suddenly blew up out of a clear sky. If I hadn't believed in spirits before I certainly did now: God was angry!

'Go to the toilets in your formation then return to your squad rooms!' Team Leader Jiang shouted, scared out of her wits.

When we got to the toilets I realised that, like me, Wang Ke and another Falun Gong practitioner named Xia Jing were crying. As we came out of the toilets we saw all the women from Squad 2 squatting alongside You Min in the fierce wind.

'Sit down!' Team Leader Jiang shouted sternly when we returned to our cell.

Normally, if we made the slightest mistake we were punished by having our campstools taken away and having to squat for several hours. This punishment, which didn't apply to group leaders, was meted out for transgressions such as inadvertently looking up when someone walked past the window. Now, though, they were telling us to sit down when we had surely 'committed a major error'. Somehow we knew they were anxious to get us 'fixed', so that they could go to torture those in Squad 2. Without saying a word we all remained standing.

'Sit down!' Team Leader Jiang shouted again.

Xia Jing raised her right hand.

'Reporting, Team Leader,' she said in a small voice. 'I wish to go and squat with the students in Squad 2.'

'No! Sit!'

It began from my sitting on the ground crying and regretting my own cowardice, then spiralled up and up through my brain, becoming more and more intense, and finally 'Lunyu' burst from my mouth like a torrent:

The Buddha *Fa* is most profound; among all the theories in the world, it is the most intricate and extraordinary science. In order to explore this domain, humankind must fundamentally change its conventional thinking. Otherwise, the truth of the universe will forever remain a mystery to humankind, and every day people will forever crawl within the boundary delimited by their own ignorance . . .

I couldn't hear whether I started first or all seven of us started together bringing forth the most powerful, the most steadfast resonance from life's deepest recesses. At last, after all this time, we were shouting the most powerful sound of our lives! Oblivious to our surroundings, seven voices as one poured our entire lives into the mighty Buddha Law:

Then, what exactly is 'the Buddha *Fa*'? Is it a religion? Is it a philosophy? That is only the understanding of the 'modernized Buddhist scholars', who merely study theories. They regard it as a philosophical category for critical studies and so-called research. Actually, 'the Buddha *Fa*' is not only the tiny portion documented in the scriptures, for that is simply 'the Buddha *Fa*' at an elementary level. 'The Buddha *Fa*' is an insight into all mysteries. It encompasses everything and leaves out nothing—from particles and molecules to the universe, from the even smaller to the even greater. It is an exposition of the characteristic of the universe, 'Zhen-Shan-Ren'[17], expressed at different levels with different layers of meaning. It is also what the Tao[18] School calls the 'Tao', or what the Buddha School calls the 'Fa'[19] . . .

This was a solemn and sacred moment: the first time the mighty Buddha Law had been voiced in what I believe was the darkest concentration camp of our day. Seven voices, seven lives, came together as a moral force to smash the darkness, to surmount the firmament, to break through the layered heavens. Instantly, those wicked forces

---

17 *Zhen* (truth, truthfulness); *Shan* (compassion, benevolence, kindness); *Ren* (forbearance, tolerance, endurance).
18 1. also known as 'Dao', Taoist term for 'the Way of nature and the universe'; 2. enlightened being who has achieved this Tao.
19 Law and principles in the Buddha School.

that relied on violence and coercion to change the will of the people were scared out of their wits; they were reduced to flying ashes and smouldering smoke.

This was the most 'serious' thing that had happened since the despatch division was set up. The police were in chaos; Wolf and Bei were flustered and panicked. They all rushed into our cell and screamed at the tops of their voices, 'SHUT UP!'

In the melee I felt my physical self dissolve as my will was transformed into a gigantic and indomitable spirit of limitless courage and determination. Firm and unshakeable, I went on reciting:

As advanced as the present human science has become, it is still only part of the mysteries of the universe. Whenever we mention specific phenomena of 'the Buddha *Fa*', someone will claim: 'This is already the electronic age, and science is very advanced. Spaceships have already flown to other planets, yet you still bring up these outdated superstitions.' To put it frankly, no matter how advanced a computer is, it is still no match for the human brain, which to this day remains an unfathomable enigma. However far a spaceship may fly, it cannot travel beyond this physical dimension in which our human race exists. What can be understood with modern human knowledge is extremely shallow and tiny; it is far from truly coming to terms with the truth of the universe. Some people even dare not face, touch upon, or admit the facts of phenomena that objectively exist, because they are too conservative and unwilling to change their conventional thinking. Only through 'the Buddha *Fa*', can the mysteries of the universe, time–space, and the human body be completely unveiled. It is able to truly distinguish what is righteous from evil, good from bad, and eliminate all misconceptions while providing what is correct . . .

By this time the officers had brought out their electric prods, but just as they reached the door an even fiercer gust of wind dislodged the sign saying Squad 4 and, blessed coincidence, it fell with a clunk right on top of them. If this wasn't a sign of indignation from heaven, what was?

Team Leader Liu waved her prod in my face and a thought flashed through my mind. I remembered someone telling me once that it wasn't the large electric prods you had to worry about; it was the small ones that did the most damage. And the prod in Team Leader Liu's hand was a small one.

I suddenly stopped reciting and the others all stopped at the same time, almost as if it had been written into the score. The last stanza of 'Lunyu' remained unsung.

ENCOURAGING OTHERS TO DO GOOD

Team Leader Jiang, Team Leader Liu, Wolf and Bei breathed a long sigh of relief and it was some time before anyone spoke.

'Zheng Zeng! Go to the office!' Jiang eventually growled.

As I crossed the courtyard I saw that the people from Squad 2 were no longer squatting at the wall. I wondered if they had been sent back to their cell while we were reciting 'Lunyu'; otherwise who knows how long they would have had to squat for. The Falun Gong practitioners in Squad 2 told me later that they were moved to tears by our chanting as they squatted in the howling wind.

'Did you start this thing today?' Team Leader Jiang asked, her face serious. 'Do you know what the consequences are?'

I had been crying the whole time we were reciting 'Lunyu'. I had felt something majestic and indescribably moving as my entire life seemed to dissolve into the glorious Buddha *Fa*. And I knew that 'earth-shaking, enough to make the spirits weep' was the only way to describe this courageous, heroic assault against all wicked oppression.

'Actually, it was all of us wanting to do it,' I answered slowly, with tears in my eyes. 'But if you really want someone to have been the one who started it, then I don't mind if it's me and I'll accept whatever punishment you see fit. If I had been afraid I wouldn't have come here in the first place.'

The wind suddenly dropped and a gentle rain began to fall, as if God were weeping with me.

Another officer came in.

'Don't you have any consideration at all?' she said to me. 'Team Leader Liu was letting you have a song out of the goodness of her heart to give you a bit of a break and you go and cause this commotion. How do you think she's going to explain this to our superiors?'

I mustered all the compassion I was capable of.

'Team Leader,' I said to her, still in tears, 'we don't want to sing; we want only to practise. You've been a police officer for a long time and I'm sure you can tell at a glance who's a good person and who's a bad person. Do you see anything bad in these old ladies? Why have good people like this been brought here?'

She seemed to be moved by this and murmured that they were only doing their job and had no say in state affairs.

'Did you know,' I went on, 'that during the Tian'anmen Massacre many soldiers threw their rifles to the ground and deserted rather than obey the order to shoot? That was the wisest choice for them to make. Yes, you are implementing policy and I know you are in a very difficult position, placed between mistaken government decisions and innocent people. But you could still treat us with some magnanimity and leniency. The section head in the detention centre chose not to see us when we practised Falun Gong there and what could they do to her? She was the really clever one.'

'Oh, so now you're trying to straighten me out! Do you realise who you are? Do you know how serious this affair today is?'

'I do know, Team Leader. I'm only thinking of you.'

'Go back to your cell.'

When I got back I found everybody concerned for me, not knowing what was going on.

But that was the end of the matter. It was never mentioned again. We thought later this was probably because what they feared most was our acting as one body, so they tried to pretend it hadn't happened.

On June 6, a second group of twenty or so women arrived and they kept coming after that, usually two groups a week, some large, some small, until all the cells were full.

'All squads close doors!' Wolf and Bei would yell before each group arrived.

It was suffocating inside but we had to keep on reciting Order 23, presumably so that the sound of our own voices would drown out what was happening outside. We would recite the whole day, until the newcomers had been put through what we had been put through on our first day, and only after they had finally been installed in their squad rooms could we open our doors and get some air.

Whenever we heard the shout and a new group filed past with

their heads lowered we would sneak a quick look through our little window to see if we could pick out any Falun Gong practitioners. They were fairly easy to spot and, as with our group, made up the vast majority of newcomers.

One afternoon two tall thin women arrived, clearly sisters. They were searched and their belongings were inspected, then Wolf led them over to the large board to read the *Points for attention for people entering the re-education through forced-labour camp.*

The sisters read the first few points out obediently after Wolf.

Then Wolf shouted out the next one. 'Four: I plead guilty and admit my mistakes. I accept re-education.'

The silence was deafening.

'You gone dumb?' Wolf raised her voice a notch. 'Say it. "I plead guilty and admit my mistakes. I accept re-education!"'

'Making a peaceful appeal does not make one guilty,' a clear voice said softly.

We glanced at each other, sure now that they were Falun Gong practitioners. Everybody who had come into the division so far had been knocked into shape quickly. Unable to offer any resistance, they had been compelled to knuckle under and follow procedures to the letter. This was the first time that established procedure had not been followed.

Like a madwoman, Wolf bellowed for Bei.

Squad 4 was on the southeastern corner of the block, closest to the board, and we heard everything while the other squads kept reciting Order 23. We strained to hear as Wolf and Bei took the sisters over to the wall, gave them a good kicking, and then made them squat.

Just then another group of women arrived and Wolf and Bei had to attend to the later arrivals. It was after dark before the sisters were allowed to get up and come into the building but they still hadn't said, 'I plead guilty and admit my mistakes'.

'Just the two of them!' Wang Ke said bitterly. 'Twenty of us and what did we do? Those two are better than all twenty of us.'

The next morning we got up as usual, did our ablutions and started reciting Order 23. At eight o'clock, when the day-shift officers came on duty, there was a whiff of something different in the air. And, indeed, not long after we heard the shout from Bei.

'Close doors! Recite Order 23!'

In the normal course of events, new people wouldn't come two days in a row so why, we wondered, were they ordering us to shut the door? We soon found out.

The two sisters who had refused to admit their guilt were taken to the little courtyard at the end of the building. Company Leader Wang Li went to supervise as Wolf led them through the *Points for attention*.

Again, a deafening silence when it came to 'I plead guilty and admit my mistakes'. But this time the police officers were ready and they sallied forth with their electric prods. For a good while all we could hear was this crackling and we had no idea what was happening.

Suddenly the silence was shattered by a horrible shriek that broke my heart almost in two. Then the prods started up again and we heard the sound of people running in the courtyard. Soon another cry came.

'Ahhhh . . .!'

There was the sound of something being lifted up and flung heavily to the ground with a muffled moan. The moans grew in intensity and the scream kept on.

'Ahhhh . . .! Ahhhh! . . .'

The piercing cries tore at my heart. I looked around and saw Wang Ke in tears. Everyone else, except the drug addict Yang Jianping, was crying, desperately trying not to make a sound, and finally my tears began to fall, too.

The screams, the sound of the prods, the moans as something was thrown to the ground over and over went on and on, until I felt I could stand it no longer. I'll rush out, I said to myself, and shield them from the blows with my body. Three are stronger than two and when the prods run out they'll have to let us go. I got up and was about to dash out when Wang Ke pulled me back down onto my campstool. She was crying so much she couldn't speak. Reluctantly I stayed where I was, desperately trying to think of something else I could do. The police were beside themselves, running back and forth past our door.

That's it! I thought. I'll ask outright to talk to them. Yes, 'Report my thoughts!'

'Team Leader!' I called out. 'Team Leader!'

Several officers walked away, seeming not to hear me. One paused for a moment then walked off.

The noises continued outside and I just kept calling out until eventually the officer I had earlier encouraged to treat us with some magnanimity and leniency heard me.

'What do you want now, Zheng Zeng?' she said as she opened the door to our cell.

'I wish to suggest an idea to Team Leader Wang.'

'Later. Team Leader Wang is busy.'

'No. Please go and speak to her. I have to make a suggestion now. It has to be now!'

She gave me a look, realising that something was going on, then turned around and left.

Not long after, Wang Li appeared at our door, prod still in hand.

'So it's Squad 4 again,' she said, a certain languid truculence in her voice. 'What is it?'

'Team Leader Wang,' I said, making a supreme effort to remain calm, 'I want to suggest an idea to you.'

'Suggest an idea! What idea, eh?'

'I suggest you shouldn't treat them this way.'

'You "suggest"! Well, that's big talk. Do you know who you are? Do you understand that people being re-educated must unconditionally obey those in charge? Huh! You "suggest"!'

'So may I *request* that you not treat them this way?'

Someone barely contained a sob.

Wang Li looked around at us, apparently somewhat surprised at our reaction.

'I'm in charge here,' she said. 'What business is it of yours?'

I lifted my head and looked her in the eye.

'They're here because they practise Falun Gong, Team Leader Wang,' I said. 'Anything to do with Falun Gong is our business.'

'We are against corporal punishment.' This firm statement came from the mouth of Li Zhiru, an older woman with a voice normally the size of a mosquito who hardly ever said a word. There was a chorus of agreement. Common feeling had never run so high in a despatch division.

Wang Li took half a step back.

'I may consider your suggestion,' she said with her haughty air. Then she paused and took another step back. 'I accept your suggestion and now you must do as I say or you will be guilty of insubordination. I order you to sing. You start them, Yang Jianping. Sing *Socialism is good*.'

Yang Jianping lifted her head.

'*Socialism is good*,' she began. 'Ready, one-two!'

Socialism is good. A great sadness welled up within me and I burst out crying. How could socialism be good when people were being electrocuted to the point of screaming? Everybody stopped, unable to go on.

By this time, however, Wang Li had sauntered off, cradling her electric prod.

A LIVING CORPSE

A few days later a pathetic figure appeared in the little courtyard, someone who couldn't keep up. She looked to be in her early twenties and was about 165 cm tall but she was even more emaciated than those African famine victims you see in films. She would have weighed no more than 35 kilos. Her hair was all tangled and her skin had a deathly pallor. Her lifeless eyes stared unseeing on a world that no longer concerned her, her whole being so lethargic that she was more living corpse than human being.

When the detainees in her squad lined up to go and do their ablutions she would totter along several metres behind, looking for all the world as though a breeze would blow her over at any moment. The entrance corridor into our single-storey building was only about 5 cm above courtyard level. Others would easily step up without even noticing its existence. But to her, this tiny step presented more difficulties than climbing the Himalayas. She would stand at the entrance swaying, mustering all her strength and will. Then all of a sudden she would fling her left foot onto the sill, almost losing her balance. This would set her rocking quite severely but she would eventually regain her balance and stand there swaying until she managed to bend down and place her hands shakily on the floor. She would stay like that for a while to catch her breath and then, propping herself on her hands for all she was worth, she would suddenly and with great daring throw her right foot forward. But this wasn't the end of it. There she would stay, on all fours, swaying precariously, and we would watch with our hearts in our mouths until she finally managed to stand up straight and proceed into the building with faltering steps.

After many days we still couldn't work out who she was; all we

knew was that her name was Liu Shuying. I suspected she had
become so thin and weak through using drugs, but then one day we
saw her sitting in the little courtyard copying something from a
green-covered book.

We knew this green-covered book. The police made us study it
because in it were the Ministry of Public Security's six prohibitions
as well as some articles 'exposing and repudiating' Falun Gong written by former Falun Gong practitioners who had been 'reformed'.

We wondered why Liu Shuying was copying things out of this
book. Surely she hadn't been a Falun Gong practitioner? I didn't
think that was possible but what was odd was that we never did find
out who she was or what she had done. 'Don't fill the rest of your life
with everlasting deep regret!' I wanted to call out to her whenever
I saw her hunched over in that chair, copying things down.

But she seemed to have departed this world long ago for, although
she was copying things down, her heart, her soul and her mind were
elsewhere. I felt that she was only a shell, a body whose life force no
longer had the capacity to be called back.

———

On the Clearwisdom website I later read something a Falun Gong
practitioner had written about his time in Panjin re-education camp
in the northeast:

> I don't want to record every beating I suffered. Each account of
> every beating is almost the same. But to the victim, every time is
> different. Although they might beat me with the same baton every
> time, being hit once and being hit dozens of times are different.
> Being tortured once and being tortured every day are two differ-
> ent things. Although I don't want to repeat each one of these atroc-
> ities, the evil ones continue to repeat their crimes. If we were to
> write down the details of every beating that each person received
> in the Panjin City Forced Labor Camp, we would fill volumes.

It was the same with the 'socialism is good' issue in the despatch
division of Beijing. With the arrival of each new group, a new round
of atrocities was enacted, culminating in what they did to an unmar-
ried female practitioner. She was tied to a chair, then several burly
policemen with flashlights applied electric prods to her vagina, her

breasts and the top of her head until she lost control of her bladder and sphincter. She was unconscious for several days and for a long time was unable to walk because of the damage to her genitals.

Then there was the practitioner from Jiangsu province who passed out the first day from sunstroke. Thinking she was malingering, an officer applied an electric prod to her head for a considerable length of time before realising the woman really was unconscious. The officer panicked and had her sent to hospital. There they found that her pupils were dilated 1.5 times greater than normal and they didn't think they could save her. She was in intensive care for 24 hours before she eventually regained consciousness. She, too, was unable to walk for a long time.

Despite or perhaps because of these episodes of unadulterated brutality, there was a certain black humour to be found in the despatch division.

At the height of Beijing's summer the temperature soars to about 40°C and the metal frames of our bunks would get scorching hot, while the sweat poured from us morning till night. We were allowed just two minutes a day to wash and we wore the same unwashed clothes day in, day out. I was still wearing that tattered and holey pair of pants; really not a pretty sight. We were soon caked in a thick layer of dried sweat and dirt that you could chip off in chunks. Our white shirts had turned yellow and the sweat stains made our blue shorts look like maps. Our clothes were so stiff they could almost stand up by themselves when we took them off.

It got so bad that one day we asked the little sentry Chun Ling to ask Officer Sha, who was sitting in the cool courtyard, to give us a little time to have a wash. We had made friends with Chun Ling over a period of time. The day I had been dragged away and electrocuted, the other Falun Gong practitioners in my squad had all stopped reciting Order 23 on my behalf and Wang Ke had been the first to be given collateral punishment.

'Ai-ya!' Chun Ling is reported to have said. 'You lot really are all of one mind.'

From then on she had gradually become a sort of accomplice.

Officer Sha's nickname was Sha-sha, meaning 'Kill-kill'. She was deputy team leader of Company 4 and it had been she who had helped Wang Li electrocute me that day. The drug addict Yang Jianping had come up with the nickname Sha-sha.

We couldn't hear how Chun Ling phrased our request but we did hear Sha-sha's answering bellow.

'How dare you ask for so much? Be grateful that you are still alive!'

Chun Ling turned and fled.

Wang Ke nodded. 'Well, we've finally found the perfect spokes-woman for Chairman Jiang Zemin's human rights ideology. Chairman Jiang says China's most fundamental human rights problem is the problem of existence. Our team leader Sha-sha says be grateful that you are still alive! So incisive! I am filled with admiration. Clearly, Sha-sha really understands Party policy.'

Many women got so hot sitting all day in stuffy little cells they nearly fainted. Occasionally squads were issued with a dish of cool water to splash on their faces so they could cool down a bit but when the women got really thirsty they would resort to drinking the water in which they had washed their faces.

In the end, during the hottest period, the police let the women strip and remain naked in their rooms. When members of the leadership or male officers turned up, Wolf or Bei would yell from the courtyard 'Get dressed!' and there would be a bit of a scuffle as women rushed to get into clothes in time.

Anyone who has visited the remnants of the Nazi concentration camps can visualise Jewish women, stripped of their clothing, being herded into the gas chambers. But it is hard to imagine this sort of thing happening in the twenty-first century—human rights' 'finest' hour—in Daxing County just twenty or thirty kilometres from Tian'anmen Square, the heart of 'new China'.

THE GREAT MEN'S AND WOMEN'S RE-EDUCATION CAMP RESHUFFLE

Not long after we arrived in the despatch division a little sentry told us that inmates were usually held there for ten days to two weeks before being sent on to a re-education camp. We were there for over a month, however, and the eleven squads were full to overflowing, with the last group forced to sleep on the floor because there weren't enough beds. Yet there was no indication that they were going to send us on.

We sensed that this overcrowding was making the officers impatient as they waited for instructions. One afternoon we finally heard some secondhand information from the little sentry. The women's re-education camp wasn't big enough to hold all the female Falun Gong practitioners so a swap was being arranged between the men's and the women's camps. In other words, the women were being moved into the men's camp and vice versa. All personnel and physical paraphernalia had to be moved, which was no small thing. In addition to the heavy lifting, the re-education camp staff had to ensure that strict precautions were in place to prevent escapes. It was no wonder there was a delay in our being sent on.

Those of us who had arrived in the first group could claim ourselves to be more 'fortunate' than later arrivals as the staff became even harsher towards the newer inmates. In addition, in August they ran out of summer-weight uniforms and new intakes had to wear the autumn-weight uniform. This had long sleeves and long trousers and must have been absolutely unbearable in the stifling heat of high summer. After we left they were forcing twenty women into the eight-bed cells so that the overflow had to sleep squeezed into the space between the bunks, and under the bunks. It was too bad if you wanted to go to the toilet in the middle of the night, because the floor was littered with sleeping bodies.

———

At noon on July 7, 2000, as we were rinsing our bowls in the ablutions block, we became aware that something was going on outside. Shortly afterwards, another of the little sentries with whom we were on quite good terms came in.

'This time you're really going,' she said to us. 'A big van has come for you. Just remember: whatever you do, do not lift your heads on the way or you'll get the electric treatment!'

We were told to return to our cells and saw that the police had already started to call the roll. As soon as your name was called you had to get your things and line up outside.

The despatch division had always been the very model of 'good order', but suddenly there was about it an air of disorderly retreat. It was as noisy and confusing as Judgement Day may be, with names being called, people answering, registering who was going and who wasn't, asking who was going and who wasn't, leaving messages, bidding farewell to one another, collecting belongings, retrieving articles that had been put in safekeeping. All of the customary rules of behaviour went by the board as everybody ran around in circles, with luggage strewn all over the small courtyard. The sun beat down and it was very hot. There was tension in the air, as if a war was impending.

Eventually, Wang Li took control.

'Attention!' she shouted at the top of her voice. 'Get into line in the order in which I call your names!'

Mine was the first of 51 names to be called out. Thirty of us were Falun Gong practitioners; eighteen were drug addicts; and there were three others.

We stood in a line that stretched from west to east right across the courtyard. While Wang Li continued to call out names, the police assigned to the job of handing back our personal articles got us to sign for them, one by one. The sweat just poured off me. When someone behind me lifted her head as she signed the list, Team Leader Jiang gave her a burst with her electric prod.

'Keep your head down,' she shouted.

'You haven't gone yet!' Bei shouted. 'Just remember who you are.' It was obvious that she was not happy at the idea of us no longer being answerable to her.

When all the formalities had been attended to we were ordered to walk out of the courtyard. We then had to squat with lowered heads, clasping our heads, while the male officers into whose hands we had been placed called the roll again. Then we were handcuffed in pairs and herded onto a large coach, the cold metal of the cuffs heavy on our wrists.

Once on the coach we squatted in pairs in the aisle or between the seats; our free hands had to remain behind our heads. The coach was tightly sealed and my head was under a seat so I couldn't see a thing; all I could hear was the wail of the siren. Our clothes were drenched in no time; our legs were trembling; and it was like being in a sauna.

Half an hour or so later when the coach slowed down and stopped I realised we had at last arrived at the Tiantanghe Re-education Through Forced Labour Camp.

2

I AM INCARCERATED
IN TIANTANGHE

THE INDUCTION PROCESS AT TIANTANGHE Camp was the same as for the despatch division except that the body search was conducted in the washhouse, where I seized the opportunity to gulp down several mouthfuls of tap water, ladling it into my mouth with my grimy hands.

It was dark before all of the formalities were completed and we 51 new arrivals were formed into a new company—Entry Company—comprised of four squads with about a dozen of us in each squad. Wang Ke and I were put in Squad 3.

There had been only Company 1 and Company 2 in Tiantanghe before the crackdown. Company 1 then consisted entirely of drug addicts, hence its nickname 'the powder company', from white powder or heroin. Company 2 was made up of miscellaneous felons, mainly prostitutes, thieves, robbers and women dealing in pornographic CDs.

The first Falun Gong practitioner arrived at the camp in October 1999 and the second in November. Several women came in as a third group at the Spring Festival of 2000 and a group of 30-odd on May 26. They had been integrated into Company 1 and Company 2.

There were two four-storey dormitories ten metres or so apart in the camp. In front of each building was an exercise area bounded on the other side by an electrically operated gate. Behind the dormitories were ranged the mess hall, another hall that could seat

400 people, a boiler room and two workshops. All this was enclosed by a high grey wall topped with an electric fence to prevent anyone from climbing it, and right up against the wall were some dilapidated single-storey structures.

To the east of the tightly closed gate was a small building that housed the clinic and the visiting room (for relatives) known as the 'reunion' building. To the west was the 'prison within a prison' where the training and solitary confinement rooms were. This six-sided modular building was obviously quite new and had a weird and secretive air about it.

Training and solitary confinement are standard punishments in the forced-labour camp for those who commit new crimes, violate the regulations of the camp or disobey the police. The so-called training usually lasts for three months. During this period, inmates must get up earlier and go to sleep later than other 'normal' inmates. But no matter how hard they work, they cannot earn a single merit point. They eat the worst food, without any vegetables, and are not allowed to meet or write to their families. Those put into solitary confinement have the length of their punishment added on to their sentences, so the inmates dread both training and solitary confinement.

The Entry Company, Company 1 and Company 2 occupied one dormitory building, one company per floor, so that there was no interaction. The other dormitory building housed forty or so teenage male offenders—the 'young re-educateds'. They had not been involved in the changeover of male and female accommodation, probably because there had not been room for them with the adult male offenders.

Chun Ling had told us we would be able to wash at the re-education camp and, sure enough, our new little sentry took us along to the washhouse, saying we had twenty minutes to have a wash before going to bed.

There were no showers, just two rows of hand basins, and only four of the eight taps worked. The drug addicts in our squad commandeered three of these, leaving us eight Falun Gong practitioners to share a single tap. We took turns at the tap to fill up our washbasins, knowing it wasn't going to be easy to wash off a month's accumulated grime in twenty minutes. I quickly stripped and got to work but almost immediately heard the little sentry calling me.

'Zheng Zeng! The team leader wants to see you. Quickly, get dressed!'

Before I could pat myself dry, I was hustled over to the duty office, where a young officer was on duty by herself. She had a cranky look about her and asked me a few questions absentmindedly before she seemed to change tack.

'What's the point of putting up with all this suffering?' she asked, half bewildered and half sympathetic. 'Do you think the state is going to pay any attention to you? You're all taking this punishment for nothing.'

For a moment, as I looked into her youthful face, I didn't know how best to answer.

'We can't expect everything to be the way we want it,' I finally said, 'but we seek to keep our consciences clear.'

She frowned but didn't seem able to think of a suitable reply.

'Go on back!' she barked instead.

I realised later that this was the beginning of the ruthless and protracted re-education camp process of mind games, brainwashing, forced reform and the arduous struggle for Falun Gong practitioners to resist them all.

For a non-Falun Gong practitioner, being in the camp was just a question of doing what was required, trying to accumulate merit points to get out early, or leaving when your term was up. It was a totally different story for Falun Gong practitioners.

IF VIOLENCE DOESN'T WORK, TRY DECEPTIVE PERSUASION

When I got back, the others had washed and returned to the squad room where they were sitting about on their stools. My fellow practitioners immediately asked what had been done to me and were very relieved to hear that nothing had happened apart from a brief conversation. At the despatch division we had gotten a jolt of electricity or a beating for no reason at any time. You would often see people with bruises all over their bodies. After a while, we had become accustomed to such things without even realising it. Thus the others had expected something worse to happen to me.

I gradually came to realise that this was a meticulously designed trap. The police at the despatch division played the 'bad guys'. The repressive measures through which they enforced their cruel discipline— electric prods, not allowing us to speak, look up, shower or wash our clothes, making us squat and stand for long periods—deprived us of every last shred of human dignity and freedom, and pushed us beyond our psychological limits. Now the police at the re-education camp would play the 'good guys'. They didn't make us lower our heads and clasp our hands any more; they let us have five minutes every day to wash and change our clothes, and so on. Just when we were expecting even crueller treatment in these new surroundings, they suddenly presented a 'kind' and 'caring' face, and caught us completely off guard. The sharp contrast between the strict regime and this new, 'relaxed' attitude put us at a psychological disadvantage and it was at this point that they started talking to us, very softly.

'What is better, now: Falun Gong or the re-education camp? You're in here for practising Falun Gong, but Li Hongzhi is eating and drinking to his heart's content overseas. He's not coming to rescue you, but we team leaders are here with you. We don't see you as criminals; we just want to turn your ideas around. As far as the government is concerned, you are still one of us if you change your thoughts.' The truth of the matter was that Li Hongzhi had taken up residence in the United States before the crackdown in 1996, and was living a quiet and simple life there.

Some people who had withstood all the cruelty of the despatch division would collapse under the psychological pressure of this gentle approach. And if gentleness didn't work it wasn't too late to try toughness again. They had all the time in the world to 'fix' us.

A practitioner who arrived several months later, in December, was reformed in this manner. It had been unbearably hot while we were at the despatch division, but by December the temperature was regularly falling below zero, and the women arriving at the division trembled from the cold. Their luggage had been searched and any padded jackets and thick sweaters confiscated and put into storage. They had been left with only one thin sweater each. The doors were kept wide open all day so they sat shivering in the cold wind that blew ceaselessly through their rooms, freezing their facecloths stiff. Their teeth chattered day and night and it was impossible to get warm. One practitioner had developed severe chilblains on her toes. By the time she arrived at the re-education camp she couldn't put her shoes on. She had difficulty walking and by nightfall her feet were unbearably itchy, yet she had endured all of this without a word of complaint.

Then the company team leader put on a show of concern for her. She allowed the practitioner to wear slippers inside her room; she took her to the clinic to get medication for her chilblains; she kept asking after her feet. So accustomed was this practitioner to being ground down that she simply couldn't take these small kindnesses without crumbling. Weeping, she fell into a carefully contrived psychological trap, and was 'reformed'.

I WRITE A GUARANTEE IN A FIT OF PIQUE

On my first day at the camp, the battalion team leader also summoned me for a talk. Team Leader Hou was in her forties, a very dark and emaciated woman, devoid of all femininity and independent thought or judgement. The Party had succeeded admirably in shaping her into a tool devoted entirely to carrying out orders. She herself had no idea of this.

She started off by giving me a good dressing down, but when she saw this did not have the desired effect and I showed no sign of repentance, she contained her anger and simply told me to leave. Almost as soon as I got back to our squad room the camp leader arrived and I was summoned to his presence. It must have been one or two in the morning by then and after being tossed about for an entire day, I was feeling both mentally and physically exhausted.

The camp leader was also a tool, but an even more sinister one as he was quite willing to do anything at all for the regime. He was infinitely more self-possessed and more 'patient' than Team Leader Hou. He told me he hadn't the slightest doubt that he could reform me, but then never mentioned the word again. Instead, he asked me if I knew Yang Jing. She, too, was a postgraduate student, he told me, very capable and reasonable and had been 'reformed' not long after arriving here. She had been released in June to serve out her sentence outside the camp, but she would be returning in a few days to have informal discussions with the students[20] and he asked me if I wanted to be part of this.

I remembered having read a story in an internal newspaper put out by the re-education camp about two Falun Gong practitioners who had been released after being 'reformed'. Yang Jing had been one of them.

I told the leader no, I was not interested. He clearly knew what he

---

20 The detainees in the re-education through forced-labour camp are referred to as 'students', implying that they are in the camp to be 'educated'.

was doing and didn't pursue the matter any further. He asked me very politely to write a guarantee stating that I would observe discipline in the re-education camp and not practise Falun Gong while I was there.

I had several rash thoughts. So, I said to myself, it's writing a guarantee, is it? So you think that my writing a guarantee is tantamount to giving up my practice? No way! Besides, what you mean by not practising Falun Gong is just not doing the exercises, isn't it? What does it matter if I don't do the exercises? Cultivation is about cultivating moral character. Don't you understand? So, if you want a guarantee I'll give you one.

So I wrote a guarantee and he was quite happy to let me go. Perhap this rashness of mine was just superficial, however; the real reason was that I knew by some instinct how terrible his 'politeness' was. Or perhaps I was just exhausted to the point where I was no longer capable of normal thought and determination.

As I walked back along the corridor I saw a dozen or so practitioners standing facing the wall. The drug addicts in my squad told me that they were the women who had refused to write guarantees. 'They did the right thing,' I thought vaguely. 'I should go out and stand alongside them.' But I was too exhausted to hold on to that thought. 'Tomorrow,' I said to myself.

Then my head hit the pillow and I was dead to the world.

We got up at precisely 5:30 the next morning because that was the time we had to get up no matter what time we had gone to bed, and no matter whether we had slept or not. The only exception was when there was to be an inspection or an official visit to the camp, when we would be roused at 4 a.m. to clean the place thoroughly first.

The camp was surrounded by dilapidated graves, rubbish dumps and undergrowth almost two metres tall. It had been decided that Tiantanghe Re-education Camp was to undergo an 'accreditation' process in order to be recognised at a military level as a 'civilised labour camp' by October. In order to achieve this, the labour camp had to have a 'facelift'. Therefore, our first task was to transform the surrounding abandoned graveyard into a lush grassy area.

It is light by 5:30 on summer mornings in Beijing and July is the hottest month of the year, so it was already muggy when we got up. I am sure there were more procedures to be followed when inmates went outside the camp to work than when an emperor left the palace. The number of individuals going out, what they were going to be doing, how long it would take—all this had to be reported and then arrangements made for sufficient guards and escorts to ensure none of us escaped. There was a lot to be done even before we got that far, however. We had to count ourselves off in the corridor and again as we went out of the building; then we had to line up at the gate as the police accompanying us handed an exit note to the entrance guard. We counted ourselves off a third time and the numbers were checked. When the guard was satisfied as to our identity the gates slowly opened with an ear-splitting screech.

Security was even tighter once we were outside. Fully armed policemen patrolled on motorcycles and little sentries grasping coloured banners were posted all around. Our police escort didn't dare blink because they had to keep one eye on us and the other eye on the little sentries in case they took it into their heads to make a run for it.

And so, under the triple gaze of guards, police and little sentries, we began our career of hard forced labour. The occasional passer-by would stop and also cast a curious eye over us as we worked.

Before we could plant the grass we had to pull up the weeds that were there already. These weeds were as tall as small trees and too much for one person to uproot. It took two or three of us, all tugging together, to get each one out. In no time I had big blisters on my hands. Once we had uprooted the weeds we had to clear the area of rubbish and stones. The grass we were to plant came in big squares, like a carpet. After unloading it from the truck we would carry it piece by piece to where it was to be planted. Then we would painstakingly tease out each little plant and put these carefully in the ground 10 centimeters apart. This was the most difficult part; the lines had to be dead straight, like soldiers on review, and time after time we had to take plants out and replant them until they were straight.

We had no tools and had to dig the holes by hand, so we started hunting through the rubbish we had just cleared away for any fugitive fragments of tiles or twigs. Even a broken floppy disk became a valuable tool. We tried pocketing these little tools for later use but were searched as we returned to the camp and our hard-won finds confiscated, apparently to prevent us using them as weapons or a means of committing suicide. We took to stashing them away on the site in the hope we would be able to find them when we went back.

It was very hard work. We had an area of several thousand square metres to plant and sometimes we worked for more than ten hours a day. At one stage we were getting up at 5:30, working through until meal time, queuing at the mess hall, then going straight back out to work. We would squat on our haunches all day in the hot sun, our clothes drenched with sweat, but we weren't allowed to stop work to have even a drink of water. All our bodily fluids evaporated in sweat, which saved us the bother of going to the toilet. (But then there weren't any toilets outside the re-education camp, so in all that time we were out there planting no one actually asked to go.)

One day Company Team Leader Su Rui took us out to work. Several of the drug addicts who were doing their second stint in the re-education camp knew her, so they were brave enough to ask if we could have a little rest in the middle of the day. She agreed and we plonked down on the ground not caring how dirty it was. It was so muggy we could hardly breathe and we actually felt worse for the short rest. Far off on the road we saw a taxi.

'How I'd love to catch that taxi home,' Yang Jianping said longingly.

'Team Leader Su,' one of the other addicts said, 'can we sing?'

'Go ahead.'

As if by tacit agreement a dozen drug addicts started singing a song they had composed themselves, a song that was sung in all the drug clinics and detention centres. It was called *I want to go home*.

Behind those prison doors, prison life's so hard.
Steamed corn bread to eat, a cold hard plank to sleep on.
My eyes are full of tears; I cry for my father and my mother.
Tears of grief drip down their child's face.
I want to go home, I want to go home!
I want to go home to see my mother.
I am the darling of her heart,
Who will go to see her if I don't go . . .

Tears fell as they sang and Team Leader Su called out to them to stop, fearing for the morale of her troops.

———

For me, the harshest, most difficult part of each day was not squatting in the hot sun until my legs turned to jelly or digging holes with my blistered hands. It was not even carefully planting grass only to discover it was crooked and then having to pull it out and replant it. The worst part of the day for me was that first moment when I awoke from sleep. Even though I was half-dead from exhaustion I still dreamt every night. It was always the same indescribably painful dream—I was in prison and every time I was released they put me back in, like an endless *Groundhog Day*. So my first thought on waking was thank heavens it was only a dream! But in that same instant it would hit me that my reality was far worse than my bad dream. Not only was I actually in the re-education camp but another endless day of hard forced labour lay before me.

Everywhere I turned I was imprisoned. There was nowhere for me to hide, nowhere for me to run to, and the pain was more overwhelming than any dream. All my leaden body wanted to do was just sleep a little longer. And if I hadn't driven myself on with the affirmation, 'I am a Falun Gong practitioner,' exerting every last ounce of will to roll over and get up, I would probably have simply fallen to pieces.

'I PLEAD GUILTY AND ADMIT MY MISTAKES': THE WEAK LINK

Those of us who were more sensitive had immediately felt the eerie gloom that penetrated the chilling atmosphere of the camp, the presence of something sinister that couldn't be seen, something that wasn't in a hurry to do anything to us because time was on its side. But sooner or later it was surely going to get us.

I wasn't aware of it until the police started to force us to write 'I plead guilty and admit my mistakes' statements. What frightened me about this was not the statement itself but that, for the first time, differences of opinion surfaced among the Falun Gong practitioners.

Those in favour said it really didn't matter, because we had already disobeyed the Ministry of Public Security directive not to put up banners bearing the words Falun Gong when we did just that in Tian'anmen. Pleading guilty and admitting our mistakes was no big deal; we weren't saying we would stop practising.

This started me thinking. I felt we had come to the crunch, that something was not quite right. I couldn't put my finger on what the problem was or how serious it was; all I knew was that I strongly believed we simply must not write statements pleading guilty. We must not cross that line. We must not retreat or we were finished. And

I suddenly realised I had been wrong to write that guarantee. Doing exercises was part of practising Falun Gong, so surely by guaranteeing not to do the exercises I was implicitly guaranteeing not to practise Falun Gong.

On the anniversary of July 20, I wrote a formal retraction of my guarantee. Su Rui didn't lose her temper when I handed it to her because by then they had formulated their policy of 'divide and demoralise; destroy one by one'; clearly it wasn't my turn yet.

One day Wang Rong, a Falun Gong practitioner in our squad, was taken away and held for quite some time. She was about twenty and so shortsighted that she had to hold things a few centimetres from her face to see them and would trip unless someone guided her.

'Look at you, you worthless soul!' the police and little sentries used to taunt her. 'You're doing Falun Gong but how come your eyes aren't fixed after all this time? You eat but you don't work; all you're good for is producing shit! You'd better hurry up and reform so you can go home and save the camp some food!'

Wang Rong's sight was so bad that the only job she could do was separate the grass plants by feel. As she made her stumbling way over to where we were working, to give us the plants, she would invariably trip on the uneven ground or over anything that was in her way. If we had our heads down and weren't looking she would have to crawl about feeling for the plants that had spilled. Yet she always had a smile on her face and however hard people tried to humiliate her she never got angry or sank into self-pity.

I didn't pay any special attention when she came back that day she was called away, but I slowly began to feel something wasn't quite right. A couple of days later I was sitting beside her and happened to see through the open collar of her shirt a big dark patch on her upper chest. Then I realised what had been troubling me: the smile had gone from her face.

'What's the matter, Wang Rong?' I asked her. 'Who hit you?'

Tears spilled from her eyes but for the life of her she wouldn't say what had happened. Two days later she was moved to Squad 2 and was in tears as she took her bedding away.

Some time after that we heard through the grapevine that the team leader of Squad 3 had fixed on Wang Rong as the weak link through whom she could get us to plead guilty. This team leader handed Wang Rong over to some drugged-up little sentries who took her to a vacant room alongside the training unit and beat her up. Then they made her 'ride the motorcycle' and do the 'gecko on the wall' and 'fly'.

These were the names of punishments. The first two are fairly self-explanatory and consist of holding certain poses for long periods of time: standing with your legs apart as if you were straddling a motorcycle, and pressing yourself spreadeagled against a wall. To fly, you stood facing a wall then forced your head down, bending at the waist until your whole spine was against the wall in a U shape. Then you lifted your arms up and pressed them back against the wall. You were supposed to hold this position, without moving. Most people could only do it for a few minutes but I know that the record was over 40 minutes.

Who knows for how long Wang Rong flew before she wrote her guilty plea? What I do know is that she almost died of shame at being the weak link and that whenever we spoke to her she simply burst into tears and wouldn't speak.

———

A few days later the camp leader summoned me again and went over the same thing: the informal discussion with reformed Falun Gong practitioners was an opportunity not to be missed and it would be a pity if I didn't go.

This time I didn't insist that I wouldn't go and not long afterwards a little sentry called out my name and told me to meet her in the corridor. There were two other Falun Gong practitioners with her. One was Gu Hua—she, Wang Jin and I had been in the first group from Chongwen District to be sentenced to re-education through forced labour. The three of us fell into line behind Team Leader Su and were escorted out the main gate to the administration building.

As I entered the room where the discussion was to be held I saw another familiar face. This woman was in her thirties and I had met her at a fellow practitioner's place. We had been talking about going to Tian'anmen on the anniversary of April 25, but she had said she couldn't wait a day longer and wanted to go on the thirteenth. Nobody, it seemed, could stand in the way of her determination and I was filled with admiration for her courage. Seeing her now I felt a warm glow as if I were meeting up with an old friend in a distant land. I nodded to her and, apparently recognising me, she gave me a nod in return. I walked over and quickly sat down beside her before the police had time to tell us where to sit, trying to figure out how I could manage to talk to her. I saw from the card pinned to her breast that her name was Hu Xiuying.

All the seats around the big oval meeting table were soon taken. There were a dozen or so labour-camp inmates and the same number of police officers. Slices of watermelon were set out on the table and something like *So-and-so, welcome back for a discussion* was written on the blackboard in coloured chalk.

The camp leader, who was chairing the meeting, said that they had invited the former Falun Gong practitioners Yang Jing and Tang Shuzhen, who had 'reformed' and been released in June to serve their sentences outside the camp. Unfortunately, Yang Jing was tied up at work and had been unable to get away but Tang Shuzhen was going to speak to us. However, he would like to say a few words first. Tang Shuzhen was not highly educated and not much of a speaker, he told us, so he would appreciate it if we would all remain disciplined and not interrupt her. If there were any points on which we didn't agree we were to leave them for later discussion; this applied especially to his three new inmates—and here he gave me a meaningful look.

I was quite surprised at the non-appearance of this Yang Jing of whom we had heard so much, but a month or so later I would hear something even more surprising. It had not been her workload that had prevented this role model of reform from coming; it was because she had been placed in confinement in the forced-labour re-education camp. It turned out that after she was released her local police asked her to visit the local police stations to reform other Falun Gong practitioners. But in the end those very practitioners 'reformed' her right back. Immediately after she 'de-reformed' she went straight to the underground railway to hand out Falun Gong leaflets and was arrested.

The only person in the room in civilian clothes, Tang Shuzhen was a timid, soft-spoken woman in her forties who was clearly not very articulate. She was obviously nervous about speaking in public, and talked about how good it was to reform, about how her family rallied around when she got home, and about the effect on her family of her imprisonment because of Falun Gong.

After a bit I raised my right hand and asked the camp leader if I could ask her some questions. He was a little taken aback but, not wishing to puncture the 'fine spirit' of 'reformed Falun Gong practitioners having a cordial conversation' that he had so carefully constructed, he suppressed his anger and agreed.

'Whether you wish to practise or not is up to you as an individual,' I said to Tang Shuzhen, looking her in the eye, 'but you once practised Falun Gong and you have read our teacher's books. I would just like you to search your conscience and answer one question: Did our teacher assert that the world was going to explode?'

This stumped her. While the camp leader was busy figuring out how to rescue the situation, I was busy thinking where I should go from there. And then the most unexpected thing in the world happened.

Sitting right alongside me, Hu Xiuying suddenly broke the silence.

'On page 18 of *Zhuan Falun*,' she began, 'Li Hongzhi says . . .'

And off she rattled in a loud voice, hardly taking a breath, for at least half an hour. She spoke in a malicious tone, her words sinister and with vicious intent. What she said was far, far worse than the clumsy fabrications of the *People's Daily* editorials; she was carefully playing tricks with concepts and misleading her audience. She distorted the part in *Zhuan Falun* about prehistoric civilisation, making it sound like a plea for the world to blow up, and then proceeded to twist every single thing in the book. After that she condemned Falun Gong as an out-and-out evil cult, abusing Li Hongzhi as 'not truthful', 'not compassionate' and 'not forbearing'. The ruthlessness and contemptuousness of her words came from the most unexpected directions and places.

My life suddenly seemed to split into several levels. On one level I was stunned, as if I had run towards this old friend I found with both arms outstretched and she had whipped out a dagger and cut me to the bone. How could someone who just three months before had cared for nothing but going to Tian'anmen and who would have risked her life for Falun Gong have turned around to such an extent that she had become a devil? Was I deranged, or was she? I was almost reeling on my chair from shock.

On another level I was perfectly at rest, as if I had expected this. I looked nonchalantly out the window at the sky and the fields almost as if I hadn't heard a word she was saying.

A third level of me said, 'This is the genuine, the most rigorous test. As soon as I go back I must tell the other practitioners about this; it can be their vaccination shot, to help them prepare psychologically.'

When Hu Xuiying finally fell silent, I raised my hand again.

'May I discuss what I have learned from this talk?' I said to the camp leader. 'I have just three things to say.'

This time he was in excellent spirits. As far as he was concerned, Hu Xiuying's speech had been more than enough to turn the tide and had indeed rescued Tang Shuzhen and the discussion.

'The first thing I have to say,' I went on as soon as he agreed to let me speak, 'is that I am most surprised Hu Xuiying hasn't been released to serve her sentence outside the camp since she has clearly "reformed" most thoroughly.'

Before the camp leader had time to speak, Team Leader Hou broke in hurriedly to explain why Hu Xuiying had not been released.

'When my husband came to see me this morning,' Hu Xiuying interrupted, 'I warned him not to get too excited, because I wasn't going home just yet. I want to stay here and help the team leaders reform other Falun Gong practitioners.'

Mentally, I asked her, 'In your speech just now, you accused yourself of selfishness in being detained on account of Falun Gong and letting your husband worry so much that his hair turned grey; so why don't you blame yourself now for choosing to stay when you can actually go home?'

However, I knew that she was no longer a person to reason with; so I ignored her words and went on.

'The second thing I have to say to Hu Xiuying is "Thank you"...'

Team Leader Hou interrupted again, assuming from this that Hu Xiuying's spiel had reformed me and I had broken free from the 'spiritual shackles' of Falun Gong.

I managed to wait for her to finish before continuing.

'I'm sorry,' I said. 'I hadn't finished my second point. For Asians cultivation is enlightenment; for Westerners it is faith. I wanted to thank Hu Xiuying for helping me cultivate my faith. This is my second point. The third thing I want to say is what I have learned from practising Falun Gong. I believe that Truthfulness, Compassion and Forbearance are the highest principles of the cosmos and regardless of whether or not others practise them, I practise them. This is my third point. Thank you.'

My third point was directed at Hu Xiuying's personal attack on Li Hongzhi. I had no intention of becoming entangled, in that setting, in a discussion of our teacher's personal behaviour for 'when a scholar and a soldier run into each other neither can clearly explain his *raison d'être*'.

I felt so at ease after putting my points forward that I reached forward for a slice of watermelon and sank back into my chair to eat it—this was, of course, the only slice of watermelon I ever had in the forced-labour camp. Some other people began to speak and I realised that almost everybody in the room was already 'reformed'. Eventually the camp leader moved to bring the meeting to a close, saying that he was very happy with how it had all gone. He said that if we had any questions or suggestions in future, we should simply raise them to ensure the smooth running of the labour camp. The meeting was over and team leaders were to take their charges back inside.

Suddenly I remembered the bruise on Wang Rong's chest and I raised my hand for the third time.

'If that's the case,' I said, 'I have a question. May I raise it?'

The camp leader frowned but agreed, somewhat reluctantly.

'My question is this: are inmates allowed to beat other inmates in the despatch division or in the labour camp?'

I may as well have lobbed a hand grenade into the meeting. The police were all on their feet ready to leave but now surprise, embarrassment and anger flickered across their faces. Two of them, a man and a woman, simply stared at me, their faces betraying nothing.

I saw all this out of the corner of my eye, as I focused on the camp leader's face and waited quietly for his reply. He seemed rattled and rambled on, not answering my question directly. Essentially, he said that if there were specific instances these would have to be looked at on their merits; if anything came up the relevant team leader would have to be notified; we mustn't listen to rumours; and so on. Our meeting then came to a 'satisfactory end'. I didn't have a chance to discuss with Gu Hua and Wang Jin how they felt as we were not in the same squad.

My fellow practitioners were stunned when I told them what had gone on. I said that I now knew what we must cultivate at the forced-labour camp: being steadfast in the *Fa*.

We were just starting to get somewhere with the grass planting when the police of the camp dreamed up another method for reforming us: a series of six lectures, in twelve sessions. The lectures consisted of going over and over the *People's Daily* editorials and were given by police and by philosophy lecturers from the university; several police equipped with electric prods were also in the 'audience'.

I recognised the policewoman giving the second lecture. She had been head of the corrective section in the despatch division. I had never spoken to her but I remembered her well. She had glared in our window one day as she walked past, a fleeting glance but one of such malevolence, from black eyes that seemed to take in everything in one quick sweep.

She started her lecture by enumerating every single infuriating thing every single evil cult in the world had ever done. She followed this up with the *People's Daily* allegations of Falun Gong 'suicides' and 'harikari'; death after death after death—all caused by Falun Gong. Her voice was full of hatred and couldn't have got any louder; amplified through the loudspeakers it was as if the whole auditorium was shouting with her. So strenuous were her exertions when she got really excited that she almost fell off the podium.

I was doing my best to control myself and not be affected by the venomous clamour filling the hall when a loud, clear voice suddenly rang from the back of the hall.

'Falun Dafa is the righteous *Fa!*'

Turning to look, I saw several police officers converging on a woman in her fifties who had risen to her feet. Clapping their hands over her mouth and wrenching her arms, they bundled her out of the hall. Officers wielding prods followed and the rest of the prods in the hall crackled to life.

Order was quickly restored and the lecturer continued her diatribe. Several months later someone saw the older woman who had cried out. She was in the forced-labour camp hospital by then. On the day of the lecture, however, she had been taken straight from the hall to the training unit. Nobody knew just what went on there but when she was admitted to hospital she had several large wounds on her head through which her skull could be seen.

THE SWEATER-KNITTING FOOL

The lecture series was still going on when the sweater work started. I had often seen the women from Company 2 knitting away as they walked to and from the mess hall, with plastic bags full of balls of yarn dangling from their arms or the buttons of their clothes. That's a bit over the top, I remember thinking at the time.

One day, we were informed out of the blue that Company 2 had taken on an urgent knitting job and we had to share the work by making 40 sweaters. Each squad in the camp had its own 'labourer', a person who was responsible for learning production skills, technical processes and quality requirements and passing them on to everyone else in the squad. This task was shared in order to maintain the quality of what was produced.

I was elected as the Squad 3 labourer for this knitting job. Off I went to the office and found the quality controller from Company 2 already showing several others what to do. Zhang Lei had a tape measure draped over her neck and tiny drops of sweat hanging from the tip of her nose. She was only in her twenties but her hair was already grey. It was she who had made that comment about her bed in the forced-labour camp being dearer to her than her mother. She was in for two years, for trafficking in pornographic CDs. Of the 'three schools of thought and the nine religions'—the people of various walks of life and callings in the labour camp, those peddling pornography were tantamount to nobility and, like nobility, didn't have much respect for others. As far as ordinary inmates were concerned, porn traffickers ranked with squad leaders, little sentries and quality controllers.

The West has long condemned the system of forced labour that operates in Chinese re-education camps and jails, but many inmates accept the reasoning indoctrinated in them: they have committed a crime against society, and therefore must work with all their might to reimburse the state that is 'feeding' them. Also, the slump in some sections of the economy has caused many factories to close down because of lack of orders. Forced-labour re-education camps have an annual profit target but negligible labour costs, which has given them an unbeatable competitive edge. Tiantanghe's steadiest customers are local village and township enterprises, who take on export orders and pass the work on to the camp for very little outlay, making a tidy profit in the process. Two brands I know of that do this are Shunhua and Fenghuang (Phoenix) knitting mills and sweater factories. Foremen from these processing factories were in and out of the labour camp teaching inmates new technology and checking on quality, so that quality controllers such as Zhang Lei were on very familiar terms with them.

Zhang Lei was a painstaking teacher: my knitting, for example, was too loose to begin with and she had to unpick it for me three times. After a night's work, however, I had gotten the hang of it. The most difficult part was the measurements. The technical requirements were very strict as these products were for export. For example, 100 rows of knitting had to measure 50 cm, with a margin of error of only 1 cm. If we were out we had to unravel it and do it all again. This was the hardest thing to master and many of us became quite tearful as we unpicked our work over and over again.

It was even harder for those of us who had never knitted, a bit like a child learning to write. First we had to learn how to hold the needles, then we'd clack away for ages and still not produce a good piece of knitting, so we'd get anxious and break out into a sweat, which would ruin the yarn, the once white thread coming off our needles almost black.

We knitted flat out for days, from 5:30 in the morning until one or two the next morning, every day. It almost killed us but we managed to finish the job on time. I no longer felt that Company 2 was overdoing it, knitting as they walked; instead I regretted not having a plastic bag in which to keep my yarn so I could do the same.

We finally handed the 40 sweaters over and waited anxiously that night for the order to go to bed. We waited and waited, and eventually got word that 39 of the 40 sweaters were not up to standard! The order was to be flown out the next day and the delivery date had to be honoured.

The little sentry responsible for production stood at the door looking at our exhausted, despairing faces.

'I know there is no earthly way you will be able to fix them on time,' she said, in an effort to sound fair, 'so this is what I suggest. I will ask Zhang Li from the training unit to help you if you send two people from each squad to assist her. Tomorrow I'll ask for permission to let you have a nap during the day.'

I was so exhausted I thought I was going to be sick, but I was the fastest knitter in our squad so I struggled hard to say that I would go.

'Great!' the little sentry said. 'That's really terrific!'

She led me and another Falun Gong practitioner to the confinement room, across from the training unit, where the rush job was to be done.

Inside the confinement room were three iron cages, each about waist high. Anyone held in these would spend the whole time bent over double. The cages took up only part of the space; the rest was stacked with returned sweaters. A small paper tag giving the reason it had been rejected had been sewn to each sweater: the sleeve seams were not smooth; the collar was two rows short; the pattern was wrong; the measurements were wrong, etc.

Zhang Li was in for taking drugs. Just twenty, she was due for release soon. She had become a tremendously skillful seamstress in her year or so in the labour camp. Very methodically, she would check the tag on each sweater then snip, unravel, and sew in just the right places before handing the item over to us with clear and detailed instructions on what we had to do. She chatted as she worked, saying this was nothing, just a small job, and this sort of thing was going to happen more and more often.

'At the busiest times we'll have three people knitting the back of one garment,' she said, 'and these will be sewn together to make one piece in order for the sweaters to make the plane on time. If you want to get by at the labour camp you have to learn to sew, so you can cut away mistakes and sew them up correctly. Nobody has the time to unpick it and do it all again.'

This sewing she spoke of is usually called 'invisible mending' and takes considerable skill. It involves cutting out the flawed section, re-knitting it and then sewing the new piece back into the garment in such a way that it is impossible to detect the mend. I would later learn how to sew plain pieces, but the skill of mending patterns always eluded me.

That night I went to work on the knitting assigned to me for all I was worth, longing for matchsticks to prop my eyelids open. I knitted and knitted, aware only of a white haze before my eyes and of constant nausea. I was terrified that if I lost my concentration my head would drop and I would pass out. I gradually began to feel as if I were a fool in one of my dreams, conscious of nothing but furiously knitting the sweater in my hands.

I don't know what time it got light and I don't know whether the rush job got finished or even what time we finished. All I was aware of was the emptiness within, the feeling of having been cheated when we were summoned to line up in the corridor with the others, before filing over to the mess hall for breakfast. There was no sign of the little sentry who was going to ask that we be allowed to have a nap during the day, and the police who had just come on duty made us go as usual to plant grass. As the day wore slowly on I had to force myself to move from one moment to the next. I floated in a dream world, aware only of a vague dread somewhere deep within my brain, a dread that my will would disperse with the wind, a dread that my nerves would fray, and a dread that I would become a mere fool, furiously knitting wherever she went.

From that day forward the fear of not being allowed to sleep was deeply engraved on my heart.

SLEEP DEPRIVATION

On July 27, some three weeks after I arrived at the forced-labour re-education camp, there was a sudden commotion in the corridor. It turned out that some of us were being moved. After some general anxiety we finally found out that nine Falun Gong practitioners who were considered particularly headstrong—Wang Ke was one of them—were being transferred to Company 1. The rest, including me, were going to Company 2. Essentially, the drug addicts of each squad were staying put; they acted as group leaders of the squads and the police wanted them to manage the next group of Falun Gong practitioners due from the despatch division.

Soon after, I was told to get my things and move my bedding to Company 2 on the second floor. Five of us—Wang Rong, Zhang Qing, Zhao Ying, Cheng Lan and I—were being transferred to Squad 5 of Company 2. Zhang Qing was 29, a graduate of the People's University and as slender as a young boy. Zhao Ying, a small woman in her fifties, had been a technician with a large state-run factory before she retired, and 39-year-old Cheng Lan was a kindergarten teacher.

Squads normally had twelve people at most, and the beds, cupboard space and mess-hall seating were all organised around this number. Squad 5 already had seven women in it. Gu Rong, the squad leader, was in for trafficking in pornography. Zhang Feng was in for prostitution. At 50 or so, Old Mao was the oldest non-Falun Gong inmate; she had been brought in for running a brothel. Shao Hong, a woman in her forties, and quality controller Cui Fen were in for theft, while there were two teenagers in for robbery.

Once beds and cupboards had been assigned, bedding organised and our things put away, Gu Rong asked us if we had all written a guarantee. We shook our heads. Having suffered the agony of shame and self-recrimination after writing her guilty plea, Wang Rong had retracted both that and her guarantee.

'Well, what a pity. I'm going to miss out on sleep again, and just when I was thinking I'd be out of here!' Cui Fen said, with a sigh.

I looked at her in bewilderment but the other six clearly understood her meaning.

'Let's roster our shifts,' Gu Rong said, 'starting with me.'

That night I learnt why Cui Fen had sighed and what rostering shifts was all about. It was a rule in Company 2 that Falun Gong practitioners who had not written a guarantee were not allowed to sleep, and this rule was enforced by the inmates who had committed 'other crimes'; in other words, by inmates who were not Falun Gong practitioners. Gu Rong and the others were obviously very practised at implementing this policy and took turns going on duty without the police having to say a word. What Cui Fen had meant by 'just when I was thinking I'd be out of here!' was that if she could get her sentence reduced by qualifying for an award when the points for the first half of the year were awarded, then she would be going home in a few days.

There was a strict system for keeping score of rewards and penalties in the labour camp. If you completed the amount of work allotted to you each day you earned a specific score; squad leaders, little sentries, kitchen staff and quality controllers received a fixed number of points every day. If you exceeded your production quota or if you rendered meritorious service as an informer you got extra points, while any mistake or infringement of the rules would cost you points. Every six months, everybody was ranked according to their point scores. If you were in the top 30 per cent your sentence might be reduced.

Before any Falun Gong practitioners came in, all forced-labour re-education camps relied on this system to control the inmates. Newcomers cottoned on very quickly and would always have a fair idea about how they stood in the prize stakes. If they felt they had a chance they would be on their best behaviour and would work very hard with an eye to perhaps becoming a squad leader. If they realised they weren't in the running they just wouldn't care any more. They muddled along day by day, not working very hard and constantly making small mistakes while avoiding big ones, just surviving until their term was up. But all this changed with the influx of Falun Gong practitioners. If a Falun Gong practitioner wouldn't 'reform', it didn't matter how hard they worked. They could never earn a merit point.

After everyone else went to bed, Gu Rong placed her stool by the door and told the five of us to stand in a line inside the room.

Geng Xiu, the little sentry on night duty, popped her head in after a while to have a look and came back about midnight.

'You're not very smart, you know,' she said with a smirk. 'Everybody in Squad 7 has written a guarantee and they're all asleep now. There's just you five, standing here. If you don't believe me I'll take one of you along to have a look.'

Zhang Qing went with her and they were back in a couple of minutes.

'There you go,' said Geng Xiu. 'Ask Zhang Qing. Everybody in Squad 7 is asleep, aren't they?'

None of us said a word and nobody moved as Geng Xiu walked off with a strange grin. Many days later we understood the reason for her peculiar expression: she had told Squad 7 to go to bed, but pretended to us that they had written their guarantees. A few days later when we in Squad 5 were sleeping she played the same trick on Squad 7.

We stood for two nights. The following day we were escorted to the auditorium for our first conference on 'exposing and repudiating Falun Gong through citing our own experience'. There must have been 80 Falun Gong practitioners in the labour camp by then and we were seated in our separate company formations, and surrounded by police and male guards equipped with electric prods.

I looked across to the units in Company 1 and saw that Wang Ke had become so wan and sallow in the two days since I last saw her I hardly recognised her; her large eyes, once so full of intelligence, were now clouded with confusion. I tried to catch her eye but she simply did not see me. It was obvious that she was suffering so much that she was turning into a 'fool'. I heard later that, like us, the women who had been transferred to Company 1 were not allowed to sleep. They had to stand in the corridor with a bowl of water on their heads and if they spilled one drop of this precious liquid they would get a beating. I also heard it was the drug addicts who had dreamed this torture up.

The drug addicts who were in the forced-labour re-education camp were there because they had failed to respond to the mandatory drug rehabilitation program. At the drug clinic everyone had to 'walk the plank'. Their cell mates would either throw 50 basins of cold water over them or slap them across the face 50 times. That was just for starters; then they would take it from there. Many people emerged from the drug clinics really damaged, wanting to inflict upon others the same mistreatment they had received, and then some. So the inmates at the labour camp, supported by the police, were honing their skills on Falun Gong practitioners who wouldn't hit back when attacked or talk back when insulted. Once, when I was refilling the water in the boiler, I bumped into the team leader of my squad in Entry Company.

'I was really wrong about you, Zheng Zeng,' she said. 'If I had known how stubborn you were I would have put you under those drug addicts and they would have fixed you long ago. You'll be getting a 74-center if you continue to be as stubborn like this!'

'What's a 74-center?'

'What's a 74-center?' she laughed. 'A bullet! Seventy-four cents each! You're one of the ones that should be shot!'

TEARS OF YEARNING

One day early in August, the atmosphere crackled with excitement from the moment we got up. This was the only day of the month on which visitor privileges were allowed.

Just after eight o'clock they started calling us into the corridors. As each woman's name was called she would shoot out of her room and stand in line waiting to be led over to the visiting room. Those whose names were not called stood at the window, gazing longingly towards the main gate.

Some of the women came back from their visits in tears, others were elated, while yet others were quite composed. Friends told each other what their families had said and what items they had brought along but women with no family became very upset, either withdrawing into themselves or picking fights. It was a day or two before the excitement and the sadness wore off and things returned to normal.

I knew that Falun Gong practitioners who had not 'reformed' were not allowed visitors so I watched the others coming and going with the detachment of an outsider. I could hardly believe my ears when my name suddenly echoed along the corridor during the afternoon. It seems that Tiantanghe had realised that denying family visits was not really helping the 'reform' process and had therefore changed its policy. They must have hoped that family visits might have some 'reforming' effect. A police officer once said that since the sole purpose of our going to the forced-labour re-education camp was for us to be 'reformed', they did whatever was necessary for that to happen.

And there behind the thick glass panel was my husband's face, pale and intent. We communicated by telephone, with police officers able at any moment to listen in on our conversation. The four months since we'd been separated had been very difficult for him. He had made dozens of enquiries at the despatch division after I was transferred from the detention centre and driven out to Tiantanghe countless times in the car, only to be turned away.

He had put away all the photos of me around the house so there would be nothing to remind him of me. He had to be strong, with the whole family as well as everybody at work depending on him. He had adopted the approach that what the eye doesn't see the heart doesn't grieve for and it worked well for quite some time, until one day when he was about to ring a friend. As he flicked through his address book for the number he came across something I had written in the book, my scribble starkly childish alongside his graceful script. In that instant he was undone: he thought he had constructed his defences so as not to be completely overcome by grief and longing, but how was he to know these scribbles would carry so potent a message?

Seeing him was not easy. I could tell he was choking down all the things he wanted to say. He could only sit there staring at me. Eventually he marshalled his thoughts. He had been reading a book about the Cultural Revolution, he said, and there was a bit about how the heroic and outspoken Zhang Zhixin had died rather than submit and how her vocal cords had been cut just before she was killed to prevent her from speaking. Anything can happen in prison, he told me. What was really worrying him was that when it came to the crunch I would be pig-headed. He couldn't really bring himself to believe my purpose in practising Falun Gong was to be a 'revolutionary martyr'.

He stopped. Then, fearing he would forget if he didn't tell me now, even though he knew the police might be listening in, he hurriedly hinted to me that he was using his connections to find some way to get me out of there. I had to cooperate, though; be sure to cooperate; otherwise all his hard work would come to nothing. He had thought of every possible way of getting my sentence reduced: ringing people in authority, trying out all his connections, using his pull.

'Relax,' a senior cadre friend of his had assured him. 'Leave it to me.'

A few days later this friend had come to see him, somewhat crestfallen.

'You don't know how sorry I am,' he said. 'If your wife had killed someone I could get her out, but not if she's an unreformed Falun Gong. Get her to write the guarantee and go a bit easy; then I can do something for you.'

When my husband told me this I quickly said that if he wanted to help me he could get a lawyer so I could sue the forced-labour re-education camp. 'They've beaten me, electrocuted me, put me to hard forced labour,' I said, turning my neck to show him where the prods had raised blisters. He looked in the direction of my neck but couldn't bear to see and his eyes slid away, glistening with tears. But in his unruly heart another pair of eyes opened, looking out at me through his chest. They could see immediately everything I had been through, and this pair of eyes began crying tears of blood.

'How is Shitan?' I asked, hurriedly changing the subject.

He returned my gaze with an effort.

'She's fine . . .'

'Does she know where I am?'

'Yes. I didn't tell her but somehow she knows.'

'Well, you must tell her that her mother is a good person, that she is innocent. Tell her about Zhang Zhixin. She must never, ever be ashamed of my being in the forced-labour camp for that might damage her psychologically.'

This was the point when, finally, I too burst into tears, thinking of my 7-year-old daughter, held precious her whole short life by her grandparents and her parents with not a dark cloud in her heart. And now suddenly to burden her with what had happened to Zhang Zhixin! Yet if we didn't talk about this with her she would never understand that her mother was innocent . . .

Our twenty minutes were soon up and the police called out that all visitors were to leave. My husband stood up, but his gaze was locked on my face. All of his strength, his love and his pain were gathered and expressed in his eyes, as if he wanted to draw me into them so that he could take me away with him; as if, if he never took his eyes from me, then I could remain with him forever . . .

When he left the camp he got in the car and just kept driving. He drove right out of the city and was 100 kilometres away when he finally pulled over. He turned the radio up full volume and lay down on the back seat longing to weep but the tears wouldn't come.

For myself, I regretted telling him I had been electrocuted and I regretted letting him see me cry.

THE STUBBORN ONES

On August 9, a police vehicle arrived with its siren screaming. It was still high summer but this new group of women were fitted out in autumn-weight clothing and the smell could have knocked you over at twenty paces.

With their arrival, Entry Company became Company 3 and the few women left in the original Entry Company were assigned to Company 2. This was when the camp began to get seriously overcrowded. There were now sixteen women in each squad. More beds were brought in; the minuscule cupboards had to be shared; sixteen women had to squeeze into seating meant for twelve at mealtimes and Company 3 had to wait to eat until Company 2 was finished. At the despatch division newcomers had to sleep on the floor because more people were being brought in than were being sent on.

The women in Company 2 were shuffled about as well. I was moved to Squad 3 while Zhang Qing, Wang Rong and Zhao Ying were moved to Squad 7, apparently to allow the 'reformed' women in that squad to go to work on them. However, when a week had gone by without any results, the three of them were hurriedly moved out in case they 'de-reformed' the 'reformed' Squad 7 women! They were put in Squad 3 with me. Cheng Lan was seen as a 'reform' hopeful so she was sent to be 'nurtured' by the women in Squad 2, which had been set up especially for 'reformed' women.

Squad 3 was becoming a special squad for stubborn cases. The three original stubborn ones in this squad had arrived in the group before us. Li Wen, at 63 the oldest woman in the camp, had been a university laboratory technician. Zhou Jie was in her thirties and Song Mei, a fairly recent university graduate, in her early twenties.

Li Wen had been widowed when her son was just two years old and had known great hardship raising her child alone. Her own health was not good but her son was very sickly and had given her no end of worry. After mother and son took up Falun Gong their illnesses disappeared, and she did not have the words to express how grateful and devoted she was to Falun Gong. There was no point even mentioning 'reforming' to her.

Zhou Jie was very quiet and almost simple-minded. When I asked her about the many black circles on her arms she simply said, with a smile, that they were 'from shocks'.

Song Mei was quite talkative by comparison. She said that every night in the month or so between their arrival at Tiantanghe and being moved to this squad they were forced to stand lined up along the corridor facing the wall until four in the morning. They had been allowed to sleep for an hour then had to get up at five and work all day digging holes almost two metres deep in which to plant trees. They were so exhausted all they could do was crawl along the ground.

'We were sleeping standing up every night in the corridor,' she said, 'and our heads would go clunk as they hit the wall, waking us up. All night long you would hear this clunk, clunk, clunk echoing along the corridor. Every day I really thought I couldn't hold out for another day.'

The other nine occupants of Squad 3 were in for crimes such as prostitution, gambling and theft. Three of them were teenagers in for robbery and fighting.

The squad leader, Hao Ying, was in for porn trafficking, but it didn't take me long to realise that she was the best squad leader in Tiantanghe. The police gave squad leaders absolute authority over Falun Gong practitioners. Unlike most of her peers, Hao Ying did not abuse this power. On the contrary, she often quietly looked after us, especially Li Wen, without drawing any attention to herself.

Thirty-two-year-old Li Chun had the chivalrous air of a highly skilled martial artist. She had been in the forced-labour camp six times—more than anyone else—each time for stealing money. Since she was thirteen years old she had spent more than ten years in forced-labour camps and, as a result, had become a superb knitter. She could spot a wrong stitch at twenty paces; she could fix the most complicated mistakes without unravelling the entire piece; and she was the fastest knitter anyone had ever seen. Yet she had a very calculating streak and was quick to take advantage of others. Although she was skilled, she would bluff her way through her work and for this reason the 'upper class' had little time for her. The other inmates didn't normally have much to say to her either, but as soon as someone was having trouble with a pattern or had made a mistake that required invisible mending, there was nothing anyone could do but call on her.

'Call the party when you're in trouble!'[21] she would say jovially, patting herself on the chest, and she would have the problem fixed in a flash. However, if she was in a bad mood she would make you knit a sleeve for her before attending to even the simplest problem; for her this was a fair exchange, and she wasn't prepared to let anyone profit in the slightest way.

SITTING ON A BED OF NAILS — NETS ABOVE AND SNARES BELOW

When I think back to my first few days in Squad 3, I hear the phrase 'start knitting as soon as the eyes are plucked open' and I always see three women perched on the top bunks with mountainous balls of yarn behind them. The fine 9-ply yarn they are winding onto their left hands as fast as they can is looping and dancing several metres across the room to skeins of yarn stretched across the knees of several other women sitting on small stools below. Their heads are down and they are knitting as fast as they can. The only woman on the floor not wielding knitting needles is blind Wang Rong, who is holding out her skein with both hands.

Twenty-seven strands of yarn in three lots of 9-ply was passing through the hands of those on the bunks, stretching up from the knees of the knitters on the floor. It was a 'splendid' sight, the small room draped with yarn as if nets were spread above and snares deployed below. At the time I joked that after I got out I would write a book about the camp, and when it was made into a film I would make sure this scene was in it.

We did it this way because we had no time to sit holding the skeins on our outstretched hands. It took a while, however, before I

---

21 A political slogan used in China. 'The party' is the Communist Party.

could knit and keep an eye on the skein on my knees at the same time, to ensure the yarn didn't tangle as the winders above pulled on it. I gradually became very skilled at it and, eventually, could knit patterns requiring different colours, handling several different yarns at the same time with both hands. Only a few people in the camp could manage this.

Our eyes had to be 'plucked open' because we were so tired that we felt our eyes couldn't open naturally without being 'plucked open' by some external force.

For over three months we kept on knitting, producing every manner of sweater and all sorts of patterns. From the time we got up at 5:30, we sat on our little stools and knitted, with time out only for meals, going to the toilet and attending lectures. In the end, I wouldn't even wash my hands after going to the toilet because the yarn wouldn't run freely through my fingers if they weren't completely dry. After sitting for almost twenty hours each day, I felt as if the thin layer of flesh between the stool and my bottom had almost worn away, leaving only two sharp bones that dug into the hard wood of the stool. The weight of my whole body pressed down on these bones, causing me continuous pain. I developed many stool sores that eventually spread, so it was impossible to avoid sitting on them. I guarantee whoever coined the phrase 'sitting on a bed of nails' never knew what it felt like to have a hard wooden stool dig into the sores on your thighs and buttocks.

For a long time the only thing I looked forward to was sleep. One night I volunteered to sit on a bunk and wind balls of yarn because I was too tired to go on knitting. When I was dopey with fatigue I would always find mistakes in my work the following day and it wasn't worth having to unpick it. Winding yarn wasn't part of our workload that we got points for, so not many people wanted to do it.

I wound and I wound, and at one point I think I fell asleep. With a start I realised the yarn no longer felt like 9-ply, and I was suddenly fully awake. I knew that if I bungled winding the balls of yarn others would be producing wasted work. Since everybody was so tired, my fault would be too great to bear.

I stopped and counted the threads in one ball. Eight strands. The two other women were still winding at their fastest speed. Feeling guilty about having stopped, I anxiously counted again. Ten strands! What had I done? I clenched my teeth and counted for the third time. Eleven strands! I was devastated. Here I was, having done calculus at university, and now I couldn't even count to nine! Desperately tired, I had to give up and climb down into the bunk, too exhausted to care whether or not this particular ball was actually OK.

TAMING A WILD HORSE

The police designated non-Falun Gong practitioners as 'forced-labour re-education camp inmates who have committed other misdemeanours'. But these people just called themselves 'regulars'.

'If writing a guarantee meant I could go home,' a drug addict once said, 'I'd write 10,000 of them!'

So in their eyes, people who wouldn't even write one guarantee were anything but regular. Perhaps they unconsciously felt that under normal circumstances Falun Gong practitioners would not be in the forced-labour camps.

Ever since we had been moved to Company 2, the regulars had but one thing on their minds: when would the awards be given? Five of the nine regulars in Squad 3 were in the running and four of these (Li Chun was the fifth, non-eligible, one) would be released immediately if they received awards so it was no wonder they couldn't think about much else.

They waited and waited. August passed, September passed, and still the awards had not been announced. It became clear that the police were being distracted from calculating the awards by having 'talks' with Falun Gong practitioners, sorting out Falun Gong practitioners' files, trying to establish model 'reformees' and writing reports. They were also preparing for the early release of the first group of 'reformees' before October 1, National Day, to encourage the ones who had not 'reformed' yet.

When the regulars who were in the running for awards could stand it no longer they delegated Hao Ying to question the company leader.

'The Falun Gong certainly deserve some consideration,' she said, 'but don't we count, too? Ever since the Falun Gong came we've had to put up with lack of sleep just to reform them. Even 16-year-old Kuai Wei has been rostered to watch them and she's so exhausted she falls asleep while sitting on the ground. It's so hard to reform one; but as soon as they are reformed they're treated like royalty while we don't get any credit whatsoever! We wouldn't mind so much not getting any credit but we've worked dreadfully hard, and willingly done extra shifts while other people slept, just to win a few extra points so that we can go home a little earlier. The government promised we'd get awards! The team leaders said that the national emblem they've got on their caps makes them the government's representatives and now they've deceived us.'

'The government has not deceived you,' was the reply. 'The awards will be made so please be a little patient. Falun Gong has been made a priority for the camp and there's nothing we can do about that. It has become a very important national issue with international repercussions and we hope regular inmates will be patient until team leaders deal with it, as they have been instructed.'

Hao Ying came back in tears. I really felt sorry for these regulars. Just about all of them had been sent to the labour camp before the crackdown on Falun Gong and had no idea of the fuss it had caused. All they knew was the system of grading that was dangled in front of them and that if they got an award they might be able to go home. They couldn't work out how these people they'd been ordering about all this time could be having any international repercussions!

'Huh!' Kuai Wei said crossly. 'Just wait till I get out. As soon as I walk out that main gate I'm going to sit right down on the ground and practise Falun Gong. And then as soon as they arrest me I'm going to reform!'

One day, about noon, a woman in our squad started quarrelling with 18-year-old Zheng Jia and in the ensuing fracas suddenly shoved one of the bunks, jamming Li Chun's hand between two bunks. The pain brought tears to Li Chun's eyes and she started swearing. But suddenly her eyes fell on Song Mei and she immediately fell silent.

Shortly afterwards, Li Chun went over to Song Mei, who was sitting on her stool, and half knelt before her. She extended her red and already swollen hand for Song Mei to see.

'How's that?' she said, like a spoilt child. 'I came out pretty well today, didn't I? Before, I would have cursed her ancestors to kingdom come. I can take anything except getting the worst of things; I would never have let her get away with that before.'

Song Mei was younger than Li Chun but she spoke to her as an adult would to a child.

'Mmm. You didn't do too badly. Keep being good.'

I was surprised by this and wondered as I quietly watched them

202 • Witnessing History

how Song Mei had subdued this 'wild horse' who now so fervently wished to perform well for her.

As time went on I found out more about Li Chun. She had run away from home when she was twelve and no longer able to tolerate her stepfather's abuse. She stole to get money for food and first went into a forced-labour re-education camp when she was thirteen. In the nineteen years since then she had struggled to be a good person; she once had had her own small business and a decent boyfriend. After her fifth stint in the labour camp she had gone straight for quite some time. She got into the clothing business and eventually managed to save a tidy sum—more than 20,000 *yuan*. And then somebody stole it. The more she thought about this, the more outraged she felt that she, elder stateswoman of the trade that she was, should herself have been so deceived. As some form of retribution, she in turn stole a wallet and was unlucky enough to be caught. As a habitual offender she got three years for stealing 400 *yuan*. She considered harming herself by banging her head on the radiator after she was arrested, but was afraid it would hurt too much.

By the time the Falun Gong practitioners began to come in she was an 'old hand', which meant she was charged with the important task of guarding them. Fairly early on she had told Song Mei that even if she were a hooligan, she had very high standards for people and even higher standards for her friends. She said that very few people nowadays were really worthy people but she would risk half her life for those who were; for those who were worthy of being her friends she would risk her entire life. People like Song Mei, who would challenge the police and go to the electric chair rather than write a guarantee but who treated petty thieves like her with genuine human respect, were her idea of really worthy people.

Later on she told Song Mei she wanted to practise Falun Gong too. She didn't talk about it and most of the time remained her usual self, laughing and joking, but I could see that deep down she cherished Song Mei. She so treasured the things Song Mei told her that she didn't dare speak of them, fearing that she would disappoint Song Mei if she didn't do well.

One day another group of women arrived from the despatch division and the little sentry notified Song Mei and Li Wen to get their things together and move to Company 4, which had just been set up. There was something of a commotion in the corridor as women from other squads prepared to move as well.

We all pitched in to help Song Mei and Li Wen pack. Kuai Wei got out her coat-hangers and insisted that they each take some, and a regular who had been responsible for keeping guard on Li Wen shed silent tears as she folded Li Wen's quilt. I was miserable as well. In none of the other squads had the regulars and the Falun Gong practitioners been on such good terms. Here, we had looked after each other and encouraged one another. Once we were separated, we wouldn't even have a chance to talk to each other anymore.

At some stage Song Mei went outside. She returned deeply distressed and in tears. It really surprised and worried Li Chun to see her in this state but she didn't know what to do. So she silently took her hand, not daring to ask why she was crying.

After a few minutes Song Mei was finally able to cry out, 'They've tortured her to such an extent!'

'Tortured who?' I asked quickly.

'Liu Shuying. I used to know her; we went to Tian'anmen together. She was so pretty, and now look at her! She didn't recognise me when I spoke to her just now.'

I eventually realised she was talking about the 'living corpse' we had first seen in the despatch division copying from a green-covered book, the dreadfully frail woman from whom all vitality had been drained. So she *had* practised Falun Gong. This woman had been a friend of Song Mei's and had just arrived at the camp. Song Mei started sobbing again but for the life of me I couldn't connect the Liu Shuying I had seen with the word 'pretty'.

With the little sentry outside hurrying her on, Song Mei managed to pull herself together. We were deeply disturbed as we stood at the window watching them all file across to Company 4, clutching their quilts. Company 4 was in the other building, along with the juvenile labour re-education unit. With the increase in our numbers, established practices had gone out the window and now male and female inmates were to be housed in the same building.

3

A PERILOUS TIME

On our second day in Company 2 we were lining up along one side of the corridor ready to go to the mess hall when one of the women across from me in another unit suddenly glared at me.

'Work hard to reform!' she hissed.

This woman had been seated on my right during that 'informal discussion' when Hu Xiuying had been on my left. She hadn't spoken at the time except to whisper to me that she had just written her guilty plea but felt somehow it was not a proper thing to do and was thinking about retracting it. I had agreed it certainly was not the proper thing to do and had said she should retract it immediately.

So her words now as we came face to face were completely unexpected. My reaction also surprised me: my heart raced as if I had received a really bad fright.

Earlier, a new police officer with an electric prod had visited our squad.

'I hear evil prevails in this squad,' she had said, walking around the room brandishing the live prod. 'My prod is an expert at punishing evil!'

She was waving the crackling prod in our faces, the dull blue phosphorescent sparks centimetres from our noses, but I didn't even blink and my pulse certainly didn't race. I had actually found her quite ridiculous.

Yet for some reason this inmate's 'Work hard to reform!' really jolted me. It began to gnaw away at me and I sensed some insidious, omnipresent thing that was more frightening than an electric prod, more evil than a demon. The sinister sensation I had felt before was suddenly much stronger.

Just after that episode I heard that Gu Hua had 'reformed'. A few days later I heard that Xia Jing had 'reformed'. Then I heard that some others had 'reformed' . . .

Hu Xiuying's treachery had been a dagger in my heart but I had never really known her to begin with. Gu Hua and Xia Jing were different. Our hearts beating as one, we had shared a common destiny, friends who would have died for each other. They were my fearless fellow practitioners. What could have made them both 'reform' overnight?

I felt so desolate and empty that it was as if my very soul had died. I could rise above the *People's Daily* rumours; but the 'reform' of my dear fellow practitioners really made my heart sink.

I forced myself to keep going. I put my head down and knitted for all I was worth every day, paying no attention to anybody and not listening to what was being said around me. But I couldn't escape the excitement the 'reformed' ones showed after 'reforming'. Their chatter about it being right to 'reform', about 'reform' being a more advanced level of practice, swirled around me and seeped into my head. Their words thudded into my body like poisoned arrows, leaving me utterly defenceless.

'Surely reforming isn't right, is it?' I started asking myself. 'Perhaps they really do know something I don't? Am I really wiser than they are?'

As soon as these thoughts occurred to me, I felt a hand reaching into my brain, seeking to grab my will and my thoughts and drag them away. I broke into a cold sweat, clenching my teeth as I struggled to stop my self from disappearing. I focused my entire will on confronting this terrifying hand in a fearful tug-of-war. I staggered like a drunken person. With my last shred of clarity, I told myself that if I relaxed just the tiniest bit this hand would yank me over the line and into that place that was called 'breeding demons in one's own mind'.

I never dreamed that two petty thieves would be my salvation in this crisis. Every time that hand gained ground in its tug-of-war and I felt I was going under, I would look at Li Chun and Feng Yulan sitting beside me.

'What would they think if I reformed?' I would chant to myself fiercely. 'How would they react?'

Feng Yulan had come from the despatch division the day Li Wen and Song Mei were transferred to Company 4. In her forties, she was in for theft. A Falun Gong article had been found in her luggage on her first day in the despatch division and this had earned her an immediate session with an electric prod. She didn't say a word in protest though.

'What were you doing with Falun Gong articles if you don't practise Falun Gong?' an officer had said to her several days later. 'Are you suicidal? And why didn't you say right off you don't practise Falun Gong? If you had said that, you wouldn't have gotten a beating.'

'I'll be honest with you, Team Leader,' she had said quietly. 'There were many things in among my belongings that the Falun Gong people gave me but I didn't know there were Falun Gong articles. I can't read, you see. I met a lot of Falun Gong practitioners in the detention centre and I thought they were pretty good. I wouldn't mind learning with them, so if you want to consider me a Falun Gong practitioner that's okay with me. I won't blame you if you shock me as a Falun Gong practitioner.'

As for Li Chun, it had just seemed natural that I would fill the gap for her when Song Mei went. She and Feng Yulan both trusted me and regarded me as a person to depend on. My every word and deed, my very thoughts and ideas, nothing escaped their scrutiny. Everything I said and did represented for them the whole body of Falun Gong. Lacking the opportunity to read Falun Gong books, they had to rely on my words and actions. I believe they didn't grasp all that talk about how right it was to 'reform', about how 'advanced' it was. Their logic was very simple: if you reformed you weren't a practitioner and all you had said about good being rewarded with good and evil being rewarded with evil, about stealing people's things being immoral and having serious consequences, all that was just deceitful. It meant that those who reformed no longer believed in any cosmic principles. And that meant that if they had to steal, then they had to steal, and that was all there was to it.

Even in my befuddled state I knew with absolute clarity that the most terrible thing any individual could do was not believe in cosmic principles and the most heartening thing was to have proper faith. Any person who was willing to begin practising would be saved for ever and ever. I couldn't harm those two. I couldn't ruin them.

As I thought this through, my mind became so much clearer and my will so much stronger that I found the strength to tug against that large invisible hand. If I had thought a little bit more about myself and my 'advancement', and a little bit less about others, I would have been completely done for in that tug-of-war against those thousands upon thousands of demons.

PLEASE, GOD, DO NOT FORSAKE ME

A day or two after Li Wen and Song Mei went, Zhou Jie was also transferred away, leaving only four Falun Gong practitioners in our squad. Divide and demoralise was clearly the policy of the day.

Every night after we had climbed into bed, utterly exhausted, the little sentry would come to our room and give Zhang Qing a light tap on the shoulder.

'The team leader wants you,' she would say.

Zhang Qing would be taken to the main office, where she would have to copy out material smearing Falun Gong or copy out Order 23 a certain number of times or simply stand there as a punishment. She would come back after 4 a.m. and get up at 5:30 with dark circles under her eyes. She was already thin, but now she was growing wan and sallow.

Cheng Lan from Squad 2 also stood every night in punishment. About midnight one night she suddenly threw up, a river of vomit gushing from her mouth. She was shaking and crying and when the officer who came to see what was happening showed her a little concern she immediately 'reformed'.

'If they want to increase the punishment, let them,' she had said only the day before. 'They can make it a hundred years for all I care.'

Zhang Qing saw with her own eyes what happened that night and told us all about it the following day.

'If this keeps up,' she added in a despairing voice, 'I won't even be able to trust myself.'

'If I were the only one left,' Zhao Ying piped up resolutely, 'I would still defend Dafa!'

I didn't say anything. But each night when the little sentry came to get Zhang Qing I couldn't help wondering if it would be my turn next, if they would come for me the following day. When I was on the point of utter exhaustion I feared nothing except not being allowed to sleep. Yet the daily terror that the next day they would come for me almost made me hope they would take me to stand in punishment instead of Zhang Qing

This went on for about two weeks. During the day we tried to look out for Zhang Qing and give her a break from work but she struggled on with her workload the same as before, trying very hard to keep on smiling. Then one day when I was called away I came back to find her gone—she had suddenly been sent to the training unit.

I looked at the empty beds—Zhang Qing, Li Wen, Song Mei, Zhou Jie, all gone—and I felt unutterably lonely. Squad 3 had been known as the stubborn squad but there were very few of us left now. My heart was heavy: perhaps tomorrow it would be my turn. As I filed across to the mess hall I gazed up at the luxuriant poplar trees outside the high brick wall, topped by an electric fence.

'How many changes of season will I see those trees pass through while I am in here?' I asked dully.

I didn't know the answer. My heart ached as never before and I echoed the cry of Jesus as they placed Him on the cross, 'My God, why hast Thou forsaken me?'

SWEET SPRING WATER IN THE DESERT

This all happened just before the Mid-Autumn Festival. Usually the rewards would have been announced by then, and regulars who had received awards would be able to go home and spend the Mid-Autumn Festival—traditionally a time for family reunions—with their families. This year, however, as the festival approached and the awards still hadn't been announced, these women grew increasingly restless. To quell popular indignation, it was quickly decided that some of the women who were in the running for awards could go home for two days during the festival.

This threw everyone into an even greater tizzy, but after a week or more of asking, discussing and tussling, the dust finally settled. It ended up that in our squad only Hao Ying and Li Bin were to enjoy this privilege and, to everyone's surprise, not one of the Falun Gong women who had 'reformed' were to receive this special honour. Apparently the forced-labour camp still didn't trust them. The regulars finally felt a little more balanced.

In the end, very few inmates were allowed to go home and life went on as before for the rest of us. One afternoon, there was some unusual activity in the grounds, however, and we could see a sound system and a rostrum being set up. It looked as though there was to be a mid-autumn party that evening.

The regulars were all very excited and couldn't settle down to their work, waiting for the little sentry to call us out into the corridor. When the call finally came, everyone took their stools and filed out to the performance area.

As I remember it, several armed police from nearby stations and some retired cadres had been invited to perform; they were certainly nothing to write home about. I had no idea how we were supposed to relax and enjoy ourselves when we had to sit bolt upright like soldiers on parade, in a high-walled courtyard surrounded by police.

Nevertheless, the last item was announced as 'police and inmates tripping the light fantastic together to share a happy mid-autumn'. The music played on for several minutes and still no one from Company 2 had got up to dance on the sparsely populated floor. Desperate to move things along, Team Leader Hou rushed up and, with a radiant smile, asked me if I would like to dance. I could see Song Mei, whom I hadn't seen for over two weeks, in the middle of the floor looking over at us as if she wanted to say something. This was an opportunity not to be missed so I stood up and said to Team Leader Hou that not only could I dance, I could take the man's part, so I would lead. Grasping her thin body, I waltzed her around the floor a few times then steered her over towards Song Mei.

Song Mei said not a word; she just went on dancing. Suddenly I felt a wad of paper in my hand, but by then she had danced off.

I lay on my bunk that night forcing myself not to fall asleep. My bed was directly opposite the open door and the little sentry and police on night duty could wander in at any point on their twenty-minute rounds. The camp guards also made periodic patrols, as much to check on the little sentries and police as the inmates.

I bunched up some clothing at the head of my bunk and, sheltered by the little nest this made, I opened up the wad of paper Song Mei had slipped to me. It was all crumpled and torn, clearly having passed through many hands. Both sides were covered in closely written characters, written with a ballpoint pen. There was no heading and I couldn't make out an ending. In the dim light I started reading:

Your current performance as Dafa disciples is magnificent. All of this is your goodness (*shan*) made manifest, and it is what evil fears most, as those who attack goodness are bound to be evil. The actions they are now adopting in the persecution of Dafa and its students are extremely evil and shameful, and they fear these will be exposed. You must let the world's people know about their evilness—this is saving people, as well . . .

I realised this was a new article from our teacher. After more than a year I was finally hearing his voice again! But, more to the point, I understood the value he was placing on our stepping forth to clarify the real situation.

Li Hongzhi had remained silent for ten months after the crackdown. During that time there had been a great deal of disagreement between Falun Gong practitioners as to whether or not to appeal to the authorities. Would appealing to the government and exposing the persecution we were suffering be counted as being involved in politics or disrupting society? Both were against the requirements of Falun Gong practice. Now, reading these recent words of our teacher, I felt warmed and at peace.

For the next three nights I lay on my bunk struggling to stay awake after everyone had gone to sleep, trying not to wake my companions or to alert the patrols. In that time I committed to memory this article whose title I did not know. The labour camp was searched periodically, so it was not safe to hide anything anywhere. I wrote several copies of the article out from memory and at the first opportunity passed them on to fellow practitioners. There was never any shortage of pens and paper in the camp, as we were always being forced to write 'thought reports'. Each time we had to sit through a 'lecture' or to 'study' an article or broadcast attacking Falun Gong, we had to write a report about the conclusions we had reached after our 'study'. Sometimes we even had to write a thought report after a family visit.

POISON

Many of the 'reformed' women gradually became part of an 'education group' that filled in for the police-run discussions by 'educating' women who had not reformed. I was called to the main office one day and surrounded by this group, one of whom was Xia Jing.

After lecturing me on the advantages of 'reforming', they discussed these advantages among themselves, using all the appropriate Falun Gong words, terms and concepts. Their message was simple: it was right to 'reform' and 'reforming' did not mean you were renouncing Falun Gong; it just meant you were practising on a more advanced level. Their distortion of the concepts of Falun Gong was so subtle that at times it was difficult to realise just what they were doing.

I was sent to several of these 'help sessions' and each one left me with an inexplicable lassitude that I had never felt after any police interrogation. It was the sort of malaise that overtakes martial arts heroes in swordsman fiction when they are given poison. To rid themselves of the poison they have to resort to the potency (*gong*) they have painstakingly cultivated over a lifetime.

Just when I thought I couldn't bear it any longer, things took a turn for the better. We were all squatting in the courtyard one day, doing the weeding, when Assistant Team Leader Cheng Cui poked her head out of a dormitory window. She called out to the officer supervising us that I was wanted in the dormitory duty room.

'Look who's here,' Cheng Cui said. 'I've invited two guests from Company 4.'

These two, dressed like me in labour-camp garb, turned out to be ace 'education aides', one of whom was named Xiao Yu.

Whenever I had been subjected to 'help sessions' before I had not taken in much of the discussion, because what they were saying made me feel unwell and I rejected it out of hand. I would just end up feeling pained, unwell and a little despondent. This time, however, when Xiao Yu started to talk my mind came alive with a vigilance that sprang from deep inside. Every cell in my body was instantly combat ready, like a warrior who has not fought for a long time but instinctively recognises a truly worthy opponent.

'OK,' I said readily. 'Now tell me why you reformed.'

She started to give her reasons, an argument couched in brilliant rhetoric and illustrated with copious quotes. She cited and analysed almost the entire content of *Zhuan Falun*. She was clearly the camp's greatest exponent of the theory of reforming, having taken her predecessors' theoretical stance to its ultimate point.

I listened quietly, weighing in my mind each of her points and contrasting them with my understanding of *Zhuan Falun*. Sometimes I could see where a point was wrong even before she had finished making it, or where her bias lay, why she was biased, or the attachment that was causing her bias. I mentally refuted each of the hundreds of points she made, even as they tumbled from her mouth, like a warrior cutting down foes one by one as they came at me. The sequence of my opponent's ideas was crystal clear to me. I was quick but not impatient; and I was not thrown into disorder by the sheer number of issues she raised. When she reached her conclusion, referring to the well-known 'the more secrecies you see through, the more enlightened you will be', I nodded to myself: I had finally experienced what our teacher spoke of as 'breeding demons in one's own mind'.

All of a sudden I was full of optimism; all the pain that had been oppressing me disappeared without a trace and I felt so light-hearted I wanted to sing. A split second later I became aware of a separate pain that all the suffering in my heart had overshadowed, a pain I had not recognised, or had not wanted to acknowledge. And this was that the mansion in which all my beliefs were housed had actually been shaken by the cruel reality of so many people 'reforming'. It had wobbled ever so slightly, not enough for me to notice, but the very fact that it had wobbled could have brought me down totally.

In that split second when my thoughts shifted and I realised this, the mansion of my beliefs ceased wobbling and my pain vanished. I knew now that it did not matter how many reformed, because each of them was wrong. Their reasoning did not have a leg to stand on, so how could they not be wrong?

I will never be able to describe that moment of happiness nor how blissful I felt. The delicious irony was the police could never have anticipated that this 'expert education aide' would help me walk free of my heart's predicament.

After that, the words of the reformed women no longer made me ill. It didn't matter what they said when they came to educate me or what I might inadvertently hear; their words ran off me like rain off a pane of glass.

I remember this as the period when I was most frequently chosen to do additional heavy work. This included collecting rubbish, sweeping the courtyard, moving bricks, moving soil, hoeing, planting grass and watering the flowers and lawns. This was also when

Tian Yong, head of the corrective section and second only in status and authority to the labour-camp director, began to summon me.

Tian Yong was short and stout with dark skin and a large mouth and he walked with a rolling gait. He was extremely self-assured. He was the last police officer to summon me for a talk when I was in Entry Company. He was also the only officer to summon me for a 'talk' after I was transferred to Company 2. I had recognised him instantly as the policeman who had coolly appraised me when I asked at the informal discussion whether inmates were allowed to beat other inmates in the labour camp.

This man was terribly conceited. He only ever summoned university graduates, never anyone who had not trained for a profession. Such was his conceit that he believed his 'civilised scholarship' and skill in psychological warfare were all that were needed to fix me and that was why he would summon me, again and again. In the end he had only to appear in the corridor of Company 2 for someone to inform me, 'Section Head Tian is here again, Zheng Zeng.'

He would always plan our talks with meticulous care. How best to build ramparts for protection, how to attack, how to dig a pit and then how to push me into the pit. And, when things weren't going his way, he would work out how to outflank me, how to find my weakness and once he had done so, how to formulate rules for the talks most favourable to him, and so on. 'Talking' with him was very tiring but even though we crossed swords many times it would always end up with him losing it.

'You know who are the hardest people to reform?' he thundered at me one time, tapping his forehead. 'Uneducated oafs! You've wasted all that time reading all those books and you've learned nothing. You're worse than an uneducated oaf; you're just a bag of gristle!'

I didn't understand what he meant by this so I asked Li Chun when I got back to our room. She said it was a term of abuse that referred to meat that was too tough to slice or to cook.

When, after several days, he summoned me again he just asked me one question.

'What would you do,' he said, 'if everybody else in the labour camp reformed?'

'When I first decided to practise Falun Gong, Section Head Tian,' I said, with the utmost sincerity, 'I didn't discuss it with anyone. I made my own decision. In the matter of my practice I don't consult others.'

That uncertain look he often got during our talks stole across his face and he remained silent for a long time.

'Mmm,' he said finally. 'People like you are really very rare. . . . It is a pity . . .'

He left without saying anything further.

STORM THE FORTIFICATIONS

About a week before October 1, 2000, China's national day, something was up in Company 2. There was a sudden flurry of name calling in the corridor.

'If you hear your name called, get your things together and assemble downstairs! You're going for training!'

Zhao Ying's name was called and so was Wang Rong's. I pricked up my ears but did not hear my name echo along the corridor.

Eventually, I learned that all of the Falun Gong practitioners in my group and in the group after us who had not 'reformed' had been assembled downstairs for training. All, that is, except me. I was the only one left. I felt a shiver of dread. I would rather have gone with them; at least then we would meet our fate together.

I watched from the window as Wang Rong and the others, clutching their meagre belongings, lined up and were escorted to the gloomy modules of the training unit. I decided not to try to work out why only I had been left behind, or to think about whether they had kept me back as part of a more frightening way of dealing with me. That was a sure road to despair.

A few days later, at dusk on September 29, an officer escorted me to the garden at the front of the building to water the flowers. As I hosed the rows of Chinese roses I looked around and saw a line of inmates, holding their quilts, walking towards me from the training unit. Escorting these inmates was none other than Su Rui, the team leader of former Entry Company who at some stage had been transferred to the training unit. Su Rui looked at me, scornfully, as she walked past.

'Ahh! Tiantanghe's great prospect!' she said sarcastically. 'Postgraduate student who waters the flowers, waters the lawn, collects rubbish!'

I realised that the inmates she was escorting were those from Company 2 who had been sent for training. Then I found the familiar face of Wang Jin and our eyes met.

I shall never forget the expression on her face at that moment. Her hair was tousled and she still had the rosy cheeks of a young girl, but those cheeks had lost their shine and innocence. They were tarnished, as if a veil of humiliation had fallen across her face. Her expression, the look in her eyes, cried out wordlessly in the misty twilight.

'Dear one! Dear one!' her eyes told me, 'I have fallen into the hands of traitors and my purity is gone! I . . .'

My heart sank. Within one second I knew what had happened to her—she must have been unable to endure the torture and written a guarantee. With heavy steps and in evident despair she walked out of my sight.

And then I saw Zhao Ying and Wang Rong. I cannot describe the look on Zhao Ying's face except to say that I hardly recognised her. There was a queer look in her eyes, which told me that she must have 'reformed'. Expressionless, she walked past me as if she didn't recognise me, or perhaps she really didn't see me. Ever after, each time we met it was as if she had never seen me before.

Blind Wang Rong couldn't see me as she walked with wide-open but unseeing eyes. I could not read her story from the traces of distress on her placid face.

I couldn't help wondering, as one by one they walked by, what had gone on in that maze of a place in little more than a week?

By the time I returned to our room, Li Chun had found out that half of the people who had been sent to training had 'reformed' already. The entire 'reform' operation had been planned and executed by a few 'ace reformers' who had complete control over the form it would take. Apart from sleep deprivation there were beatings, 'flying', 'bottoms up' (bending over with your face touching your shins) and squatting. Wang Jin acknowledged that she could bear being beaten by regulars, but could not for the life of her bear being beaten by 'Dafa practitioners'. That someone who had once been one of us would suddenly no longer be on speaking terms was one thing, but it was beyond her understanding that they would be even more ruthless than regulars. Actually, this was another tactic they used to 'reform' us. Many of those so-called 'Dafa practitioners' were, in fact, plants. Their unexpected 'about-face' put us at a psychological disadvantage and achieved better 'reforming' results than mere physical torture.

What none of us expected was that Wang Rong, the first of the inmates to have written a guilty plea, should now have stood firm and that Zhao Ying, who had always said she would defend Dafa even if she were the only one left, would suddenly capitulate and utterly 'reform'.

The regulars had a lot to say about all of this but it had knocked the stuffing out of me and I couldn't say anything. Word got around that those who had been to training would be assigned to different squads when they got back. And indeed, Zhao Ying was put in Squad 6; Wang Rong went to Squad 5; and I was the only Falun Gong practitioner left in Squad 3.

I hadn't recovered from this business when Cheng Cui suddenly told us to take our stools out to the drill ground. Over 100 of us sat around in a big circle. This was something new and none of us could tell what she had up her sleeve.

After two months of anxious waiting, Hao Ying and a few others had become privy to a piece of classified information: the awards were to be given the following day and those who received them were to be released immediately after the ceremony. The police had let these people ring their families on the quiet to tell them to bring clothes when they came to get them. We were losing four regulars from Squad 3. A group of 'fully reformed' Falun Gong practitioners was to be released as well.

We sat on the drill ground waiting. Kuai Wei lightly touched the hand of Hong Xue, who would be leaving the next day, and started softly singing a song of parting. Tears fell as they told each other to take good care.

I, too, felt the pain of loss and cried along with the others. After almost two months of living together, Squad 3 had become our family and we had no idea what sort of people would be coming in to replace those we were losing. Tiantanghe would probably never see the likes of Hao Ying as a squad leader again; our lives would be very difficult if someone vile were brought in to replace her.

Cheng Cui appeared in the middle of the circle to explain the purpose of this emergency gathering. It was to give us an 'unexpected pleasure'. Apparently several stubborn Falun Gong practitioners in the training unit had finally reformed and they wanted to perform a sketch they had written themselves.

Xiang Hong came on first; she played the heroine. Next was Wang

Run, who had been the one to introduce Li Chun to Falun Gong and who, it was said, had not been induced to 'reform' even when electric shocks had deformed her head. She was playing the role of Xiang Hong's husband. Two others were playing the roles of Xiang Hong's mother and her daughter.

We watched Xiang Hong chant the story of how she had been 'obsessed' by Falun Gong, how she had been more stubborn than anybody, how she had gone through four different training units where she had remained, unreformed, while others came and went and how this had broken the hearts of her husband, her mother and her daughter. The sketch included an extremely heart-breaking scene where the family came to visit, amid much weeping and wailing. The four actors cried all over the place, tears of apparent pain and remorse. Xiang Hong gave a remarkable performance. She shouted herself hoarse, repented and caricatured her 'pre-reformed' self as both an out-and-out buffoon and a mental case.

I was in tears myself even before this travesty. Now realising that several of the most stubborn practitioners in the labour camp had completely and utterly reformed, I was heartbroken. I was crying tears of blood as they defiled and distorted the wonder and sanctity of Buddha Law practice by portraying it through a buffoon. I didn't want to cry with them but I was unable to hold back my tears.

A pall of grief hung over the grounds, as many of the other inmates too were crying. In my distress I didn't notice when the sketch finished and I didn't hear Cheng Cui announce that, because they had reformed, Xiang Hong and the other three were being let out of the training unit immediately and would return to Company 2. I don't remember anything until I was halfway up the stairs and I suddenly heard someone behind me fall with a thud. Another woman and I whirled around to see what had happened.

It was Li Chun who had fallen. In my grief I had forgotten her; I had forgotten that Wang Run had been the first to introduce her to Falun Gong; I had forgotten that she had modelled her resolve on Wang Run; I had forgotten how she idolised Wang Run. And I had not given a thought to what a blow Wang Run's reform must have been to her. Li Chun had been crying even harder than I until, almost comatose with agony, she had hyperventilated and passed out.

It so happened that the other woman who helped her up was Wang Run. Together we got her onto her bunk, where she quickly came round. When her eyes fell on Wang Run she started sobbing again. Wang Run murmured something inaudible, as if trying to soothe her, but Li Chun turned to me, her nostrils quivering and red from crying.

'I can't accept it,' she moaned over and over. 'I can't accept it.'

I will never forget the look on her face at that moment. She was an orphaned soul who had finally found a resting place after a lifetime of wandering, only to be mercilessly driven out again. All of her innocence, her helplessness, the terrible injuries she had suffered, the agony of being deceived and sold out by the person she trusted most, her despair and her grief—all of this was written all over her tear-streaked face.

I looked into Wang Run's eyes and challenged her, from a place of deep indignation.

'Do you know that she took to heart everything you said to her before?' I said. 'Do you know the implications for her of your performance tonight? You might as well have killed her!!'

It was only then that I noticed the tell-tale burn marks of the prods on Wang Run's face and arms. Her whole face was black, the whites of her eyes startlingly bright by contrast. She lowered her head.

'You'll understand later,' she said listlessly and then she was gone.

As soon as she was out of the door, several women hastened to tell me that the police in the training unit had used several prods on her simultaneously for long periods. These officers' hands had been so affected by the electricity leaking from the prods that they were unable to lift their hands for several days afterwards.

I sat silently by Li Chun's bunk wondering how I could share her suffering. It wasn't long before the little sentry told me to take my stool with me to the main office.

Chaos reigned that night. Company 2 seemed to be bursting at the seams, with the insufferably arrogant Xiang Hong and the others who had just returned from the training unit running about on sinister errands. I found out afterwards that everything that happened that night, as well as all the operations leading up to it, had been meticulously planned. Because October 1 was the national day, there had apparently been a week of 'storming heavily fortified positions' to ensure that the unreformed all reformed. My being summoned to headquarters was the final thrust at my heavily fortified position.

As soon as I sat down in the police dormitory I was surrounded. The woman who had played the role of Xiang Hong's daughter launched the first attack. She was believed to have been the one who 'reformed' Wang Jin. She may have been small but she was ruthless when she got going.

I cleared my mind of all thought and just kept my head down, calmly going on with my knitting as if I had no doubt whatsoever she wouldn't dare raise a hand to me.

It so happened that she really didn't; what's more, her tone grew softer and more gentle as she went on. In the end, she was squatting in front of me stroking my leg and bending her head down to get her face in my line of sight.

'How about it?' she said finally, in the most patient voice you could ask for. 'What do you feel about what I've said?'

I stilled my hands and looked at this very small person, not daring to believe she could really hit someone and feeling no hatred in my heart for her.

'I don't want to say anything,' I said very slowly, 'yet four words have come into my head. And since thinking something is the same as saying it, I'll tell you what they are: "A load of nonsense".'

I went on with my knitting. Someone suggested I shouldn't be knitting because it was preventing me from listening properly but someone else said that I could hear every word perfectly well even though I wasn't raising my head.

Shortly afterwards the police wanted to take a break and I was taken into another large office. I was still surrounded by a large group of people and I saw that Zhou Jie and another practitioner named Bai Lian were in the same office, each surrounded by their own group of people. Bai Lian was in her fifties and both she and Zhou Jie had arrived with the last intake.

At some point I finished my knitting and with idle hands came a weariness so complete that I could have gone to sleep there and then. I had experienced many emotions already that night. I had seen the violation written all over Wang Jin's face; I had sobbed in agony during the sketch; I had helped get the barely conscious Li Chun into the dormitory; I had ferociously challenged Wang Run. The long periods of heavy forced manual labour and chronic lack of sleep had also worn my body and my spirit down to the point of exhaustion. I barely had the strength to hold my head up so I stretched out on the chair alongside me.

My adversaries, on the other hand, were bringing in fresh and combat-ready troops who seemed to have taken some sort of stimulant. They made a terrific noise, abusing me in the most frightful language. If I didn't reform I was sabotaging the Dafa and harming the master, they said. I was an evil cult follower, a demon from hell, selfish, attached to consummation, a coward, greedy, harming my loved ones by selfishly pursuing consummation, going down in history as a byword for infamy, filthy, going to die without a place for burial, and so on and so forth. This stream of abuse continued for several hours but was actually quite varied and the tone did not lower as they interwove their charges with surprising coherence. They seemed to think I really was the most evil person in the world.

Utterly exhausted, I lay across the chairs feeling like a tiny craft adrift on a Force 12 tsunami, about to capsize under the violence of their attack. Yet in my soul a little lamp burned steadfastly, throwing off a gentle radiance they could not extinguish.

As the night wore on it grew colder and the chill began to bite, seeping into my bones. And suddenly there was Hao Ying's head in the door. She was holding my coat. She had been too excited to sleep and was saying her goodbye to her friend, the little sentry Zhang Lei, in the corridor. This, of course, was not normally allowed but because she was going home the following day the police were letting her do as she pleased. She had started to feel cold and remembered that I had gone out with just a light short-sleeved top. So she had fetched my coat for me.

She marched straight across the room, throwing a withering glance at my tormentors, and handed me my coat. I put it on, too moved to thank her for her compassion, which had cut through this vicious bombardment.

Cheng Cui woke up about 3 a.m. Hair all dishevelled, she came to watch the battle but then she grew furious as soon as she realised I was showing no signs of imminent reform.

'What's going on here?' she shouted. 'Separate them! Put them in three separate rooms. Don't let her sit down. You sure are working hard at educating her—here she is, asleep on a chair!'

So I was taken to another room, where I was not allowed to sit or lie down but had to stand and pay attention to their yelling and their attacks. By this time I knew that all this yelling was not important. The real battle was taking place in some other space. There, the demons controlling these people and my moral character were engaged in a fight to the death. Their demon nature was a deadly weapon, but they had to find a chink in my heart through which to pierce me.

I paid no attention, but bent and laid my head on the only table in the room, trying to gain what little support I could. So exhausted and weak was I that I no longer had the strength to care for my physical being. At all costs, though, I had to concentrate my energy and will to shield that bright lamp in my heart.

That night seemed to last for centuries but as dawn's rays crept across the sky the demons finally lost their potency. Dishevelled but ever hopeful, Cheng Cui returned to the scene only to see head after drooping, dejected head of her vanquished education aides. Hope changed to despair: she seemed unable to understand, much less accept, this failure of her eloquent senior staffer Xiang Hong.

I raised my head from the table. Although utterly exhausted, I knew with total clarity that I had just had a very narrow escape from a battle about life or death. During that endless and crazy night, the tsunami could have smashed my fragile craft into pieces at any moment.

4

REFORM

ANOTHER BUSY DAY HAD ALREADY begun by the time I arrived back at the squad room. It was a day like no other, a day of awards and of liberation from the camp for those who had earned it. Those who were leaving were light of heart and even those who were not leaving felt some excitement for them.

My head was swimming and I felt as if I were sleepwalking as we carried our stools down to the auditorium; they couldn't fit us all in, so some of us were sent back to our dormitories.

This was nearly as good as a pardon. With almost everyone in the auditorium it was very quiet, and Li Chun said she would keep a lookout for team leaders while I had a sleep on Kuai Wei's bed, which was in a corner which couldn't be seen from the corridor. This was the bed of choice when regulars wanted to have a bit of a loaf. Sleeping in the daytime was absolutely forbidden, of course, and if you were caught you were in all sorts of trouble.

I lay down to sleep, putting all that aside. I knew that I had to get whatever rest I could in preparation for continuing my fierce nocturnal battles. If they were really going to torture me for a long time by depriving me of sleep then it would be a battle to the death.

I didn't sleep soundly; it's always a little strange sleeping in the daytime. I was also cold because I couldn't risk covering myself with a quilt. There were a great many rules in the labour camp and one that was never breached was that during the day everybody's quilt had to be folded square and flat. You had to get someone to help you if you couldn't do it properly when you first arrived and then you treated your folded quilt with the respect accorded ancestral offerings: you didn't dare disarrange it; you didn't dare fiddle with it. And during the night you dared not open and use it but curled your legs up underneath you. It was preferable to suffer the cold than to have to fold the quilt again in the morning.

I dozed for a while until, half awake, I discovered someone had covered me with a large bath towel. This towel was Kuai Wei's treasured possession—she was the only person in Squad 3 to have such a homely item. It wasn't that we couldn't ask our families to send us such things; it was just that there was nowhere to keep them. We weren't allowed to put anything on our beds except our quilts and, with two people sharing them, the little cupboards were full as soon as we each stuffed in a change of clothes. Kuai Wei had given a lot of thought to this towel and to acccommodate it had shifted a number of things into other people's cupboards.

Once again my heart swelled with gratitude but I couldn't sleep any longer.

By that night I was mentally prepared for being laid siege to, but all was quiet on that front, as it turned out. For several days afterwards, still nothing happened. It was almost as if Cheng Cui and her team had forgotten me.

Everybody but us was having national day holidays during which 'the whole nation celebrated joyously' with a week-long break. The police were also rostered on leave and things in the camp were a little less tense than usual. I certainly didn't expect a problem to arise for me during this lull.

Nor surprisingly, I felt I had surmounted a major hurdle, and I allowed myself to relax mentally in this less fraught atmosphere. I recall that twice in those few days the food in the mess hall improved and the police put on a show for some visitors by taking us to the games room on the fourth floor, a room normally out of bounds to inmates. No one even mentioned the word 'reform'.

During this lull, however, everything I had seen and heard and experienced since coming to the labour re-education camp began to run through my head. It's too dark, a voice cried. How many people will be destroyed by all of this, each one having once let go of life and death and practised to the level of an enlightened being, yet losing their minds through this senseless reforming, and forfeiting their future forever? The master says that once you breed demons in your own mind you are irretrievably lost. I want to get out! I want to get out! I want to expose this darkness to the light; I want to stop this evil. I want to save these innocent and precious lives.

I had already worked out exactly what I was going to do when I got out even before I had thought of a way to get out. I had seen too much of the darkness—I would write a book which would bring it into the light. I would leave the country and seek asylum. I would confront the Western media, go to the United Nations, give testimony as a witness. I would reveal everything to the whole world!

Yes, I could do this, and I would do this! But how was I to get out?

From far away I heard my husband's voice ringing faintly in my ears.

'Get her to write a guarantee—it doesn't matter how flaky it is—and I'll find a way.'

'Write a guarantee.' This voice startled me and my first impulse was to ignore it but it wouldn't go away. Over the next few days it grew louder and louder. Life went on around me while I struggled to reconcile my new aspirations with my conviction that once I had written a guarantee I would no longer deserve to be called a disciple of Dafa. This internal dilemma was to me a thousand times more difficult to endure than the torture I had experienced.

As this intense battle raged, around me time seemed to stand still. It was chilly outside and my heart was icy, too.

'If I don't do it, who will?' The words echoed in my mind.

Finally, I decided to renounce my identity as a disciple of Falun Dafa, to abandon my practice in order to free myself of this conflict.

Forcing myself to remain completely objective and not think of its future effects on me, I began to weigh the pros and cons of 'reforming'.

First was the negative impact it would have on Falun Gong. The authorities would undoubtedly use my 'reform' as propaganda; but after I got out I could write a statement declaring it to be invalid. If I could get my book out I could strike them a deadly blow!

But what about the mental turmoil it would cause other practitioners and the pressure it would place upon them? Those practitioners who remained firm were extraordinary and would not be affected by whatever I did, just as I had resolved not to be influenced by anyone else. Besides, I might have a chance to explain my motives to them.

But what about Li Chun and Feng Yulan? I could risk telling them what was really on my mind; I could tell them that Falun Gong spoke the absolute truth. If I explained that I was doing this *for* Falun Gong they would understand.

And what if they used me as a tool to reform others? My mouth was mine and I decided what came out of it. If it came to the crunch I could cobble together a few phrases that had no import and throw them in.

For days I struggled with all of this, unable to come to a decision.

Eventually I came up with a compromise plan. I would ask Company Leader Wang Zhao to pass the message to Tian Yong that I wanted to see him. I would then persuade Tian Yong to arrange for me to see my husband once, alone, and I would ask my husband how confident he was he could get me out. Then I would reform or not reform according to how he answered. I was not planning to make a losing deal.

The next day I heard Wang Zhao's voice in the office. I decided to proceed with my plan. I walked along the corridor with leaden steps. I was not about to recant but I could not deceive myself. Where was this taking me? Where was my life headed? Would the damage and humiliation my actions caused Falun Gong be greater than their positive effects? Would I be able to do what I planned after I got out?

I did not know the answer to any of these questions and I felt I was walking a tightrope from which I could topple at any moment and be smashed to smithereens.

I gritted my teeth and walked on, against my better judgement.

Wang Zhao had just come on duty and was wiping down the desk as I explained what I wanted.

'Why do you have to talk to Section Chief Tian?' she said in a neutral voice. 'Why can't you talk to one of the team leaders?'

I realised then how naïve I was. Wang Zhao was about 40 and had just been appointed as the acting team leader of Company 2. The former team leader had been seconded to Masanjia Forced-labour Re-education Camp in Liaoning province to gain from their experience in 'reforming' Falun Gong practitioners. Wang Zhao was, naturally, very keen to work her way into the position of company leader. Her eyebrows were plucked to a fine arch and looked quite feminine, but her little triangle-shaped eyes were sharp and fierce, hard to reconcile with her gender. She had a husky voice, because she was always yelling.

I could see that Wang Zhao wanted the credit for 'reforming' me and that it was fruitless asking her assistance to meet with Tian Yong. I also knew she would not agree to my seeing my husband alone. She had always been wary of me. She had not summoned me once for a talk since I was put in Company 2 but her eyes had followed me everywhere. Tian Yong, in his self-appointed role of man of letters, was eminently more approachable.

I had no idea how to get around this impasse, except to persist in wanting to see Tian Yong.

'I know, I know,' she said coldly, in the end. 'Now go on back.'

'Oh, my goodness,' I said to myself as I came out of the office. 'I've done it!'

My head was spinning and I almost collapsed. I leant against the wall, completely drained, a soft empty shell that anyone passing by could have blown over with a single puff. I stayed there for some time but no one came along the corridor and I was thankful that the little sentry had gone off somewhere and couldn't see me standing there like a corpse. When I finally decided to move, I found I didn't have the strength to stand unaided. The rule was that we had to walk along the right-hand wall of the corridor but I couldn't manage the almost 2-metre gap across so I inched along the left-hand wall. It seemed to take years to travel fifteen metres.

'I have reformed, I have reformed,' I chanted to myself over and over, as if possessed.

Tian Yong came to see me two days later. When I told him I wanted to see my husband he asked me why, and I said I wanted to discuss something I had been thinking about. He persisted, asking me if I was thinking of reforming.

I didn't say anything, but I didn't deny it, either.

'You're really something,' he said, peering at me. 'A major thing like this yet you don't look concerned.'

I knew what he meant. The first few people to reform had experienced quite violent reactions to the sudden collapse of their beliefs, some laughing hysterically, others sobbing inconsolably. Those who had reformed because they could no longer endure physical torture usually fell into deep despair.

I don't know how I looked at that moment; but said to him apathetically, 'I've already suffered; only you didn't see it.'

He looked at me suspiciously for a while, realising there was no point in questioning me further. He seemed to be weighing things up. The worst case scenario was that I would remain unreformed after meeting my husband, so he really had nothing to lose. In the end, as I had expected, he agreed.

Early the next morning I was called to the office, where I found both Tian Yong and Wang Zhao.

Somewhat shamefacedly, Tian Yong told me that he had thought about his responsibility for my being able to live an independent life after my release and that the team leader had thought about it, too. They decided not to let me see my husband.

'Someone in her thirties should be able to make a decision without having to discuss it with her husband', was how he put it.

I knew straight away that Wang Zhao had been pouring her mistrust of me into his ears. She fixed her little eyes on me.

'So, tell us,' she said. 'What is it you can't talk to the team leaders about but that you have to discuss with your husband?'

Unable to lie, equally unable to speak the truth, and with four sharp eyes boring into me, I didn't know what else to do but burst into tears.

Tian Yong burst out laughing. In the many times we had talked together he had always been confident of success but had walked away empty-handed. I had always argued him into silence; he had never reduced me to tears. If this wasn't a 'reformed' me, what was it?

Confident that he had everything under control, he said magnanimously that they wouldn't make things difficult for me. They would give me a day to think it over and would talk to me again tomorrow.

Once again I returned to my room in a state of collapse. Before I went to see Wang Zhao I had told Li Chun my secret plan. I am placing my life in your hands, I had said to her, because I trust you and because I don't want to destroy your faith in Falun Gong. A look of concern had crept over her face as I explained my reasons for 'reforming'.

She was waiting for me on my return, and she asked me what had been said and if they were going to let me see my husband. I told her exactly what had happened, that I hadn't relented or said anything, and that they had given me a day to think it over.

'Think hard about it,' she said, taking my hand with a worried look.

I knew what she was worried about. She understood the forced-labour camp only too well and was concerned that once they knew what I was up to they would have it in for me. 'Deceiving team leaders' was considered a serious crime and carried a hefty penalty.

As I got into bed that night I decided to think it all through carefully, as I still had time to reverse my decision. But despite my resolve I fell asleep straight away. Perhaps the battle that day had taken it out of me; perhaps insufficient sleep over a long period had robbed me of will power; or perhaps I fell asleep at the crucial moment because my thoughts were blocked.

In the morning, Li Chun told me she had been so worried about me that she had hardly slept and that she had had a nightmare just before she woke up. She dreamed she saw Zhang Lei kill somebody but the murder was pinned on me and the police were looking for me, to kill me. Li Chun hid me and the police seized Kuai Wei instead. Li Chun and I sneaked into court the following day to see her trial and discovered that the judge was the real murderer, Zhang Lei!

As I tidied the folds of my quilt I thought about Li Chun's dream. It was rather symbolic that the judge was the murderer; but why had Kuai Wei been seized instead of me? Had I harmed her? Suddenly I was overwhelmed by a dread of such cosmic proportions that I wanted to hurl my quilt to the ground and rush to Wang Zhao shouting, 'No! No! I am not reforming!'

Instead, I broke into a cold sweat, and clutched my quilt to me as if my life depended on it.

That day I forced myself to sit quietly in our room trying to work out where that dread had come from. I soon thought that I had discovered the reason: I was afraid I could not bear the responsibility of sabotaging Dafa. I was afraid that I was making the gravest of mistakes, and that I would regret it in the future. Then I counselled myself forcefully: No, do not let fear of retribution stop you doing what you have to do.

That night I wrote a report on my thoughts that I titled 'A new understanding in New Peace Camp'. (Tiantanghe Forced-Labour Re-education Camp, originally battalion-sized, had grown so large that it had been upgraded to an independent Forced-Labour Re-education Camp and renamed Xin'an or New Peace.)

After beating about the bush I finally came to the part where I had to write those words my brain demanded but my heart refused. My pen found a compromise, writing it as 'no longer exercise Falun Gong'.

I felt slightly sick after writing this phrase but also a little bit satisfied. Not acknowledging the practice of Falun Gong as cultivating moral character, the government always referred to Falun Gong practitioners as 'Falun Gong exercisers'.

'Did I "exercise" Falun Gong?' I asked myself. 'Never. I "practise"; I do not "exercise". I have not lied.'

The date was October 10, 2000.

I felt I had been flayed alive several times over by the time I handed over my guarantee to no longer exercise Falun Gong. The question that now confronted me was how I was going to comport myself: how was I to adapt to my new label? If I continued to act strictly in accordance with what was demanded of a practitioner, surely I would be corroborating the lie upon which reforming rested: that you could be a good person, as before, after you reformed. I did not want to become a 'good reformed person' for that would only confuse incoming practitioners even more. But that didn't mean I had to become a 'bad reformed person', did it? Knowing what being good entailed, I could not just discard all self-discipline.

I experienced considerable angst before resolving to act as before in all things except rescinding my guarantee. That way, when upon my release I declared everything I had previously written to be invalid, perhaps the police, the regulars, and the 'reformed' Falun Gong practitioners would all think back on how I had been while I was in the camp. She was pretty good all around, they might say; she was a good person. Why did such a good person do what she did, they might ask; and the answer might be that perhaps there's something in this Falun Gong.

Then one day, out of the blue, I had a sudden flash of inspiration: I could still cultivate. I could still cultivate!

Yes, I could still cultivate because I wanted to, because every cell in my body was used to practising cultivation, because it was simply impossible for me not to cultivate. This is how Zhang Qing had put it in a thought report: 'Cultivation is my only form of existence'. This sentence brought tears to my eyes when I read it. Yes, cultivation was my only form of existence, too; on the deepest level, my life demanded it.

Yes, the *Fa* was still lodged in my heart and I hadn't forgotten a word of what my teacher had said. No matter how many mistakes I had made, who could stop me if I wanted to change for the better?

Li Hongzhi had also spoken of the perfect harmony of Dafa being evident in its transformation of bad things into good things. This great cosmic Dafa was undoubtedly able to harmonise perfectly everything I did.

The life that had been lost to me, the life essence that had been lost to me, surged silently from the innermost recesses of my heart, filling my entire being in an instant. No shocks, no surprises; perfectly naturally and perfectly calmly I seemed to return to how I had been before 'reforming'.

DECEIVING MYSELF AND DECEIVING OTHERS

I believed I had perfectly 'harmonised' my reforming and would be able to continue on in that way. It took me sixteen months to realise how horribly, how shamefully wrong I was, what an appalling line of fallacious reasoning I had followed. When I did realise what I'd done, burning hot tears rolled down my face and I sobbed uncontrollably. I vowed a thousand times over that I would die rather than ever make the same mistake again if I were to put into the same environment.

After cooling down from my bitter regret and shame, I managed to see objectively that, if at the beginning I still knew that writing the guarantee rendered me unworthy of being a Dafa disciple, I became one of those reformed people I had always felt so bitterly sorry for; and I began to profane the sanctity of Dafa and cultivation from that moment. I believed I was still cultivating Dafa but in fact I identified as a reformed person. This conduct that 'originated from Dafa but failed to validate Dafa' was the most serious blasphemy and had nothing whatsoever to do with Dafa. But it was such a minuscule deviation that I was entirely ignorant of it for the entire sixteen months to follow.

In the article 'Buddha-nature and demon-nature', contained in

Essentials for Further Advancement, Li Hongzhi discusses certain dimensional levels in the universe where two different kinds of substances exist, 'pervading certain dimensions from top to bottom, or from the microscopic level to the macroscopic level'. The lower the level the more marked the mutual opposition, giving rise to the principle of mutual generation and mutual inhibition through which appears the opposition between kindness and wickedness, right and wrong, and good and evil.

According to this, the higher the level, the less marked will become the mutual opposition between the two substances, so that at certain times there may be a very small distance between Buddhas and demons, between the Buddha *dao* and the demon *dao,* between truth and falsehood.

There are also critical junctures in cultivating that do not necessarily appear in this dimension but that may appear in other, predictable, places. Once the thought of acting wrongly occurs, you are doomed for many lifetimes and there is no escape. Shakyamuni vanquished untold numbers of external demons as he sat for 49 days beneath the bodhi tree before he was able to succeed in his cultivation and become enlightened. At the critical moment, those who cultivate the *dao* through 'setting up a bodily crucible and furnace to make *dan*[22] using gathered medicinal herbs[23]' enter a dimension of delusion where they attain whatever they most desire: for example, those intoxicated by lust would see the man or woman of their dreams; murderers and robbers see themselves seeking refuge as monks to avoid being thrown into prison, only to be told when they meet some local people that upon his ascension the new emperor had declared a general amnesty. Once the thought of acting wrongly occurs, however, their world of illusion ceases to exist and by the time you have quite woken up to reality you have probably lost your chance forever. The most frightening thing is that the individual is always unaware of the demonic forces creeping in.

Those who feared cruel torture were beaten cruelly; those who

---

22 *Dan* (dahn) is the energy cluster in a cultivator's body, collected from other dimenions.

23 'Setting up a bodily crucible and furnace to make *dan* using gathered medicinal herbs' is a Taoist metaphor for internal alchemy.

did not have a clear understanding of the principles of *Fa* were befuddled with false reasoning. I had experienced and survived these trials, but was finally fooled by my own delusion of 'doing it for Dafa, doing it to expose evil'.

Where was the chink in my armor? It was my attachment to *doing* things. During that period when I wrote my 'divorce statement' and left home, when I pressed fearlessly on in the spirit of the solitary hero, when I was travelling all over the place with my fellow practitioners, I had utterly abandoned my attachment to the physical things of this world. But instantly, I had replaced it with an attachment to *doing* things. Seeing so many of my fellow practitioners being unsure of how to guard Dafa, as I had once been, and then marching purposefully forth after hearing what I had to say, I allowed the mantle of leadership to settle on my shoulders. Such attachments were extremely difficult to detect since they seemed to be part and parcel of my resolute and indomitable spirit. I could not see it, however, and those of my fellow practitioners who felt a little uneasy about my inappropriate zeal didn't know how to broach the subject with me.

I had seen myself as a leader, as special and different. My being isolated at the detention centre, my not being sent to the training unit with the other steadfast practitioners at the labour camp: all this was to strengthen my attachment and to lead me eventually to destruction. I had sat in the corridor weighing up the pros and cons of 'reforming', coldly assessing each of the practitioners who remained steadfast, and I had said to myself, 'If I don't do it, who will?' I was quite unaware that my megalomania had grown to such outrageous proportions.

Even in senior middle school I had been concerned about being first. And although I was not particularly interested in making a name for myself in the ordinary world, after I started cultivating I took to reckoning up my successes and failures and my achievements in cultivation. I noted that I was in the first group in the Beijing area to be sentenced to the forced-labour re-education camp and in the first group to be sent on from the despatch division. My article was quoted by the *People's Daily* and top-ranking leaders in Beijing knew of me. I even noticed that mine had been the first name to be called when we were to leave the despatch division and that I had been the first to be summoned for talks with the police at the forced-labour camp. I had reckoned up so many firsts, and now I had become the 'first' to discover further false grounds for 'reforming'.

Another major reason was 'insufficient righteous thoughts', not being able to distinguish what was my true self, and the 'chink' that existed while I was studying *Fa*. I had been intoxicated with the image of myself as an accomplished military master, penetrating with consummate ease Xiao Yu's false defences of reform even as she advanced them, one after the other. It had never occurred to me that in fact one righteous thought can subdue a hundred evils and that as soon as righteous thoughts go forth to battle the evil demons self-destruct. There had been no need for me to analyse those false grounds and reveal precisely where they were wrong just so that I could continue to be steadfast. That far-off voice that told me to write a guarantee was not my voice; I was tempted by the bait of exposing evil and I fell for it.

I was aware that intellectuals who treated *Fa* on a purely intellectual level always came a cropper, but I had never realised that I, too, had this weakness because it was so well concealed. After I had dealt with Xiao Yu, this 'method' of resorting to theory to refute evil reached a dead-end.

Even in those perennial battles of wits with Tian Yong, hadn't I confused intellectual posturing and bravado with clear-headed spiritual wisdom?

What was even more frightening was that I believed I had undergone ordeals and passed tests, had let go of life and death. I had told myself that was why I could do what others couldn't. And because I had undergone those ordeals and was up to standard it was a waste of time for me to remain in the labour camp.

This was a typical case of breeding demons in my own mind. No being in the universe could say it no longer adhered to the cosmic *Fa* principles. The dread I had felt after hearing Li Chun's dream must have been innumerable beings in some invisible space beating their breasts in agonised supplication. But I didn't realise this, nor did I recognise it for what it was—an instinctive warning from my true nature. We must at all times remain in awe of heavenly principles.

Furthermore, was I really so staunch, so immovable? The night of my battle with the reformed practitioners, I had managed to talk to Hao Ying when meeting her in the toilet. I had asked her to contact my husband after she got out and tell him that they had started to torture me. She was to tell him he had to think of something quickly, since I would die rather than 'reform'.

I hadn't realised I was already afraid; afraid of being deprived of sleep. That dread had been etched on my heart since that sleepless night of the rush job in Entry Company. So perhaps all that rationalising had been nothing more than an attempt to hide from myself and everybody else the dread I felt.

This was truly what Li Hongzhi described as being put 'through a comprehensive and destructive test that targets all human thoughts and attachments'. Ohh! All my failings that had not yet been rectified and all my new attachments were now laid bare to great effect, fuelling the fire by leading me to the path of evil enlightenment where I could not remain firm in righteous thoughts. This was the bitterest lesson of all for me and for many other practitioners in the forced-labour camps.

THE LITTLE DEMONS ARE THE DIFFICULT ONES

Li Chun's first reaction when I told her I was thinking of 'reforming' was that as soon as I did so they would move me to another squad, and she didn't want that to happen.

This was indeed what usually happened in Company 2; their policy was to keep people of like minds together and pick us off one by one. But after I handed over my guarantee, the expected transfer didn't eventuate, nor was there the fanfare I had expected would accompany the reform of such a die-hard; it was almost as if no one actually knew I had reformed. I was a bit surprised but didn't give it a great deal of thought because I was happier to remain with Li Chun than to be put with the other reformed women.

However, shortly afterwards a new addition to Squad 3—Fu Lai—told me she had just reformed and that she would be going home within the month. I had groaned inwardly when Fu Lai joined our squad because she was always wanting to share experiences and exchange views with me, probing into the ways in which Falun Gong was 'heretical'.

This particular day, Tian Yong had brought a guest around to Squad 3 and, not without pride, had introduced me: 'And this is our brilliant Beida graduate.'

'I hear that you used to be particularly stubborn?' the guest responded, addressing me directly.

'Yes.'

'Then what happened?'

'Then I started thinking differently about things.'

'So what's your current view of Falun Gong?'

'As a citizen I must adopt the stance of the nation and the people in thinking problems through.'

At this, Tian Yong led the guest off, looking very satisfied.

Fu Lai had been listening closely to this exchange and as soon as they had gone she started.

'You certainly have a way with words, don't you?' she said. '"Adopt the stance of the nation and the people in thinking problems through"! Let me ask you. Is Falun Gong an evil cult?'

Suddenly filled with emotion and ready for a quarrel, I returned the compliment. 'What point is there in my saying it is or it isn't an evil cult?' I said to her. 'The government says it's an evil cult!'

Seeing I was on the verge of giving myself away, Li Chun quickly interrupted.

'That's enough, you two,' she said. 'Listen! What's going on outside?'

I realised straight away that I had been wrong to get worked up. What she said was her business and I didn't have to get caught up in it. Nor should I be speaking to anyone in an argumentative tone of voice.

'You have to be careful,' Li Chun said to me quietly when we were alone. 'It's easy to deal with the king of hell; it's the little demons that are difficult. She might be a plant and you don't want her informing on you to the team leaders.'

Regulars despised informers, preferring to sort things out between themselves rather than involve the police.

Two days later Feng Yulan was summoned to the office.

'I ask you,' Wang Zhao growled at her. 'Has Zheng Zeng reformed? No, she hasn't! What do you two whisper about all day long? If you don't tell me I'll give you so many shocks you won't know what's hit you!'

But Feng Yulan wasn't intimidated.

'We don't whisper about anything,' she replied in her distinctive measured tones. 'She's a postgraduate and I can't even read; what could we possibly whisper about? Sometimes I ask her advice when I've got a problem with my knitting.'

'That's all? She hasn't "widely spread *Fa*" to you? Tell me! What is Falun Gong?'

'I haven't studied it. I don't really understand; I just know it's been called a cult.'

'Listen. If you're taking me for a ride you'll really pay for this!'

When Feng Yulan told me about this I didn't take it too much to heart, but then one day about noon the quiet corridor echoed with the ring of the telephone.

'Zhao Ran!' the officer who answered it called. 'Quick! Someone's ringing to get the names of those who have not reformed.'

'The people in Company 2 who have not reformed,' Zhao Ran shouted in response, 'are Bai Lian, Zhou Jie, Wang Rong, Zheng Zeng...'

My heart sank and I thought I would die from dejection and irritation. They still counted me as unreformed! Here I was, having sold my soul completely and gone through all those agonies, and they still had me recorded on their lists as unreformed.

All that afternoon I felt my heart was being pulverised by a giant roller and my chest heaved as if some filthy object were lodged in it. I felt sick and in deep distress, unable to catch my breath. A voice in my head jeered over and over: You tried to steal a chicken and you've ended up losing the rice.

A HEROIC DEED

There was a commotion outside our room on the night of November 4, a Saturday. First the little sentry was changed, then no one was allowed out of their rooms or even permitted to open their doors.

Most nights we were cut a little slack. During wash time and when people were coming and going the regulars would slip off to have a few words with friends in other squads or would arrange to meet for a chat in the toilet block. Usually the police and the little sentries would turn a blind eye.

That night, however, the moment 18-year-old Zheng Jia poked her head out the door, the new little sentry shouted down the corridor: 'You're not allowed out of your squad rooms! Get back inside!' Grumbling and swearing, Zheng Jia did as she was told. I didn't pay much attention and went on with my knitting. It didn't affect me because I never went gadding about anyway. They kept a close watch on Falun Gong practitioners so whenever I wanted to contact practitioners in other squads I would get Feng Yulan to be my runner. At such times, her plump body would become as agile as a young girl's and she would look as excited and proud as a child entrusted with a major mission.

Zheng Jia grumbled on and slowly I began to feel something was up. It was only when Fu Lai came back, right at bedtime, that I realised she hadn't been in the room all evening. Her face was flushed and she seemed strangely stimulated.

'Did you know?' she said to me excitedly. 'There's a big battle on tonight—we're educating Bai Lian! I've come back to recharge my batteries; then I'll go back and relieve Xiang Hong and the others. This time we have to drive out the evil in her.'

So they were doing this! And they had actually found a theoretical basis for beating people: to drive out evil!

I lay sleepless on my bunk, my heart in turmoil. I thought back to that dreadful night they had surrounded me. Summoning all my strength I had barely been able to withstand only verbal attacks; how could Bai Lian bear something even worse? Listening as hard as I could, I heard muffled voices and sharp cries coming from the office. I didn't dare imagine what they were doing and I kept tensing up then weakening, and breaking out in a sweat. I wanted to rush out and get the police; I wanted to rush to the office and lean protectively over Bai Lian. But . . . I had 'reformed'. How could I do that now?

Now I really understood the meaning of torment and I knew what hell on earth was.

The next morning at breakfast I saw Bai Lian sitting a table away from me. The whole left side of her face was purple, her lips were swollen and her face was covered with the imprints of fingernails. Tears trickled down my face and when Feng Yulan, who was sitting opposite me, turned and caught sight of Bai Lian she, too, started crying.

I looked away out the window, eating my *mantou*. I didn't dare stop eating and I didn't dare wipe away my tears. There were no offi-

cers near me to see my tears but I couldn't count on them not noticing any unusual gestures. I couldn't let them know I still harboured
any sympathy for people who had not reformed.

That night Li Chun was called away after we had done our ablutions. Fu Lai was missing, too, as usual. When Li Chun came back she
looked angry and scared.

'What's up?' I asked her.

'What's up!? They just called a meeting and they want me to go
with them tonight to do some educating, that's what's up. They said
there is still evil in Bai Lian and they're going to stick needles in the
tops of her thighs, her armpits and the soles of her feet because that's
where they said evil things hide. And they're going to stuff garlic in
her mouth . . . I've always been afraid of ghosts. What they said really
frightens me. What am I going to do? Tell me what I should do! I'm
not game to say I won't go, because they'll tell the team leader
straight away.'

All those years in the forced-labour camps and the poor woman
was more afraid of team leaders than of demons. She was so agitated
she was almost in tears.

'Kneel down before her!' I blurted out. 'As soon as you kneel they
won't be able to beat her.'

'Right! That's what I'll do. Damn it! The nerve of them, getting
me to go. And see if I'll let them get what they want!'

Once Li Chun had set her mind on cultivating Falun Gong, she
had resolved to mind her speech, as required of practitioners, and
she had stopped using foul language. She had been appointed squad
leader of Squad 3 after Hao Ying left and had devised a rule to stop
herself as much as anybody else using bad language: the penalty for
bad language was sweeping the toilets. It had been extremely effective in cleaning up just about everybody's language. But this time,
when long-time non-perpetrator Li Chun broke her own rule I
didn't have the heart to bring it to her attention.

After she had gone my mind was awhirl, worrying that my suggestion was a truly stupid idea. If Li Chun knelt before Bai Lian while
they were trying to get her to write a guarantee, might this not exert
even greater pressure on her than a beating would? What if it made
her write one? Heavens, I thought to myself, what have I done?

Seeing me in an obvious state of agitation, Feng Yulan grabbed
my hand.

'Zheng Zeng,' she said, looking into my eyes, 'remember the date—November 5. When you get out and write that book, don't forget today is November 5.'

Li Chun came back just before dawn looking exhausted but content. She couldn't wait to tell me what had happened.

'What a great idea!' she said gleefully. 'To begin with I didn't pay any attention to them and let them carry on. Then, when they were just about to strike her, I just plonked myself down and knelt before her, boom! "Bai Lian," I said, "we've been together in the same squad and it's been really good. You're old enough to be my mother; adopt me as your daughter!" Then I just went on kneeling there. They couldn't really beat her; all they could do was stand there and urge her to write a guarantee and say that if she didn't I'd suffer from all that kneeling. Hah! Fortunately I was wearing padded trousers, because I was on my knees for over two hours. She didn't write it and I couldn't very well get up. This couldn't go on forever, and Team Leader Su came and took Bai Lian and me on a tour of the training unit. One, she wanted Bai Lian to see what it was like, sort of get the wind up her a bit. And two, it got me out of a hole. I'd been kneeling for so long I could hardly walk. Bai Lian hadn't slept for two nights and she insisted on carrying me! I really *would* like her to adopt me, you know. When Team Leader Su wasn't looking I whispered to Bai Lian. "Whatever you do," I said to her, "don't write a guarantee. I really admire you standing up to this many people. It was worth kneeling before you!"'

News of Li Chun's 'heroic deed' spread through the company as the morning progressed. The police praised her willingness to do her bit for the company; the regulars expressed their pleasant surprise at her—this hooligan—coming up with such a smart move; the 'reformed' people commented on the compassion Li Chun exhibited despite not having practised Falun Gong. But the unreformed Falun Gong practitioners understood that she had done what she did purely to protect Bai Lian. Suddenly, in everybody's eyes Li Chun was a good person and she, who had never in her life impressed anybody, was very proud of herself.

———

A few nights later the corridor suddenly rang to the sound of Wang Rong's agonised voice.

'Reporting, Team Leader!' she shouted. 'Someone's being beaten!' This was immediately followed by another voice.

'Get back inside! How dare you report to the team leader! Are you going to go on being difficult? Can't you take even this?'

It sounded as though someone dragged Wang Rong back into the room, and quiet was restored. A few days later I heard that Wang Rong had finally reformed and had written a renunciation.

My first thought on hearing this was that I had to see her straight-away lest there be some mishap. No opportunity presented itself for a couple of days but then I got word through a regular from Squad 5 that Wang Rong wanted to see me. Another day passed and despite my anxiety I still couldn't find a way to see her. The regular who had brought the message urged me to go and see her.

I finally got my chance on the fourth day, when Squad 3's TV set broke down and we were told to take our stools to Squad 5 to watch the news. The CCTV news was our compulsory daily lesson in pol-itics; if there were items attacking Falun Gong we would have to watch these several times.

And there was Wang Rong, in Squad 5, sitting lifeless and expres-sionless among the crowd. I placed my stool beside her and she moved along mechanically to make room, not seeming to have any idea who I was, or to care. After everybody was settled and the news had started I leaned over to her.

'Wang Rong,' I said softly. 'It's me.'

Because of her poor sight her hearing was very acute and she heard me immediately, although I had spoken too softly for others to hear. She grabbed my hand as if she feared I might run away. It was no surprise when she indicated she planned to kill herself; she had wanted to see me one more time before she did it.

'Whatever you do, you must not act on this thought, Wang Rong,' I whispered to her. 'You cherish Dafa, don't you? If you cherish Dafa you cannot think like this. If you killed yourself they wouldn't admit they had hounded you to death; they'd say you had died from prac-tising Falun Gong. And this would harm Dafa, wouldn't it?

'I know the agony you are going through,' I went on. 'Don't think about yourself so much; if you think more about Dafa and about others you will be able to go on. Your living on is witness to this per-secution. When you get out you can expose everything you went through in the forced-labour camp. Your life is valuable; you can't die, no matter what. Besides, our teacher has said practitioners shouldn't take any life, didn't he, let alone their own? He even said that suicide is a crime, didn't he?

'You might think that you are no longer worthy to be a practitioner since you wrote a renunciation but let me tell you, you still know in your heart that writing a renunciation statement is not right. In this sense you are so much better than those who thought they could only reach consummation by "reforming"! You cannot die, no matter what!'

I had been holding her hand while I was talking to her, until tears spilled from her dispirited eyes, as if all of a sudden she had regained feeling within her that pained her again. I knew then she had finally given up the thought of killing herself. The TV announcer prattled on. Some of the women were listening to the TV, others weren't paying any attention as they chatted among themselves, but none of them was aware how close the forced-labour camp had come to costing a life.

THE ECONOMIC BENEFITS OF 'HELP SESSIONS'

One afternoon in mid-November I was sent out to do some watering, escorted by Wang Zhao.

The higher-ups were very satisfied with the reports of 'reforms' in the forced-labour camps. Previously they had been unable to come up with an effective way of dealing with Falun Gong practitioners, many of whom had been in and out of detention centres without missing a beat in their practice. But now reforms were actually taking place and the reformed people were ready and willing to lend the government a helping hand in educating others! Hadn't the forced-labour re-education camps rendered outstanding service?

Since October, all the major ministries and commissions in Beijing had sent the Falun Gong practitioners in their employ to the labour camps to attend 'help sessions' (brainwashing classes). The labour camp had ceased running lectures, which had not been very effective and were therefore a waste of money, and had instead opened the auditorium as a help session venue where education aides plied their trade.

Those whose work units were below ministerial level were not sent to the camp because this would have required more education aides than were realistically available. The first group to be 'cared for' were from the Chinese Academy of Sciences, the Chinese Academy of Social Sciences and organisations directly under the Central Committee. Some of them were the heads of their work units, the lowest-ranked departmental heads. Once upon a time the forced-labour camps had dealt only with petty thieves and prostitutes; they had never seen so many prestigious figures in one place before. Shuttling back and forth all day between these politically important people bearing red 'Distinguished Guest' cards on their chests, Tian Yong walked around the camp with even more of a roll in his gait.

A great many of these people refused to be 'educated': some had had to be forced into vehicles by unit leaders; others were tricked into thinking they were to take part in political studies of one sort or another. Some refused to get out of their vehicles when they saw they had been brought to a forced-labour camp and had to be lifted out bodily.

Things were relatively civilised at first but as time went on these people were subjected to the same methods as were used in 'reforming' inmates. They were not allowed to go home at night but were kept under guard in the visitors' room. They were deprived of sleep for days and nights on end, then bombarded with that load of false invective; they were beaten, abused and physically punished in whatever way those 'educating' them wished. 'Reform study classes' ran for a term of fifteen days and those who did not reform were re-enrolled for a second term. If they still hadn't reformed after a third term they were given a one-way ticket to the forced-labour re-education camp on the spot.

Quite a few people were 'reformed' in this way. The key to it was that for every individual who was brought into the reform classes the labour camp received 10,000 *yuan* in 'tuition fees' from that individual's work unit. Ten thousand *yuan* each! Soon the forced-labour camps were making a fortune. Each year the labour camps were given a profit target. If a camp didn't meet it the police didn't get their bonus.

I don't know what the figure was for our Xin'an camp but I recall reading in the internal labour-camp newspaper that the targets for Shuanghe and Tuanhe camps were one million and 500,000 *yuan* respectively.

As a point of comparison, it would be interesting to know just how much Xin'an camp earned in from our knitting. It was probably a pittance. It took us on average fourteen to fifteen hours to knit a flawless cushion and for this the camp received 80 cents. In February 2001 the camp received an urgent order from Nestlé for 100,000 toy rabbits. At least 30 processes taking over 10 hours were involved in making each one; the camp got a measly 30 cents per rabbit. So, it took several hundred people working flat out and overtime for two or three months to make 100,000 rabbits for which the camp received 30,000 *yuan*. The police had to stand guard while we worked and this wearied them as well. They had to be extra-vigilant while we were wielding sharp tools in our work, to make sure no one got violent or committed suicide.

But this! Who wouldn't want to be in a business that required no capital but raked in 10,000 *yuan* per person accepted for 'reforming'? The manual labour involved in knitting couldn't compete with this sort of economic performance. That's why Wang Zhao beamed with joy every time she looked at those expert 'education aides' who were earning so much for the labour camp.

There was another regulation in the camps, and this was that if any reformed person 'turned over' within six months of being released the police officer who had signed the release form was fined 5,000 *yuan*, or more than six months' salary.

('Turning over' was when 'reformed' Falun Gong practitioners declared any guarantees they had written in a forced-labour re-education camp to be invalid and resumed their practice.)

'TURNING OVER'?

It is obvious from this, now, why Wang Zhao fixed her little eyes on me in such an unsettling way that day she escorted me out to do the watering. It was an awkward situation and I kept my head down as I went silently on with my task.

'Zheng Zeng,' she said finally. 'I can see you're not as obsessed with Falun Gong as some people are. They have genuinely stepped forward to protect *Fa* but what are you up to? What was your purpose in coming to the labour camp? What do you intend to do when you get out? A person must be patriotic, you know. What good does it do to throw the nation into turmoil? You're too inexperienced to get mixed up in politics. I haven't paid much attention to you all this

244 • **Witnessing History**

time, but you'd better not play the team leaders for fools, thinking you're so clever. Think carefully about what I've said today and write a thought report clearly stating where you stand.'

I felt a shiver run through me. How did she know what was on my mind? This was dreadful!

When I got back to the squad I thought her questions over. If I looked at it from her perspective, I could understand her saying I was not 'deeply obsessed' with Falun Gong. But why ask me what my purpose was in coming to the labour camp? That was really wronging me. What purpose *could* I have had? To protest against my being put to forced labour and having to endure electric shocks, of course! But why had she phrased it like that?

Suddenly I remembered joking about writing a book and making a film, but this had been before I 'reformed'. This must have somehow got back to her; perhaps she believed I had come to the camp to observe and to gain real-life experience, not because I was a genuine Falun Gong practitioner. And she probably believed that now I had gained about as much as I could from being there I had simply written the guarantee in order to get out.

When I initially joked about writing a book, I envisaged that I would remain absolutely steadfast until the day I could, with dignity, walk out of the labour camp after Falun Gong's name was reinstated; I had not really meant to write one. However, after I decided I really would write a book and wrote my guarantee, I never said another word about it.

But where had all that stuff about 'patriotism' and 'getting mixed up in politics' come from? She surely couldn't know I was thinking of leaving the country and applying for refugee status? She must have been bluffing.

I went over these questions again and again, but I couldn't come up with any answers and I was at a loss as to how to respond. In the end I posed myself some additional questions: Why was this happening? Why did they still count me among the unreformed when I'd written my guarantee more than four weeks ago? The only answer I could come up with was that I had been wrong and that I shouldn't go off on these wild tangents. Dafa didn't need me to get out and write a book; adhering to the principles of a practitioner was more important than anything.

OK, so should I turn over right then and there? It wouldn't be such a big deal, would it? And I suddenly felt no more desire to escape the labour camp.

I picked up my pen and straight away wrote five pages, in which I calmly acknowledged that I had not reformed and that I had written my guarantee for the sole purpose of getting out and exposing the darkness of the forced-labour re-education camp.

When I finished I didn't feel elated or distressed, just very ordinary and at peace. My head was completely empty and I had given no thought at all to what would happen after I handed this report in. As I walked to the mess hall I looked at the modular training unit and a thought flashed through my mind: even if I want to make more mistakes, after this I will never have the chance.

NOT 'TURNING OVER'

Wang Zhao did not come to work the following day; Cheng Cui summoned me to the office instead. The expansion of the labour camp had led to a special education section being established for the task of 'reforming' Falun Gong practitioners and she had been appointed its section head. She had come back especially to see me. She had a thought report I had written after I reformed and said it was so well written that she would like me to make a copy for her to use in her work.

I forget my exact words in that report; I think it was about citizens having to be patriotic and law-abiding. I had beaten about the bush a lot in everything I had written since reforming, mercilessly dissecting my own weaknesses and errors but never mentioning Falun Gong and not using any Falun Gong terminology.

A voice started up in my head when I returned to my room after copying out the report. See, it said, Team Leader Cheng said your thought report was pretty good. She has approved your reform so there is a hope you will actually get out. You must not turn over, whatever you do. And I started torturing myself again. Turn over? Don't turn over? Turn over? Don't turn over? Hamlet and his 'To be or not to be' had nothing on me; I was in an absolute agony of indecision.

Eventually I gritted my teeth and got out the five pages I had written the previous day. I tore them up and started again.

I began by saying that I had not come to the forced-labour re-education camp with a purpose. I was at home asleep when I was arrested and I had no idea I would end up doing forced labour. If my purpose in practising Falung Gong had been to come to the forced-labour camp I would have put up banners in Tian'anmen, but even that was no guarantee that I would be sentenced to forced labour. I was not the one who had set up the forced-labour re-education camp, I wrote, so how could I plan to come and go as I wish? At the despatch division I had been rendered unconscious with electric prods because I refused to accept the forced-labour re-education verdict. Team Leader Wang could verify this for herself.

Then I wrote that had I not been patriotic I could have left the country many times. My postgraduate tutor and my fellow students had all gone to America and it would have been extremely easy for me to have done the same. I chose to remain in China simply because I loved my country and I loved its traditions and culture.

Had I wanted to be involved in politics, I wrote, I would have stayed at the State Council's Development Research Centre. Two other postgraduates had been assigned there at the same time as me: one was now a deputy mayor and the other deputy director of a ministerial-level provincial committee set up to reform systems. I chose to leave because I *wasn't* interested in politics and it didn't suit me there. I wrote that while Team Leader Wang might think me arrogant and full of smart suggestions I did possess sufficient self-knowledge to know that I didn't have what it takes to be involved in politics. I reminded her that she had said this to me herself.

Also, my entire family enjoyed considerable social status and was quite well off. You could say, I wrote, that we have profited from the economic reforms and the opening up of Chinese markets, so there would be no point in me being disruptive, or 'throwing the nation into turmoil'.

I went on in this fashion, responding to her questions one by one. I was exhausted by the time I had finished and felt slightly sick, but satisfied at the same time. There, I said to myself, I had not told a single lie and it was up to her what she made of it.

Wang Zhao came to see me the day after I handed in my report. She asked why I had written what I had written. Why would the team leaders suspect I had an agenda in coming to the labour camp?

This was a stroke of luck. Whatever she thought of the rest of it, at least she believed I had not come to the forced-labour camp to experience 'slice-of-life' realism and gather material for a book. This was good.

'Is that right?' I replied. 'You didn't suspect me? It must have been me being neurotic then.'

She went on to tell me that because I was a postgraduate, Section Head Tian had pinned great hopes on me but I had never come up with the goods. She also wondered why I wasn't writing anything now, when I had written so well before. She believed that if I straightened out my thinking I could write wonderful thought reports, but I obviously lacked motivation. She suggested I give it some consideration.

'EXPOSING AND REPUDIATING'

A few days later, Team Leader Cong from the education section called all the 'reformed' women in Company 2 together—including me, this time—and gave us a very long questionnaire. It asked:

'How did you start practising Falun Gong?'

'Why did you want to practise Falun Gong?'

'What sensations and changes did you experience after taking it up?'

'What sort of activities did you participate in to appeal for Falun Gong after it was banned?'

'What were your thoughts on first coming to the labour re-education camp?'

'Why did you not reform?'

'What was it that later convinced you to reform?'

'What was your attitude towards Falun Gong after you reformed?'

'What are your future plans?'

Team Leader Cong told us this was part of a special research project on Falun Gong as a social issue that the Chinese Academy of Social Sciences had been instructed to carry out to support the government's anti-Falun Gong struggle. She hoped everyone would give detailed answers to all the questions but they were especially interested in the process that had turned around our stubborn adherence to Falun Gong and how we had shaken off its spiritual shackles.

What particular thing was it that a particular person had said and in what specific situation that had led us to reform? What were the key factors? Team leaders were especially interested in this, she said, because they frequently found that the sample scripts the aides had written out merely said that they were 'reformed' with the help of other practitioners. But the details of the 'reforming' process that happened in one's mind were never mentioned, which was very frustrating, so it was important that we give full details this time.

At this, several of the reformed women glanced at each other and smiled. While I, of course, *could* not say what I really thought, they *would* not say because they believed the principles behind their 'reform' to be secret.

Some time earlier, Zhang Qing had discovered this secret that these reformed women kept to themselves.

'Heavens!' she had apparently exclaimed, as if she had just discovered a new continent. 'So these compatriots of mine see "reform" as a continuation of their practice. While they're writing their renunciations—"I want to break with Falun Gong"—they're thinking, "I've broken with a lower level and moved up to a higher level."'

Zhang Qing had decided she must 'expose and repudiate' this deceitful behaviour. So she presented to the police a thought report 'exposing and repudiating' the statements these women had made when they reformed. However, there was absolutely no reaction from the police when they read Zhang Qing's report. This was probably because the police didn't care what anyone thought so long as you wrote a renunciation, for then they had another reformed person to add to their statistics to help them achieve their 'reforming quota', which for Xin'an camp was 95 per cent.

As I returned to my room with the questionnaire I remembered that a few days earlier an officer had told me I must write an 'exposure and repudiation' of Falun Gong, something I hadn't yet done. Perhaps this was why they didn't consider me really 'reformed', because I had never been willing to write such a statement. All I knew, though, was that Falun Gong did not call on us to do anything other than practise Truthfulness, Compassion and Forbearance. Our teacher had not taught us anything else but to do good, to do more good and in everything to take an upright path. Where on earth would I start if I was going to criticise this?

I sat there numbly for a while then started to answer the questions methodically. The first ones were easy and I answered them frankly. When I got to why did I reform, I said I had realised all of a sudden that it was not easy for the state to support a postgraduate student. With all that learning I shouldn't be wasting my time in a forced-labour re-education camp but should go out and use my knowledge for the greater benefit of the people.

Next question: what was my attitude towards Falun Gong since reforming? I knew what they were expecting me to say, but I wouldn't write those words even if they killed me. I laid my head down on the page, surprised that I hadn't died yet or gone mad. Li Chun was watching me with concern.

Some time later I lifted my head and finished writing a passage about my understanding of Falun Gong in one breath.

I was playing with words again. But I could hardly call it 'playing with words', as anyone who took this passage at face value would think that I was criticising Falun Gong. Only I knew that I was actually saying in various permutations that *the government* said Falun Gong posed this danger, *the government* said Falun Gong posed that danger . . .

I was deathly pale when I finished this passage, sure I now understood how a young girl would feel after being violated.

I wrote eighteen pages 'exposing and repudiating'. Why, I wondered grimly, had I ever gone on to postgraduate studies? I had never wished so desperately to be illiterate.

5

真善忍

STORMY SEAS

SQUAD 3 WAS CHANGED AROUND again in mid-November. Fu
Lai was released and Feng Yulan was moved out. Wang Zhao had
never got any information out of Feng Yulan but, fearing she was on
my side, she took the opportunity to move her to the newly created
Company 5. Fortunately she had no such qualms about Li Chun.

Newcomers arrived nearly every fortnight and were squeezed
into the existing companies as well as into the new Company 5.
Squad 3 no longer had the luxury of empty places, but most of our
newcomers were Falun Gong practitioners. Wang Zhao still wanted
to keep me separate from the other students, in case I was de-
reformed by the newcomers, or 'reformed' the old 'reformed' ones
in other directions. Her solution was to transfer Squad 7, the cookhouse squad which was made up entirely of regulars, to Squad 3, then
put the newcomers in Squad 7.

The cookhouse squad kept different hours from everyone else.
They had to get up even earlier, then they were escorted over to the
mess hall every morning to prepare meals. There had been twelve in
the squad when the labour camp had housed only 200 people and
there were still twelve, even though the number of inmates had
expanded to 1,000 with the arrest of so many Falun Gong practitioners. It wasn't that more people couldn't be assigned to the squad;
it was more a matter of real estate. The kitchen ranges were only so

big and there were only so many woks. More people would have only gotten in each other's way, working in such a confined kitchen space. The mess hall was so small that every piece of equipment and every person was constantly on the go just to prepare three meals a day.

The regulars said that it used to be that if you had money you could get stir-fry, and have fancy steamed rolls quite regularly, but Falun Gong had ruined this for them. They could no longer get anything good to eat. The food was getting worse all the time, as well. A dish on the menu board might be called 'Chicken and potato stew', but when it was ladled out into your bowl it was just plain old potato stew, without the chicken pieces. One time Kuai Wei was feeling really hungry.

'Oh,' she said, with a big sigh, 'when will they ever give us "Chicken and chicken stew"!'

It took me ages to get the joke.

Because the cookhouse squad got up so early and worked so hard, they also went to bed earlier than everyone else, which was why they had been originally allocated to Squad 7, at the end of the corridor.

There was a lot of swearing and bad feeling when these regulars were transferred into Squad 3. Theirs had been a special squad and now they were having to room with people who didn't keep the same hours. Also, Squad 3 was right in the middle of the corridor, which was obviously going to affect their sleep.

All of this was a bit difficult for the original occupants of Squad 3, too, who had grown accustomed to sharing the room with only three or four other persons. Fortunately, however, the cookhouse squad women were not there at all during the day and, since we were not able to pick and choose, everybody adapted fairly quickly.

Two other regulars had moved into Squad 3 along with the cookhouse squad. One was a 17-year-old who was in for trafficking in porn. The other was the youngest inmate in the labour camp but also the one who had committed the most serious crime. Thirteen-year-old Huang Fang was in for murder. She had been sentenced to three years, which was the longest term you could spend in a forced-labour camp; it was known as 'the full score'.

Huang Fang's appearance in Squad 3 caused quite a stir. Women found excuses to come to our squad just to have a look at her. She was from rural Anhwei province, a very poor area, and used to go to the market with her brother and his wife, where they killed and sold chickens. Her brother got into a fight over a customer with another family in the same business. During the brawl her sister-in-law had incited her to stab the other family's son, who was only two or three years old. So she grabbed the knife they killed the chickens with and stabbed the child several times in the back, killing him. Because she herself was still a child, she got only three years' forced-labour re-education for the crime.

Because of her age and the nature of her crime, a 24-hour suicide watch was placed on young Huang Fang, a task assigned to the few remaining original occupants of Squad 3. Days were no problem; it was the nights that were hard. There were only four of us—Li Chun, Kuai Wei, Zheng Jia and me—to share the roster and the only way to keep a constant eye on her was to break the nights into four equal watches.

Huang Fang was only a child but apart from some tears in the first few days, most nights she just slept. Those of us on duty watching over her grew more sallow by the day, however.

In the dead of night I sat on my bunk fighting to stay alert. As I listened to the others' even breathing I thought back to when we used to take turns on night duty at the detention centre and how I would use the time to practise Falun Gong exercises. And now I really wanted to practise again. I might have written a guarantee and even written a report 'exposing and repudiating', but I somehow felt I had acted in 'perfect harmony'. I had not said I would not practise Falun Gong, nor of course did I see myself as having given it up. It was several months since I had practised the exercises; how could I let this opportunity slip? I didn't give a thought to what the repercussions might be.

I slipped down from my bunk, did the exercises, then climbed back up to sit in meditation. The little sentry only patrolled every twenty minutes and I could perfectly fit in my exercises in the intervals.

Thus was I able to resume doing my exercises at night. As for the daytime, as I knitted I would tell Li Chun what *Zhuan Falun* was all about. I had read it so many times that I practically knew it by heart and as near as I could I repeated it to her in the original wording. I was no longer worried about anyone informing on me now that Fu Lai was gone. With nobody to poke their noses into our business, this was a heaven-sent opportunity.

MOUNT TAI COLLAPSES BEFORE MY EYES

A day later something unexpected happened.

Tian Yong summoned me that night to tell me that Professor Qin had been extremely happy to hear I had reformed and was probably going to come with a reporter from Beijing TV to see me.

'You're a woman of the world,' he said, 'so this won't be a problem for you, will it? There's no need for me to tell you what to say. Professor Qin appreciates talent and we in the labour camp hope you might be able to get out a little early, so we hope you won't let this opportunity slip by.'

My husband had become friendly with Professor Qin, a man in his sixties, after I was arrested. They were planning to set up and run a college together and he seemed to have considerable social connections. Not long after my husband's first visit to the labour camp Professor Qin had used these connections to arrange a 'back-door' visit and, with my husband, had come to see me outside visiting hours. He admired my husband and was happy to do whatever he could to get me out early.

When I heard he wanted me to go on TV I wanted the earth to open up and swallow me.

I have no idea how I managed to finish the talk with Tian Yong. This was all so overwhelming that I was numb when I went back to our room, with not a thought in my head. I remained in a daze for the rest of the night. When it was my turn to go on night duty I did the exercises again, standing in the middle of the room with my eyes shut. I was up to the third exercise when I suddenly heard a voice.

'Zheng Zeng!' it hissed. 'What are you doing?'

I had been discovered. The voice belonged to Cui Rui, a woman in her forties from the cookhouse squad who was in for trafficking in porn. She had woken up to go to the toilet and seen me.

Several others stirred at her voice.

'What was that, Cui Rui?' one of them said sleepily.

'Nothing,' she replied. 'I must have been talking in my sleep.' And she got out of bed and went outside.

I stood there blankly. Should I go and have a chat with her, asking her not to tell the police I had been practising? But then it occurred to me that she had said she was talking in her sleep. Did this mean she wasn't going to say anything? Neither thought made much sense to me, though. Cui Rui came back from the toilet and went back to bed without a word. I finished my shift and then I, too, went to bed without a word.

Wang Zhao summoned me to the office as soon as she came on duty the next morning, her sombre dark face seething with fury.

'How have you been these last few days?' she asked noncommittally.

'Good,' I replied, my scalp crawling.

'Haven't been feeling unwell?'

'No.'

'And last night. What were you doing?'

What was I doing? Cui Rui must have reported to her. But Cui Rui had gone to the mess hall before Wang Zhao came on duty; how could she have had time to do that? I was still trying to work this out when Wang Zhao suddenly raised her voice several decibels, erupting like a volcano.

'How dare you deceive team leaders! How dare you practise Falun Gong half the night!' she yelled. 'You have abused the trust of the team leaders! You must be tired of living! You . . . !'

She had been sitting at her desk about to make some tea when I came in. In her fury her hands began to shake uncontrollably, spilling some tea leaves on her uniform. It was some sort of nourishing tea, with Chinese wolfberry in it, and a speck of red wolfberry caught my eye against the dark blue of the cloth.

Wang Zhao had been on her guard with me all along, worried that I might expose what went on in the forced-labour camp. The one and only time I had a visit after I 'reformed' she had not let me communicate with my husband by phone in the reception room as the others did. Instead, she had taken me to a small room and sat us down on either side of a table. Then she stood there staring at us without a hint of embarrassment. My husband and I couldn't talk, yet we couldn't remain silent; it was an extremely difficult twenty minutes. Now, just when she was almost ready to believe that I had really 'reformed' she was hit with the news that I'd been up half the night practising Falun Gong! It was like watching Mount Tai burst apart to see her vicious rage erupt.

I didn't move a muscle. I stood quietly looking down at her.

'Team Leader Wang,' I said calmly, pointing to the fleck of Chinese wolfberry on her uniform. 'You've dropped some wolfberry.'

Dumbstruck, she looked down to where I was pointing. Then she automatically plucked the tiny red wolfberry from her uniform and dropped it into her mug. By the time she looked up again her hands had stopped shaking and the rage seething under the volcano seemed to have been restrained and melted. She puffed and blew, unable to pull herself together sufficiently to launch another attack.

'Go and write me a good solid self-criticism,' she said eventually. 'And you know the consequences if you don't account fully for that business last night!'

I went back to my room and began to write a self-criticism, acknowledging for the second time that I had not 'reformed' and indicating that I was prepared to accept the consequences of this. Teardrops rolling down my face, I wrote on and on.

The first time I wrote my five-page 'turning over' report I had felt extremely calm; this time my feelings were very complex. On one level I was happy, relieved to have escaped the dreaded TV interview. I couldn't possibly be their 'model reformed person' now and if I had been forced to go on TV I would never have been able to redeem myself. On another level, I was filled with remorse. In an effort to get myself released I had given away what was most precious to me and had died a thousand deaths because of it. Here I was ruining all that, just for several days' exercises. I thought I would never be able to forgive myself.

Another reason for my remorse was Li Chun. I had just finished telling her what the fifth lecture in *Zhuan Falun* was about and had four to go. I had no doubt I would be placed in solitary confinement this time and who would finish *Zhuan Falun* for her then?

After Fu Lai was released I had written out from memory as many of the poems and articles from Falun Gong texts as I could and had given them to Li Chun, who hid them in her clothing to take out and read whenever an opportunity presented itself. One time there was a big search of the squad rooms and we were told to sit in the corridor while the security police went through our bedding and our cupboards, strewing our things everywhere. Then they searched us, one by one.

As it was coming up to Li Chun's turn I saw her slip off to the washroom when no one else was looking. Even though it pained me I felt sure she was going to destroy the articles, for that was the only thing she could do. When she returned from the body search in the main office I couldn't resist asking her if she had thrown the articles away.

'No need,' she chuckled. 'I had them in the lining of my autumn-weight clothes and they didn't find them!'

This moved me almost to tears. Li Chun had taken great risks for those Falun Gong articles, since we could be searched at any moment. Yet through my own simple carelessness I had forfeited the opportunity to tell her the rest of *Zhuan Falun*. She was not a bad person but had spent so many years in forced-labour camps that she had developed some bad habits she herself was unaware of. She wouldn't listen if just anybody were to point them out, but I had gained her trust. She had a mind ripe to cultivate but without books to guide her it rested entirely with me to tell her what was in the teachings. If there was no one to take care of her, who could say she wouldn't just drift with the tide? Naturally, I regretted not having fulfilled my obligation to her.

Li Chun had been watching me all this time as I wavered tearfully between happiness and remorse. It took a long time to bring myself to tell her of the events of the previous night and that morning. She was furious.

'Why didn't you wake me up?' she said. 'Something major like that, if I had said something to Cui Rui she wouldn't have ratted on you! You might not be on good terms with her but I've helped her out quite a few times and she owes me. Why didn't you wake me up?'

I have to admit it had never occurred to me and I didn't know what to say except that I hadn't had the heart to disturb her sleep. Which, actually, was true. With us sharing the night watch, lack of sleep was a genuine concern.

'No, it wasn't that,' Li Chun responded. 'I know you still look down on me and you don't see me as a fellow practitioner. If Song Mei was still here you wouldn't have hesitated to wake her up to talk about it. If Feng Yulan was still here you would have woken her up, too. You didn't ask me. You don't think I'm worth . . . anything.' She was so angry she was almost in tears. 'But what you don't know is that Cui Rui is trash and so am I, and because we are both trash she'd have to do me the favour …'

She was heartbroken, tears pouring down her face.

Nor could I hold back my tears. I had no idea my not waking her would wound her so. Yet I couldn't deny that I hadn't thought of her as someone I could discuss things with. Apart from my tears, what more could I say?

We sat facing one another, crying and unable to speak, as if we were parting forever. Suddenly, there was the sound of Tian Yong's cheery voice outside the door.

'And our brilliant Beida student?'

Beaming, Tian Yong walked into Squad 3 with a guest in tow. I didn't have time to wipe the tears from my face before standing up, in accordance with the rule of the camp that inmates must stand up when police entered the room, nor did I really want to wipe them away. One look at my face shattered Tian Yong's good mood. Without a word he turned on his heel and shoved his bewildered guest out the door before him.

None of us knew what would happen next. After dinner, the little sentry announced I had a phone call. Who could be ringing me, I wondered. This was a new development.

The voice on the other end of the phone was so soft and gentle I could hardly believe my ears when it claimed to be Wang Zhao. People say there's nothing worse than a hypocrite and this may be true; all I know is that Wang Zhao's soft and gentle telephone voice upset me more than her furious barking that morning had.

She said she had already knocked off work and was having her day off but was ringing on her own time because she really cared for me.

'I didn't mind my manners very well with you this morning,' she went on. 'I hope you didn't take offence. The team leaders are all looking out for you; if you leave without reforming completely, next time we may very well have to send you to our opposite number.' By this she meant Beijing Women's Prison, somewhere opposite the forced-labour camp, where the criminal offenders were kept.

'Now, about this practising Falun Gong exercises,' she said. 'You needn't worry too much about that. I'll be honest with you; you're not the first to have a relapse. Team leaders understand that people don't necessarily think straight after reforming. I'll get a few people to come round and have a chat with you soon and if there's anything troubling you that you don't feel comfortable talking to the team leaders about then you can discuss it with them. You can talk freely with them; they're like you.

'I haven't been taking enough care of you,' she continued after a slight pause, 'but I'm going to get the duty team leader to transfer you to my squad and then I'll be able to care for you better. After all, students and team leaders are all one big family, aren't we?'

I suspected that all of this talk of how she would take good care of me was the aftermath of Tian Yong coming upon me in tears and realising what had happened. He must have given her a good tongue-lashing about her oversimplified and crude methods and how she had no idea about handling someone like me. How would I present a good mental attitude for the TV journalists in a couple of days' time if she intimidated me like that? He would have pointed out that if this major event went awry the higher-ups would be looking for someone to blame, and he would have asked her meaningfully whom she thought that someone might be.

And sure enough, not long after Wang Zhao hung up some education aides she trusted called me to the office to help me resolve my ideological problems.

I was quite exhausted by then, what with those bouts of crying and not having had much sleep for several days. I set my stool down by the window and hunched over the radiator, turning my back on them. How on earth could they help me resolve any 'ideological problems' I might have?

Wang Zhao had obviously instructed them not to be rough with me and as a consequence they had no idea what to do with me. This stalemate went on for some time until finally they must have thought I'd gone to sleep. They started talking softly among themselves about how pitiful I looked, how dreadful it was, how I still had not come to my senses, how I wouldn't break completely with the past but still wanted to practise Falun Gong and how this attracted evil things, and so on and so on.

Listening to them I didn't know whether to laugh or cry and I wonder now how long this farce would have continued if Tian Yong hadn't turned up just then.

'Ahh!' he called out as he came in. 'Still up and at it! Look who's here, Zheng Zeng. You have quite a reputation.'

Behind him stood Ma Hao, the newly appointed deputy director of the labour camp. He was only about 30, extremely young to have done so well in his career and from the look on his face he felt just fine about it. I had seen him at large meetings but he had never lowered himself to speak to any inmate in the company.

'How's it going?' Tian Yong asked, with what he hoped would pass for concern. 'How's the chat progressing?'

'She won't talk to us,' one of the education aides responded.

'Well, you'd better be sensible and go back home,' he said with an attempt at humour. 'Let's see if Camp Director Ma and I have what it takes.'

When the others had gone Tian Yong adopted a confidential tone, asking me why I hadn't said anything to them.

'Because all they were saying about practising Falun Gong exercises attracting evil things is just ludicrous,' I told him, adding that I believed Falun Gong exercise to be good for the health.

Ma Hao took this point up. He said the state had not yet organised research on the health effects of the Falun Gong exercises and still not enough was being done. So in that respect, he said, I had probably reformed much better than the others, because I had dared to think for myself while they were not yet thinking outside the practice.

He went on to say he had read all eighteen pages of my 'exposing and repudiating' report and thought it was pretty good; it was obvious that I was a graduate of Beida. The camp's leadership were very serious about the TV interview coming up very soon, he said, and people from the department also wanted to come because the state valued talent.

'No,' I said. 'I don't intend to see the journalists. I have written a self-criticism for Team Leader Wang . . .'

'Tear it up!' he broke in. 'Wang Zhao is a brute. She doesn't understand shit. I'll handle this from now on.'

Tian Yong added that my practising Falun Gong exercises was a serious breach of discipline for which I would normally be sent to the training unit or solitary confinement. But we were in the business of 'educating, persuading and rescuing', he went on, and since the director had raised this matter we should act on the principle of 'reducing major issues to small ones and minor ones to nothing'. He suggested that none of us should mention this matter again and we should set about remedying the situation. He said I should go and have a good rest and that Professor Qin would be waiting to hear some positive news.

This time I didn't intend to turn over. At this point the only thing I could do was to 'push the boat along with the current'—to make use of this opportunity to gain my own ends.

It was very late by the time I left the office. The little sentry told me not to go to Squad 3; they had moved my things already and I was to go straight to Squad 1, Wang Zhao's squad.

I WALK THE TIGHTROPE AGAIN

I was summoned to the duty office two days later, about two o'clock in the afternoon. Tian Yong was there, intercom in hand, agitated, and breathing hard. There was a strong smell of alcohol about him. He must have just come from a big feast.

'She's here!' he said excitedly as soon as he saw me.

I wasn't much troubled at seeing him so agitated and just thought to myself, what's so exciting about a journalist's visit?

'Xie . . .,' he mumbled as his bottom sank onto the sofa, '. . . wife has arrived.'

I couldn't catch what he said.

'Professor Qin's wife has come, too?' I asked.

'No! Xie Juezhai's wife!' he exclaimed. 'Wang Dingguo, the wife of the veteran revolutionary Xie Juezhai, has arrived! She is an 85-year-old revered Red soldier and she took part in the fabled Long March!' It looked like he had only just found out she was here. The labour camp was run along military lines and he was probably not privy to such confidential matters.

I remembered studying something Xie Juezhai had written in junior middle school but I couldn't recall what positions he had held. Very few of the female Red soldiers of the 1934–35 Long March were still alive so an 'honour' such as this would have been a first for the forced-labour camp.

'How long will the visit last?' I asked him.

'Don't get anxious. It won't be long. Ten minutes or so at most. Now everything depends on you. We'll go downstairs to welcome them.'

As I went out the door I saw an officer hurriedly bringing Xiao Yu upstairs. Not surprisingly, they were afraid I wouldn't be able to handle such a big occasion and had rushed over to Company 4 to get Xiao Yu as a back-up. If anyone in the labour camp had the gift of the gab it was she. By the time I got downstairs the senile veteran of the revolution—supported by two helpers—was tottering in the front door, followed by a great crowd of people. Leaders from bureau level right down to section level were there, together with the journalists and Professor Qin. And there, at the very back of the crowd, was my husband.

We went to the large meeting room, which had been made ready, and Xiao Yu and I were given pride of place. The event was billed as 'Veteran of the revolution comes to our camp to see reformed Falun Gong practitioners' so we two clearly were the headliners. My husband was allocated a seat at the other end of the room.

When everyone was seated all eyes and cameras turned to me. In the detention centre I hadn't even given a verbal undertaking not to go to Tian'anmen, yet here I was facing this circus. I knew I was supposed to say something. The day before, Tian Yong had brought a group of visitors around, heads of various large detention centres in Beijing. Tian Yong's first remark on walking into Squad 1 had been that all of the Falun Gong practitioners there had reformed. Unconvinced, one of the visitors asked an inmate he recognised from his detention centre if she had reformed.

She nodded.

'You've really reformed?' he persisted.

She nodded again.

The visitor looked as if he wanted to shake her.

'Why is it that in the detention centre nothing short of death would have made you say you'd stop practising,' he said to her, 'yet here in the labour re-education camp you've reformed? What's their trick?'

The woman gave a mysterious smile but said nothing. The visitor turned to Tian Yong for some explanation but he, too, simply smiled and ignored him, which infuriated the visitor, of course.

I also remembered a team leader by the name of Jiang who had recently been moved from Company 2, before I 'reformed'. After she was put in charge of Squad 3 for a few days, she got each of us to write an account of ourselves for her. I braced myself and wrote several detailed pages about my life, why I wanted to practise Falun Gong, my understanding of Falun Gong and where my thinking was right then. She called me to the office a few days later and said she had read my account several times; she had even taken it home for her husband to have a look. She had been deeply affected by the part about calmly making sacrifices for the sake of truth.

'Here and now,' she said to me, 'the relationship between us must be that of team leader and inmate. Were we not here, however, I would wish to be your friend, your sister.'

I had felt so warm towards her that the old adage 'a long acquaintanceship that never ripens; a cordiality as of old friends' came to mind. From then on, she did treat me like a sister and with deep respect. When I resolved to 'reform' I rejoiced in the fact that she had already been transferred away.

Reflecting on these two things finally gave me my starting point for my talk. I said that after our visitors had left the day before I had begun to think about why Falun Gong practitioners reformed in the labour camps and not in other institutions. I believed I had found an answer. It was the special atmosphere of the labour camps (very special!), the tenacity of the team leaders ('I won't let up until you reform!') and the help sessions (really 'poison sessions'). In such an environment an iceberg would melt (who wouldn't melt with eighteen electric prods coming at them?) and insensate rock would shed tears (trust me!).

Then I started talking about how Team Leader Jiang had cared for me like a sister and how moved I had been by that. I went on to cite the example of Section Head Tian, who had devoted endless effort to my case, and spoke of how he had meticulously planned and choreographed every discussion we had ever had.

I stopped at that point, certain that Tian Yong would jump in and expand on what he had done, saving me a little work. My word juggling was not over yet and I was running out of ammunition.

Right on cue, he picked up his end of the pole.

'What is so noticeable about Zheng Zeng,' he said, after a few appropriately modest introductory words, 'is her outstanding patriotism. The people she studied with have all gone overseas yet she has remained here to repay her motherland for its kindness.'

He went on to say how much care and support I had received from Professor Qin, and so on.

As soon as he had finished all eyes turned to me again, so on I went, saying how Professor Qin had treated me like my teacher and just as a daughter can never repay her parents so, too, I could never repay him for all he had done. How heavily this thought weighed on my mind, I said. How could my heart not be heavy, I thought, wondering how it would affect him when I was released and immediately turned over? I believed all I had to do, I said, was simply do better from now on and devote all my energies to repaying society; that was the only way I could repay the professor (but I had my own definition of what constituted 'doing better').

I spoke slowly, a resolve forming in my mind: after I got out I would do everything in my power to redeem this day.

One of the journalists suddenly put his camera down.

'As a reporter,' he said, 'I'm not supposed to say anything. But Zheng Zeng's words have moved me almost to tears and I cannot help saying something. I had no idea such good people were in labour camps! This in itself is just too much for me. But I don't understand why a highly educated person like yourself would practise Falun Gong? I hear that Li Hongzhi only went as far as junior middle school.'

I looked at the journalist, thinking what a good person he must be. Most of the people in that room probably thought that my talk of repaying society was simply a parroting of the old Party line. I resolved to tell him why I practised Falun Gong but just as I opened my mouth Professor Qin interrupted.

'Oh,' he said, with a wave of his hand, 'she had been unwell.'

As I opened my mouth a second time, he pre-empted me again.

'He's a friend of mine,' he said, referring to the journalist. 'Let's talk to him about it when we get home.'

At that moment someone from the bureau spoke up about how the government had begun looking into ways of resettling Falun Gong practitioners who had reformed. It was about 'giving them a way out', he said, 'about giving them a policy'.

While he was talking I sneaked a look at my husband. His face was ashen and he looked ill. He looked as if too many dead weights were lying on his mind and his soul had left his body. He refused to look at me or even catch my eye. This was rather depressing because he must have been thinking how all his efforts to make me any less extreme had failed, and here in the labour camp they had somehow managed to get me to reform! He must have been racking his brains and come up with the only possible answer: I had undergone something beyond his wildest imagination and more dreadful than death.

He had always told me not to be so extreme but then he would tell the police and friends that I was much nobler than he. It must have been incredibly strange for him to see me sitting there chatting away quite calmly after having reformed. I didn't dare wonder whether he also felt as if he had been raped.

The ten minutes were up by the time the bureau person had had his say, and in deference to the age and infirmity of the veteran Red soldier the 'informal discussion' drew to a close.

This tightrope act had been dangerous but I was quite satisfied with my performance. Not once during the entire ten minutes had anyone made a direct attack on Falun Gong, and Xiao Yu, who had the most profound knowledge of the 'principles' of reform, had not had a chance to open her mouth.

But still, I was on tenterhooks for quite some time, watching the TV for a report that never materialised. There was an item in the camp newspaper about a veteran Red soldier and a Beida professor coming to visit inmates, but my name was not mentioned, nor was the fact that they had come to see reformed Falun Gong practitioners. I imagine the authorities must have realised afterwards that there wasn't any direct attack on Falun Gong during the entire 'informal discussion', so from their point of view the whole thing was pretty pointless. Their doubts about the legitimacy of my reform might also have made them think twice about mentioning my name.

SELF-IMMOLATION IN TIAN'ANMEN

Anyone would be excused for thinking that this, my crowning success, would have earned me a ticket home. But no, things had to follow their proper course. By this stage I had completed only three of the five components of reform, the 'guarantee', the 'renunciation' and the 'exposing and repudiation'. I still had to 'go public' and 'be an education aide'.

'Going public' involved reading out the 'exposing and repudiation' article on the stage of the auditorium in front of all the camp's inmates. The whole process is recorded on video and archived. 'Being an education aide' means helping the police to reform others.

The time was approaching for me to 'go public' when the 'self-immolation' incident in Tian'anmen Square shocked the world.

On January 30, 2001 we were crowded into our room as usual, watching the evening TV news after dinner. Suddenly there on the screen were the horrifying pictures of the 'self-immolation' of five[24] supposed Falun Gong practitioners in Tian'anmen Square: the billowing smoke, the human forms in flames running about wildly, the charred faces, the agonised screams of the little girl with her face horribly burned. Involuntarily, I closed my eyes against this tragic scene.

---

24 The number was later changed to seven by Xinhua News Agency.

Surely Falun Gong practitioners were in enough of a mess already! Surely enough unrighted wrongs had been laid at our feet! How much more hatred was this going to breed in the minds of the people? Who could be capable of such a thing?

Everybody around me was busy voicing an opinion while I squeezed my eyes shut and said nothing. In my extreme grief all I could think of was a very ordinary phrase: It never rains but it pours.

When I eventually pulled myself together, something occurred to me. Apparently this had happened seven days ago, on January 23; why had it taken so long to air the story? Why had such a major news item been suppressed for seven days? There was something fishy about this!

I didn't have to think twice, of course, to know that no genuine Falun Gong practitioner would do a thing like that. Only someone who feared that Falun Gong had not been exterminated could stage such an event.

However, if lies are repeated often enough they become the truth, and the 'self-immolation' was played over and over on TV, the announcers sounding as if they wanted to wipe out the lot of us. They would show clips of large mass criticisms, with all sorts of people raising indignant voices in condemnation of Falun Gong, interspersed with the shocking images and the voice of the 12-year-old survivor calling out 'Mama! Mama!' over the charred body of her mother. Who, seeing these images, would not have loathed Falun Gong? This blanket coverage was nationwide, and many people who had not cared one way or another about the suppression of Falun Gong began to believe that we had indeed incited this young girl's mother to set herself on fire. This was such an evil thing that the government ban began to look good; it began to look excellent; no, it was top-notch!

My heart ached. Every time they showed those programs I would close my eyes—I had never liked seeing ugly images of any kind. In my grief I didn't at first notice how flawed the report was. But overseas Falun Gong practitioners soon discovered many inconsistencies in the story by watching video footage recorded from CCTV news reports. Tian'anmen Square is huge—it can hold a million people—and it has a large police presence. But, Chinese people do not normally set themselves on fire, so the patrols have never been equipped with fire extinguishers, nor have cameramen strolled about there with cameras on their shoulders. So how come the police, almost 30 fire extinguishers and fire blankets, cameramen, cameras, actors and props all arrived at the scene of the fire in less than a minute? How did the police get distance shots, mid-range shots and close-ups of the 'self-immolation' from various angles and from multiple cameras unless it had been prearranged? Chinese officials later tried to claim that CNN had taken the shots but CNN immediately denied this. CNN reporters were indeed present at the scene but their film was confiscated in Tian'anmen Square by the police and has never been shown to the public.

There were other obvious flaws, which again I didn't pick up at the time. There was the blow to the back of her head that the woman who was said to have 'burned' to death—Liu Chunling—received. There were the discrepancies in the sitting posture and the shouted slogan, 'Everyone in the world must practise Falun Dafa,' of the main self-immolation protagonist, Wang Jindong—they were clearly not consistent with Falun Gong practice. There were the worrisome details that he could sit up straight and call out in a loud strong voice while he was on fire; that the burn victims were seen wrapped in bandages; that someone was able to sing after a tracheotomy, as the 12-year-old was supposed to have done. Nor did I see the many other obvious flaws. The pre-immolation Wang Jindong was not the Wang Jindong we saw setting himself alight; his hair did not catch fire; the plastic bottle of petrol on the ground did not explode in the fire.

What is interesting is that, ten years before this all happened, the mainland writer Wang Lixiong had written a futuristic political novel called *Yellow Peril*. Published by the Canadian publisher Mirror Books and the Taiwan-based *Fengyun Times*, the book described the collapse and recovery of Chinese society. It also depicted a self-immolation incident in Tian'anmen that was almost identical to the one that took place in January 2001. In the book, the Ministry of Public Security bribes a woman with a terminal illness and sets up her self-immolation as a pretext for a crackdown. The woman has late-stage cancer and has had a double mastectomy, and the Minister promises to give her family three million *yuan* after she dies. This is the relevant plot line:

'June Fourth . . .'The girl opened the black hole of her mouth and her voice trembled. It was part of the deal that she was setting herself alight to reverse the verdict on the June Fourth affair, not for some other business. She had memorised any number of possible slogans but couldn't call any to mind at the critical moment. '. . . reverse the verdict . . .' was all she could manage.

Fortunately, that would do. The flames burst from the lighter. It was a windproof lighter and had been tested over and over again to make sure it would work first go. But just as the flames burst forth a gigantic hand grabbed the lighter. Lu Haoran almost cried out, so near yet so far! [In the book, Lu Haoran is the highest-ranking person in the Communist Party.] The flames had not reached the petrol and the girl had not ignited. Two other big fellows had grabbed her. She struggled but she was no match for three big gorillas. She quickly lost the desire to struggle and fell still. The whole thing was over in a few seconds. He saw the lighter in the hand of one of the men. Suddenly, a flash, and boom! The girl burst into flames. Flames engulfed the three goons. From the ball of fire came the voice of the girl, like the wail of a wild animal, but he could only make out two words: 'deceived . . . me'. She flew at the crowd.

This is incredibly similar to what Liu Chunling did ten years later when she ran about in agony in Tian'anmen after catching fire and before she was knocked down by a blow to the back of her head.

On February 4, 2001, twelve days after the 'self-immolation', the *Washington Post* in the United States published a front page article by Philip P. Pan called 'Human fire ignites Chinese mystery—motive for public burning intensifies fight over Falun Gong'. The author had gone to the city of Kaifeng in Henan province, where Liu Chunling had lived before her fiery death, and his article contained some amazing revelations:

- Liu Chunling was not a native of Kaifeng and made a living as a hostess in a nightclub;
- Liu Chunling would beat her elderly mother and young daughter from time to time;
- No one ever saw Liu practise the Falun Gong exercises.

And on August 14, 2001, in a formal statement to the United Nations, the International Education Development Office said:

> The regime points to a supposed self-immolation incident in Tian'anmen Square on January 23, 2001 as proof to slander Falun Gong. However, we have obtained a video of that incident that in our view proves that this event was staged by the government. Interested parties are welcome to have a copy of this video.

The Chinese delegation is said to have remained silent out of fear; what is certain is that they did not attempt to deny this statement.

Another interesting thing is that after the self-immolation affair the novel *Yellow Peril* was suddenly banned. The authorities might as well have erected a sign over it saying, 'No 30 *taels* of silver buried here!'

However, locked away in the labour camp I knew nothing of all this. After I was moved into Squad 1 for practising Falun Gong exercises, Li Chun had been demoted from her position as squad leader of Squad 3 and relegated to commoner status in Squad 2. One day after the 'self-immolation' she managed to find a chance to sneak into Squad 1. You would have thought I had forgotten to repay a large loan from the tone she adopted as she asked me immediately what this 'self-immolation' was all about.

I could see it had really rocked her faith in Falun Gong. All I could do was remind her that practitioners were not to take life; and, of course, they were not to take their own lives. I also reminded her about true Falun Gong practitioners. A practitioner, I said, is not just someone who does the exercises; true practice is when you have attained what is required of a practitioner.

'Well, why would they want to go and set fire to themselves?' she asked me, her tone warning me that if I wasn't straight with her she would no longer believe in Falun Gong.

I told her about the only obvious flaw I had noticed at that point.

'Why do you think they didn't broadcast this news until the thirtieth when it happened on the twenty-third?' I asked her. 'Don't you think there's something fishy about that?' (I discovered when I got out of the camp that Xinhua News Agency had released the news to overseas media two hours after the event.)

'So just what do you think this is all about?' Li Chun persisted.

'Let me say this. I bet it was people the Party sent to infiltrate as practitioners and they incited some confused people to do it. Only the Communist Party would wish for people to burn themselves to death. Infiltrators do whatever they can to cause disruption. What about the people in here who "reform" and then beat others: would you still call them Falun Gong practitioners? Disruption takes many forms, and this is the most devastating. I'll bet you anything you like they're not Falun Gong!'

This got her thinking.

'You know what?' she eventually said. 'What that Liu Baorong[25] said on TV didn't make sense to me. She pulled out of the "self-immolation" at the last minute but she said something about when virtue burns it gives off white smoke. Well, everyone knows that when petrol burns it gives off black smoke, don't they? So what's all that about white smoke? I think she's mad!'

'That's right,' I said. 'You can say that again. No way would Falun Gong tell people to do this sort of thing.'

Li Chun's problem may have been solved but I still had one. Would the next group of people to go public to expose and repudiate be expected to include self-immolation in their criticism?

After considerable thought I finally remembered what Zhang Qing had once said: 'I have now discovered that it is the Communist Party that is the most evil cult. It is banning Truthfulness, Compassion and Forbearance and if that isn't the act of an evil cult then I don't know what is. Throughout its entire existence the Chinese Communist Party has been making people suffer. How many of them has it killed in movement after movement? And you don't call that a cult?'

All right. That was the tack I would take in my forthcoming public talk. No matter what they said, in my heart of hearts I knew that the Communist Party was very probably behind this affair, but even if the Party had not deliberately provoked it I would not be wrong

---

25 Liu Baorong is a woman who was not included in the 'five Falun Gong practitioners' but was added later as one of the 'seven Falun Gong practitioners who were involved in the "self-immolation"'. She appeared on the TV repeatedly, telling her story about how she suddenly changed her mind after she saw the 'black smoke' enveloping those who had set themselves on fire. She also said that she immediately 'reformed', on the spot.

in calling the self-immolators 'disciples of an evil cult', because I did not believe they were genuine Falun Gong practitioners. So that's what I would call them, disciples of an evil cult (by which I meant the Chinese Communist Party), and I would criticise them severely, saying they should not slaughter life. More word games!

As I went up on stage I wanted to get it over as quickly as possible. However, I couldn't help crying when I reached the part about self-immolation because of the frightful effect this affair was having on Falun Gong. Woven into that occasion and my text, my tears made an impression that I was deeply regretting having practised Falun Gong.

6

'COERCION CANNOT CHANGE PEOPLE'S HEARTS'

Li CHUN WAS A LOST soul for a long time after she was parted from me. Whenever she ran into me she would put on a pained expression, frown and piteously mouth, 'I miss you . . .' Eventually, however, she found a new companion in Liu Shuying.

Liu Shuying was much the same when she came into Company 2 in early August as she had been at the despatch division. She kept her head down; she didn't speak; she didn't even look at anyone. She still had difficulty walking and it was a struggle for her to line up with everyone else to go to the mess hall for meals. She depended on the other students for everything.

In time I learned a little more about her. She, too, had gone to university and she had been arrested for putting up banners in Tian'anmen. She had been taken to the Dongcheng District lockup, where she had gone on a hunger strike. After eleven days of this she had been hauled away and subjected to electric needles, a punishment in which electrodes are attached to the acupuncture points on a person's body and a strong electric current run through them. It is a frightful torture, much worse than electric prods.

As soon as they turned on the current, Liu Shuying passed out. She was *non compos* when she came to and her memory had completely gone. She had been sentenced to labour re-education a few days later and sent to the despatch division. It was there that by some lucky chance we had come upon her in her pitiful state.

She was in Squad 2 when Zhou Jie was moved there and Zhou Jie was deeply upset by her pitiful condition. Although she had no idea whether Liu Shuying could hear her or whether anything was going on in her head, Zhou Jie didn't want to give up and would recite the *Hongyin* collection of poems to her softly every day. At first there was no reaction, but a month or so later she suddenly spoke.

'It is wrong to expose and repudiate our teacher,' were her first words.

Later, she told Zhou Jie that she remembered the police at the despatch division getting her, dazed as she was, to copy something out of some book every day. She hadn't known what she was copying but was certain now that it was draft statements exposing and repudiating Falun Gong.

All this got straight back to Wang Zhao and Zhou Jie was immediately sent down to the training unit. Then Wang Zhao organised a group of people to give Liu Shuying 'help sessions'.

Day after day these people took Liu Shuying to the office, where they surrounded her. Wang Zhao took part in this, too.

'Good,' she said to her. 'You've come back to life. When you first came here looking half dead I didn't even want to have you in my company. The team leaders have taken good care of you, haven't they? They haven't made you knit sweaters; they haven't made you recite Order 23. You really have had it good. And now the first thing you do when you come back to life is to refuse to acknowledge the things that you yourself have written. Have you no shame? OK, so now that you have come back to life you have to really get down to your studies.'

Wang Zhao proceeded to punish her by not letting her sleep for days on end. She made her sit in the dimly lit corridor copying out Order 23 until three o'clock in the morning. Poor Liu Shuying had only just started talking again. She still had difficulty holding a pen and her writing was all over the place. She would huddle up on her stool in the corridor, shivering in the freezing autumn nights. After more than a week of this she simply couldn't take any more.

'I am a cripple now,' she said to Wang Zhao, 'and my body has completely collapsed. I have trouble maintaining my human dignity and I don't have the courage or the ability to endure anything more. I am only alive because I haven't died just yet. I will write whatever you want me to write but in my heart I know it is wrong to expose and repudiate our teacher.'

Wang Zhao was beside herself with rage. She got Xiang Hong and her gang to take Liu Shuying to the main office and give her a beating while she stood at the door, arms folded, watching. In her fury, however, she forgot there was someone squatting in the corridor. Eighteen-year-old Ni Bei was in for stealing but was currently being punished for passing notes to a boy in the juvenile labour camp. She saw everything and told us about it.

I don't know whether or not Liu Shuying ever said it was right to expose and repudiate our teacher, but she was beaten until once more she became a living corpse.

Li Chun had sized up the other occupants when she was transferred to Squad 2 but didn't fancy the two regulars and had no time for the other reformed women. Silent Liu Shuying alone stirred her gallant heart and she treated her with the greatest care in all things, as if they belonged together.

I complimented Li Chun on her kindness, enjoining her not to stop and saying it was crucial to find some way of reviving Liu Shuying's will to live. Within a day or so Li Chun reported that it was hopeless: she had tried everything to get her to talk but Liu Shuying had just ignored her. Still, she felt there was a spark of understanding in there somewhere.

Then a group of the education aides returned from an outside assignment with the news that Li Hongzhi had just put out a new article, entitled 'Coercion cannot change people's hearts'. The police had told them about it because they wanted them to write a criticism of it. When the women suggested it might be difficult to critique something they had not read, the police replied that they would explain what was in it.

The gist of it, the police said, is that you can deceive the government, that you should work hard at deceiving the government and that he, Li Hongzhi, will still want you when you have done all your deceiving. So, on the basis of this 'explanation', the education aides wrote a thought report criticising the article.

You must remember that after the crackdown, access to overseas Falun Gong websites was denied to mainland Falun Gong practitioners and to the public. The police and those who worked in the

610 Office must have had the pleasure of reading those sites day after day. New articles that appeared on the Internet would have been studied with great concentration to see how they could be distorted, all with the aim of reforming more people.

I here quote a passage from the 'Coercion cannot change people's minds' article to demonstrate just how 'neatly' the labour-camp police had explained it.

For over a year, the evil has utilized the bad people who have been used as its tools and who employ all sorts of torture instruments and methods to beat cruelly and torture *Dafa* cultivators. Although many people have been beaten to death, beaten to disability, or sent off to mental hospitals, this has still not changed true cultivators' steadfast, righteous thoughts. [The bad people] produce fake scriptures, don't allow students to sleep, fabricate charges, frame students, spread lies, and so on. Being threatened severely, deceived, and pressured greatly by all those indecent means, some students have written things like the so-called 'guarantees to stop practising' or 'statements of repentance' when they were not in their right minds and forced. None of those were genuine expressions from the students' hearts—they were done against their will. Although they had attachments, were momentarily taken advantage of by the evil, and did what a cultivator should not, a cultivator ought to be looked at in his entirety. I do not recognize any of those things. When they return to their senses, they will immediately start doing again what a Dafa student should do during this time, and, in the meantime, will declare as null and void everything that they said and wrote when they were not in their right minds due to intense persecution, and will declare that they are determined in cultivation. A large number of declarations from students all over the country have appeared daily. The last hope of attempting to change Dafa disciples' righteous thoughts through coercion and deception has been completely shattered. The evil no longer has any way to change the determination that Dafa disciples have developed from their true understanding of the *Fa* through cultivation and from their Buddha-nature after the elevation of their *benti* [true being] in actual cultivation.

While I had not seen the article, I could make an educated guess about what it said, going by the title and the police's explanation of it. I believed that Li Hongzhi had publicly stated that he did not recognise anything that took place in the forced-labour re-education camps and those who had been forced to write guarantees should still have the opportunity to cultivate. Yes! That must be it. Surely people who had been forced through indecent means to write guarantees would not really be ruined beyond redemption?

The first person I thought of when this realisation hit me was Liu Shuying. I knew I had to tell her this news straight away—it might be her only hope of survival. But I didn't know how to get to talk to her. Then it came to me that the knitting might be the answer. Since moving to Squad 1 I had been assigned the task of 'single order', the same as Li Chun, and I was currently working on an item that I could say I needed Li Chun's guidance with. This might give me the access I needed to Squad 2. It did.

Li Chun's bunk was in a corner and when I arrived that night she quickly realised I had come to see Liu Shuying. She pulled Liu Shuying over to her bunk and plonked a pile of knitting books on the bed as if she was giving instructions to me. Then she casually placed her stool at the head of the bed so she could keep an eye on the passageway outside. This effectively screened Liu Shuying and me from the others.

Liu Shuying sat passively beside the bunk, her entire being a void.

'Liu Shuying,' I whispered fiercely. 'Listen. Our teacher has put out a new article. It's called "Coercion cannot change people's hearts" and in it he says he doesn't recognise anything that's happened in the labour reform camps and that all those who have been compelled to write guarantees are still able to practise. It's true! You can still practise. Come on, pull yourself together.'

She sat motionless in the shadow of the bunk, gazing at me. With what seemed a supreme effort she finally spoke.

'It's true?' she asked, her voice flat and croaky from lack of use.

'Yes, it's true. It's absolutely true. The article has been published. It's clear from the title "Coercion cannot change people's hearts". And it's genuine, too, because the team leaders told it to some education aides when they went out on a job.'

She went on staring at me, and after an eternity a miracle of beauty appeared before my very eyes. She compressed her lips and smiled at me.

It lasted but an instant but it had a profound effect on me, this flash of light in our dim cell, like a brilliant patch of blue through black clouds. It was as if a spring flower had suddenly blossomed in the tundra, full of joy and brimming with delicacy.

When Liu Shuying had first come from the despatch division nine months before, Song Mei had burst into tears at the sight of her. She had been so pretty, she sobbed. But I saw now that Liu Shuying was far more than pretty; her smile, even so faint, made her very beautiful.

Slowly, in that croaky voice, she shared with me a secret she had locked away in her heart. After she had come back to life that last time and Wang Zhao had beaten that life out of her, she had been having nightmares. In these nightmares she and some other people were rolling about on the blood- and pus-soaked ground and then she died in agony. She was absolutely convinced that what she saw in her dreams was her inescapable fate. You could see why she showed no interest in anything.

'Our teacher always told us to take the *Fa* as our teacher,' I said to her. 'He never told us to take dreams as our teacher. You will only end up destroying yourself through self-loathing if you believe those dreams.'

'So you're saying that just as I am I can still practise?' she said quietly. 'But my health is completely ruined.'

'Of course you can,' I told her. 'Just think of all the people all over the world who haven't even started practising. Why don't you just start at the beginning, like them? Didn't our teacher quote the saying "Having heard the *Dao* in the morning, one can die in the evening?" There is no saying that practitioners can't recover from broken health. It doesn't matter so long as you believe Dafa. You'll be going home in just over a week. If you practise the exercises as soon as you get out you'll quickly get better.'

'All the Dafa books I had at home have been confiscated.'

'I've got some. I'll give you a set!'

In no time we had arranged everything: how I would contact her after we got out, how I would get the books to her, and so on. I didn't dare write her phone number down so had to commit it to memory. I repeated it to myself every day so I wouldn't forget it.

I had no trouble contacting Liu Shuying when I eventually got out and gave her a set of the books and the practice tape. She recovered incredibly quickly, the colour coming back into her face and that beautiful smile blossoming and playing about her gorgeous lips. Nobody who had seen her a year before in the despatch division could ever have imagined that this was what she really looked like.

In no time she had put her solemn declaration up on the Clearwisdom website, declaring null and void the guarantee and everything else she had written in the forced-labour re-education camp. With great determination she chose to leave home so that she wouldn't be rearrested. I would never have believed she could so quickly muster such resolve after the horrific damage that had been done to her.

I should mention that in the forty-five months from New Year's Day 2001 to September 2004 over 146,000 people put their solemn declarations up on the Clearwisdom website. Some Falun Gong practitioners who had been forced to write guarantees but had no one to put their declarations on the Internet wrote them out as big-character posters, put their names on them and stuck them up in busy shopping centres.

The police kept a constant watch on the Clearwisdom website and some people were rearrested the day after their solemn declaration appeared. Apparently the probationary period for reformed Falun Gong practitioners released after serving their full term has now been extended from six months to three years.

If you visit the Clearwisdom website these days you will see dozens and sometimes hundreds of solemn declarations going up every day. They are from people of all walks of life; some are short; some are long; some are very bland and some are written in blood. It is sometimes difficult to imagine the profoundly disturbing events that spawned these declarations.

Where has Liu Shuying, with her radiant smile, ended up? Has she fallen once more into the devil's clutches? In this far-off foreign land, I hope with all my heart that she remains steadfast.

I AM WITNESS TO A TRAGEDY

When I became part of Squad 1, I learned a secret that explained why so many newcomers were succumbing to reform for no apparent reason. Apparently a rule had come into being that all newcomers had to write a guarantee and that they were not to be allowed to sleep until they had done so, no matter how long this took. It was so simple, nothing like the lectures that had been put on for us just after we arrived. By July 2001, the record for going without sleep was said to have been an entire month.

A Falun Gong student named Ma Rong was tied to her bed at the despatch division in the height of summer for over 50 days for practising Falun Gong exercises. The muscles and skin of her whole back and arms went putrid and when they untied her she couldn't move her arms or walk. The little sentry assigned to watch her while she was tied down had frequently jumped on top of her and slapped her face. Yet this woman did not submit. She became famous in the despatch division as someone who would never reform, no matter how much she suffered. But when she came to the labour camp they kept her awake for five days and five nights, with supplemental beatings from time to time to instil their principles. She just couldn't soldier on and she gave in. Another student at the despatch division had been held down by four or five police—they actually stood on her—and given shocks. The current was so strong that her body bucked, even with the police standing on her, and her chest had ended up looking like the fried underside of a pancake. She had black scorch marks all over her chest and her back but still wouldn't renounce her practice of Falun Gong. But at the labour camp she, too, collapsed when she wasn't allowed to sleep.

When I was initially transferred into Squad 1 I wasn't included in the business of reforming others because I wasn't considered to have fully reformed myself. So while the education aides took turns in ensuring newcomers did not sleep, I hid my head under the quilt, like an ostrich.

Battalion 7 was formed not long after the self-immolation incident. Due to the increased numbers in the labour camp, all of the companies had been upgraded to battalions and a juvenile re-education unit had been added. The two dormitories were full and the storage room and the office had been converted to dormitories. Wang Zhao was placed in charge of the new Battalion 7, taking with her the reformed women in Squad 1 she had come to rely on as education aides.

Our new team leader then ordered me to be part of the brainwashing classes, or 'help sessions'.

The first person I had to help educate was He Jiang, a woman in her early twenties from Gansu province in the far northwest. My friendly manner probably led her to believe that I was not reformed, for as I was taking her to the ablutions block she asked me if I had been frightened when I first got to the camp.

'No,' I said. 'Are you?'

'Yes, I am,' she replied. 'I'm frightened of being reformed.'

We hadn't known anything about reform when we arrived, so it had not weighed on our minds, but the police in the despatch division had since started telling inmates things. You're tough now, they would say, but you'll reform, too, when you get to the labour camp. Tougher people than you have, so don't think you won't. Then newcomers were thrown in with reformed women and I thought back to how astonished I had been at the things I had heard after Hu Xiuying reformed; I had been aghast at the pressure they must have brought to bear.

He Jiang bore up the first night and the second, but I could see that mentally it was becoming more difficult for her.

The burden on me was no less heavy. Knowing full well the import for Falun Gong practitioners of reforming, I had to keep telling myself that if I didn't do it then someone else would, and it was better I did it because I was on her side.

I was rostered on for the first shift on the third night. By then her eyes were unfocused and she didn't appear to be taking anything in. She just stood there in silence, resolved not to reform.

Squad Leader Cui Rui finally lost patience a little after midnight. You lot go to sleep, she told us, and let me have her. Cui Rui had been transferred to Squad 1 a week after me and had been taken off mess hall work, which was very tiring and thus the reason you earned extra points for doing it. Cui Rui had long ago gained sufficient points to be eligible for an award so she didn't need any more, but her requests to be transferred had always fallen on deaf ears. Now, however, Wang Zhao had stepped in on her behalf after Cui Rui turned me in for practising Falun Gong exercises. She had topped this off by promoting her to squad leader of Squad 1.

Incredibly relieved, I went to wash my hands, anticipating a good sleep once I had been to the toilet; I was really exhausted after three days of this hardship. In sleep I could go on putting my head in the sand.

Everybody seemed to have gone to sleep, but as I emerged

from the washroom a mournful wail pierced the deep quiet of the corridors. I heard a heavy muffled noise then a tangle of sounds—footsteps, pulling, a stool overturned, a reprimand, abuse.

I went weak and my legs almost buckled beneath me. Holding onto the wall I made my way back to the squad and there I saw He Jiang lying unconscious on the floor, with several people crowding around her and Cui Rui pinching her to bring her round.

The sounds I had heard after her wail had been He Jiang running headlong into the wall as hard as she could. Cui Rui had enlisted the help of a newly arrived drug addict from Squad 1 to force He Jiang to do the flying posture hard up against the wall, just to make her suffer a bit more. Three days and nights had passed and He Jiang still had not reformed; Squad Leader Cui's patience had reached its limit.

He Jiang had finally reached the limit of her endurance after a few minutes of flying. But her horror of reforming had pushed her to a decision: it was better to finish herself off than to become a Judas by reforming. So she had asked to go to the toilet. Cui Rui had agreed and followed her out the door, whereupon He Jiang had given a great wail and rushed headlong at the wall.

She didn't die, of course, but knocked herself out. She came round quite quickly in response to Cui Rui's pinching. The police were called and they gave He Jiang a right royal tongue-lashing before handing her back to Cui Rui. He Jiang was forced to go on standing and one way or another she got through the night.

On the fourth night, Cui Rui removed her Squad 1 helpers from the task, saying they were being too kind, and handed He Jiang over to the education aides of Squad 2 with the request that they lend a friendly hand. Ever since I had gone to Squad 1 I had been up front about my opposition to hitting people, and the education aides in that squad had never hit anyone. At one stage I had discussed this issue with the deputy head of Battalion 2. I had said that the team leaders had always claimed the Clearwisdom website reports were just rumours but I wanted to know if beatings did in fact occur in the labour re-education camps. Her response was that it really didn't matter since once someone reformed they wouldn't say anything when they got out. After everything Ma Rong had been through, for instance, once she reformed she indicated that when she got out she would not say a word about what had happened in the labour camp.

The education aides from Squad 2 lent a friendly hand by taking

He Jiang to the team leaders' duty office. About midnight Cui Rui instructed me to go and see how she was and whether she had written her guarantee.

It was obvious when I got to the main office that He Jiang had just been beaten. She was standing before the education aides with an air of righteous indignation.

'I started practising Falun Gong once I decided to be a good person,' she was saying. 'You want me to reform? To reform to become thugs like you? I'll die before I do.'

The aides took no notice but went on feeding her their lies. I sat down with my knitting, watching her as I worked. She hadn't slept for four days and four nights and the clout she had given herself the previous night had almost exhausted her reserves of energy. Her face looked very sallow.

When next I glanced up she had a strange look about her. Her eyes had become confused and as she listened to the aides she seemed more and more befuddled, until this stupid expression settled on her face.

No! I wanted to shout at her. Whatever you do, don't listen to them. Don't listen to them!

But it was too late. In a flash the stupid look in her eyes had been replaced by the queer light I had once seen in Zhao Ying's eyes and hard on its heels came an odd little laugh.

'Aha!' she said to her antagonists, as if it had suddenly dawned on her. 'So that's it. Why didn't you say so earlier? This makes it all clear to me. Thank you, thank you so much!'

My hair stood on end. I had never been present at that instant at which somebody was reformed. Tragedy may be seeing the destruction of something beautiful but nothing in the world is more terrifying than the sight of an angel suddenly becoming a devil, of an ordinary person being driven mad.

She sat straight down at the table and wrote whatever she was told—guarantee, renunciation, exposure and repudiation—in one go, without turning a hair. In a very short period of time she became more zealous than any of her tutors. She became the expert 'education aide' member of Squad 1 and was constantly seen with the most experienced members of the 'study classes'. She also became a financial asset to the camp.

Cui Rui, who was not beyond throwing kitchen knives from

time to time, claimed that after this she developed a dread of new students. No matter how you look at it, He Jiang's headlong rush into the wall had frightened the life out of Cui Rui because she knew she would have to answer for it if she had hounded someone to death. Should something have actually gone wrong, the police might have shifted the responsibility onto her, making her the scapegoat. But then she would have been shirking her responsibility if she didn't force a guarantee out of newcomers; at the very least she was unable to sleep either, before a guarantee was written.

She didn't know then of the verbal instruction that had come down that 'Falun Gong practitioners who have been beaten to death are to be counted as suicides; their bodies are not to be identified and they are to be cremated immediately'. All she knew was that in the normal course of events she could be expected to hound people to their deaths; it is no wonder she would dread new students. With each one a similar, terrible story would be played out.

MY INTEGRITY IS SHATTERED

That was how I involuntarily became an accessory and witnessed tragedy after tragedy. When I became distressed beyond measure I would clench my teeth and repeat to myself: 'The rain will fall; you can't change the inevitable; just let it go'. And when I wasn't able to convince myself, I would tell myself that when I got out I would expose all of this.

I gradually began to feel that my integrity was coming apart. I felt nauseous, and deep within I knew I was terrified that one day my spirit would shatter completely because of this irredeemable shattering of my integrity.

I think it was in mid- or late March that I was told I was to be released eight days early as a reward for having reformed. A group of people had already been released ahead of time after the Spring Festival. Gu Hua, who had come in at the same time as me, had been released then, more than two months before her sentence was up, because she had reformed quite early on.

The other side of the coin was that people who had not reformed had their sentences extended, initially for six months. This had already happened to two groups of people. The first included three male students who had served their full time; they belonged to a group of six particularly stubborn men who had been moved from Tuanhe labour re-education camp to Xin'an women's camp. The other group was all women and included Bai Lian and Li Wen.

My last full day in the labour camp was April 3, 2001. Those of us being released ahead of time were to go straight home early the following morning after an awards ceremony. By this stage I was emotionally numb and just carried on with my knitting. I had become used to this mechanical work and much preferred being allowed to work away quietly in the squad to being part of the help sessions.

As night fell, Cheng Cui called me to the main office. She had been transferred back when Wang Zhao was moved on.

'I've been wanting to have a chat with you ever since I came back,' she said, 'but I haven't been able to find the time. What I wanted to ask was why you never wrote the heading "Exposure and repudiation" on anything you wrote? Also, I've noticed that you choose your words very carefully and there seems to be more in what you write than meets the eye. Is this a habit you developed when studying science and engineering, or what?'

'It's probably habit,' I said, concentrating on my knitting.

'So how do you see Falun Gong at present?'

'I do not intend to engage in politics.' I could feel her watching me but I just kept on knitting and didn't look up.

'You're very clever,' she said eventually. 'I think you do understand everything, so I won't say any more. Take good care of yourself when you get out. Since you're going tomorrow, though,' she went on, and I felt she was somehow testing me, 'will you do one last thing for the labour camp? Instead of going to bed tonight, will you watch Wang Bo for me? She comes from Shijiazhuang, and your primary task will be to get her to wear the labour-camp clothing.'

Just nineteen, Wang Bo had been expelled from the Central Conservatory of Music, where she was a talented student, for practising Falun Gong. She had been sentenced to labour re-education and kept in Shijiazhuang labour camp, a little to the south of Beijing. Falun Gong practitioners there had apparently refused to wear camp garb because they would not acknowledge that they were inmates. First thing that morning, on April 3, the police had summoned Wang Bo on the pretext of wanting to talk to her but instead bundled her off here to Xin'an. She was not at all prepared mentally. She hadn't brought anything with her and had only the clothes she wore and the shoes on her feet. She had just started her period and didn't even have any sanitary pads.

When I arrived to watch her she looked utterly exhausted. The police had held her in the main office for the whole day, and had kept forcibly dressing her in the labour-camp uniform. Wang Bo kept taking it off. Now, late at night, she still wasn't wearing it. By now the population of the camp numbered 984 and there wasn't a single empty bed in Battalion 2, so Wang Bo had to remain in the main office until those of us who were being released the following day had actually left.

Her emaciated young face reminded me of a verse in the film version of *The White-haired Girl*, which I had seen as a child: 'The lamb enters the tiger's den; how can these difficult times be endured?'

I sat in the duty office knitting, trying to work out how I could subtly indicate to her how important it was that she not listen to their distortions, but she sat hunched over the table, worn out. The only way that I was able to help her was to persuade the other woman watching her to let her rest for a while.

By three o'clock in the morning even I was feeling a bit faint and I hadn't been under pressure all day, as Wang Bo had. Fresh from a good sleep, Cheng Cui appeared in the doorway; she frowned when she saw that Wang Bo still hadn't put on the camp uniform and told the two of us who were on guard to return to our quarters.

I had just climbed into bed when an ear-splitting round of abuse poured out of the office. There was a bit of a racket and ten minutes or so later Cheng Cui came and told us to go and keep watch on Wang Bo again. When we got to the office I saw she was finally wearing prison garb. I suspected that, suddenly separated from the fellow practitioners with whom she had gone through so much, and exhausted by her confrontation with both savage police and reformed practitioners, she had reached the end of her tether.

Daylight found a haggard Wang Bo in prison clothes and shoes standing in line for morning drill. For my part, I was worn out and feeling not an ounce of joy at the prospect of going home. I wondered how Wang Bo would manage in this hellhole. After just one night of hardship she had already begun to look 'pale, with dull eyes and unkempt hair, hysterical', which was how CCTV and a Xinhua article would describe her appearance as a Falun Gong practitioner a year later, before she reformed and became what they called the 'typical reformed student'.

Later, I tracked Wang Bo down on the Internet and found out what had happened to her. After she reformed at Xin'an Labour Re-education Camp she helped the police trap her father, who was also a Falun Gong practitioner, and have him put into a brainwashing facility. As part of their *Focus Interviews* series, CCTV later broadcast a program called 'From destruction to rebirth—Wang Bo and her parents'. This program described how the Party and government policy of 'caring, educating, and saving', which they likened to 'life-giving spring breeze and rain', had given Wang Bo and her family a new life and reunited them. However, after Wang Bo's father, Wang Xinzhong, escaped from the brainwashing centre he posted on the Clearwisdom website an article exposing the misleading content and lies contained in the CCTV program. In this article he said that the TV program was a complete set-up and that he and his wife and daughter were brought together and photographed for the sole purpose of making the TV program. They were separated immediately after making the program: his wife was taken back to the labour camp, where she remains, while he and Wang Bo were returned to the brainwashing centre. When the three of them met at the TV studios, this is what Wang Bo said to him:

> Father, I suffered tremendously when I was at the labour camp. They abducted me to the Xin'an labour camp in Beijing. On the way there, I almost jumped out of the train. I didn't know if I would be able to endure the persecution that was to come. At the Xin'an labour camp, to forcibly brainwash me they deprived me of sleep for six consecutive days and forced me to watch videos that distorted Falun Gong and contained lies that reversed black and white. One policeman in the labour camp said these words to me: 'We are simply using the methods that we use on spies to make your mind collapse!' . . . Father, do you know how I came through all of this? After being transformed [i.e. reformed], my internal turmoil and mental depression made me feel I'd rather be dead. At times I felt like a person over 60 years old and I felt as if I had already died mentally quite a number of times.

Wang Xinzhong was rearrested in October 2002, after he published his article. His present whereabouts are unknown, nor is it known if he is alive or dead. Wang Bo was reinstated as a student in September 2002 through the 'solicitude' of the Party because she had been nominated as a model reformed person. However, a month later she was escorted to Hebei brainwashing centre and up until the autumn of 2004 was still being accompanied wherever she went by police officers and 610 Office personnel.

I AM RELEASED

One-two-one! In a daze I marched alongside Wang Bo at morning drill. I felt no happiness, no ease, no sense of freedom, only the certainty that if I had to spend another day in the camp I would go mad. All of a sudden I understood why I had been able to keep my cool and not even blink when a high-voltage prod had been waved under my nose, but had gone to pieces when I heard He Jiang's wail as she rushed headlong at the wall. It was because I had played a part in pushing her to that extremity.

After breakfast, those of us who were being released were escorted to a dank building to fetch our belongings. Along with selected representatives of the labour camp, we were taken by coach to the award ceremony at Tuanhe Men's Labour Re-education Camp, where 'birds sang and flowers gave forth fragrance'. The ceremony was being held there, apparently, because of the tame rabbits they kept. They looked good in the background of the TV coverage, giving the place the air of a scenic convalescent home and proving that the Party was providing the highest standard of humanitarian concern for Falun Gong practitioners.

I sleepwalked through the ceremony and have forgotten everything about it. I do remember that afterwards they took us to a small building by the main gate. In sacks laid out on the ground outside the building were the clothes our families had sent us.

When we had each found the sack with our name pinned on it we were taken to a room to change our clothes. I took off the labour-camp clothes I had worn for a year and removed the card carrying my photo and my name that I had worn on my chest. I was about to throw it away but changed my mind and stuffed it in my pocket as powerful testimony to the persecution I had suffered.

We lined up facing the gate and as it slowly opened we saw a great crowd of people outside craning their necks to see us. My husband was there, holding a bunch of flowers, and alongside him was Professor Qin.

Part V

EXILE

1

STATING THE FACTS

I THOUGHT **I** HAD GAINED my freedom but I couldn't have been more wrong. Barely had I taken the flowers my husband had brought when I saw the familiar faces of Niu Jun and Wu Bing. They had both aged. Then I found out I would not be going home in my husband's car, as I had imagined, but in a minibus.

Time is no respecter of humanity. Niu Jun and Wu Bing were not the only ones to have aged in the year since I had seen them; my husband had, too. Physical and mental exhaustion were written over all three faces. While I had been surviving in the labour re-education camp they looked as if life had not been too good to them either. This was the first thing that had a major impact on me. My husband and I have never discussed the impact my appearance had on him. Some things are just too painful to put into words.

My husband and Professor Qin had come in the local police station's minibus and we all returned together to report to the local police station. There was one unfamiliar face in the minibus and it bore the look of one even more determined than Niu Jun had ever been to seek personal advancement. This was Director Dai of the District Commission of Politics and Law, also in charge of the 610 Office and currently responsible for Falun Gong. Apparently I was to take Director Dai's presence as a sign of respect.

Director Dai was very enthusiastic about my release, saying that the reform squad for the entire district was extremely depleted, and only Gu Hua was doing education aide work. My youth and educational attainments would greatly strengthen the district and it was hoped that I would join in the work of the squad very soon and do my very best for the government.

Do my best for the government?

Five days later a family crisis saw me leave Beijing—my younger sister had escaped from custody and gone into hiding after being arrested for practising *qigong*.

MY SISTER IS ARRESTED

I went to Xinjiang in the far northwest first, then made my way down to Chengdu, the capital of Sichuan province, where I located my sister. She was in hiding in a small wine bar.

My younger sister had been the director of the law court's policy research room in our home town. She had been on maternity leave the last time I was arrested and when she heard I had been sentenced to labour re-education she had immediately set out for Beijing to see if she could provide me with any legal assistance. Before leaving, however, she had written to her work unit stating her views on the crackdown on Falun Gong. This letter gave those in charge of the law courts such a fright that they had driven the couple of thousand kilometres to Beijing non-stop to bring her back home before she could do anything foolish.

They were anxious because my sister was an outstanding worker of many years' standing. She had been nominated as an 'advanced worker' nine years in a row, had enjoyed a special government allowance and was popular with her fellow workers. They used the fact that she was on maternity leave to protect her after the crackdown, reporting to the authorities that 'no one in the law courts is practising Falun Gong'. Assuming she would be grateful for this, they said no more about it. They weren't to know that as soon as a shot reverberated in this silence—my arrest and sentencing—she would be off to Beijing.

So they had brought her back under cover of darkness and asked her to write a guarantee that this sort of thing wouldn't happen again, because they didn't want to have to report her. She had refused, and the affair had to be made public. She was sacked from her job, expelled from the Party and held in detention for a month, even though at that stage she was still breastfeeding her 5-month-old baby.

Six months after she was released from detention she had decided to go to Beijing again to make her voice heard. Not two minutes after they had started their exercises, she and three other Falun Gong practitioners were arrested in Tian'anmen Square for practising Falun Gong exercises. They were held in Beijing while her local police asked her husband for a 3,500-*yuan* 'repatriation fee' for them to go to Beijing and escort her back home.

Her husband didn't have this kind of money but the families of the other three practitioners paid up. One of them was forced to hand over more than 8,000 *yuan*. The police would usually have travelled by train, but now they had so much money at their disposal they flew both ways and had themselves quite a time in Beijing before escorting the three other practitioners home.

A few days later my sister seized her chance and escaped from the Beijing office. She had immediately been placed on the Ministry of Public Security's wanted list: her home phone was monitored, as were those of our parents and all our relatives, and the police kept dropping by to search for her. Our mother had been so incensed by this that at one point she took to sleeping fully clothed on the sofa by the front door to make it easier to open the door to any police who might honour her with their presence.

My sister had fled to Chengdu and eventually managed to get work in a small wine bar. She mixed drinks, served meals, washed up, swept the floor, handled the money, did the accounts, answered the phone, played the music and placed orders. She worked late and couldn't go to bed until the last customer had gone because she had to push all the tables back to make room on the floor for her bedding.

The local police would come to the wine bar from time to time. They would ask her where she was from and tell her to take her ID card to headquarters to get a temporary resident's card. Whenever this happened she would take off to some small town and hide for a few days. Then she'd ring the owner of the bar and go back when the coast was clear. But the police were becoming suspicious.

She had been in hiding for over four months by the time I caught up with her. She didn't have room for me to stay at the bar so we booked in at a little hotel and talked all night. The next morning, as we walked out of the hotel we bumped into a man who took one look at my sister then turned and walked away. He had been at the police academy with her ten years before and he was now a policeman in Chengdu. He was obviously aware that the Ministry of Public Security had set a price of 30,000 *yuan* on her head.

We immediately cancelled our hotel room and spent the rest of the day in a teahouse. I caught the last train back to our home town that night and my sister returned to the wine bar.

It took me several days to organise everything, but I eventually contacted a safe house and arranged to meet my sister on the train from Chengdu when it passed through our home town. We were to go on to Taiyuan in Shanxi province, where we would change trains. I had had to arrange all of this by public phone because the phone at home was being monitored, so it was all quite complicated.

When the train pulled in to the station on the night we were to leave, my sister did not alight from the carriage with the ticket she had bought for me, as arranged. This didn't look good, but I used my platform ticket to get on the train and by the time we pulled into the next station—over 50 kilometres away—I had searched right through the packed train without finding a trace of her.

I had no alternative but to get off the train and pay for my ride. So there I was at three o'clock in the morning, the rain pouring down, in an unfamiliar town. I had nowhere to go, no fallback plan, and my heart was as heavy as lead.

I got back to my parents' home about midday the next day. Without anything definite to go on I found it hard to believe my sister would just go missing like that. As I walked in I saw luggage scattered all over the floor and my mother, her hair standing on end, sorting through it.

'Your sister was arrested yesterday,' she said numbly. 'Her husband has just brought her belongings back from the detention centre. Here's the list of what they found when they searched her.'

Highlighted on the list were: a number of Falun Gong texts, two train tickets to Taiyuan, one railway luggage ticket.

'Go! Quickly! Go!' my father said to me as he scooped up my bag and pushed me through the door. 'Get on a plane. Don't wait until they find out who the other train ticket was for.'

I looked at my mother, her face grown so old in just a year, hair grey at the temples from worrying too much, her eyes full of despair. She shed no tears, only because I think she had no tears left. I longed to stay and console her but, gritting my teeth, I shouldered my bag and left.

There was no airport in my home town so I caught a coach to Chengdu. It was the day before the International Labour Day holiday on May 1 and the airport was packed with tourists.

I couldn't find anywhere to sit in the airport lounge so I went to a nearby Internet bar to wile away the time for a few *yuan*. It might sound strange that I had hardly ever accessed the Internet or sent emails, given that I had just spent a year in jail for 'using the Internet to voice grievances on behalf of Falun Gong'. I had only used my computer for work purposes. All I ever did was access the securities brokerage branch's terminal to view stock market quotations, perform simple transactions and handle correspondence.

Knowing I wouldn't be able to access the one site I wanted to, I idly clicked on the URL the previous user had visited. An obscene image appeared on the screen. People were coming and going in the bar and I didn't know what to do with myself. I was starting to get really flustered when in walked several burly policemen. I could see them walking towards me but I simply couldn't remove the image from the screen. In desperation I yanked the power cord out. The police looked at me suspiciously for a while and then left.

I sat at the computer physically and mentally exhausted, the pain of separation almost breaking my heart. The labour camp, my sister's arrest, her daughter cheerfully calling me 'Mummy', my mother turning grey and silent before my very eyes, my father's spirit crushed. Everything that had happened in the last few days seemed designed to test my endurance all over again.

The government had created an army of Internet police some tens of thousands strong; it had bled the people and had even bribed transnationals, developing some sort of firewall and blocking access to any website it didn't approve of. It arrested anyone who visited these sites or posted reactionary opinions on the web. It intercepted citizens' emails and sentenced people who downloaded prohibited material from the Internet to over ten years' imprisonment. Yet obscene websites like the one I had stumbled upon were accessible at the click of a mouse and they had not been removed. I hadn't seen who had been using the site I had just visited by accident—and what would my daughter have made of it had she seen it?

My flight got me to Taiyuan earlier than the train I was to have arrived on, so I was still able to contact the person who had come to meet me. I visited the ancient Buddhist temple sites and national treasures on Mount Wutai but any sense of sanctity was destroyed for me by the unbearably vulgar 'Grant whatever is requested' bronze plaques nailed all over them and the crowds of peddlers hawking their wares at the tops of their lungs. Yet for some reason the Buddhist chants playing over the sound system in the tourist shop cut through the din and moved me to tears. I was overwhelmed afresh by the pain of my sister being thrown into that den of monsters and the age-old sorrow that is encapsulated in the expression 'I look back—I do not see the ancients; I look ahead—I can't see the generations to come'. Holy Buddhist temple buildings and sacred canons had been traded countless times for banknotes but there seemed to be nowhere in this vast world where genuine practitioners could find a resting place.

LOOKING BACK

It was close to a month before I was finally in a position to start writing my book. One of the people I had been to university with had gone to live in America and when he heard of my desire to write about what I had been through he immediately arranged for someone to bring me a laptop computer. He was not a Falun Gong practitioner, he told me, but he was not a supporter of the Communist Party either. He had been in the Muxidi area on June 4, 1989 and when the troops had opened fire a bullet pierced the chain guard on his bicycle and wounded a person alongside him. This stranger died in my friend's arms just as they reached the hospital in a taxi.

It took me almost a week to write the preface. Overwhelmed by grief, I would sit at the computer unable to go on as the tears rolled down my face. I worked day and night on the manuscript and I also found a way to access the Clearwisdom website through another fellow practitioner overseas. At last I was able to read the new articles Li Hongzhi had put out since the crackdown.

Almost daily I read on the Internet of who had been persecuted to death and who had been arrested. I also learned that as soon as I had left the labour camp people were saying mine had been a 'fake reform', that I had not done my best in the brainwashing squad, that I had gone into hiding from the police, that a report about my sister (which I had written) had appeared on the Internet, and so on. All of this had aroused the suspicions of the police and they were looking for me. I knew that they might appear any day and if they found out what I was up to it wouldn't be the labour re-education camp this time. It would probably be just as Wang Zhao had predicted: the women's prison across the road.

But I had to write this down. I was prepared to be arrested again at any time, but in the meantime I was careful to copy what I wrote every day onto a floppy disk, which I carefully hid, and then delete that text from the hard drive.

I also printed out an English version of *Zhuan Falun* so I could brush up on my English, which I hadn't used since I had graduated, ten years before. I was getting ready to speak to the media in English about the horrors of the prison camp once I left the country.

At the same time I put my affairs in order. I wrote a solemn declaration and an open letter to the labour-camp police and sent these to my fellow practitioner overseas. I also sent her my manuscript in instalments as I went along, asking her to publish it the moment she knew I had been arrested. That way I felt I had done everything I needed to do.

2

A SACRED MISSION

MY EXIT VISA CAME THROUGH almost five months after I was released, by which time I had written down everything up to my time in the despatch division—almost half of the story. Before I left the labour camp I heard that everybody had to go back six months after their release to write a thought report and to check that their 'reform' had really taken and that they had stabilised. One Falun Gong student I knew of had reformed and been let out early on what was recorded as 'serving the sentence outside the labour camp'. When she was brought back to write her thought report she had said something that did not quite meet the standard required of a 'reformed' person and, therefore, was sent to the training unit instead of being released.

My visa came through just in time, because I knew my local police were interested in me, as were the labour-camp police, who were making enquiries as to my whereabouts. I had been able to apply for a visa because at that time very few Falun Gong practitioners had escaped the country to expose the crackdown, so the authorities hadn't thought of taking precautions yet. In addition, Chinese law allows even criminals who have fully served their sentences to apply for a visa to travel overseas. Nevertheless, I arranged everything for my departure very carefully, not knowing if I had been blacklisted by Customs. I carried nothing that had anything to do with Falun Gong except the labour-camp evidence necessary for applying for refugee status and my precious English-language copy of *Zhuan Falun*. I wiped my hard disk completely and sent the partly completed draft of my book and other necessary material to myself at an electronic mailbox.

Just before dawn on September 1, 2001 my flight from Guangzhou approached the city of Melbourne in Australia. The view as I peered down from the dark sky was of a city still asleep, but as the plane flew lower on its approach to the airport I could pick out the lights of houses and I saw a splendid city already full of life. I was exceptionally calm and felt hardly any excitement or sense of freedom, or even happiness, for this calm was tempered by my need not to forget my fellow practitioners still in prison and my responsibility to them and my family, still in China.

I had chosen Melbourne because some distant relatives I had never met lived there. An hour after arriving at their place I phoned Simon, the Melbourne contact person I had found through the Falun Dafa Contact List (Worldwide) page on the Clearwisdom website before leaving China. In English, I asked him if he was Chinese or a Westerner. A Westerner, he replied. Since my spoken English was still a bit shaky, I asked him if he could get a Chinese-speaking Falun Gong student to ring me back. It wasn't long before someone rang back and I explained my situation briefly: I was from the mainland; I had recently come out of a forced-labour re-education camp; and I wanted to meet and share experiences with local Falun Gong practitioners. She said someone would come and pick me up that evening.

My relatives were wary and peppered me with questions.

'Who was that who rang you? What was her name? How long have you known her? What is she up to? How long has she been in Australia?'

Their degree of anxiety surprised me. My relatives went on to warn me that Australia had its fair share of swindlers and that they themselves had often been cheated and even been beaten up. They said that because I had fled my country I should be extremely careful, to the point of telling no one where I was living.

I found out later that my relatives had come to Australia two years previously with limited English and had been cheated out of a considerable sum of money by an unscrupulous immigration agent; they had even been involved in physical fights.

This made me realise I was being much too impatient. Here I was, not in the country two minutes and trying to contact strangers of whose background I knew nothing. The person who was coming to pick me up that night rang first but, because my relatives did not want him to come to the house, we arranged to meet at the local railway station.

My relatives lived in an outer suburb of which I saw very little as they drove me to the darkened station. There was no one about, just one lone car parked there waiting. It was like a scene from a movie. We went up to the car and out hopped two Westerners: Simon and his girlfriend, Kate.

It was a very cold night so we all got into Simon's car. He told us that Melbourne Falun Gong practitioners were gathering that night for a reading group and asked if I would like to go and meet them. Glancing at my relatives, I asked him when the next gathering would be.

'In two weeks' time,' he replied.

That settled it. I certainly wasn't going to wait another two weeks. Sensing my mood, my relatives took a closer look at Simon and Kate in the wan glow of the streetlights. Perceiving Simon to be a gentle person and his girlfriend, Kate, a decent young university student, they finally agreed to let me go with them.

It took us quite some time to reach our destination, a brightly lit room in a large building, where several dozen people were reading *Zhuan Falun*. Only one or two of them looked up as we walked in. I found an empty seat beside a young woman. Seeing I didn't have a book, she rose slightly from her seat and moved her book so that we could share it. I read along with the others.

About half the people there were Westerners and it was quite strange the way the readings were done. The Chinese would read a passage in Chinese; then the Westerners would read a passage in English; then the Chinese would read a passage in Chinese and so it would go on, the Chinese and the English dovetailing together so smoothly one would have been forgiven for not realising it was not all the one language.

When we reached the end of that lecture we started sharing our experiences. Simon introduced me and I spoke briefly of my experience in China and of the brutality of the labour camps. Others spoke and I recall a young Western man who had just started university telling of the planned SOS! Emergency Rescue bicycle tour in which people were going to cycle around the state to draw attention to the persecution in China.

During the break quite a few people approached me, asking when I had arrived in Australia, what sort of visa I had and if I was going to seek asylum, some offering assistance and many giving me their phone numbers.

My gaze was somehow drawn to a very elegantly dressed middle-aged Chinese woman at the other end of the room, her hair coiled on top of her head in a bun. There was about her a certain air of trustworthiness, and I could sense she was very capable. I went over to her and told her that I had just arrived that very day.

'There are three things on my mind,' I said to her. 'First, to contact the media. Second, to apply for refugee status. And third, to find a quiet place to live where I can write my book.' I asked her if she could help me.

She was very gracious. Yes, she said, she could help me. I could stay at her place but she couldn't come to get me for a few days because she was going to take part in a 36-hour protest fast outside the Chinese consulate.

And so in one fell swoop all my needs were met. And that was how the Falun Gong 'organisation' worked.

The testimony of SOS!

Three weeks later, with the help of fellow practitioners I had prepared my application for asylum and submitted it to the Department of Immigration, thus formally becoming a refugee in the international community.

A little over a week after that I caught a plane to Brisbane, the capital of Queensland, to attend a large Asia–Pacific Falun Gong experience-sharing conference. Over 1,000 practitioners from a dozen countries attended and at the press conference held during the conference I had my first meeting with the media.

The press conference was held on October 5 at Centenary Place, an open park in the city centre. It was a warm spring morning and as the sun burned off the light morning mist female Falun Gong practitioners in their white skirts were quietly busy with their children, filling balloons with helium and preparing for the conference. I sat by myself under the shade of a tree going over my material. I had written a draft in English of what I was going to say but I wanted to memorise it instead of reading it out. I had never spoken in English before this many people so I was as nervous about my pronunciation and my grammar as about forgetting my lines.

Just before the press conference began I learned that it had been timed to be a welcome for six Falun Gong practitioners who had taken 34 days to walk the more than 1,000 kilometres from Sydney to Brisbane as part of the SOS! Global Rescue Walk.

Once the podium was set up, people flocked into the park, many of them wearing white skirts or yellow T-shirts and holding banners proclaiming 'SOS! Urgent Rescue', 'Stop the deaths through maltreatment', 'Truthfulness, Compassion, Forbearance' and 'Falun Dafa'. The crowd filled the park, leaving a narrow passageway down the middle, and I sat at the back of the podium feeling it was all a little unreal.

The crowd suddenly erupted, applauding the arrival of the six Falun Gong practitioners, and the press photographers swarmed around them. When the walkers reached their appointed place the press conference began. As the MC introduced the SOS! walkers I gazed down at their deeply tanned faces, so different from the faces in the crowd. One of the six, a woman, was moved to tears by the occasion. I did not know whether her tears were for the hardship she had endured on the walk or for her fellow practitioners dying through maltreatment in Chinese prisons, but I shared her pain and could not hold back my own tears.

One of the walkers later told me that it had been very hot when they set out and as they walked along the highway under the blazing sun with not a soul in sight the back-draught of the long-distance coaches as they whizzed by would nearly blow them over. Their SOS! T-shirts were wet through and some of them got blisters on their feet, which made walking very difficult, but they physically supported one another and walked on through their pain. One old Chinese man who had lived in Australia for many years said it had been a long time since anything had shaken him until he saw those six small figures quietly supporting each other on their long journey by foot along the relentless highway.

Not enough books could ever be written on what Falun Gong practitioners outside China have done to alert their governments and their fellow citizens to the brutal persecution that has taken place since the crackdown. Countless numbers of people have been touched and many nations have made a stand but many others, guided by economic motives, have remained apathetic and made only token protests. It has sometimes been difficult for others to understand what these overseas practitioners have been doing and yet they have created a great deal of sympathy for their cause. They have quietly persevered with their task, oblivious to public acclaim or the lack of it. Just like Falun Gong practitioners in China who do not hit back when attacked or talk back when insulted they, through their own peaceful tenacity, have slowly begun to have an impact on the most brutal and seemingly powerful regime in the world.

Some have said it is nothing less than a miracle that a fearless and non-violent group of reasonable people who are not rising in rebellion but who equally are not prepared to submit to terror should have made their presence felt in China, where one violent regime has replaced another. This is a guilty China, a China that is prepared even now to dip 'a steamed *mantou* roll in the fresh blood of its compatriots' and eat it to cure its sickness, which is precisely what the famous writer Lu Xun accused 'old China' of doing to young revolutionaries in his 1919 short story, 'Medicine'.

All of a sudden I heard the MC announcing that I would speak next. Tears streaming down my face, I walked to the lectern and managed to say in English only 'I am so happy to be able to speak here today' before I was choked with sobs and could not go on. I had come so far for this!

That night my speech, which I eventually managed to finish, was broadcast nationally on radio and TV. It was the first time I exposed to the media the cruel persecution of Falun Gong practitioners in China's labour re-education camps.

A few days later I flew to Sydney, the largest city in Australia and the news and cultural hub of the country. My fellow practitioners thought that this would be the best place for me to tell my story.

I was billeted in Sydney with a Western Falun Gong practitioner named Myrna, a woman in her fifties who had migrated to Australia from Chile 30 years previously. Her husband, Tim, was English and they had opened a furniture store in the heart of the city. Myrna had started practising Falun Gong after being attracted to a group she saw meditating in a park, a few days before the crackdown in 1999. She noticed that numbers dropped dramatically a few days later and asked the lad instructing her why this might be. He told her it was because the Chinese Government did not allow people to practise Falun Gong.

Myrna was wide-eyed in astonishment at this. Why on earth would somebody living in Australia who had chosen to practise a form of *qigong* they enjoyed reverse that decision because of a decision made by a foreign government? For her it was a simple question of to whom do you owe your loyalty: to yourself or to a foreign government that for some inexplicable reason concerns itself with ordinary people doing *qigong*? This strong-willed woman who had always lived in Western society, with its emphasis on the individual, found it almost impossible to understand why Chinese people who had migrated to Australia would take any notice of the Chinese Government.

Myrna welcomed me warmly, in true South American style. She took me upstairs to a small bedroom and told me it was my room. The three of us talked about everything under the sun during my stay there, me in my Chinese-accented English, Myrna in her Spanish-accented English and Tim in his perfect native English.

One day Tim told me, only half joking, that he used to be racist and had kept his distance from Chinese people, with their yellow skin. He had never imagined he would have any contact with them or that he would ever have a Chinese person living in his house, much less place his home, his person and his life in her hands (this was in reference to the fact that I was alone in the house when they went to work during the day). If I hadn't been a Falun Gong practitioner, he told me, he would have said, Forget it!

Myrna had two young grandsons, a 5-year-old and a 3-year-old, and whenever they came to visit they would come up to my room to see me. When they found out I came from China they began to call me 'China' and for a long time after I left they would always ask 'Where is China?' when they came to visit their grandparents.

They loved my computer and as soon as the Chinese writing appeared on the screen they would sing out '*Fofa! Fofa!*' (meaning 'Buddha Law'). The 3-year-old would sit on my knee as I typed and with supreme assurance would pronounce everything as it appeared on the screen to be *Zhen, Shan, Ren* (Truthfulness, Compassion, Forbearance).

I discovered that Myrna had taught them this. She could not read

Chinese but had a lot of Falun Gong material and leaflets in Chinese in her house. She also displayed bundles of a brief synopsis of Falun Gong, in both English and Chinese, in their furniture store for customers to take if they wished. She would point to the characters on the leaflets and say to her grandsons *Fofa, Zhen, Shan, Ren* and naturally enough they thought that was how all Chinese characters were pronounced.

I have since come across many Western Falun Gong practitioners who have developed quite an obsession with Chinese culture and who will happily try a few Chinese words no matter how awkward their pronunciation is. They treat Chinese people like me who can give an extensive and clear account of things Chinese as some sort of authority.

A day or two after going to stay with Myrna I discovered that she was in frequent email contact with other Falun Gong practitioners about a matter that seemed to be important. She didn't say much to me about it, however, and I didn't ask.

'Did you know that I had seen you before you came to Sydney?' she said to me one day, out of the blue. 'After you gave your talk at the press conference in Brisbane a journalist interviewed you by yourself and I was right there listening. I don't think you noticed me, though. After I while I said to myself: "Everything she's saying is precisely what I would say. Why should I have doubts about her? Why am I doing this? It is quite silly." So I walked away.'

I looked at her for some time, piecing together what I had heard with a vague feeling I had had. Slowly I began to understand what she was talking about and why I had been billeted with a Western student. It was an anti-espionage measure.

There were two aspects to this anti-espionage: one was to keep them safe if I was a spy and the other was to keep me safe from spies.

This had never entered my mind. I had always thought of Australia as the land of the free; once I got there, I had said to myself, everything would be just fine. But the reality was quite different. The tentacles of Chinese communism stretch across the world. Just over a year later, the United States Department of Justice would arrest Chen Wenying, an overseas Chinese and resident of Los Angeles, and charge her with being a double agent. This was just the tip of the iceberg and people began to wonder just how many agents the Chinese Communist authorities might have stationed overseas to suppress Falun Gong.

As head of the Los Angeles–Guangzhou Friendship Association, Chen Wenying had been prominent in Chinese circles in Los Angeles and had maintained close ties with the higher echelons of the Chinese Communist Party. She had met Jiang Zemin at the airport when he visited America in October 2002 and he had let it be known that he acknowledged her alone of all the Los Angeles Chinese. She was arrested in April 2003 on a charge of stealing confidential documents belonging to the United States Federal Bureau of Investigation and passing them on to the Chinese mainland. The foreign media were surprised at the sumptuousness of her Los Angeles villa, but they were even more amazed that the Chinese Communists would bring in an elite spy at the national level to counter Falun Gong.

By definition, spies generally keep a low profile but after the crackdown Chen Wenying put out articles hurling abuse at Falun Gong, called meetings of overseas Chinese to attack Falun Gong and was a very aggressive opponent of Falun Gong in general. This was so unusual that it is hard to believe she had not received specific instructions on how to handle Falun Gong.

The foreign media also reported that the Jiang [Zemin] government had despatched over 1,000 spies to North and South America and Canada alone, at considerable cost. How much of this is true is not the issue. It is an open secret that the Chinese Communists have for many years assigned large numbers of people abroad as journalists, merchants and spies. What is more unsettling is the huge amounts that have been poured into these activities and the influence they have exerted on local media. During Jiang Zemin's visits to Iceland, Russia, Lithuania, Latvia and Mexico in 2002, Falun Gong practitioners from many other countries blacklisted by the Chinese Communists were denied entry visas and were thus unable to stage peaceful appeals. Falun Gong practitioners from Taiwan were not allowed through Customs when they tried to attend an experience-sharing conference in Hong Kong. Spies placed overseas had clearly devoted a great deal of effort to Falun Gong matters.

Since such activities were so difficult to guard against, it is no wonder that I should have been suspected of being a spy. After all, I had appeared out of nowhere and no one knew anything about me. On the other hand, if I really were human testimony to persecution, then I needed protection to prevent real spies discovering my whereabouts. This, then, was the reason I had been billeted with a Western Falun Gong student, since most Chinese Communist spies infiltrated the Chinese community rather than the Western.

Myrna then told me that she was discussing with some Western students the possibility of their going to Beijing to present a petition on behalf of Falun Gong. I knew at once this was no small matter, nor was it something that could be bandied about, so even though she had raised it I didn't pursue it, waiting for her to bring it up again.

'I have cashed in my ticket to China,' she said to me one day. 'I don't think I'll go.'

'Why not?'

'All this talk and discussion is too much like some kind of an organisation. The practice of Falun Dafa is not an organisation, as you know, and now I just feel I don't want to go.'

'May I tell you what I think?' I asked, even though I could see from her face that she had already made up her mind not to have anything to do with any 'organisation' or with politics.

'If you go,' I said gently, 'it will be tremendously encouraging to the Falun Gong practitioners in prison and they will be so grateful. You would be going to present a peaceful petition, wouldn't you? And the more people who know about the petition, the better, isn't that so? Therefore if everybody goes together it will have a far greater impact. Do you really have to contact the media beforehand? Each of you is a free agent and there is no compulsion, so would it still feel like an organisation if you made contact as and when required? You don't have a political purpose or a political agenda, do you?'

She looked at me for several seconds then turned and went downstairs. We came from different cultures and I couldn't tell whether she felt what I had said was inappropriate. Also, she was so independent she did not take kindly to advice or sermons.

Five minutes later she came back upstairs.

'It's all arranged,' she said, with the faintest of smiles. 'I bought another ticket. It only cost an extra $1,000. But I'll be travelling by myself; I couldn't get on the same plane as the others.'

I was surprised that she had made such a major decision so quickly. I walked over to her and gave her a hug and as I pressed my cheek to hers I whispered, 'I love you for that.'

———

I saw Myrna off on her journey to Beijing on November 17, 2001. She looked very calm but there was something different about her. We had not given much thought to the consequences of her actions but as she set off in her taxi she turned to me.

'The world will never be the same again,' she said.

She had written a declaration entitled 'Why I am going to Tian'anmen' to which she had appended her name, her date of birth and her passport number. She had given it to a close friend and asked him to contact the Australian Department of Foreign Affairs should she be arrested.

She hadn't told Tim what she was going to do in Beijing, nor had she told any of her fellow practitioners who were not directly involved, apart from me. I translated her declaration into Chinese, her last words ringing in my ears: The world will never be the same again.

Myrna and her companions were due to make their appearance in Tian'anmen Square at two o'clock in the afternoon on November 20, 2001, Beijing time. I didn't know how many people from how many countries were taking part and I didn't know how the Chinese authorities would handle this unprecedented situation.

Five minutes before the appointed time I sat at my computer and from a calm heart sent blessings to them for their endeavour. At precisely 2 p.m. I uploaded my translation of Myrna's 'Why I am going to Tian'anmen' to the Clearwisdom website.

I do not remember the day I made this decision; all I remember is knowing that I would be there. Within me, I know the benefits derived from practising Falun Dafa, and consequently I cannot understand this senseless persecution. Day by day, I try to follow the teachings, although at times it is hard to change old habits and not fall short of the mark. Practising Truthfulness, Compassion and Forbearance is a challenge for any individual, but one tries and, with practice, one is bound to succeed. We all know that in many ways we are encouraged by society to deviate from these principles. The pursuit of absolute wealth and power are fast becoming the trademarks of this new century. I feel that in the 21st century, with all its scientific and technical advancements, there should be peace on the earth. Sadly, things are getting worse.

Due to the terrorist attack, America is on full alert and there are conflicts in most countries around the world. Worst of all is the situation in China, where thousands upon thousands of Falun Dafa practitioners are imprisoned without trial, and many others are persecuted in one way or another. The reality for female practitioners in forced-labour camps is physical abuse—and, in some instances, rape—while some pregnant practitioners are faced with the horror of forced abortions. Many healthy, vibrant practitioners have been tortured to death. To Western societies, these people are only names and statistics. The human rights abuses that are taking place in China are beyond our understanding. We cannot comprehend how human beings in our day and age can carry out acts so inhuman that they belong in the dark ages.

Falun Gong practitioners are being used as scapegoats in the struggle for power within the Chinese Government. Jiang Zemin has indicated Falun Gong is to be eliminated. Thus people who want to be good, and to be of value to society by following and practising this cultivation system are persecuted. Upholding the fundamental principles of Truthfulness, Compassion and Forbearance is not a crime. If Jiang Zemin were to succeed in obliterating Falun Dafa, the universe and the world would indeed be very dark places. Some people say this has happened before in history, that this is nothing new or strange. Is this a good enough reason for us to be silent or inactive? As people of conscience, should we not raise our voices and tell everyone that these kinds of violations of human rights are no longer acceptable?

Why are children still being born into a world full of violence? My belief is that in some small way we can all contribute our good thoughts to make a difference. Some people have looked briefly through the pages of *Zhuan Falun* and adopted an uninformed opinion of its contents, without any in-depth understanding. Some have sensationalised what they thought to be controversial. It surprises me that the truth of what lies within the pages of *Zhuan Falun*—the goodness, compassion and benevolence of Master Li—have not become public knowledge. Falun Dafa is a beautiful experience, and it does make a difference in one's life.

Like everything that is good for us, it is not easy; but neither is it too difficult. Everything hinges on one's heart and determination. In an effort to awaken the minds of the Chinese population that are being brainwashed by the vicious, poisonous propaganda campaign that was launched in 1999, I have made this decision. As a Falun Dafa practitioner, I feel it is my duty to travel to Beijing and join other Western practitioners in making it known that Falun Dafa is good, that it is practised throughout the world, and that it belongs to everybody.

That evening I read on the Clearwisdom website the joint declaration issued by the 35 Western Falun Gong practitioners from twelve countries who had gone to Beijing to present a petition:

Today, we gather here in Beijing's Tian'anmen Square as Falun Gong practitioners from 12 countries. We are here to appeal on behalf of tens of thousands of innocent people who suffer imprisonment, torture or even death at the hands of their own government in China.

We make five demands.

First, we call upon China's government to abolish the '610 Office' and other administrative offices that were created for the sole purpose of directing violence against Falun Gong practitioners.

Second, we demand that China's police immediately stop attacking Falun Gong practitioners with torture, rape and sexual violence, criminal psychiatry and other forms of cruelty that have reportedly caused over 1,000 deaths; those responsible should be held accountable and brought to justice.

Third, the government must immediately and unconditionally release all Falun Gong practitioners who have been detained, whether in prisons, labour camps, mental hospitals or elsewhere. It must restore to them their basic freedom of belief and right to practise Falun Gong in peace.

Fourth, the government must restore Falun Gong's legal standing, and remove all the malicious labels it has affixed to the practice.

Fifth, China's government must also cease its treacherous campaign to slander Falun Gong and our respected teacher, Li

Hongzhi. The name of Mr. Li must be cleared, and the ground-less warrant to arrest him withdrawn; he should be allowed to return to see his students in China.
(<http://clearwisdom.net/emh/articles/2001/11/20/15954.html>)

The media began reporting the matter a few days later. Thirty-five Western Falun Gong practitioners from twelve countries—who had never met before—suddenly appeared in Tian'anmen Square and proceeded to take group photos in the usual tourist fashion. Then some of them sat on the ground in the Falun Gong meditation pose while others stood behind them and quickly unfurled a large banner reading, in English and Chinese, 'Truthfulness, Compassion, Forbearance'.

Within fifteen seconds they were surrounded by police and police cars. According to witnesses, the police knocked some students to the ground and hauled them into a minibus. One woman was knocked unconscious and a CNN reporter at the site was also arrested.

They were taken to a nearby police station and locked in a small basement cell. They were shocked not so much by the violence and harassment as by the harsh reality of the crackdown. The young police officers they came in contact with were completely ignorant of the outside world, believing as gospel that Falun Gong was bad and that they could do whatever they liked with Falun Gong practitioners. They even thought Falun Gong had been banned all over the world.

The Chinese Government had probably never been faced with such a knotty diplomatic problem: the likely consequences of seizing foreign citizens of twelve different countries. They acted quickly, however, and deported the 35 foreign practitioners, prohibiting them from entering China for five years.

THIS DAY WILL GO DOWN IN HISTORY

Two days later—on November 22, 2001—I saw Myrna at a 'welcome home' press conference in Sydney for her and the other two Australians who had gone to Beijing.

What Myrna had experienced in that short time may have jolted her more severely than anything she had gone through in 50 years. As she stood at the microphone to tell her story, holding out the blouse that had been ripped by the Beijing police, her hands and her voice shook and she couldn't go on. I could understand what it must have been like for someone from a Western country where even mistreating animals is against the law. The violence visited upon them was really difficult for them to accept, not because of the slight personal inconvenience but because of its implications. If citizens of foreign countries could be roughed up like that in broad daylight, what sort of treatment in prison could their Chinese fellow practitioners expect?

Seized by a sudden impulse I plucked up my courage and walked over to the MC to ask if I could say a few words. I stammered and stuttered a bit because this was impromptu and I was speaking in English, but the gist of my speech was as follows:

This day—November 20, 2001—was a great day that will go down in history. Over the years the Chinese people have seen the cannon balls of the Opium Wars, the sacking of the Old Summer Palace—the Yuanming Yuan—and the killing and pillaging of the invading Japanese army. We have also seen Western missionaries bring the teachings of Christianity to China. But the Chinese people have never seen anything like this before: 35 foreign Falun Gong practitioners from twelve countries gathering in Tian'anmen Square holding aloft the same Truthfulness, Compassion, Forbearance banner as thousands upon thousands of Chinese have done before them. They have done this in support of a form of practice that originated in China and are requesting that the Chinese Government release its own people.... I am so proud to be Chinese today, for today the Truthfulness, Compassion and Forbearance of Falun Dafa, which has its origins in China, have transcended national borders. They have transcended language, culture and race to reach beyond ideologies and social systems to every corner of the globe.

The press conference made the TV news broadcasts that night and marked my second appearance before the media talking about my experiences.

I AWAKEN FROM MY DREAM

Australian practitioners made it possible for me to go to many different places to tell my story after that. When I wasn't on the radio or on TV, I was talking to newspapers, to members of parliament, to human rights groups, research groups or university groups. In the meantime I went on with my writing.

When I got to the part about reforming I found it hard to continue. Knowing it was utterly wrong for a practitioner to reform, I could pinpoint just where the others who had reformed had gone wrong, but subconsciously I had always felt that *my* reform was somehow different. This was coming through loud and clear in my book.

In March 2002 Falun Gong practitioners held the First World Congress of Future Science and Culture at Cambridge University in England. I had rushed to finish writing, thinking I could present the manuscript at the conference, and sent sections off to the organising committee as I completed them. About three weeks later I received a letter saying they had been through the manuscript and had decided against it.

This was a dreadful blow and after reading the letter I sat at my computer and cried. Many of my fellow practitioners had tried to tell me that my 'bellicose battle of wits' with the police in the labour re-education camp had not been worthy of a practitioner, but I had been unwilling to really acknowledge the truth of what they said, convinced that their experience was different and they could not really understand mine.

I woke up the next morning with phrases from *Falun Buddha Fa: Lecture at the First Conference in North America* running through my mind. I had been reading it the night before and something had begun to stir in my brain.

'Don't tell me I really was wrong?' I asked myself incredulously. 'Me! Me, who put her life on the line? How could I have made such a mistake, such a preposterous mistake?'

Almost immediately I realised that I was, in fact, absolutely, totally wrong, and if I continued to harbour the notion that I was right, no matter how many books I wrote, how many facts I exposed, I could no longer be counted as a genuine practitioner. Our practice is not about surface deeds, but about our true state of mind.

To put it another way: if every Falun Gong practitioner took the same path as me, that is, to reform as soon as they were arrested and then renounce their reformation as soon as they were released, could they still be called practitioners of 'Truthfulness, Compassion and Forbearance'?

Zhuan Falun states that 'no matter how the moral standard changes, this characteristic of the universe remains unchanged, and it is the sole criterion that distinguished good people from bad people. As a practitioner, one must then conduct oneself by following this characteristic, rather than the standard of everyday people'. However, I had allowed myself to be seduced from the standard I had willingly chosen for myself and had instead acted as those who would 'use whatever methods to achieve the goal'.

I believe that the reason why today's society has so many problems is that people's criteria for evaluating good and bad are declining so that people's moral standards can only decline. Faced with this, Falun Gong practitioners' only weapon is their flesh and blood bodies, but they have to face a regime with all the resources of a nation at its disposal and which has 'made use of all its experiences in every past campaign and struggle, along with evil means of all times and all lands'.[26] We practitioners can only overcome this ordeal if we walk a righteous path at all times, if we demand of ourselves the highest personal standards. If we do not, then we will be suppressed or forced to accept 'amnesty' and 'serve the ruler'. All our efforts would, therefore, be in vain.

This realisation caused me to sob uncontrollably. The agony and humiliation I felt outweighed all the sufferings I had experienced in the labour camp. A fellow practitioner who had gone through the same experience once said that 'nothing hurts more than repenting'. He had spoken prosaically, but now I knew the pain that lay behind his prosaic tone.

I recovered from this initial onslaught of emotion, but shame, remorse and self-reproach would attack me without warning, the violence of the assault reducing me to painful tears.

Twice my writing came to a complete halt, the second time after completing the first draft. I was faced with a logical dilemma: I had written the guarantee in the first place in order to be able to

---

26 Taken from Li Hongzhi's lecture on the *Fa* at the International Conference in Washington, DC, 2001.

write this book, but when I thought back to everything that had happened in the labour camp after I had written the guarantee I knew I couldn't bear to confront these events and tell the whole thing all over again.

Once I wrote a short article about my experiences in the labour camp and sent it as an email. As soon as I clicked on 'Send', I immediately wanted to stretch my hand into the screen and drag the text back. I felt almost sick about stating in the article that I had once been 'reformed'.

I often went on the Internet, reading other practitioners' stories, some of which moved me to tears. The experiences of many practitioners were so dramatic and stirring that I thought perhaps I should write a novel, a blend of their stories and my experience, describing this slice of history through a fictional heroine. But in the end I abandoned that idea because I was not a professional writer and I lacked the necessary imagination. Besides, practice is an internal process and while I might be able to tell the bare bones of other people's stories I could never describe their inner journeys.

Eventually I realised that by allowing myself to be surrounded by all these negative feelings, I was allowing the persecution I had experienced in the labour camp still to have an effect on me. Why did the Chinese government persist in arresting and 'reforming' practitioners when our teacher had said that he did not recognise any of the recantations extracted from practitioners under duress? Their true purpose must have been to destroy our wills by playing on our remorse for having done the wrong thing.

If I could teach myself to think more of the need to expose the truth of the persecution rather than the effect it was having on me, I could escape this mental dilemma. In order to represent the story and journey I had taken vividly and truly, I would have to return to the past and write until the tears were streaming down my face, until I felt that all my strength had been poured into my manuscript and all that was in me had been emptied. To do this, I had to realise that the 'me' in the labour camp was not the 'me' of today. This would allow me to examine 'her' rationally and dispassionately, to tell the story that had to be told.

Yes, I could save face by glossing over my experiences after reforming, but if I did this I would not be exposing the cruellest part of the persecution. I would not be able to show my readers why the 'saving grace' of the police in the labour camp could drive people to insanity and death.

So after stopping twice I started again, telling my own story. Initially, my motive was to expose the brutality of the crackdown and present the facts. I believe there is nothing wrong in that. To be overly concerned about my own 'greatness' or about whether my experiences might give readers a misrepresentation of Falun Gong was simply another attachment. My experience as an individual cannot be taken as being representative of the practice of Falun Gong, but I wanted to pluck up the courage to deliver an entirely authentic account.

I BRING CHARGES AGAINST JIANG ZEMIN

A lot happened after that. Together with six other Falun Gong practitioners from five other countries, I was party to a lawsuit against Jiang Zemin's crackdown on Falun Gong filed with the United Nations. This was announced in October 2002 when Jiang Zemin arrived in Chicago, the first stop on his visit to the United States. At the same time, he was served with a separate subpoena: another group of Falun Gong practitioners had filed charges against Jiang Zemin in the United States District Court, Northern District of Illinois, for the crimes of genocide, crimes against humanity and cruel torture.

Four days later my husband was arrested in Beijing. His house was searched and his computer and other items were confiscated. The authorities kept his whereabouts secret and no one knew how long he was to be detained, whether he was to be given a heavy sentence or what sort of mental and physical suffering he was being subjected to. His mother lost over ten kilos in less than a month; our terrified daughter spent her tenth birthday without either of her parents; and I was in greater torment than when I was thrown into prison myself. But those feelings are far too ugly for me to describe here, even if I could. I struggled to get out of bed in the mornings but I couldn't give in to grief and anxiety; I had to do everything in my power to rescue my husband.

My story hit the headlines again and several overseas journalists interviewed me by phone. In China, my family, friends and even people I had never met learned through these foreign news reports of my filing charges against Jiang Zemin and of my husband's arrest.

Many people could not understand my actions and some suggested

I was simply trying to make a name for myself. I got phone calls from distant relatives passing on threats from other relatives that if I continued to carry on like that they wouldn't be so nice to me next time . . . I don't want to write about that either, not because I don't understand it but because, after enduring so many years of violent abuse of power, too many Chinese people are no longer capable of choosing between what is honourable and what is evil.

I can understand why the people of China were appalled at an ordinary person filing charges against a Chairman who had taken for himself total Party, political and military authority. After what I had experienced and witnessed, however, I had not the slightest hesitation in making that decision. I believed those sorts of crimes had to stop.

Back in early 2000, when I had found out that a Falun Gong practitioner had been persecuted to death in Beijing's Chaoyang District lockup, I had drafted a letter to Jiang Zemin. (This was before I was sent to the labour camp.) The letter was intended for joint signature and at the end we had suggested he take the blame for the damage he had caused the nation and the people and immediately resign. We had reserved the right to prosecute him through the International Court of Justice. Copies of the letter were circulated widely among Falun Gong practitioners, many of whom, including me, had signed the letter with their real names and addresses. We had been planning to present the letter to the Petition Offices at Zhongnanhai when we got enough signatures but I was arrested soon afterwards and don't know what became of it.

Yet, despite all I had been through, I still underestimated the savagery of those bandits. It never occurred to me that they would strike at my husband.

NOTHING LIKE THIS HAS EVER HAPPENED BEFORE

I think many people will agree that the events surrounding Falun Gong are unprecedented. The nation has spent one-quarter of its financial resources on maintaining this bloody crackdown aimed at 100 million practitioners. The daily expenditure on maintaining police patrols and vehicles in Tian'anmen Square and hiring unemployed people to help is over one million *yuan*. When I was in China I heard some classified information: by April 2001 some 830,000 Falun Gong practitioners whose names and details are known had been arrested, but there were no statistics on the number of unnamed people. So many people have gone to Tian'anmen to display banners but the longest time any were displayed was two minutes, the shortest a few seconds. Some people were arrested before they had brought out their banners and even some tourists who did not practise Falun Gong had been arrested when they pulled out red scarves to wear in photographs or when they shaded their faces with their hands to get a clearer look at something. Imagine the number of people it takes to maintain this level of surveillance in that gigantic square. The country's police force has been on overtime and complaining about the heavy workload since the crackdown. Detention centres and labour re-education camps nationwide are full of Falun Gong practitioners, with real criminals being released early to make room for them. Where there is still not enough room, 'study squads' are being started up or people sent home to live under surveillance, effectively being placed under house arrest.

To prevent Falun Gong practitioners visiting Beijing at all, each level of government has its own methods to keep those below under control. The central government controls the local authorities, which control the work units, which control individuals. In my home town, for example, a medium-sized city of 600,000 people, the guideline issued before January 1, 2001 was that if more than six people from the city visited the capital at New Year's, the mayor would have to step down. The mayor had to pass the guideline on down, of course, and the head of a large state-run factory employing several thousand people ended up being sacked because more than the quota from his factory visited Beijing. Then some work units created new regulations. To get their pay, all Falun Gong practitioners had to complete a certificate from the local police station stating that they had been behaving well and that they wouldn't go to Beijing after they were paid. Some units started paying their workers fortnightly instead of monthly so that they wouldn't have enough money for train fare.

Things are even tougher in the countryside. In one place, the village head ordered the villagers to demolish the house of their only Falun Gong student so that he had no option but to stay with the village head, who could then watch him 24 hours a day. The only thing the head didn't do to stop the man going to Beijing was bind himself to him with rope.

At Changchun Railway Station the trick was to print 'Falun Gong is an evil cult' on the back of the tickets. Passengers were required to turn their tickets over before getting on the train and read out what it said. If you didn't? Well, well, here's another one; arrest her! Then they refined it even further by putting a portrait of Li Hongzhi on the ground at the ticket entrance so passengers had to tread on it before getting on the train. If you didn't? Well, well, here's another one! If you somehow made it onto the train, the police patrolling it would ask any suspicious-looking people to mouth obscenities or to swear. If you didn't? These days only Falun Gong practitioners are stupid enough or pigheaded enough to not be willing to mouth obscenities.

If you find a wallet and take it to the police station, the first thing they'll ask is if you practise Falun Gong. Not very many people hand in money they've found these days and anyway you can be sure that those who try to be good people under any circumstances are Falun Gong practitioners, or so the reasoning goes.

Of course, suppression is only part of the Party's 'protracted, multi-faceted and arduous struggle' against Falun Gong. There is also brainwashing. Falun Gong books have been confiscated and burned, so ordinary people have no way of knowing what Falun Gong really is and can only go by what the Party tells them, which is contrived and increasingly sensationalised, including stories of self-immolations, suicides and murders.

The propaganda is aimed at all levels of society. The Party has also written out 'prescriptions' for various 'magic potions' designed for different strata of society. So you have vested interests in reform and opening up, do you? OK, your prescription is that Falun Gong is in the business of disrupting society. And you, you consider yourself an intellectual, do you? OK, your prescription is that Falun Gong is feudal superstition fit only for ignorant peasant women. As for you, you're a patriot, aren't you? OK, yours is that Falun Gong is receiving money from anti-Chinese Westerners for the purpose of overthrowing our mighty fatherland. Now you believe in family, don't you? OK, yours is that Falun Gong practitioners are cold-hearted creatures who disown their families and friends. You consider yourself pretty smart, do you? OK then, yours is that only people who practise Falun Gong are stupid enough to be cannon fodder for someone else. Oh, I hear you say that some senior intellectuals practise Falun Gong? Well, there's no guarantee that people with learning can't be spiritually barren, is there?

All of this is aimed at adults, but for middle school and primary school students there is a much more streamlined package, piped straight into the classroom. Special classes, signature drives, protest movements—it takes me back to primary school when we had to join our teachers in criticising Lin Biao and Confucius to counter the 'right deviationist tendency'. Deceiving little children is a cinch but if older ones don't succumb to this deception, there are questions on Falun Gong in all political exams and college entrance exams, and to continue their schooling candidates must answer them in the prescribed manner. My then 8-year-old daughter, for example, immediately assumed responsibility for 'educating' me when I was released from the labour camp. She didn't approach me directly, for fear of wounding my pride, but left a note on my desk. 'Mama,' it said, 'I recommend you don't practise Falun Gong any more. Please read this book.' 'This book' had been distributed by her school and was full of vicious attacks and contemptible lies. When I tried to tell her that her mother was not a bad person, that the government's propaganda was just rumours, she burst into despairing tears.

'I know you are a good person, Mama!' she cried. 'But the TV says everyone who practises Falun Gong is bad. I don't know who to believe!'

In her eyes I saw despair. What had her young soul gone through in the time I had been parted from her? What did she say when her teachers and her classmates asked her where her mother was? Who will she choose: her mother or the entire nation's propaganda apparatus? She is but a child!

By December 15, 2004, a total of 1,224 people had been persecuted to death; this figure only includes the cases which are known and have been verified through independent sources. These deaths have occurred throughout China, in every province, autonomous region and municipality directly under the central government. According to classified internal statistics, more than 7,000 Falun Gong practitioners had died in custody by the end of 2002—an average of 7 people per day. At least 6,000 had been sentenced nationwide and over 100,000 were doing forced-labour re-education illegally. Thousands had been forced into psychiatric hospitals, where their health was ruined by medication that damaged their central nervous system. A large number had been kidnapped and sent to brainwashing classes where they were mentally tortured, while many more had been beaten and subjected to corporal punishment and financial extortion by so-called 'legal personnel'. Untold numbers had been forced out of their homes, while their families, friends and work colleagues had been implicated to varying degrees, some of them even brainwashed themselves.

What effect has this wasteful and protracted crackdown had? Let us look at China first. Petitioners continue to stream into Tian'anmen Square and they have moved into the streets and lanes and homes of the people. Labour re-education camp police officers find Falun Gong leaflets on their doorsteps when they go home. At the Spring Festival of 2002 in Beijing it was said that you weren't a Beijinger if you hadn't received Falun Gong leaflets. Falun Gong banners and slogans keep on appearing in remote villages and busy shopping centres. If you make a call from a public telephone you will find a sticker on the receiver displaying the Falun Gong web addresses or addresses of proxy servers through which people might break through the Internet blockade. Time and again Falun Dafa broadcasts are made outside labour re-education camps. In Li Hongzhi's home town of Changchun an amazing thing happened on March 5, 2002. The Falun Gong programs *Falun Dafa Spreads All Over the World* and *The Facts About the Self-immolation in Tian'anmen* erupted simultaneously on all eight cable TV frequencies at prime viewing time. One transmission ran for over 50 minutes before it was cut off and who can say what effect it would have had on the million viewers who saw it. This sort of thing was once unthinkable—let alone doable—under the iron hand of the Communist Party. Yet the same thing happened in Heilongjiang province, in Qinghai province, in Beijing, in Heibei province and in Gansu province. A great many people who have come into direct contact with Falun Gong practitioners—and this includes police and criminals in prisons—recognise the crackdown for what it is. Under that brutal monolithic rule Falun Gong practitioners have been faced with the prospect of losing everything, even their lives, but through it all they have remained firm, defying with a peaceful smile all those lies, evil and violence—the antithesis of Truthfulness, Compassion and Forbearance. It is from the clear knowledge and practical application of these *Fa* principles that they derive their wisdom and courage.

And what effects have the crackdown had on the world outside China? As one commentator put it, 'Overseas, Falun Gong becomes more courageous as the battle progresses'. In Taiwan alone, the number of practitioners increased from about 5,000 at the time of the crackdown to hundreds of thousands, just three years later. By February 2004, *Zhuan Falun* had been translated into 25 languages, while *Falun Gong (Law Wheel Qigong)* had been translated into 30 languages. There are 'foreign' Falun Gong practitioners in 60 countries around the world. Falun Gong has received over 1,000 commendations in various countries and Li Hongzhi has twice been nominated for the Nobel Peace Prize. Increasing numbers of governments and nongovernmental organizations have come out in support of Falun Gong and against the crackdown. Research students in universities have begun to write dissertations on Falun Gong. In Indonesia, 3,000 followers of Islam have taken up the study of Falun Gong and in Rome the Pope blessed Falun Gong on the tenth anniversary of Falun Gong's introduction to the public. High-ranking Chinese officials on overseas visits can depend on being greeted on their arrival by practitioners bearing banners, peacefully appealing. By September 2004, lawsuits had been brought against 27 of those responsible for the crackdown, including Jiang Zemin, while they were on overseas visits, forcing them to beat a hasty retreat to China; four of these people have now been pronounced guilty by the international courts.

Since the first group of Western practitioners petitioned in Tian'anmen Square on November 20, 2001, a second group has gone to do the same, and a third and a fourth. Some are groups of several dozen; sometimes a lone hero goes. They say that for a long time now the police patrolling Tian'anmen Square have been looking harder at foreigners than at Chinese.

On the first anniversary of July 20, about 1,000 practitioners took part in a commemoration in Washington, DC; three years later, in 2003, over 5,000 took part and they came from over 60 countries. They held experience-sharing conferences, parades and a mock trial of Jiang Zemin, while over a dozen members of parliament from several countries addressed the gathering and over 30 non-governmental groups offered direct support.

'This is indeed a strategic turn of events,' one analyst said.

Falun Gong offered only passive resistance to the Chinese Communists' crackdown before but now they are on the offensive, laying charges against Jiang Zemin and sentencing him. A global encirclement of China is now in place and the impact on Chinese society and politics of this change cannot be overestimated.

The New York Times also carried a review article under the banner 'International Pioneer Forum':

No one would have predicted the stunning resilience and tenacity of the movement four years ago, when it was targeted by China's then-leader, [Jiang] Zemin, as the biggest threat from within. No dissent movement had managed more than four days of resistance before. The pro-democracy movement in 1989, when a million people gathered openly, was crushed within a day and remains marginalized to this day.

It is increasingly evident that, as a spiritual force, Falun Gong can never be suppressed and that the attention the crackdown has focused on Falun Gong has placed it centre stage, where it has become a global faith. And once this bloody suppression has ended, history will recognise the significance of this period for humankind.

So that is my story. Far away in Australia, my every move is noted by Chinese Communist agents and authorities, but this doesn't worry me any more.

My husband managed to find a guarantor and, a month after he was arrested he was released, pending trial. I had been busy on his behalf overseas but at home in China his friends rallied round, calling on their connections and spending a huge amount of money to make his release possible. It is very hard for us to know what the decisive factors in his case will be. He is still under strict surveillance and has to report to the police every time he leaves Beijing.

After 22 months of waiting, I was granted refugee status on July 1, 2003. Thanks to the Australian government, my daughter Shitan was finally able to join me on April 4, 2004, exactly three years after my release from the forced-labour camp. We hardly recognised each other when our eyes first met at the airport. She was travelling on her own, escorted by a stewardess, and had grown up so much since I last saw her. In the last photo she had seen of me I had long hair, and here I was with short hair, she complained. How could she be expected to recognise me!

We didn't talk about Falun Gong for the first few days. However, when she did hear one of my fellow practitioners mention Falun Gong she did say something along the lines of 'I don't believe in Falun Gong'.

I didn't say anything, or try to influence her. One month later, in May, when she heard that we were going to have a big parade to celebrate the twelfth anniversary of Falun Gong's introduction to the public, she begged me to take her with me. Before the parade, we met the son of a fellow practitioner who had been introduced to Shitan earlier. When he saw her, he said, indignantly, 'Why are you here? You told me you are not a Falun Dafa practitioner!' The boy must have thought that only practitioners were allowed to take part in the parade, so Shitan had no business there. Poor Shitan was absolutely aghast. Five years of relentless of propaganda against Falun Gong had left such a deep impression on her mind that she had never expected to be discriminated against for *not* being a Falun Gong practitioner! However, she was quick to respond, 'But my mum is!'

Several days later, she told me, without making a big scene, 'Now I am a Dafa practitioner as well.' I never expected it would happen so soon.

One day, after reading some material on the Internet, she exclaimed, 'Oh, I feel so bad!'

'Why?'

'Because I am finding out how cheated I was in China.'

Shitan is now studying in an English language school in Sydney and I will never be able to express my gratitude adequately towards those who made this happen. Although she misses her father, friends and teachers back in China very much, she has adapted quite well, and she and I are enjoying sharing our new freedom in Australia.

My mother-in-law passed away on September 9, 2004. She was diagnosed with cancer shortly after my husband's release. The doctors said that the shock was too much for her.

My sister was sentenced to eighteen months' re-education and sent to Nanmusi Women's Forced-labour Camp in Zizhong City, Sichuan Province. Although she was released in 2003, she is still under close surveillance and it is difficult for me to contact her or my parents as their mail is monitored and their telephones tapped.

As for myself, as a practitioner I have no worldly needs and hope only that people will come to know the facts about Falun Gong. My special hope is that those who are hostile to Falun Gong because they have believed the lies, or those who for whatever reason have become witting or unwitting accessories to the crackdown, will adopt a more kind-hearted stance once they know the truth. I hope they will reject falsehood and violence.

I believe that these things are what I have to do.

Postscript

I WOULD LIKE TO MAKE two final points.

The first is that all those who cultivate Falun Gong with an attentive heart sense a distinct change within themselves. This change begins at the most microscopic level and may be barely perceptible on the outside. People will readily believe in the crude and cold instruments manufactured by theories and hypotheses, but they dare not believe the things that this most marvellous, perfect and complex instrument—the human body—perceives through its sensory organs. Taught for so many years through the prism of materialism, we differentiate between a subjective and an objective understanding of things and people, drawing simplistic conclusions about right and wrong. However, surely the reality is that we bring our own subjective understanding to all of these things that we define as 'subjective' or 'objective'?

Throughout the ages Daoists have spoken of the unity of heaven and humankind, describing the human body as a 'small universe'. In both the human body and the universe, 'all matter in the cosmos is formed through sequential formation of microscopic substances and particles that constitute bigger particles until they reach the level of cells—particles the size of molecules that can be observed today by humans'.[27] In other words, just as Falun Gong practitioners expe-

---

27 Li Hongzhi, *Falun Buddha Fa: Lecture at the First Conference in North America.*

rience immense changes in the microscopic recesses of their beings, earth-shaking changes, in fact, have been taking place in even more microscopic dimensions in the universe. Because of these changes, substances and lives that have degenerated from the true nature of the universe—Truthfulness, Compassion and Forbearance—are able to return to and conform with the higher standards of the most original, magnificent and pure cosmic *Fa* principles. I believe such a renewal is rapidly advancing towards the dimension in which humankind exists.

According to *Falun Buddha Fa: Lecture at the First Conference in North America*, 'every level of matter below the surface level is composed of microscopic matter. And when the microscopic matter disintegrates, the matter at the surface level also disintegrates and disappears; its disintegration is unnoticeable and imperceptible, just like that of mist and smoke'. With this advancing towards our human dimension, all those things people cannot presently see and do not believe in may suddenly appear, to our amazement. In fact, many changes have already been taking effect in this dimension in which we live, such as the unprecedented astronomical changes that scientists have observed and the many strange phenomena that people have seen with the naked eye.

Falun Gong practitioners are displaying banners in Tian'anmen, handing out leaflets in the streets and sitting in meditation outside Chinese Embassies all over the world. All of these activities, however, have nothing to do with worldly power, worldly politics or systems of government. They have a much more profound significance. There are going to be fundamental changes in all aspects of society, from the scientific to the cultural, from ideologies to the way we live, and I believe it will be Falun Dafa that brings these changes about.

The second is that everything in this book is my own personal understanding of Falun Gong and should in no way be taken as representing Falun Gong itself. While I have quoted Li Hongzhi, it is sometimes difficult to avoid taking things out of context and reducing his message to my level of understanding. Also, everything I did after I went astray in the labour re-education camp was far removed from the standards required of a Falun Gong practitioner. I would advise anyone who is really interested in understanding Falun Gong to read the original text—*Zhuan Falun*. It is available on the Internet as a free download at http://www.falunDafa.org/eng/books.htm

I would like to thank all of my fellow practitioners and my friends who gave selflessly of their help and support while I was writing this book. I am particularly grateful to Zheng Qingcheng, that elegantly dressed and gracious woman I met the day I arrived in Australia. She made it possible for me to concentrate on my writing and attended to my well-being the whole time. Whenever I began to doubt myself or wanted to quit she would encourage me to go on.

I am also especially grateful to CNW, a fellow practitioner, and the editors of the Clearwisdom (http://www.clearwisdom.net) and Pure Insight (http://www.pureinsight.org) websites. CNW wrote a nearly 10,000-character critique and review of my manuscript. Over a year later I am still deriving benefit from the suggestions in that critique.

And, of course, my beloved family, who have shared all my sufferings throughout my most painful ordeal and who, in their different ways, have given me immense support.

The person I most want to thank is my respected teacher Li Hongzhi, but since I cannot properly express my sincere gratitude to him I must simply preserve it in my heart.

Falun Gong chronology

13 May 1951 Li Hongzhi, the founder of Falun Gong, born in the city of Gongzhuling, Jilin province, China.

13 May 1992 The first Falun Gong study classes held in the city of Changchun, Jilin province. Li Hongzhi begins teaching Falun Gong.

December 1992 Li Hongzhi and his disciples attend the 1992 Oriental Health Expo in Beijing. Falun Gong's ability to heal illness creates enormous interest. Li Hongzhi receives more awards than any other *qigong* master.

April 1993 Li Hongzhi's *Falun Gong* (*Law Wheel Qigong*) published.

1993 The China Society for Research on Qigong Science formally approves Falun Gong as a genuine school of *qigong*. The Falun Dafa Research Association is established as a branch of the society. The China Society for Research on Qigong Science confers the title of *qigong* master on Li Hongzhi.

December 1993 Li Hongzhi and his disciples attend the 1993 Oriental Health Expo in Beijing as members of the expo organising committee. He receives the expo's highest award—the Frontier Science Advancement Prize—and the Special Gold Prize and is named most popular *qigong* master.

September 1994 Falun Gong instructional videotapes, published by Beijing Television and Arts Centre Press, officially released.

13 May 1992–21 December 1994 At the invitation of official societies for research on *qigong* science, Li Hongzhi conducts 54 Falun Gong courses, each lasting about ten days. Tens of thousands of people attend his classes.

4 January 1995 Li Hongzhi's major work *Zhuan Falun*, published by China TV Broadcasting Agency Press, a subsidiary of the State Council's Ministry of Radio and Television, is launched in the auditorium of the Public Security University, Beijing.

13 March 1995 Li Hongzhi visits Paris, France, to teach Falun Gong, marking the introduction of Falun Gong overseas.

Easter, May 1995 Li Hongzhi conducts a seven-day course in Göteborg, Sweden. This is the last class he conducts in person.

January 1996 *Beijing Youth Daily* lists *Zhuan Falun* among the top ten bestsellers in Beijing.

March 1996 Falun Gong is withdrawn from the China Society for Research on Qigong Science.

1996 Li Hongzhi emigrates to the United States.

From April 1996 Members of the former Falun Dafa Research Association apply to the National People's Congress Nationality Affairs Committee, the Buddhism Association of China and the Central Committee's United Front Department for permission to establish a non-religious Falun Gong Academic Research Association. The applications are refused.

17 June 1996 China's official media outlet *Guangming Daily* publishes the first public attack on Falun Gong, titled 'A loud and long alarm must be sounded against pseudoscience'.

24 July 1996 The Chinese News Publishing Bureau, which is under the Propaganda Department of the Central Committee, issues a restricted internal order to provincial and metropolitan news bureaus prohibiting the publication and distribution of *Zhuan Falun* and *China Falun Gong*.

12 October 1996 Li Hongzhi gives a public lecture in Houston, Texas, marking the introduction of Falun Gong to the USA.

Early 1997 The Chinese Ministry of Public Security launches a nationwide investigation into Falun Gong.

November 1997 Li Hongzhi gives his first lecture in Taipei, Taiwan, marking the introduction of Falun Gong to Taiwan.

May 1998 The National Physical Education Central Bureau conducts a nationwide investigation into Falun Gong. In September 1998, as part of this investigation, a small group of medical specialists carry out a uniform sampling survey on 12,553 Falun Gong practitioners in Guangdong province. They find a 97.9 per cent success rate in healing illness and restoring health.

May 1998 Beijing TV broadcasts an attack on Falun Gong by He Zuoxiu, a member of the Chinese Academy of Sciences. Several hundred Falun Gong practitioners write to or call at the TV station pointing out errors in the program.

2 June 1998 Beijing TV acknowledges the Falun Gong program to have been its most serious error since it began broadcasting and broadcasts a positive report to correct the error.

21 July 1998 The No. 1 Bureau of the Ministry of Public Security issues its *Circular on Investigation into the Development of Falun Gong*. The Ministry begins monitoring the phones and movements of Falun Gong assistants, places a ban on practice sites, disperses groups of practitioners, ransacks homes and confiscates property. It illegally forces its way into private homes.

20 October 1998 The head of a research group sent by the Chinese National Sports Bureau to Changchun and Harbin after the investigation into Falun Gong confirms the health benefits of Falun Gong and its role in promoting social stability and spiritual civilisation.

11 April 1999 He Zuoxiu attacks Falun Gong in his article 'Why young people shouldn't practise *qigong*', published in *Teenager Expo*, which is put out by the Tianjin Teachers' College.

18–24 April 1999 Falun Gong practitioners in Tianjin go to the Tianjin Teachers' College and other related organisations to clarify the truth about Falun Gong. Within several days, thousands of Falun Gong practitioners arrive at Tianjin to help clarify the truth.

23, 24 April 1999 Over 300 riot police from Tianjin Bureau of Public Security disperse Falun Gong practitioners, arresting 45. Some practitioners are injured.

25 April 1999 Over 10,000 practitioners gather outside the Petition Offices of the State Council in Zhonganhai in Beijing to appeal to the authorities. State Council Premier Zhu Rongji goes out to receive them. The detained Tianjin practitioners are released the same day. Beijing petitioners go home about 9 p.m.

Night of 25 April 1999 General Secretary of the Chinese Communist Party, Jiang Zemin, sends a letter to the Standing Committee of the Political Bureau of the Central Committee and to relevant leaders in which he states: 'It will be absolutely absurd if the Communist Party cannot vanquish Falun Gong'. This letter is disseminated from the highest level of the Chinese Communist government to the lowest cadres.

30 May 1999 Overseas Falun Gong practitioners launch the Chinese-language Minghui website (www.minghui.org) and the English-language Clearwisdom website (www.clearwisdom.net).

10 June 1999 The 610 Office, a special department for suppressing Falun Gong, is established.

14 June 1999 The Petition Offices of the General Office of the CPC Central Committee and the General Office of the State Council announce that people have the right to believe in any form of *qigong*. They also claim there is no truth in the rumour that Falun Gong is to be suppressed.

May 1992–July 1999 Falun Gong spreads to over 40 countries, the number of practitioners numbering between 70 and 100 million.

19 July 1999 At a high-level meeting, Jiang Zemin formally announces he wants to eradicate Falun Gong.

20 July 1999 A major nationwide campaign is begun to arrest Falun Gong assistants, ransack their homes and confiscate their property. On this day, tens of thousands of Falun Gong practitioners appealing outside the Petition Offices of the State Council are arrested and detained in large stadiums in Beijing, including Fengtai Stadium and Shijingshan Stadium.

22 July 1999 The suppression officially begins. The Communist Party newspaper, the *People's Daily*, publishes lengthy critical articles and the Ministry of Civil Affairs issues *Decision [of the Ministry of Civil Affairs of the PRC] on The Outlawing of the Falun Dafa Research Association*. The Ministry of Public Security issues the 'six prohibitions' and the Central Committee of the CPC issues the circular *On the Prohibition for Members of the Communist Party to Practise 'Falun Dafa'*. Local public security authorities continue to arrest Falun Gong practitioners, ransack their homes and confiscate their property, seize books and burn Falun Gong literature and audiovisual materials. Tens of thousands of practitioners converge on government bodies in Beijing and elsewhere to present petitions. Petitioners are dispersed or arrested.

22 July 1999 In *My Declaration*, Li Hongzhi calls on all governments, international bodies and people of goodwill to help resolve the crisis in China.

23 July 1999 Canada sends a letter of protest to the Chinese Ministry of Foreign Affairs, condemning the suppression of Falun Gong.

27 July 1999 Li Hongzhi has a signed letter delivered to the Chinese Embassy in the United States, in which he urges the Chinese Government immediately to cease its oppression of Falun Gong and to pursue peaceful dialogue to resolve the problem.

27 July 1999 The US State Department issues a statement calling on the Chinese Government to exercise restraint in handling the Falun Gong.

28 July 1999 China's Ministry of Public Security issues an international warrant for the arrest of Li Hongzhi. Interpol refuses to cooperate.

29 July 1999 American Falun Gong practitioners hold a press conference in Washington, DC, calling for a halt to the suppression.

16 August 1999 Chen Ying, a 17-year-old female tenth-grade student at Shuren Middle School in the city of Jiamusi, Heilongjiang province, is detained while travelling to Beijing to join the protests. She dies while being escorted home by the police. Posted on the Clearwisdom website on 25 October 1999, this is the first reported case of a Falun Gong practitioner being persecuted to death.

September 1999 When Jiang Zemin arrives in New Zealand to attend an APEC meeting over 200 Falun Gong practitioners gather in New Zealand to protest.

16 October 1999 The Clearwisdom website reports the first case of a Falun Gong practitioner being committed to a psychiatric hospital. Cheng Zhong, a practitioner from Jiangsu province, is taken to No. 3 People's Hospital (a hospital specialising in mental illnesses) in the city of Wujin on 28 September 1999. He is forced to take medication and subjected to electric shocks.

25 October 1999 CCTV's *News Network* broadcasts Jiang Zemin's reply to a journalist for the French newspaper *Le Figaro* during a visit to France. Jiang Zemin says, 'Falun Gong is an evil cult.' Several hundred Falun Gong practitioners who later protest in Tian'anmen Square and at the National People's Congress Hall are arrested.

26 October 1999 China's official media runs Jiang Zemin's 'Falun Gong is an evil cult' speech. Almost 1,000 practitioners who descend on Tian'anmen and the Petition Offices are arrested.

27 October 1999 The *People's Daily* publishes the article '"Falun Gong" is an evil cult', written by a special commentator. Approximately 600 practitioners are arrested in Tian'anmen. Seventeen practitioners drape a Falun Gong banner across the rostrum of Tian'anmen. The 15 Beijingers among them are later sentenced to between four months' and two years' imprisonment; the other two are escorted back to their home towns and placed in detention.

28 October 1999 Some 30 Falun Gong practitioners hold a secret press conference on the outskirts of Beijing, providing Beijing-based Western journalists with accurate stories and photographs. This is the first time detailed information on the suppression is made available to the Western media. Associated Press and Reuters run the story and the following day several other Western newspapers publish reports of the news conference, with large photos. The practitioners who hold the press conference are later arrested, among them Ding Yan and Cai Mingtao, who would both be persecuted to death in 2000.

30 October 1999 The Standing Committee of the National People's Congress passes *Decisions on Banning Cult Organizations, Preventing and Punishing Cult Activities.* The major media outlets publish *Explanation of Questions on the Concrete Application of Laws in Handling Criminal Cases of Organizing and Using Cult Organizations*, issued by the Supreme People's Court and the Supreme People's Procurator. While the *Decisions* and the *Explanation* do not mention Falun Gong, they are believed to be the legal basis for the suppression of Falun Gong.

12 November 1999 The first four Falun Gong practitioners to be sentenced are jailed for between two and twelve years. Several hundred others are sentenced to three years' re-education through labour.

18, 19 November 1999 The US House of Representatives and the Senate jointly pass Resolutions 217 and 218 urging the Chinese Government to call a halt to the suppression of Falun Gong.

19–25 November 1999 Over 100 Falun Gong practitioners from China and overseas gather in Guangzhou to convene the 1999 experience-sharing conference. On 25 November, the police arrest seventeen practitioners. One practitioner hurriedly emails the texts of conference speeches to the Clearwisdom website before throwing the laptop out the window. The speeches of fifteen of the conference participants, along with the opening address and closing speech, are later published on the website; the closing speech is written in prison.

26 December 1999 Beijing No. 1 Intermediate People's Court sentences four members of the former Falun Dafa Research Association to between seven and eighteen years' imprisonment. Over 1,000 practitioners who have come to the court to hear the verdict are arrested.

31 December 1999–1 January 2000 Several thousand practitioners from China and overseas are arrested when they practise in Tian'anmen Square and unfurl a Falun Gong banner.

9 January 2000 Three Caucasian Australian Falun Gong practitioners submit a letter of appeal to Xinhua News Agency's head office in Beijing. They are detained, interrogated, then deported under escort. This is the first time non-Chinese practitioners submit an appeal in China.

19 January 2000 The Clearwisdom website publishes a photograph of Li Hongzhi meditating in a mountain setting, with the caption 'Master Li quietly watching the world from amidst the mountains after leaving New York following July 20th, 1999'.

4, 5 February 2000 Several thousand Chinese and overseas Falun Gong practitioners petitioning in Tian'anmen Square are arrested by police, who use excessive violence.

23 March 2000 In Hong Kong, Amnesty International strongly condemns China's suppression of spiritual movements, including Falun Gong.

April 2000 On behalf of the World Citizens' Association, Falun Gong practitioners address the 56th session of the UN Commission on Human Rights on the Chinese Government's suppression of female Falun Gong practitioners.

13 April 2000 Over 200 Falun Gong practitioners are arrested in Tian'-anmen Square for appealing to members of the UN Commission on Human Rights to pass a resolution condemning China's human rights abuses.

25 April 2000 Three thousand police are despatched to Tian'anmen Square, where they arrest over 100 Falun Gong practitioners who are presenting a petition. Overseas, Falun Gong practitioners commemorate the anniversary of 4.25, the 25 April incident of 1999.

13 May 2000 Over a dozen Falun Dafa Associations in countries outside China jointly declare 13 May World Falun Dafa Day. Several hundred mainland Falun Gong practitioners petitioning in Tian'anmen are arrested.

22 May 2000 For the first time since the crackdown began, Li Hongzhi publishes his poem 'The Knowing Heart', written on 12 October 1999.

August 2000 The Falun Dafa Information Center is opened in New York.

29 August 2000 Falun Gong practitioners Zhu Keming from Hong Kong and Wang Jin from Beijing lodge an action with China's Supreme Court charging Jiang Zemin, Zeng Qinghong (head of the Organisation Department of the CPC Central Committee) and Luo Gan (secretary of the Political Bureau of the Central Committee) with violating the Chinese Constitution and persecuting Falun Gong.

September 2000 Almost 2,000 Falun Gong practitioners from over 30 countries gather in New York to petition China's delegation to the UN Millennium Summit.

1 October 2000 Several thousand mainland Falun Gong practitioners petitioning in Tian'anmen Square are arrested.

6 October 2000 Several thousand mainland Falun Gong practitioners petitioning in Tian'anmen Square are arrested.

8 October 2000 A Falun Dafa radio station run by practitioners commences broadcasting in San Francisco.

October 2000 Li Hongzhi is nominated for the 2001 Nobel Peace Prize.

26 October 2000 On the anniversary of Falun Gong being labelled an evil cult, several hundred Falun Gong practitioners are arrested for petitioning in Tian'anmen.

28 October 2000 Falun Gong TV programs made by overseas practitioners are broadcast in North America through FGM-TV.

31 December 2000 In Tian'anmen Square about 30 mainland Falun Gong practitioners unfurl a yellow banner 99 metres long by 1.5 metres wide, on which are inscribed in red the 72 poems of *Hongyin*. Approximately 1,500 petitioning practitioners are also arrested in Tian'anmen Square.

1 January 2001 At least 700 petitioning mainland Falun Gong practitioners are arrested in Tian'anmen Square. At one point, police are detaining one practitioner every two minutes.

10 January 2001 Following Canadian Government intervention, Canadian Falun Gong practitioner Professor Zhang Kunlun is released after serving almost two months of the three years of re-education through forced labour to which he had been sentenced in China. This is the first successful international rescue of a Falun Gong practitioner.

13 January 2001 The Clearwisdom website publishes the first solemn declaration declaring null and void all signed words and deeds obtained under duress.

14 January 2001 Over 1,000 practitioners from 23 countries hold an experience-sharing conference in Hong Kong and march in protest against the persecution.

15 January 2001 The European Parliament passes a resolution demanding a halt to the suppression of Falun Gong.

23 January 2001 The Tian'anmen self-immolation massacre shocks the world. One hour after the event, Xinhua News Agency releases to the world the news that five Falun Gong practitioners have set themselves on fire in Tian'anmen, later amending this to seven people. The Falun Dafa Information Center releases the statement 'China stages self-immolation act; Xinhua News framed Falun Gong with slanderous lies' and calls for an independent inquiry into the matter.

4 February 2001 The *Washington Post* publishes the article 'Human fire ignites Chinese mystery—motive for public burning intensifies fight over Falun Gong' which states that no one had ever seen Liu Chunling, who died in the self-immolation incident, practising Falun Gong.

14 March 2001 Falun Gong honoured by the US Freedom House's Center for Religious Freedom as a 'defender of religious rights'.

March 2001 Over 1,000 Falun Gong practitioners from all over the world petition the UN Commission on Human Rights, held in Geneva.

5, 6 April 2001 As members of the World Citizens' Association and Freedom House, Falun Gong practitioners speak at the UN Commission on Human Rights in Geneva against the suppression of Falun Gong.

16 April 2001 Ian Johnson wins the Pulitzer Prize for International Reporting for his reports in the *Wall Street Journal* on the suppression of Falun Gong. One week later, Falun Gong practitioner Zhang Xueling, who had featured prominently in these reports, was sentenced in China to three years' re-education through labour.

May 2001 Some 600 Falun Gong practitioners gather in Hong Kong to protest the crackdown as Jiang Zemin arrives for a conference. A further 95 practitioners are refused entry to Hong Kong.

13 May 2001 Some 300 Falun Gong practitioners petitioning in Tian'anmen are arrested.

24 May 2001 *Asia Week* ranks Li Hongzhi number one on its list of Asia's 50 most influential people.

15 June 2001 Over 600 Falun Gong practitioners from 23 countries demonstrate and hold press conferences at the European Summit in Göteborg, Sweden. Proposals are put for an 'SOS! Global Rescue Plan'.

20 June 2001 The Wanjia massacre takes place at the Wanjia Re-education Through Forced Labour Camp in Harbin, Heilongjiang province. Three Falun Gong practitioners—Li Xiuqin, Zhang Yulan and Zhao Yayun—are persecuted to death. Eight people in comas are clandestinely admitted to hospital and another four are isolated in a men's unit. Because of the secrecy surrounding the re-education office, it was at first believed that all 15 people were persecuted to death.

From July 2001 Falun Gong practitioners outside China initiate a global movement—'SOS! Urgent Rescue of Chinese Mainland Falun Gong Practitioners'. By foot, by car and by bicycle they make their way across the United States, Europe, Australia and Asia, passing through over 100 cities in dozens of countries and covering tens of thousands of kilometres.

17 July 2001 Peng Liang, a practitioner from Wuhan, files charges in the US District Court, Southern District of New York against Zhao Zhifei for the death through maltreatment of his brother Peng Min and his mother Li Yingxiu. Zhao Zhifei was head of the Hubei Department of Public Security and second in command of the 610 Office in Hubei province. Peng Liang would be arrested at the end of August along with a group of Falun Gong practitioners from the Wuchang region.

20 July 2001 The International Association of Official Human Rights Agencies calls for an end to the maltreatment and slaughter of Falun Gong practitioners.

End of July 2001 Over 130 Falun Gong practitioners at the Masanjia Re-education Through Forced Labour Camp go on hunger strike to protest the non-release of practitioners who have completed their sentences.

From August 2001 Falun Gong practitioners go on hunger strikes or sit in meditation outside Chinese consulates throughout the world, in support of those at Masanjia and in protest at the crackdown. At the time of publication, practitioners in Vancouver, Canada, are still maintaining a 24-hour vigil, which they intend to continue until the persecution stops.

14 August 2001 The International Educational Development Office declares that the self-immolation incident in Tian'anmen was staged by the Chinese Government and condemns China for persecuting Falun Gong by acts of state terrorism.

27 August 2001 Charges are filed by Boston Falun Gong practitioner He Haiying with the US District Court, Northern District of Illinois, against Zhou Yongkang, general secretary of the Sichuan Communist Party Committee, for the cruel torture and murder of Falun Gong practitioners.

13 September 2001 The European Parliament nominates Li Hongzhi for its 2001 Sakharov Prize for Freedom of Thought.

20 November 2001 Thirty-five Caucasian Falun Gong practitioners from twelve countries petitioning in Tian'anmen Square are seized and taken into custody. The following day they are deported and denied re-entry for five years.

21 December 2001 In a trial *in absentia*, the US District Court, Southern District of New York, finds Zhao Zhifei guilty of killing through maltreatment.

1 January 2002 Falun Gong practitioners in the city of Chongqing intercept cable TV to broadcast a 70-minute film on Falun Gong. Four of those involved are later sentenced to between seven and sixteen years' imprisonment; one dies in custody.

January 2001–January 2002 Over 54,700 people upload solemn declarations to the Clearwisdom website, an average of more than 140 per day. The most on a single day is 470.

7 February 2002 Charges are filed by six Falun Gong practitioners with the US District Court, Northern District of California, against Liu Qi, the mayor of Beijing, for causing physical and mental suffering and for cruel torture, inhuman behaviour and maltreatment. Charges are also filed against Xia Deren, deputy head of Liaoning province.

14 February 2002 Over 40 Caucasian Falun Gong practitioners are arrested when they petition in Tian'anmen Square.

March 2002 Public Security officials in the city of Changchun are secretly ordered to open fire on any Falun Gong practitioners putting up banners or distributing material. Police in Liaoning and Shandong later receive the same instructions.

5 March 2002 Eight channels on the cable TV network in the city of

Changchun simultaneously broadcast an uninterrupted 40- to 50-minute screening of the Falun Gong films *Falun Dafa Worldwide* and *Self-immolation or Staged Act?* The authorities later arrest over 5,000 Changchun Falun Gong practitioners. Six of them, including Li Rong, Chen Jianli, Liu Haibo, Liu Yi and Li Shuqi, die during the arrest. Hou Mingkai would be tortured to death on 21 August 2002; Liu Chengjun would be tortured to death on 26 December 2003 after being detained for 21 months. Fifteen others are sentenced to between four and twenty years' imprisonment.

7 March 2002 Ten Caucasian Australian Falun Gong practitioners are arrested as they petition in Tian'anmen Square.

19–22 March 2002 Over 700 Falun Gong practitioners gather in Geneva to petition the 58th session of the UN Commission on Human Rights. At the conference, the ministers of foreign affairs from Canada, Holland and Germany condemn China for its suppression of Falun Gong.

30 March 2002 *Guangzhou Daily*, the official organ of the Guangzhou Municipal Party Committee, publishes two of Li Hongzhi's poems. The editor of the newspaper is later arrested.

3 April 2002 A civil lawsuit is filed by 51 American Falun Gong practitioners with the US District Court in Washington, DC, against China's Ministry of State Security, Ministry of Public Security, CCTV and the Chinese ambassador to the United States. The charges are: harassment and intimidation of Falun Gong practitioners on American soil.

April 2002 During Jiang Zemin's visit to Germany more than 400 Falun Gong practitioners from 20 countries demonstrate against the crackdown.

11 April 2002 The European Parliament passes a resolution on European Union tactics towards China, censuring China's human rights record and the suppression of groups including Falun Gong.

20 April 2002 The cable TV networks in the cities of Harbin, Daqing, Shuangcheng, Qiqihar, Mudanjiang, Jiamusi, Hegang, Shuangyashan and Jixi, in Heilongjiang province, are interrupted by the broadcast of a 75-minute program clarifying the Falun Gong situation.

25 April 2002 At the 58th session of the UN Commission on Human Rights, a representative of an international society for religious freedom condemns the suppression of Falun Gong.

12 May 2002 A CCTV news program attacking Falun Gong being broadcast over satellite TV on the local TV stations in ten provinces suddenly goes dead. The interruption lasts for three minutes, until the anti-Falun Gong program is finished.

13 May 2002 Falun Gong practitioners throughout the world celebrate its tenth anniversary. Government leaders in over 30 cities in the USA, Canada and Australia honour Falun Dafa and celebrate World Falun Dafa Day.

June 2002 During Jiang Zemin's visit to Iceland, over 70 Falun Gong practitioners intending to protest the suppression are blacklisted and refused entry. In a joint statement to the press, 450 prominent Icelanders apologise to the Falun Gong practitioners and nearly 3,000 Icelanders demonstrate against the Chinese Government's flagrant violation of human rights. They also protest the Icelandic Government's refusal to allow Falun Gong practitioners into the country.

23–30 June 2002 Nine CCTV satellite channels and ten provincial stations, including those in Sichuan, Guizhou and Yunnan, broadcast a Falun Gong program showing practitioners doing the exercises and the words 'Falun Dafa is good'.

Since July 2002 The global rescue of Falun Gong practitioners who had been persecuted commences in sixteen countries. Dozens of practitioners who had been detained in China are plucked to safety in Europe, Australia and North America.

24 July 2002 The US Congress unanimously (420 votes to 0) passes Resolution 188, urging the Chinese Government to cease its persecution of Falun Gong.

1 August 2002 The International Association of Official Human Rights Agencies passes Resolution 13 condemning China's persecution of Falun Gong practitioners.

About 17 August 2002 Cable TV broadcasts in the city of Xining, Minhe County, and elsewhere in Qinghai province are intercepted to broadcast the Falun Gong program *Trial by History*.

August 2002 Two Falun Gong films are shown on a Fangshan cable TV station in Beijing and three in the eastern part of Baoding (in Hebei province). Each lasts for about 70 minutes.

23, 27 August 2002 Practitioners succeed in showing the Falun Gong TV films *Witness* and *Falun Dafa Worldwide* at peak viewing times in northern Baoding, Laishui, Yixian, Zhuozhou, Gaobeidian and Xushui. The two programs last over 70 minutes.

27 August 2002 The World Psychology Association resolves to send a team of investigators to China to look into Party authorities' misuse of mental treatment for the persecution of dissidents.

6 September 2002 A cable TV program in the city of Baiyin in Gansu province is interrupted for about fifteen minutes by a Falun Gong video.

17 October 2002 Seven Falun Gong practitioners from six countries file charges against Jiang Zemin, Zeng Qinghong and Luo Gan for persecuting Falun Gong with the UN Anti-Torture Committee, the UN Commission on Human Rights and the International Criminal Court.

22 October 2002 During his stay in Chicago, Falun Gong practitioners file charges against Jiang Zemin for cruel torture and genocide with the United States District Court, Northern District of Illinois. Over 1,000 Falun Gong practitioners gather in Chicago to protest the crackdown.

24 October 2002 The Canadian Parliament unanimously passes a motion of support for Falun Gong and demands that China release imprisoned Falun Gong practitioners.

24 October 2002 The Grand Council of the Republic and Canton of Geneva pass Resolution R461 showing concern for China's violation of human rights and, in particular, for the persecution of Falun Gong practitioners.

2 December 2002 Four Falun Gong practitioners in France bring an action against Li Lanqing, head of 610 Office and vice-premier of China.

20 January 2003 The World Organization to Investigate the Persecution of Falun Gong is established in the USA. Its first subject of investigation is the Tian'anmen self-immolation incident.

18 March 2003 The international NGO calling itself Track Impunity Always and the Swiss Falun Gong Association hold a press conference in Geneva to announce they are filing charges in Switzerland against former Chinese President Jiang Zemin.

20 March 2003 The group Fa Wang Huihui ('the arm of the law is very long') submits a 4,000-page report on the persecution of Falun Gong to the confidential monitoring apparatus of the UN Commission on Human Rights. The report includes the names and suspected crimes of over 11,000 Chinese police officers, officials of all levels and other office holders who have participated in the persecution of Falun Gong.

June 2003 San Francisco magistrate Edward M. Chen refuses to grant foreign sovereign immunity to former mayor of Beijing Liu Qi and deputy head of Liaoning Xia Deren, against whom charges have been laid. He also submits to court a report on the two officials, who had acknowledged they were guilty of overseeing the cruel torture and suffering of Falun Gong practitioners.

19–22 June 2003 Almost 3,000 Falun Gong practitioners from over 30 countries gather in Chicago to demonstrate in support of the charges against Jiang Zemin.

19–22 July 2003 In Washington, DC, over 5,000 Falun Gong practitioners from over 60 countries attend an experience-sharing conference and hold marches and a mock public trial of Jiang Zemin, in commemoration of the fourth anniversary of the crackdown. A dozen or so congressmen and about twenty NGOs lend support by their presence.

12, 13 August 2003 Chinese Education TV, CCTV and ten Chinese provincial TV stations' programs are intercepted with the message 'Jiang Zemin has been sued' and Falun Gong images.

8–18 September 2003 Charges of torture, crimes against humanity and genocide are filed against Luo Gan during his tour of Iceland, Finland, Armenia and Moldovia.

15 October 2003 Falun Gong practitioners in Spain lay criminal charges against Jiang Zemin and Luo Gan.

15 November 2003 Over 10,000 Taiwanese Falun Gong practitioners hold a public rally in front of the President's Office to 'call for the ending of the persecution against humanity; safeguard basic human rights; support the global trial against Jiang Zemin'. About 100,000 signatures are gathered in support of this campaign.

17 November 2003 Six Taiwanese Falun Gong practitioners initiates a private prosecution case against Jiang Zemin, Li Lanqing and Luo Gan with the Taiwan High Court.

21 November 2003 Forty plaintiffs, including victims of persecution, the German Falun Dafa Association and German citizens, file charges in the German Prosecutor's Office against Jiang Zemin and police officers from forced labour camps in mainland China. This is the first instance of police officers in China's forced labour camps facing a criminal lawsuit outside China.

22 November 2003 More than 600 Falun Gong practitioners from countries throughout Europe gather in Berlin to support the lawsuit against Jiang Zemin.

1 December 2003 The Australian Senate passes a motion to rescue the family members of Australian citizens. This indicates Australia's commitment to supporting the close relatives of Australian citizens who are detained on the basis that they practice Falun Gong and the importance of raising the issue in the context of the human rights dialogue.

19 January 2004 Mainland Chinese Falun Gong practitioners broadcast two hours of documentaries, including *False Fire* (about the 'self-immolation in Tian'anmen'), *Globally Putting Jiang on Trial*, *Falun Dafa around the World* and truth-clarification music videos, through a wireless TV network in Xingtai City and Shahe City, Hebei Province.

20 January 2004 An interview with Mr Li Hongzhi is aired exclusively on New Tang Dynasty TV. This was the first time Mr Li had agreed to a media interview since the suppression began on 22 July 1999.

20 January 2004 Representatives of the Canadian Falun Dafa Association and an international organisation for investigating the persecution of Falun Gong announce they have submitted to Canadian Government officials the names of fifteen people, including former president Jiang Zemin, who have persecuted Falun Gong members, together with their crimes and other relevant evidence. The Royal Canadian Mounted Police has this list, which it is treating as relating to crimes against humanity and war crimes, and is prepared to undertake a prompt investigation should anyone on the list attempt to enter Canada. By the end of January the Canadian Mounties' list of names has grown to 45.

22 January 2004 Falun Gong practitioners in Yanbian in Jilin Province hang up more than 1,000 Falun Gong banners at the airport, forced labour camps, prisons and along highways and major roads.

28 January 2004 Four Falun Gong practitioners in Paris file charges against the visiting Chinese Culture Minister, Mr Sun Jiazheng, for 'incitement of massacre and persecution'.

3 February 2004 The Ontario Superior Court in Canada finds the Deputy Consul General of China in Toronto, Mr Pan Xinchun, guilty of libelling Toronto Falun Gong practitioner Mr Joel Chipkar by saying he belongs to an 'evil cult'. The court orders Mr Pan to pay compensation to the plaintiff. This is the first time a Falun Gong practitioner has brought and won a lawsuit against a Chinese diplomat serving overseas.

3 March 2004 The US Senate House of Representatives passes Resolution 530 by a margin of 402 votes to 2, urging the US Government to introduce a resolution to the 60th Session of the UN Commission on Human Rights calling upon China to end its human rights violations of Falun Gong practitioner and of members of other religions and of dissidents.

8 March 2004 Korean Falun Gong practitioner Piao Zhongyuan charges Li Bin, the Chinese ambassador to Korea, Zhang Xin, the Chinese Consul General, and five other Chinese consular officials with vilification of character in Seoul Central Court.

12 March 2004 Professor Zhang Kunlun, a Canadian Falun Gong practitioner, submits to the Canadian Supreme Prosecutor's Office evidence of crimes committed by 22 Chinese officials, including Jiang Zemin, who have participated in the persecution of Falun Gong.

15 March 2004 At the opening of the 60th Session of the UN Commission of Human Rights in Geneva, more than 500 Falun Gong practitioners from over twenty countries stage an appeal to call attention to the suppression of Falun Gong.

6 April 2004 The World Organisation to Investigate the Persecution of Falun Gong publishes *Investigation Reports on the Persecution of Falun Gong*.

7 April 2004 The Australian Victorian Civil and Administrative Tribunal (VCAT) orders Melbourne City Council to publish an apology to the Victorian Falun Dafa Association within fourteen days in three Chinese newspapers for having barred it from the 2003 Moomba Parade, and orders it to pay court costs.

7 April 2004 Zhang Cuiying, a Falun Gong practitioner from Australia, files a formal petition with the UN Human Rights Commission requesting that it investigate the violation of her human rights in China that had taken place because she practised Falun Gong.

16 April 2004 In Switzerland, seven Falun Gong practitioners lay charges against Wang Yusheng, Assistant Director of the Chinese Anti-Cult Association.

22 April 2004 Falun Gong practitioners file a lawsuit at the US District Court for the District of Columbia against Bo Xilai, China's Minister of Commerce, during his visit to the United States charging him with 'torture, genocide and crimes against humanity'.

May 2004 Falun Gong practitioners in England file a lawsuit with the

Metropolitan Police at New Scotland Yard, charging Bo Xilai with torture.

24 May 2004 In the US District Court in Boston, Falun Gong practitioners file charges of 'genocide, crimes against humanity and torture' against Wang Taihui, Party Secretary of Anhui Province in China.

8 June 2004 Taiwan's Legislative *Yuan* passes a resolution put by 126 members demanding that China immediately release all arrested and detained Falun Gong practitioners and end the persecution of Falun Gong.

8 June 2004 Falun Gong practitioners submit a complaint to the Polish Procuratorate against Bo Xilai, China's Minister of Commerce, for crimes against humanity and torture during his persecution of Falun Gong.

28 June 2004 During the visit of Zeng Qinghong (China's Deputy National Chairman) to South Africa, Australian Falun Gong practitioners who have gone to South Africa to protest are attacked by gunmen. David Liang is shot in both feet.

2 July 2004 Falun Gong practitioners file a complaint with the Procureur de la République of the Tribunal de Grande Instance de Paris accusing Li Changchun, who was then visiting France, of being an accomplice to torture in the persecution of Falun Gong. Li Changchun is the Politburo Standing Committee Member of the Chinese Communist Party Central Committee in Charge of Propaganda and a former Guangdong Provincial Party Secretary.

6 July 2004 Minghui.net announces that at least 1,000 Falun Gong practitioners have been tortured to death between 20 July 1999 and early July 2004. Women account for 52% of these deaths and men for 48%. Their average age is 44. The youngest is Chen Ying, a 17-year-old female high-school student from Heilongjiang province, while the oldest is 82-year-old Yang Yongshou, a man from Sichuan province. The average death toll per month was approximately seventeen people.

13 July 2004 Falun Gong practitioners files a class action lawsuit in New Haven with the US District Court for Connecticut against Zhao Zhizhen, the former head of Wuhan TV and Radio Bureau in Hubei province, China. In the first case of this kind, they charge him with making films inciting hatred, violence and genocide towards Falun Gong practitioners.

19 July 2004 Chen Zhili, a former Education Minister and currently a member of China's State Council, is charged in Tanzania with 'implementing torture and maltreatment leading to death of Falun Gong [practitioners] within the "Chinese education system"'. She is summoned to court before the judge, the first instance of a defendant appearing in person.

22 July 2004 More than 1,000 Falun Gong practitioners and supporters from all over the world held a public rally on the theme of 'Uncompromising Courage' and a parade on Capitol Hill in Washington, DC. Seventeen teenage Canadian Falun Gong practitioners cycle from Toronto to Washington to promote the 'Save China's Persecuted Kids' Bicycle Parade. Their 1,200-km journey takes 23 days.

23 July 2004 Over 3,000 Falun Gong practitioners from all over the world form a human wall two miles long in Washington, DC, to demonstrate their unshakeable courage in the face of suppression and their fierce opposition to the persecution of Falun Gong. That evening, almost 1,000 practitioners hold candlelight vigils in front of the Lincoln Memorial and the Chinese Embassy in Washington to mourn Falun Gong practitioners who have died as a result of the persecution and to call for an end to the persecution.

24 July 2004 Li Hongzhi appears in person and speaks to the approximately 4,000 Falun Gong practitioners who attend the 2004 Washington DC Falun Dafa Experience-Sharing Conference.

25 July 2004 Almost 2,000 Falun Gong practitioners from all over the world take part in a 'World Alliance Against China's Exporting State Terrorism' rally and parade in Boston, Massachusetts.

5 August 2004 Three Falun Gong practitioners lay criminal charges with the Athens Procuratorate against Jiang Zemin, Li Lanqing and Luo Gan for torture and maltreatment during their suppression of Falun Gong.

9 August 2004 During Bo Xilai's visit to Russia, Russian Falun Gong practitioners file charges of persecuting Falun Gong against him with the Inquisitorial Court.

27 August 2004 Tokyo formally recognises the Falun Gong group as a 'non-profit organisation' and approves its application for registration under the name Falun Dafa Association of Japan.

28 August 2004 Approximately 400 Falun Gong practitioners form a 'Great Wall of Courage' in Manhattan, set up an exhibition depicting the torture used on practitioners and hold candlelight vigils calling for an end to the persecution of Falun Gong.

30 August 2004 The Austrian Falun Dafa Association, the International Human Rights Association, the human rights group Organisation for Threatened People, several individuals and Falun Gong practitioners who had suffered persecution in Beijing jointly files a complaint with the Vienna Procuratorate against visiting Chinese official Jia Qinglin for crimes of torture.

2 September 2004 Fifteen Falun Gong practitioners files a criminal lawsuit with the National Spanish Court in Madrid, Spain, against Jia Qinglin for the crimes of genocide and torture while persecuting Falun Gong practitioners.

15 September 2004 Ms Zhang Cuiying files charges with the NSW Supreme Court against Jiang Zemin for torture, genocide and crimes against humanity.

22 September 2004 Almost 1,000 Falun Gong practitioners participate in group practice of the Falun Gong exercises and hold press conferences outside the UN building at the opening of the 59th Session of the UN General Assembly in New York. They form a Great Wall of Courage along Third Avenue to focus attention on the persecution to which Falun Gong was being subjected.

4 October 2004 The US Senate and House of Representatives passes Resolution 304 unanimously. This resolution expresses the sense of Congress regarding oppression by the [Government of the People's Republic of] China of Falun Gong in the United States and in China. It demands that the Chinese Government immediately stop interfering in the exercise of religious and political freedoms within the United States, such as the right to practice Falun Gong, that are guaranteed by the United States Constitution; cease using the diplomatic missions in the United States to spread falsehoods about the nature of Falun Gong; and release from detention all prisoners of conscience, including practitioners of Falun Gong.

Compiled 10 October 2004.

For a more detailed Chronology please go to:
http://www.pureinsight.org/pi/articles/2004/3/14/2097.html

Appendix

Dear editors and other personnel,
I wish to express my personal views on the many articles and reports on Falun Gong that have appeared recently in newspapers, on the radio, and on TV.

I suspect that many of you have not checked the authenticity and reliability of these articles and reports, since your job is simply to publish them. Which is to say that by doing this you are nothing more than tools. However, this letter is not addressed to you as tools, but to you as people.

The newspapers, radio and TV are all saying the same thing, that 'Falun Gong is an evil cult'. This must surely put us in mind of the words of that famous Cultural Revolution song: 'The Great Proletarian Cultural Revolution, hey! It's good! It's good! It's good! It's good! . . .' It seems comical now, but many, many people sang this song with great devotion then. Isn't the media in much the same position now as it was in those disaster-ridden ten years? Are the Chinese people capable of withstanding another Cultural Revolution? Perhaps, perhaps not.

. . . The spread of orthodox religions such as Buddhism, Daoism, Catholicism and Christianity could be credited with preserving relatively stable societies and supporting the development of the past few thousand years. It is because people believe 'doing good deeds is met with good rewards, and being evil is met with evil returns' that society's moral standards have remained fairly high and that we have not created a hell on earth.

It is loss of faith that has made today's Chinese society so fearful. With human morals on the verge of complete collapse, Falun Dafa has renewed many people's hearts and restored their faith in the world. Those who truly cultivate Falun Dafa believe that the principles of 'Truthfulness, Compassion and Forbearance' are the highest nature of the universe and the sole criteria for judging good and bad. The ultimate aim of cultivators is for their thinking and their actions to be in keeping with Truthfulness, Compassion and Forbearance, renouncing past bad thoughts and behaviour. Whatever they do, they are to consider others first at all times in their thoughts and actions, so as to develop the quality of selflessness and altruism; in all of life's tribulations and conflicts with others they are to first of all look within themselves. Because they believe that 'when your character improves, your gong grows', their priority is to improve their own character and their moral standards. I ask you, are people like this a danger to society? What is just too sad is that in these times of declining morals we are no longer troubled when we hear of some boy killing his mother or of a father harming his daughter. But when people appear who do not seek personal gain, who are wholeheartedly compassionate, and who want to help others even after they themselves have achieved profound tranquillity and happiness, we will not accept that they have no hidden agenda or wild ambition, or that they are not being used. This truly is humanity's greatest tragedy!

. . . Why do evil cults appear, though? The reason people put their faith in heretical (or weird) things is that they no longer have upright beliefs and correct ideas. But Falun Dafa that has been transmitted to the world has resolved this problem. This is a stroke of luck for the nation, for the people, and for humankind. Why are the upright and the heretical not differentiated? Why is Dafa being slandered?

I was born in 1966 and the 'Criticise Lin [Biao], criticise Kong [Confucius], counter the right-deviationist reactionaries' campaign was in full swing by the time I started primary school. Even though I had not quite figured out who Lin Biao and 'Kong Number Two' [Confucius] were, I did what my teachers told me and threw myself into the movement. I copied critical articles from newspapers and modelled speeches on them, and I even wrote some derivative doggerel. I won a 'Criticise Lin, criticise Confucius, counter the right-deviationist reactionaries' activist award that was up on the wall at home for years. The first time I read the Three-character Classic at university I thought: 'Heavens! This is so good! And as a child I was forever criticising it—how absurd'. So now I want to ask you all: Have you actually read Zhuan Falun? Do you know what it's about and why so many people believe in it? Have you attempted to gather more than superficial information from a genuine Falun Dafa student? Many old idioms could be used for what *is happening today: 'Public clamour can confound right and wrong'; 'If you are out to condemn somebody you can always trump up a charge'; 'Confounding black and white'; 'Wilful distortion'; 'Spreading falsehoods'; 'Quoting out of context'; 'One hundred mouths can't explain it away'. Students of Falun Dafa fear nothing but the world not understanding Falun Dafa! So I ask you all: please get a copy of* Zhuan Falun *and read it for yourselves, or sit down and have a talk with a Falun Gong student and see what it's all about. Whatever you do, make up your own minds!*

This reminds me of something from my childhood. At one stage, the cracks in our walls at home were plastered over with newspapers that happened to be reporting the 5 April 'counter-revolutionary rebellion' of 1976. I would lie in bed reading about these counter-revolutionary atrocities, about attacks on the Great Hall of the People, about army vehicles being set alight, and my childish heart would be filled with hatred for those 'counter-revolutionary thugs'. Suddenly, however, the papers started saying that this was not a counter-revolutionary rebellion but a spontaneous mass commemoration of Premier Zhou Enlai, who had died in January of that year. This was when I first understood treachery. As I grew older, I was one of many who learnt how to read our nation's newspapers: you could read them backwards, sideways, between the lines . . . any way but straight up. Surely this is a matter of deep regret for all who work in journalism. And still today, when my six-year-old daughter asks me in bewilderment why they say Li Hongzhi is a bad man, my heart aches that someone so young is being cheated by propaganda. If I speak up, and tell her my thoughts about what is right, she will tell the older members of our family and they will be unable to sleep in peace knowing that my ideas differ from the Party's (and please note that these are ideas, not actions). Just what have we done wrong to deserve such suffering?

I have studied natural science and have a Master of Science from Beijing University, so I would like to approach Falun Dafa from a scientific perspective. It is true that modern science cannot verify the existence of higher beings, but what we must not lose sight of is that neither can science verify that higher beings do not exist. People are so very insignificant in the boundless cosmos that surely we are not the only form life can take. Why do we not have the courage to delve into this? What we call the divine is nothing more than another form of wisdom, ability and patterns of existence on a higher level than those of our earthly life; what is so frightening about that? In fact, none of the scientific disciplines raises the question of whether higher beings exist or not. In mathematics, for example, '1 + 1 = 2' does not establish the existence or non-existence of higher beings; in physics, 'distance = time x veloc-

ity' does not establish the existence or non-existence of higher beings; in chemistry, 'hydrogen + oxygen = water' does not establish the existence or non-existence of higher beings. The only place the existence of higher beings is denied is in Darwin's theory of evolution. We accepted this theory in middle school as an established fact and never doubted it from then on. But Darwin's theory is simply a hypothesis he proposed on the basis of a few fossils from various periods that he arranged in chronological order. There are serious flaws in both his evidence and his hypothesis. In terms of his evidence, no human fossils have yet been found for the period four million to eight million years ago, and the missing link between monkeys and apes and apes and humans has yet to be found. Many theoretical questions remain unexplained as well. For example, why do the tears of monkeys and apes have no salt while human tears are salty? Why is there so little difference between monkeys of different regions while so many different races of people have evolved, and with such different cultures and languages? According to the theory of evolution, the 'use it or lose it' principle applies to the organs of all living beings, yet scientists have confirmed that 70 to 90 per cent of the human brain is not used. So, why has this unused portion of the brain not degenerated? Or, perhaps, why did so many useless brain cells evolve when monkeys first evolved into humans? Moreover, scientists currently working on genes have discovered that it is impossible for monkey genes to ever evolve into human genes. Many scientists throughout the world have in fact raised doubts about the validity of Darwin's theory of evolution. Only people are too busy at making money these days that very few of them want to be bothered by such questions.

In terms of scientific rationality, all that is required of any theory is that it be plausible and that it can be tested. There is no doubt that the principles, teachings, terminology and way of thinking in Falun Dafa have great differences with modern science. But the same goes for the ideas and methods of traditional Chinese medicine and Western medicine; they are very different but they both belong to the science of medicine. The theory of Falun Dafa is undoubtedly plausible and it can explain all sorts of natural, biological, social and cosmic phenomena much more satisfactorily than many other theories can. Also, its practical value has been verified by thousands upon thousands of cultivators. On these two points it is unquestionably a science and is even more advanced than our modern proof-based sciences. This is because it can explain things that those sciences can't and it can do things that those sciences can't. It is just a pity that many people haven't realised this yet.

What is distressing is that many scientists have let their scientific success go to their heads and lost the will to explore the unknown. They either stick to their theories and refuse to entertain objective reality, or turn to politics, becoming a rod to beat people with in the hands of politicians. This really is sad and shameful for science!

I have said all I want to say in this letter; I hope you don't mind my sharing my views with you.

Zheng Zeng
A reader, viewer, and listener
November 8, 1999